T0368167

HANGIN' TOUGH

Boxing fan, big- fight analyst, tactician & historian

JAWED AKRIM

authorHOUSE®

AuthorHouse™ UK
1663 Liberty Drive
Bloomington, IN 47403 USA
www.authorhouse.co.uk
Phone: UK TFN: 0800 0148641 (Toll Free inside the UK)
UK Local: 02036 956322 (+44 20 3695 6322 from outside the UK)

Published by AuthorHouse 05/12/2021

ISBN: 978-1-6655-8505-7 (sc)
ISBN: 978-1-6655-8506-4 (e)

Print information available on the last page.

This book is printed on acid-free paper.

CONTENTS

PREFACE

Hangin' Tough is a collection of essays and anecdotes about boxing that I have wholly composed and written on the social media platform Quora. As such, the content of the book has already been subjected to mass-market crowdsourcing, and inspection of my Quora stats reveals global approval and acclaim.

Each essay is, in general, a direct response to a question which was posed to me by a hitherto-unknown person online. The vast majority of my questioners are named individuals, but some have chosen to remain anonymous. As an online sports community, we all share a passion for boxing and a desire for improved knowledge of the sweet science.

The Q & A exchanges are fairly diverse and encompass a broad range of topics. In addition to boxing, I cover topics such as mixed martial arts, bodybuilding, street fighting, and anabolic steroids. The truth of the matter is that my answers are heavily opinionated—in essence this is the name of the game. But you will find that the vast majority of my opinions are backed up by historical facts and evidence. The whole ethos behind Quora is a sharing of opinions and information which often go unreported by the mainstream media. Therefore it is safe to say that the subject matter in *Hangin' Tough* is unique, controversial, and always provocative.

An important mode in *Hangin' Tough* is humour; the essays are generally written in a tongue-in-cheek style. There are various core themes that percolate throughout. Most essays feature a famous fighter to whom fight fans can relate. Example fighters include household names such as Mike Tyson, Muhammad Ali, and George Foreman. Indeed it is safe to say that Iron Mike Tyson enjoys centre stage in many of the anecdotes; the real-life trials and tribulations of Tyson are a perfect theatrical battleground to explore the duality of humankind.

Another exciting theme that resonates through *Hangin' Tough* is hypothetical boxing matches between great fighters from different eras. These include dream fights between Tyson and Ali, Tyson and Joe Frazier, and Tyson and Foreman. Other hypothetical encounters that receive unique attention and in-depth analysis are street fights between the aforementioned gladiators. The rationale is that a street fight between two boxers will follow a different script to a boxing match, due to grossly different environmental factors.

Alternate-reality timelines are also explored in *Hangin' Tough*. Essentially these are what-if scenarios based on real-life events, but analysed through a science fiction lens.

So prepare to be shocked, amazed and sometimes horrified as I take you for a walk on the wilder side of boxing history.

CAST OF CHARACTERS

-A-

Tank Abbot: Prominent mixed martial artist and pit fighter, 1990s
Muhammad Ali: Heavyweight boxing legend
Canelo Alvarez: Current boxing legend
Vito Antuofermo: Italian middleweight boxer who had a brief stint as world champion in the late 1970s
Ray Arcel: Legendary boxing trainer
Henry Armstrong: Multi-weight old-school boxing legend
Teddy Atlas: Cus D'Amato disciple, Mike Tyson's one-time amateur trainer, and current broadcaster
"Stone Cold" Steve Austin: WWE wrestler

-B-

Sonny Banks: Early 1960s heavyweight who boxed Cassius Clay in 1962
Iran Barkley: WBC middleweight champion, late 1980s
Marco Antonio Barrera: Multi-weight Mexican boxing legend
Nigel Benn: British middleweight and former world middleweight champion in the 1990s
Trevor Berbick: WBC heavyweight champion, 1986
David Bey: Heavyweight contender, 1980s
Tyrell Biggs: Mike Tyson challenger in 1987 and Olympic gold medallist in 1984
Usain Bolt: Sprint legend in the 100 metres
Oscar Bonavena: Fringe heavyweight contender, late 1960s–early 1970s
Francois Botha: Mike Tyson opponent, 1999
Riddick Bowe: World heavyweight champion, early 1990s, and Olympic medallist
Dominic Breazeale: Modern-era heavyweight journeyman (active)
Kell Brook: British welterweight boxer (active)
Frank Bruno: Much loved and amiable British heavyweight of the 1980s and 1990s; boxed Mike Tyson twice

-C-

Joe Calzaghe: British boxing legend
Eric Cantona: French soccer player, 1990s
Bill Cayton: Mike Tyson's original manager and investor
Ezzard Charles: Old-school heavyweight great
Julio Cesar Chavez: Mexican lightweight legend
George Chuvalo: Tough Heavyweight contender, 1960s
Cassius Clay: Muhammad Ali's original name
Randall Cobb: Tough heavyweight contender, late 1970s–early 1980s
Mark Coleman: Prominent mixed martial artist, 1990s
Ronnie Coleman: Legendary bodybuilder
Gerry Cooney: Hard-hitting heavyweight contender, 1980s
Bert Cooper: Fringe heavyweight contender, 1990s
Henry Cooper: Heavyweight contender and British boxing legend, 1960s
Francis Ford Coppola: Legendary Hollywood filmmaker
Miguel Cotto: Multi-weight world champion, 2000s
Randy Couture: Prominent mixed martial artist, 2000s
Terence Crawford: Welterweight world champion (active)
Bobby Czyz: World light heavyweight champion, 1980s, and colour commentator

-D-

Cus D'Amato: Mike Tyson's original trainer and legal guardian, and inventor of peekaboo boxing
Oscar De La Hoya: Multi-weight world champion, 1990s–2000s
Jack Dempsey: Heavyweight legend
Robert DeNiro: Legendary Hollywood actor
James Douglas: Heavyweight champion, 1990
Angelo Dundee: Legendary boxing trainer
Roberto Duran: Nicknamed "Hands of Stone", legendary middle divisions brawler and multi-weight world champion

-E-

Fedor Emelianenko: Prominent Russian mixed martial artist, 2000s
Eric Esch "Butterbean": Heavyweight boxer renowned for his rotund physique, 1990s–2000s
Chris Eubank: British middleweight and WBO world champion, 1990s

-F-

Fab Four: Refers to four legendary 1980s boxers who reinvigorated the middle divisions: Roberto Duran, Marvin Hagler, Thomas Hearns, and Sugar Ray Leonard
Jesse Ferguson: Dangerous journeyman who fought a young Mike Tyson in 1986
Lou Ferrigno: Legendary bodybuilder and on-screen *Incredible Hulk* actor

Bobby Fischer: Chess grandmaster
Evan Fields: Known alias of Evander Holyfield
Zora Folley: Heavyweight contender, 1960s
George Foreman: Heavyweight legend
Mac Foster: Heavyweight contender, 1970s
Smokin' Joe Frazier: Heavyweight legend
Marvis Frazier: Son of Joe Frazier and heavyweight contender, 1980s
Julius Francis: Mike Tyson opponent, 2000
Carl Froch: Super middleweight world champion 2008–2011
Gene Fullmer: Old-school middleweight contender who fought Sugar Ray Robinson
Tyson Fury: Current WBC world heavyweight champion
Eddie Futch: Legendary boxing trainer

-G-

Arturo Gatti: Super lightweight world champion, 2000s
Andrew Golota: Heavyweight contender, 1990s
Genady Golovkin (GGG): Modern-era world middleweight champion
Royce Gracie: UFC legend and winner of UFC 1
Mitch "Blood" Green: Dangerous journeyman and one of Tyson's early professional opponents, 1980s
George Groves: British middleweight boxer, recently retired
Redge Gutteridge: Popular British broadcaster and boxing commentator, 1980s

-H-

Marvelous Marvin Hagler: Middleweight legend
Prince Naseem Hamed: British featherweight boxer and former world featherweight champion, 1990s–2000s
Lee Haney: Legendary bodybuilder
Ricky Hatton: British welterweight legend, 2000s
David Haye: British cruiserweight and heavyweight boxer who held a version of the heavyweight title 2009–2011
Thomas Hearns: Multi-weight boxing legend
Phil Heath: Modern-era bodybuilder
"Hollywood" Dan Henderson: Prominent MMA fighter, 2000s
Larry Holmes: Heavyweight legend
Evander Holyfield, "the real deal": Cruiserweight legend and Olympic medallist, 1984
Bernard Hopkins: Middleweight legend

-I-

Ike Ibeabuchi: Late 1990s heavyweight contender

-J-

Jim Jacobs: Tyson's original manager and investor
Julian Jackson: Hard-hitting middleweight world champion from the Virgin Islands, early 1990s
Mike Jameson: Mike Tyson opponent, 1986
Jack Johnson: Really old-school heavyweight great
Ben Johnson: Sprinter in 100 metres, 1980s
Michael Johnson: Mike Tyson opponent, 1985
Jon Jones: Prominent mixed martial artist (active)
Roy Jones Junior: Super middleweight legend
Anthony Joshua: Modern-era world heavyweight champion (active)
Zab Judah: Welterweight world champion, 2000s

-K-

Amir Khan: British boxer and former IBF and WBA light welterweight world champion (active)
James Kinchen: Super middleweight boxer who fought Thomas Hearns in 1988
Don King: Well-known boxing promoter
Vitali Klitsckho: Long-reigning twenty-first-century world heavyweight champion
Wladimir Klitsckho: Long-reigning twenty-first-century world heavyweight champion

-L-

Jake LaMotta: Old-school middleweight legend
Mills Lane: Well-known boxing referee
Sam Langford: Really old-school heavyweight great
Sugar Ray Leonard: Multi-weight boxing legend
Brock Lesnar: World-famous wrestler and mixed martial artist
Butch Lewis: Michael Spinks's manager
Carl Lewis: Legendary 1980s sprinter
Lennox Lewis: Heavyweight boxing legend
Chuck Liddell: Prominent mixed martial artist, 2000s
Sonny Liston: Old-school heavyweight boxing legend
DONNIE LONG: Mike Tyson opponent, 1985
Joe Louis: Old-school heavyweight boxing legend
Ron Lyle: Big-punching heavyweight contender of the 1970s

-M-

LYOTO MACHIDA: Prominent Brazilian martial artist
RAY MANCINI: World lightweight champion, 1980s, and colour commentator
DIEGO MARADONA: Argentine soccer legend
ROCKY MARCIANO: Old-school heavyweight boxing legend
ANTONIO MARGARITO: World welterweight champion, 2000s
BUSTER MATHIS: Heavyweight contender, 1960s
ZELJKO MAVROVIC: Virtually unheard-of Croatian heavyweight boxer who fought Lennox Lewis in 1998
FLOYD MAYWEATHER: Welterweight boxing legend
KEVIN MCBRIDE: Mike Tyson's last professional opponent, 2005
OLIVER MCCALL: Heavyweight contender who had a brief stint as WBC world champion, 1990s
GERALD MCCLELLAN: Big-punching middleweight world champion, 1990s
CONOR MCGREGOR: Prominent mixed martial artist (active)
BARRY MCGUIGAN: Irish featherweight boxer, WBA featherweight champion 1985–1986, and expert pundit
PETER MCNEELEY: Mike Tyson's first opponent following his release from prison in 1995
RAY MERCER: Mid 1990s heavyweight contender who had a brief stint as WBO champion
LIONEL MESSI: Argentine soccer legend
JARRELL MILLER: Current heavyweight contender (active)
ALAN MINTER: World middleweight champion, late 1970s–early 1980s
CARLOS MONZON: Argentine middleweight legend, 1970s
DAVEY MOORE: WBA world light middleweight champion, early 1980s
MICHAEL MOORER: Briefly world heavyweight champion, 1994
ERIK MORALES: Multi-weight Mexican boxing legend
TOMMY MORRISON: Heavyweight contender, 1990s, best known for portraying Tommy Gunn in *Rocky 5*
SHANE MOSLEY: Multi-weight world champion, 2000s
JOHN "THE BEAST" MUGABI: Hard-hitting middleweight contender, mid 1980s

-N-

ISAAC NEWTON: Prominent seventeenth-century mathematician
FRANCES N'GANNOU: Heavyweight mixed martial artist (active)
BRIAN NIELSEN: Mike Tyson tune-up opponent, 2001
KEN NORTON: World heavyweight champion, late 1970s
KHABIB NURMAGOMEDOV: Legendary mixed martial artist

-O-

Sergio Oliva: Legendary bodybuilder
Luis Ortiz: Heavyweight contender (active)
Alistair Overeem: Prominent mixed martial artist

-P-

Ferdie Pacheco: Muhammad Ali's personal fight physician
Floyd Patterson: Cus D'Amato-trained heavyweight, 1960s—formerly the youngest heavyweight champion of the world
Manny Pacquiao: Multi-weight boxing legend
Joseph Parker: Heavyweight contender (active)
GREGORIO PERALTA: Slick Argentine heavyweight who went the distance with George Foreman, 1970
David Price: British heavyweight boxer
Mariusz Pudzianowski: Former world's strongest man who dabbled in mixed martial arts

-Q-

Jerry Quarry: Heavyweight contender, 1970s

-R-

Hasim Rahman: Early 2000s heavyweight contender and brief stint as world champion, 2001
Alfonso Ratliff: Mike Tyson opponent, 1986
Steve Reeves: Legendary old-school bodybuilder
Jose Ribalta: Mike Tyson opponent, 1986
Sugar Ray Robinson: Pound for pound, the greatest boxer ever
Kevin Rooney: Cus D'Amato disciple and Tyson's one-time trainer
Edwin Rosario: Mid 1980s world lightweight champion
Donovan "Razor" Ruddock: Big-punching heavyweight contender, early 1990s
Andy Ruiz Junior: Modern-era heavyweight contender who had a brief stint as world champion (active)
John Ruiz: Heavyweight contender who had a brief stint as world champion, early 2000s

-S-

Corrie Sanders: Heavyweight contender, Early 2000s
Bob Sapp: Prominent mixed martial artist, wrestler, and American football player renowned for his huge size and muscularity
Lou Savarese: Heavyweight contender, early 2000s
Arnold Schwarzenegger: Legendary bodybuilder

Bruce Seldon: Mike Tyson challenger, 1996
Ken Shamrock: MMA legend and participant in UFC 1
Earnie Shavers "the Acorn": Big-punching heavyweight contender, 1970s
Kimbo Slice: Prominent mixed martial artist and YouTube backstreet brawler
James "Bonecrusher" Smith: WBA heavyweight champion 1986–1987
Renaldo Snipes: Heavyweight contender 1980s
Leon Spinks: Heavyweight, late 1970s–early 1980s, best known for his upset defeat of Ali in 1978
Michael Spinks: Light heavyweight legend and Olympic gold medallist, 1976—briefly held one version of the heavyweight crown, 1980s
Emmanuel Steward: Legendary boxing trainer
Alex Stewart: Mike Tyson opponent, 1990
Bobby Stewart: Ex-pro boxer and key worker at Tryon youth detention centre who first introduced Mike Tyson to Cus D'Amato
Braun Strowman: Current WWE wrestler
Bert Sugar: Prominent boxing historian
Tim Sylvia: Prominent mixed martial artist, 2000s

-T-

Antonio Tarver: Undisputed world light heavyweight champion, early 2000s
Ernie Terrell: Heavyweight contender who had a brief stint as WBA champion, mid 1960s
Pinklon Thomas: Heavyweight contender who held the WBC title for two years, 1980s
Elijah Tillery: Obscure heavyweight boxer, early 1990s
James "Quick" Tillis: Gatekeeper heavyweight and one of Tyson's tougher opponents, 1980s
James Toney: Super middleweight legend
Felix Trinidad: Puerto Rican boxing legend
David Tua: Big-punching heavyweight contender, late 1990s–early 2000s
Tony Tubbs: Heavyweight contender who had a brief stint as WBA champion, 1980s
Tony Tucker: Heavyweight contender, 1980s
Gene Tunney: Really old-school heavyweight
"Iron" Mike Tyson: Heavyweight legend
Sun Tzu: Ancient Chinese military strategist

-V-

Nikolai Valuev: WBA heavyweight champion, 2005–2009
Cain Velasquez: Recent, prominent mixed martial artist

-W-

Jersey Joe Walcott: Old-school heavyweight contender
Andre Ward: Super middleweight world champion, 2009–2015

MICKY WARD: Light welterweight contender, late 1990s–early 2000s
JIM WATT: Scottish lightweight, 1970s, world lightweight champion 1979, and colour commentator
CHUCK WEPNER: Heavyweight contender, 1970s
FLEX WHEELER: Prominent bodybuilder, 1990s
DILLIAN WHYTE: British heavyweight boxer (active)
DEONTAY WILDER: Former heavyweight champion of the world (active)
JESS WILLARD: Really old-school heavyweight
CLEVELAND WILLIAMS: Big-punching heavyweight contender, 1960s
DANNY WILLIAMS: Mike Tyson opponent, 2004
PETE WILLIAMS: Mixed martial artist, 1990s
TIM WITHERSPOON: Heavyweight contender who had a brief stint as WBA champion, 1980s

-Y-

JIMMY YOUNG: Heavyweight contender, 1970s
MARK YOUNG: Mike Tyson opponent, 1985

CHAPTER 1

THE INTIMIDATION GAME

ARTHUR DAVIS: Was there ever someone in combat sports more intimidating than a prime Mike Tyson?

JAWED AKRIM: Once upon a time, not so long ago, there was this dude named Charles "Sonny" Liston, and everyone feared him, even the cops. Trust me like you've never trusted anybody—you didn't want his 16-inch anvils in your face, gloves on or off. Sonny Liston was the heavyweight equivalent of "Hands of Stone", and he possessed the heaviest and most rock-solid fists in heavyweight history. He's the one and only guy George Foreman was afraid of—to the point where Foreman has admitted that Liston was the only guy to ever forcibly back him up in sparring. You can just begin to imagine how tough this guy must have been if Big George Foreman, of all people, was afraid of him. A real-life Mafioso who worked as muscle for hire for the Mob, Liston's extracurricular persona was even more menacing than his ring presence. If you didn't pay your bills on time, the Mob sent Sonny to collect.

Mike Tyson has admitted on camera that Sonny Liston was the scariest boxer ever, and if the Iron Man says so, then it is good enough for me. Other than Liston, Tyson is number two all time in the intimidation stakes. After these two, it is difficult to think of another guy who was as scary, but I suggest that George Foreman was probably number three. Where I think Tyson and Liston were unrivalled was in terms of the "hurt factor". Both guys were precision power punchers of the highest calibre. Their punches literally hurt the most. I've seen a no-nonsense interview that Tyson's former trainer Kevin Rooney gave in the mid 1980s, in which he described scenarios whereby Tyson's sparring partners regularly went AWOL after the first sparring session. They simply had not been hit that hard that often in a vital area by another fighter. He particularly cited the body shots as being the most painful.

Furthermore, Tyson and Liston were consistently able to instil copious amounts of fear into their opponents just prior to their matches. Tyson, perhaps more than any other boxer in history, capitalised massively on this fear factor. Liston was just something that came out of a Marvel comic book—a physical freak. But underpinning both their reputations was a fear of pain. Watch poor old Cleveland Williams's face when he is being surgically picked apart by Liston in round two of their 1960 rematch—it hurts, and he is grimacing in pain. Iron Mike still to this day is the only guy whom I have seen make another grown man cry in the boxing ring due to a beating: Tyrell Biggs in 1987. Tyson took tremendous pleasure in torturing Biggs that night. He admitted to carrying Biggs for at least three extra rounds of hurt and enjoyed listening to Biggs make "woman" gestures when hit by the wickedest of body shots.

—December 2018

Anonymous: What made Mike Tyson so dominant?

J. A.: There were numerous reasons why Iron Mike Tyson had easily the most dominant reign as heavyweight champion. Quite simply, he was way better than the 1980s pool of heavyweights, which has been described by some boxing experts as relatively weak. Others have described the 1980s as a boxing wasteland which was effectively cleaned up by the vastly superior Tyson. If this is the case, it is hardly Tyson's fault, as he could only fight who was put in front of him.

The main ingredients of his dominance were superior speed, power, timing, and defence. He was fantastically trained and managed by Cus D'Amato and then Kevin Rooney. He was astutely handled by his co-managers Jim Jacobs and Bill Cayton. And then there was the momentum he gained through his *Terminator*-style aura, which steadily gave him an air of invincibility. He was, for a three -year period, a virtually unbeatable fighter. I can't think of a single heavyweight champion other than Ali at his best who avoided punches better. Iron Mike, like Ali, was a master of intimidation. They just did it differently.

Something else that made Tyson so dominant at the time was his size—or apparent lack of size, as the case may be. He used his lack of height as an advantage, particularly on the inside, where he was easily the most ferocious in-fighter ever. Former lightweight world champion Jim Watt once described Tyson's punching power, saying almost in disbelief, "Tyson gets so much power into short punches that it's hard to believe."

In addition to these dominance factors, Tyson's early life and upbringing in Brownsville, New York, instilled a seriously mean and ruthless streak in him. Mike Tyson actually enjoyed beating people up, both inside and outside the ring.

—February 2018

Randy Hamme: Not asking who was the best boxer, but which boxer would you be most afraid to get in the ring with?

J. A.: Iron Mike Tyson would scare me the most. Why? Because he was a very scary guy! During his heyday, in Tyson's pre-fight stare-downs, the look on his opponents' faces was one of fear. By contrast, prime Tyson often appeared calm and nonchalant, as if he were just about to have a stroll in the park rather than engage in a boxing match.

The main reason that I would be most afraid of prime Tyson is not because he was the best. He wasn't the best. But he was certainly one of the most intimidating. At his best, he possessed a great offensive arsenal coupled with an equally solid defence. This spelled big trouble for his contemporaries, as he could land pinpoint bombs on them while taking almost nothing in return. In boxing, when you can hit and not be hit in return, rest assured that you're in a good place.

At the time of his dominance, his enormous technical skills, innate physicality, and sky-high confidence enabled Tyson to carry out boxing experimentation on selected opponents. The chosen opponents were "carried" by Tyson in order to gauge how Mike's "engine" would perform in a long fight. Two such guinea-pig opponents were James "Quick" Tillis and Mitch "Blood" Green, both of whom unusually lasted the distance against prime Tyson. Part of the reason was that Tyson was under strict instructions from his management to hold back and not knock out everybody quickly. Tyrell Biggs was also carried for several rounds longer so that Tyson could fine-tune his body-punching attacks in readiness for future tall opponents.

For an opponent, such experimentation could lead to a slow and protracted beating. In essence, they faced an opponent who could easily score a one-punch knockout but deliberately held back to prolong their demise. In other words, prime Tyson used to toy with many of his opponents.

—October 2020

Anonymous: Were people scared to fight Mike Tyson?

J. A.: Take one look at an angry and pumped-up prime Tyson circa 1986 and decide: Would you be afraid? If you saw a guy of Tyson's build and muscularity making an unusually intense and menacing facial expression during a stare-down, I'd say you would have to have ice in your veins if you weren't a little unnerved. Calling pro boxers scared doesn't quite cover it—they were fearful for their very well-being!

One of Tyson's most scared opponents was British heavyweight Frank Bruno. In the rematch with Tyson, he was observed crossing himself religiously more than twenty times during his walk to the ring. He was almost like a man being marched to the gallows. This was a world-level professional boxer with a massive build, as strong as an ox—but scared to death of Tyson. Bruno was no doubt having flashbacks of their first fight and remembering the pain and damage he had sustained.

At least two of Tyson's lesser-known opponents, Bruce Seldon and Alex Stewart, were knocked down by punches that hadn't yet landed. They exhibited behavioural responses that were inherently submissive and automatic in nature. The thought of imminent pain clearly triggered a massive and uncontrollable release of fight-or-flight adrenaline.

During Tyson's prime years, his opponents were so fearful of being hurt that they generally chose one of three boxing options: they grabbed for dear life, ran for their lives, or committed boxing "suicide". He was once voted by Sky Sports as the scariest boxer ever, and during the late 1980s, the Iron Man terrorised the heavyweight division. George Foreman once commented that he was most respectful and fearful of fighters who boxed with intent; well, peak Tyson boxed with *lethal* intent. During his reign of terror, his objective was not only to seriously punish his opponents but also to carry out such a powerful and dominant beatdown that they would never want to face Tyson again. Now ask yourself: Exactly how many of prime Tyson's opponents wanted a rematch? Mission accomplished.

—January 2019

Abhilash Pillai: Were people scared to fight Muhammad Ali?

J. A.: No, not at all—Ali wasn't that sort of fighter. Pro boxers, Joe Public, and indeed the boxing underworld were more scared of Sonny Liston. Pure intimidation wasn't really Ali's game, but it sure was the Big Bear's game. Sonny Liston has been referred to as the godfather of intimidation.

Ali had his own bag of tricks and often used sledging tactics and other psychological and distraction techniques to gain an edge on opponents. In many of his most notable fights, his main objectives were to upset, annoy, and get underneath the skin of his opponent—the rationale being that an angry opponent was more prone to making mistakes.

Generally speaking, intimidating boxers will be powerful and hurtful punchers. They have both a menacing persona and a muscular, dominant physique. They also possess a lifeless and mean stare. By heavyweight standards, Ali was probably a medium-power puncher with a medium athletic build. He said of himself, "I'm not known as a hard puncher; I am a scientific boxer." In fact, you will find that the vast majority of Ali's opponents either hit harder than him or roughly matched his power. It was probably the case that Ali was scared of some of his more heavy-handed opponents, rather than the other way around.

Apparently Ali was most fearful of Sonny Liston. At the weigh-in for their first fight, his pulse literally went through the roof when Sonny Liston stared him down. It wasn't the first time that Ali's pulse rate had red-lined. He simply dealt with the fear and used the adrenaline rush in a positive way. He was a big underdog against Liston, and many people in the industry expected him to not only lose but get beat up and brutally knocked out. The early 1960s saw a different type of Ali. He was infamously known as "the Louisville lip", and many people wanted Liston to silence his loudmouthed braggadocio.

—February 2019

Amit Jacobs: Who had a more intimidating ring presence, Foreman or Tyson?

J. A.: Tyson by a distance. When Tyson knocked out Marvis Frazier in 1986, he probably gave the most dominant and aggressive victory display ever seen from a fighter. I certainly don't think any boxer has looked this tough and intimidating straight after knocking out an opponent. The images that were captured shortly after a 20-year-old Tyson wiped out Marvis Frazier in under thirty seconds literally spoke a thousand words. Tyson went ballistic on the ring apron and for some time continued to release pent-up tension.

Tyson eventually started cooling down as the realisation that the fight was over kicked in. His manager Jim Jacobs calmed him down further. But it was still amazing to see Tyson so full of adrenaline. He was perhaps more hyper than usual, given the fact he had just erased the legend of Frazier.

In comparison, when George Foreman put the stare on Marvis's father Joe, it was a different story. While it was a cold stare-down, Frazier senior to me didn't look like he was too bothered. Now when Marvis Frazier had his father Joe backing him up and was about to face off against prime Tyson, to me both father and son looked unsettled and intimidated. The common denominator of Frazier makes it obvious to me that Tyson had a more intimidating ring presence than Foreman.

In general, if you ask most impartial boxing experts who the scariest boxer was by reputation and ring presence, then you will find that most say it is either Sonny Liston or Mike Tyson. Most polls on this topic yield this fact. Liston and Tyson are in a league of their own. Prime Foreman was without doubt a monster and very intimidating in his own right, but he trails in third place by a distance.

Another purely boxing related fact that reinforces Tyson's and Liston's menacing personas was "the hurt factor". These two guys regularly put their opponents in "the hurt locker", to the point where few if any of their beaten opponents wanted a rematch. A prime example of this was again Joe and Marvis Frazier. Tyson destroyed Marvis and sent him on his way to premature retirement. Foreman similarly destroyed Marvis's father Joe in 1973—but Frazier senior was still more than game for a rematch. So, again based on the common ground of Frazier, it appears that Tyson was more feared.

—October 2019

Steve Pierce: Why were big, hardened, top-flight professional fighters so intimidated by Mike Tyson? Surely pro boxers like that shouldn't be so fearful.

J. A.: I think the main reason was more transparent and straightforward than you might believe. Whether you're a rough and tough pro boxer or just some regular Joe Public, fundamentally we are all still human beings. I doubt very much that any normal human being wants to get beat up. In the mid 1980s, this was exactly what prime Tyson was doing on a fairly regular basis—beating up top-flight, hardened professional boxers. If you were in the boxing business and you were next in line and you just saw his last opponent get butchered, then this was bound to have a negative effect on your own pre-fight psyche. This was even more true if you happened to know one of his previous victims or had boxed them. A prime example of this common-opponent fear factor was Michael Spinks, who was terrified of Tyson. He was even more scared of Tyson because he had just seen Tyson flatten Larry Holmes. That same Holmes had gone the distance twice with Spinks.

Another major source of prime Tyson's intimidating persona was that he was possibly the most dangerous and hurtful puncher in heavyweight history. During the mid 1980s, word rapidly spread inside the heavyweight division that this guy was a seriously hurtful puncher, even in sparring with head guards on. In one interview before Tyson became famous, Teddy Atlas, one of his old trainers, explained the word-of-mouth reputation that was spreading: "I hear you got this killer called Tyson at your gym who just loves to hurt other fighters."

When you bring this kind of intent, bravado, and ultra-aggressive attitude to a mere sparring session, then it is understandable that some guys just don't want to know. At the end of the day, even if you are a pro boxer and are therefore more used to being hit, you are still only human, after all, and surely nobody in their right mind wants to get tortured in the ring. Tyson was clearly a troubled individual who used boxing as a vehicle to offload some of his ghetto-rooted frustrations.

Another major factor that made Tyson uniquely intimidating at the time was the exact manner of his knockouts. He was throwing what were known in the industry as unseen or ninja-type punches. These are the most dangerous punches because you literally don't see them coming. You cannot prepare your body for the impact as the punch is a complete surprise. More often than not, Tyson's unseen punch came from low down and travelled in an upward trajectory, so it was tailored perfectly for the average heavyweight opponent, who happened to stand around 6 feet

2 inches tall. In simple terms, if you were an average 1980s heavyweight, then you were perfect target practice for Kid Dynamite. The exceptionally tall guys who stood 6 feet 5 inches-plus were more of a challenge for Tyson because of the excessive height difference.

Finally, the concept of momentum was huge in prime Tyson's heyday. He was perfectly trained, managed, and groomed by his original team, and that gave him confidence. When any fighter or team in any professional sport becomes confident, they become better, stronger, and tougher day by day—that is, until the bubble bursts. This short-lived snowball effect was exactly what we saw with a young Tyson. The 1980s media too fanned the flames and one of prime Tyson's opponents, Bonecrusher Smith, blamed the tabloid media of the day for perpetuating Tyson's invincibility aura.

—September 2019

Nicholas Xee: Was Mike Tyson's intimidating aura a real thing that helped him win fights?

J. A.: Absolutely, 100 per cent yes. I'm guessing that you must be a young boxing fan, so you never saw him in real time during his heyday. But I can definitely confirm that his 1980s *Terminator*-type aura was genuine and contributed hugely to his victories. He was described by many journalists of the day as being a master of intimidation and as having the very desirable ability to psych out opponents before a punch was ever thrown. In reality this was a pure gangster or street-fighter mentality being brought into the professional boxing arena. That intimidation was a big part of his skill. Simply put, if you have a scared opponent, then the battle is already half won.

A prime example of a psyched-out Tyson opponent was a guy named Peter McNeely. He didn't even face prime Tyson; he was Tyson's first comeback opponent following Tyson's release from the penitentiary in 1995. McNeely was genuinely scared for his own safety and this fear factor was based on the old Tyson aura. So even years after Tyson's prime was over, that intimidating persona still loomed large—at least through the eyes of some opponents.

"Ain't no fear in me," said Holyfield to Tyson's face at the weigh-in of their first fight. Now when Holyfield specifically makes a point of mentioning fear to Tyson, this clearly indicates that Tyson's intimidating persona is tangible and real. Holyfield never said this to any of his other opponents. Holyfield of all people wouldn't have otherwise mentioned it. This was his own pre-fight psychological rebuttal to Tyson.

After losing his title to Buster Douglas in 1990, Tyson's first comeback fight was against a guy named Alex Stewart. Stewart was another very intimidated and scared fighter. I'm specifically mentioning the Stewart fight because in a pre-fight interview, Tyson threatened this guy with "a slow beating, maybe close to death". I am pretty sure Stewart heard this interview, because in the fight he literally fell over in the first round without any clean power punches connecting. This guy wasn't a bum; he was decent and had gone the distance with old Foreman and Holyfield. But on the night against Tyson, he was a shambling wreck and turned up on cue just to get knocked out. I think he took Tyson's threat literally and wanted to avoid a potentially career-ending slow beating at all costs.

In a similar manner, a guy named Bruce Seldon fell over against Tyson in the first round of their fight in 1996. Seldon was not that badly concussed, but he didn't want to get beat up, so he kind of committed boxing suicide. As far as I can see, this type of in-fight behaviour was pure fight-or-flight, adrenaline-based fear. Because there was nowhere to run or hide, some of these scared boxers simply fell over instead.

So, contrary to a lot of false speculation, Tyson's intimidatory potential didn't end after the Buster Douglas fight, but continued long into the 1990s and even into the post-prison phase of his career. What Buster Douglas took away from Tyson was his invincibility aura; that most damaging of defeats showed other pro boxers that Tyson wasn't the Terminator after all.

—September 2019

Ross Taylor: Who was George Foreman scared of?

J. A.: If he was scared of anyone, then the most likely candidate was a scary dude by the name of Charles "Sonny" Liston. Liston was the one-time heavyweight champion of the world, an ex-con, a real-life "made man", and a genuine Mob enforcer.

Back in the day, 1950s and 1960s America was a very different place. Low-level crime was rife, and in certain crime-ridden neighbourhoods, corruption was a way of life. Loan sharking and shylocking were commonplace. If you didn't keep up with your "payment plan", then Sonny Liston was the guy the loan shark would send to break your thumb.

When none other than Iron Mike Tyson admits that another boxer was more intimidating than him, then people in the know sit up and pay attention. How is this possible? Could there have been a guy more fearsome by reputation than even Iron Mike? Not only is it possible, but it is true. Sonny Liston was the most intimidating boxer in history Why?

There were various factors underpinning his provocative and fearsome reputation. Primarily, he had the largest fists in boxing history (relative to body size). No one with a degree of common sense wanted to get punched by those anvils. Secondly, because Liston learnt how to box in prison, he brought those same ruthless prisoner-type tactics into the professional arena. In the boxing ring, Liston tried to punish his opponents in the same way that a "daddy" convict sorted out the weaker inmates. There was no mercy or remorse. Since Foreman was Liston's one-time sparring partner, he knew from first-hand experience what it was like to feel the crushing power of Sonny Liston. As Foreman himself once remarked, "Sonny would get you going on that jab of his and then you were in big trouble."

Imagine Liston's shotgun jab in your face, coming off an 84-inch reach with 16-inch hammer fists, and you realise why Liston probably had the number-one boxing toolbox ever. Foreman also confirmed that Liston was the only guy ever to make him back off in sparring. So in a hypothetical boxing scenario, if Foreman would ever have ducked anyone, then surely prime Liston was that guy.

—September 2019

Michael Uzar: Was Muhammad Ali afraid to fight anyone?

J. A.: I'm no mind reader, but as far as a boxing match was concerned, I believe Ali feared no man, alive or dead. However, he may well have been reluctant to have a rematch with Big George

Foreman on US soil. Does reluctance to step back into the ring with a prime Foreman equate to fear? Probably not, although the answer is slightly debatable.

Foreman definitely wanted a rematch, but apparently Ali flatly declined. Foreman certainly had plenty of grounds to request a rematch. Shortly after his upset loss to Ali, he put forth a number of unusual excuses to explain his poor performance in the fight. These excuses were fairly wide ranging. Perhaps the most valid one was that the ring ropes had been deliberately loosened by Ali's trainer Angelo Dundee. Loosening the ropes was definitely an underhand tactic and tantamount to cheating. It has widely been acknowledged that this facilitated Ali's crazy rope-a-dope tactic.

In addition to this, the media discovered that Foreman had suffered quite a deep cut in sparring prior to the match, which was not properly treated. Another major ingredient in his defeat was believed to have been the partisan audience in Zaire, which from the outset totally detested Foreman but adored Ali. Certainly the general consensus from the Foreman camp was that the fight being held in Africa had meant that everything had been stacked in Ali's favour. In Foreman's own words, "I hated it in Africa!". Do you think Ali knew that Foreman would hate it in Africa?

But at the end of the day, I can't say that I blame Ali for declining a rematch with prime Foreman, as Foreman was a nightmare opponent. He was a truly massive puncher, stronger than an ox and possessor of a pure granite chin. By the mid 1970s, Father Time was slowly creeping up on Ali, and he was no longer the dancing master of old. To beat Foreman in 1974, he had already pulled off a minor miracle. It was his heart, toughness, and ring IQ that prevailed on that night in Zaire.

Other than Foreman, I think Ali would have stepped into the ring with anybody else at the drop of a hat. He was as brave as they came. Throughout his career, he took on all comers without ever cherry-picking his opponents. In 1980, it was widely known within the boxing fraternity that he was a shot fighter. He was universally advised to retire and to forget about facing a prime Larry Holmes. In the run-up to the Holmes fight, Ali was as defiant as ever. When questioned about concerns surrounding his health, he said, "Anything that I'm not supposed to do, then that's what I'm gonna do."

In retrospect, Ali should have retired in 1975 after the legendary Thrilla in Manila showdown, which is generally regarded as the most brutal fight in heavyweight championship history. But due to his bravery and willingness to face anyone, he soldiered on for another six years, finally retiring in 1981 after losing to Trevor Berbick. As far as bravery is concerned, for sure Ali is numero uno.

—July 2019

Alen Lutvica: Was Mike Tyson uniquely intimidating in his prime? Were other boxing heavyweight champions such as Muhammad Ali and Vitali Klitschko just as scary, or does Tyson stand out?

J. A.: Yes, in his prime Tyson was unique. He instilled preloaded primal fear into many of his opponents. Of the three solid guys you mention in your question, which guy do you reckon was most capable of provoking a "lamb to the slaughter" look on his opponent's face? Michael Spinks was probably the most scared professional boxer ever to participate in a properly sanctioned and regulated boxing match in any division in history. This guy was a former Olympic gold medallist, a former lineal heavyweight champion, and a talented and slippery boxer-mover. But on the night against prime Tyson, he literally turned up on cue just to get knocked out. Fear became his worst enemy, and the fight-or-flight adrenaline response overwhelmed him. As the great Joe Louis once said, "You can run but you can't hide."

Approximately 91 seconds after the pre-fight stare-down, Spinks was badly knocked out, having not landed a single meaningful punch himself.

Do you think Spinks had a crystal ball? Had he seen the future? Either way, his fate was sealed well before a single punch was thrown.

Tyson had much respect for Ali, but Ali would be the first to admit that intimidation wasn't his game. Ali never scared his opponents—that was primarily Tyson and Liston's game. However, if you are referring to Ali's ability to psych out his opponents—well, that is something different to pure intimidation. Ali irritated and annoyed his opponents so that they would chase after him in fights, the rationale being that an angry opponent is more likely to make mistakes. This tactic worked a treat against Foreman in 1974. Foreman literally hammered away at Ali's body in a kind of aimless, zombie rage.

As for the man mountain that was Vitali Klitschko, he was a huge, athletic guy who also happened to be a world-class boxer. When you face a man of Klitschko's size, you are bound to have a degree of cautious fear, just based on his overwhelming size. The same would apply to Lewis, Bowe, Fury, or even Wladimir Klitschko. This type of size-based intimidation isn't in the same ballpark as what prime Tyson provoked. When facing prime Tyson, guys like Spinks and Bruno were literally envisaging an ambulance taking them to an ICU.

In summary, Tyson and Liston were the top two all-time when it came to the intimidation game. In Liston's case, he was an ex-con and Mafioso who brought his extracurricular persona into the ring. In Tyson's case, he was surely the most hurtful puncher in heavyweight history.

—July 2019

Cesar Guy: Was Mike Tyson afraid of anyone?

J. A.: Tyson had a high fight IQ; that's why he feared a big dude named George Foreman. Quite frankly, if you didn't fear Foreman, then you clearly lacked common sense. Foreman was arguably one of the top heavyweight beasts in boxing history.

Truth be told, to an extent Tyson feared all his opponents, and clearly he feared some more than others. But prime Tyson used that natural adrenaline fear in a positive way. "I use fear as my friend. I reflect that fear back on my opponent; if I don't have fear, then I don't fight," said Tyson when talking about his own pre-fight psyche in 1986. Often he was more fearful of failing in front of a large audience rather than purely fearful of his opponent. Either way, there has been widespread speculation that apparently Foreman was a bad matchup for Tyson. Personally, I think that, prime versus prime, it is a 50:50 matchup. The fight would probably have been similar to the classic slugfest that Foreman had with Ron Lyle in 1976.

Other than Foreman, I don't think any fighter genuinely scared Tyson, although he was always wary of fighting very tall, strong, and athletic guys with stiff jabs who also knew how to grapple. This type of fighter could potentially keep pit-bull Tyson at bay for a few rounds and then spoil and smother him on the inside. At the end of the day, Tyson was a very instinctive boxer. First and foremost, he simply wanted to have a good old-fashioned brawl. That was when his legendary peekaboo style was most effective.

If you saw a random guy of Tyson's build and muscularity at the weigh-in of a prize fight, most people would say that fear was the other guy's problem. It has generally been acknowledged within the boxing fraternity that prime Tyson played the intimidation game better than anybody in the modern era.

—July 2019

ANONYMOUS: Is the greatly revered prime Mike Tyson overrated by fans due to intimidated opponents and his lack of competition at the time?

J. A.: Believe me, I am answering this question while biting my lip, and I'm biting so hard that I'm nearly drawing blood. But no offence intended to you. I'm not mad at you; I believe you're just young, naive, and a bit misinformed. So why don't I try and inform you of the facts—just the facts.

Tyson was probably the roughest and toughest teenager in history

The physical maturity and aggression in the juvenile Tyson conveyed the message "Come get some, all of y'all who want some. Come get some because Mike Tyson is for real." Round up Holyfield, Lewis, and Douglas at age 13 and match them against Tyson at age 13 and you know what's going down. Tyson beat up a 19-year-old guy at the age of 13!

Tyson was the youngest-ever heavyweight champion of the world at age 20

This is a record that may never be broken. At the age of just 20, Tyson was being described as a force of nature. In 1986, against the then-WBC world heavyweight champion Trevor Berbick, the primeval ferocity of Tyson in action was awe-inspiring. His whole body appeared to be one giant fist as he moved upward and forward into his punches. He was always looking to follow up immediately with either hand. Heyday Tyson was a great combo puncher and probably the best finisher in the business. If he had a man on the hook, believe me, Tyson would never let him off. This same Berbick went the distance with a peak Larry Holmes and retired an aging Ali. So Tyson demolished "the man who beat the man".

Speed kills

Tyson was the third-fastest heavyweight in history, only Ali and Floyd Patterson had faster hands. When he finished Pinklon Thomas off in the spring of 1987, he landed seventeen lethal, pinpoint punches in a row, in approximately seven seconds. This man was dangerous.

Tyson was the best defensive heavyweight of the 1980s

Correct. Textbook head movement is extremely rare among the big men. Tyson moved his head like a heavyweight version of Sugar Ray Leonard. "My defence is impregnable!"

Tyson is a legitimate candidate for the GOAT crown

Tyson is the only heavyweight in the post-Ali era who was within touching distance of dethroning the main man himself. There has been speculation that prime Tyson was deliberately derailed and destroyed by the shadier side of the boxing underworld.

Tyson is the most dominant heavyweight champion in history

Even his fiercest critics will concede without hesitation that Tyson was absolutely dominant in his prime. He had plenty of competition at the time; he was just way better than the competition. You name me another fighter—other than maybe George Foreman—who was knocking out a pro boxer every two weeks! Believe me, this takes some doing. Even if a lot of those early fighters were tomato cans, you still have to crush those cans. And just remember, Tyson's knockout streak continued at the world level—he was equally rude to the bums, journeymen, gatekeepers, fringe contenders, and champions.

Tyson is the second most intimidating heavyweight in history after Sonny Liston

This intimidation factor was key to some of Tyson's success in his prime, for sure. And good for him. If you can scare your opponents shitless, then go and do it. You will find that it is much easier said than done. Creating that fear factor, that invincibility persona, was part of Tyson's skill.

His opponents were scared for a good reason. Tyson was possibly the most hurtful puncher in boxing history. Don't believe me? Go ask some of his 1980s sparring partners. Tyson was knocking out one sparring partner per day in his prime. His handlers were literally running out of sparring partners. At times Cus D'Amato had to physically restrain him, as Tyson didn't seem to realise this was a sparring session and not a killing session. Some contracted sparring partners left after the first session without even being paid, due to injury fears!

Tyson is the number-one peekaboo practitioner in history

Peekaboo is a style that is high risk, very energy intensive, and generally regarded as suited only to young and aggressive pros. Tyson took this style and "flew it to the edge of the envelope". He had one-in-a-million boxing genetics! No one else could have pulled it off. A certain legendary trainer knew he had uncovered a diamond in the rough.

Tyson was trained by the master sensei himself

A young and skinny Lennox Lewis visited Cus D'Amato's gym in the Catskills in 1984. Although the teenage Lewis was also a good prospect, Cus knew that Lewis wasn't yet in Tyson's league.

If, after all this, you still think Tyson's overrated, then without doubt you must be a very hard guy to convince.

—March 2019

Sophio Uglava: Who is the most fearless boxer?

J. A.: This one is difficult to answer 100 per cent conclusively. But once again that man Ali has to be at or near the top of the list of most fearless boxers. Any man who set foot in the same ring with a prime Foreman must have had some serious intestinal fortitude. Ali's performance against Foreman was one of the gutsiest displays in boxing history, against a killer who was at the absolute peak of his physical powers and also had significant momentum going into the fight. On top of this, Ali was known to be at least five years past his best. And still he stood in the pocket with a guy who *Ring* magazine has described as the most fearsome puncher in boxing history.

Many fans may not realise that knowledgeable people inside the industry were urging restraint on Foreman's part. He was being told, "Be careful, George; don't kill Muhammad."

On top of this performance, Ali faced off against Sonny Liston in the 1960s. Liston was the equivalent of Foreman in that era. Ali also fought "the puncher of the century" in Earnie Shavers and faced off against possibly the most stubbornly resistant heavyweight of all time—none other than Smokin' Joe Frazier—not once but three times!

What sums up Ali more than anything else was that he literally took on all comers, no matter who they were or how they boxed. He had no fear whatsoever. This is yet another reason why he is considered the greatest. I mean, he even took on yet another Hall of Famer in Larry Holmes when Ali himself was literally washed up. The guy didn't know when to quit. Holmes was probably at his peak in 1980, and Ali was well-known to be a completely shot fighter. Yet once again he stood toe to toe with a great boxing technician. So Ali definitely gets my vote as the bravest warrior of all time, with notable mentions going to Marvin Hagler and Jake LaMotta.

—November 2018

Kinyanjui Kamau: Mike Spinks was a great fighter who beat Larry Holmes twice. Why did he not prepare better against Tyson and instead go out so quickly?

J. A.: Agreed. He was a top boxer and very underrated. Unfortunately for Spinks, he is most remembered for his final outing against prime Tyson, when he was flattened and sent into permanent retirement. He is also mostly remembered as being the most infamous victim of the prime Tyson intimidation aura. On the night, Mike Spinks was scared stiff and totally psyched out. He simply turned up to get knocked out, in exchange for an astronomical payday—pretty simple maths!

With the benefit of hindsight, I think the Tyson fight in 1988 was a fight that Spinks couldn't have won. He literally stood no chance against that version of Tyson. Tyson was way too dominant at the time. In my humble opinion, outside of prime Ali and prime Foreman, no other historical heavyweights could have beaten 1988 Tyson. He was that good. The man was a genuine physical beast and a great technical brawler. He had a great trainer and a dedicated single-mindedness that was hard to beat. On top of all of this, most of his opponents were very scared. So too was Mike Spinks.

In terms of Spinks's preparations, I think he could perhaps have hired a sports psychologist who specialised in the management of fear. Ultimately he would still have got knocked out, but with a more positive mindset, maybe he could have lasted a few rounds longer? On the other hand, in real time, Spinks maybe decided that it was better to get the inevitable over and done with sooner rather than later. I mean, no sensible human being in their right mind wants to take a slow and protracted beating.

—February 2020

Jay Harewood: Has a boxer ever been so nervous that they didn't leave the dressing room?

J.A.: In a major world title fight, the best example of a fighter not wanting to leave his dressing room because of fear was Michael Spinks versus Mike Tyson.

Shortly before the start of this fight, both Spinks's trainer Eddie Futch and his manager, the late Butch Lewis knew their fighter was psychologically broken before a punch was ever thrown. In his dressing room, Spinks was literally going berserk due to uncontrollable fight-or-flight fear.

Butch Lewis had to buy some time so that Eddie Futch could try to calm Spinks down. Lewis therefore deliberately created a "mountain out of a molehill" scene and started complaining about Tyson's hands being wrapped too soon. Apparently he had also spotted a lump in one of Tyson's gloves, and claimed to suspect foul play.

To cut a long story short, Tyson's hands were re-wrapped in front of Spinks's trainer. Lewis's charade bought Spinks a few extra minutes but made no difference to the result.

—January 2021

CHAPTER 2

THE ROCKY UNIVERSE

Anonymous: Who would win in a match between Sonny Liston and Rocky Balboa?

J.A.: To answer this question, we can use Rocky Marciano as a yardstick, given that much of Balboa's fighting character and style was based on Marciano (and of course the lesser-known Chuck Wepner). Just thinking of the pre-fight stare-down between these two legends is enough to send chills down my spine.

Breaking the fight down, most of the physical advantages go to Liston—height, reach, weight, and so on. Specifically, his reach advantage is huge and would most likely prove to be decisive.

The stylistic matchup is fairly symmetrical, since both guys are sluggers. Both guys can box and bang, but I would say Liston is comfortably the slicker boxer. He also has a big advantage in a direct comparison of jabs. Liston possessed one of the absolute best jabs in heavyweight history. Balboa will have to get used to the sight of Liston's jab, as it will be in his face all night long.

In the movies, Balboa is always a limited boxer, but he makes up for his many technical deficiencies with raw power, toughness, and heart. Like Marciano in real life, he is more than happy to take a punch to land a punch. Against Liston, this is clearly a risky tactic because Liston hits so hard. However it is a trade-off that Balboa will have to accept because he cannot outbox Liston.

Ultimately, I think the outcome of this fight depends on the timing of the fight. The only version of Balboa that can beat Liston is the *Rocky 4* version. That guy is simply too tough. He takes Drago's heaviest punches and survives. Therefore he should be able to take Liston's best punches too. Any other version of Balboa should lose by TKO. The *Rocky 4* version, however, exhibited superhuman toughness, resilience, and will to win.

—November 2020

Keith Rakofsky: Which fight out of all the Rocky/Creed movies is the most realistic? Not the most exciting, not the most action-packed, not your favourite—the most reality based!

J. A.: The opening fight in *Rocky 1* was probably the most realistic. Balboa's fictional opponent was a guy named Spider Rico, who was the epitome of a bum fighter. His nickname "Spider" was a big giveaway and perhaps hinted at a guy who was prone to using foul and covert tactics. He had very limited boxing skills, which would have been typical for a 1970s club fighter.

On top of this, Balboa was a technically limited boxer, which no doubt suited Stallone's real-life boxing skills down to the ground. The venue for the fight was a dingy but atmospheric arena, which again was a very believable setting for a local club fight.

The moment Spider Rico got frustrated, he resorted to fouling, and his go-to method was the headbutt. It is safe to say that the lower down you go in the boxing food chain, the more frequently you will see dirty tactics. The manner of his headbutt was blatant, obvious, and unforgivable, but also fairly realistic. Balboa's reaction looked genuine, and naturally he was infuriated. He went ballistic and continued beating Rico after Rico went down.

After watching this fictional fight, you can perhaps understand why Mike Tyson went ballistic after being headbutted by Holyfield in their rematch. When you're enraged, you act largely on impulse—that is, in the heat of the moment.

—December 2020

Janga Zillotin: The fight between Creed and Balboa in *Rocky 1* is obviously something from the movies. But which fight in real life comes most close to that fight?

J. A.: The fight at the end of *Rocky 1* is loosely based on the fight between Muhammad Ali and a relatively obscure boxer named Chuck Wepner. The ridiculously overmatched Wepner somehow scrounged his way to the fifteenth and final round, but in the end Ali won by a stoppage. For his part, Wepner more than exceeded everyone's expectations.

According to legend, in 1975, Stallone was ringside for this fight and was mighty impressed with Wepner's toughness and heart. And so the story of a down on his luck white underdog boxer was born. In the movie, Apollo is the personification of Ali, and Rocky Balboa is a blend of Wepner and Marciano.

The main difference between the real fight (Ali versus Wepner) and the movie fight (Balboa versus Creed) was that in the movie, Balboa lasted the full distance. But ultimately, the script of the two fights is very similar—the technically limited underdog rises to the occasion and punches well above his usual ability. The flip side of the coin is that the gifted and superior athlete underperforms due to a series of distractions and oversights.

—November 2020

Janga Zillotin: Suppose Sylvester Stallone had invested all his energy in being a boxer instead of an actor. Would he have been a force in the heavyweight division?

J. A.: Stallone had almost no chance at all. Before we even talk boxing technique, there is a very simple reason he would never have succeeded at heavyweight in real life. That's because in real life, he barely makes light heavyweight. His actual weight during the original *Rocky* movies was barely 180 pounds with loose change. But given the fact he is ripped to the bone, he is a big 180—at least on celluloid.

But to be honest, a lot of regular gym rats could be made to look bigger and tougher in a film, especially if they too strapped on a bandana, grabbed a rocket launcher, and put some fake knife cuts on their pectorals.

Stallone had one sparring session with the legendary Earnie Shavers, during *Rocky 3* auditions.

Apparently, just one mucking-about left body shot from Shavers nearly broke Stallone's ribs—and this was with Shavers taking it easy!

As you suggest in your question, what if Stallone had invested all his energy and time into boxing? I still don't think this would have made much difference. Real-life boxing is a totally different kettle of fish to choreographed boxing. If Stallone really wanted to turn pro, then I suggest his best bet would have been to become a sparring partner type of boxer. Top heavyweight contenders could perhaps have used him as a "human chicken" for target and stalking practice.

—November 2020

Jorge Buen Abad: How many people would it take to beat Drago in a one-on-one street fight?

J. A.: Three untrained, skinny guys should be enough to take on and beat Drago. Let's assume for a second that his fictional punching power of 2,000 pounds per square inch (PSI) is genuine. Also let's bear in mind that in *Rocky 4*, he generated this bone-crushing power with gloves on.

Given the fact that he is a world-class pro boxer, we can assume with 100 per cent certainty that his power punches *will* land on his untrained street adversaries. Also let's assume that Drago lands first with the power punches.

As Drago's representative in *Rocky 4* suggested, "Anything he hits, he destroys!" So let's assume that Drago's first power punch lands successfully and stretches out the first guy. According to Newton's third law of motion, Drago's bare-knuckle fist receives an equal and opposite force. Given that his punching power is 2,000 PSI, this inevitably means he ruptures his fist and has one broken hand.

The same process is repeated with the second guy. Now Drago has rendered two guys unconscious and in the process has broken both his hands. Given that he is just a boxer, we can assume he has no attacking potential with his kicks.

With Drago severely debilitated, we can conclude that the remaining adversary will overwhelm him. The moral of the story is that Drago needs to remember to wear his boxing gloves—even for a street fight!

—November 2020

Jay Harewood: What was the most unrealistic thing that happened in the Rocky movies?

J. A.: Where can you start?

The unrealistic elements of this movie franchise peaked in *Rocky 4*, starting with the chemically enhanced punching power of Ivan Drago. He hit with a mind-numbing punching force of approximately 2,000 PSI, which is in itself impossible.

In addition to this, an obvious and major plot flaw was the manner in which Drago's fictional punching power was contextualised. In round two, Drago is observed literally punching Apollo Creed to death in what was meant to be an exhibition match. Surely this could only happen in a Rocky movie—an ex-world champion being killed in the ring in an *exhibition*, right in front of the referee.

Now fast forward for around sixty minutes to the exciting conclusion of this film. In approximately forty-five minutes of non-stop ferocious action, Drago pounds on Rocky relentlessly and lands around twenty times the number of clean power punches he landed on Creed. Those same punches killed Creed—and yet Balboa is relatively unfazed and relatively unhurt? In fact, at the end of the fight, after taking the worst beating in recorded human history, Rocky isn't rushed to the hospital. Instead he is lucid enough to give a bipartisan speech that virtually ends the Cold War! By rights, if that movie had been consistently farcical, then after taking those bombs from Drago, Balboa should have had no skull left at all.

—December 2020

Jonathan Alexander: If Joe Frazier existed in the Rocky universe, then didn't Ali and George Foreman also exist in the Rocky universe?

J. A.: I suppose you could use Joe Frazier's appearance as himself in the original *Rocky* film as evidence that Joe Frazier "existed" in the Rocky universe. He only made a brief cameo appearance in *Rocky 1.* He too was from Philadelphia, like Balboa's character in the film.

The way that I have always interpreted the characters in this movie franchise are as follows:

- *Rocky Balboa* as the protagonist is apparently a composite of two real-life historical boxers: the great Rocky Marciano and the lesser-known Chuck Wepner, also known as the Bayonne Bleeder. Inspiration for the showdown at the end of *Rocky 1* was the real-life fight between Ali and Wepner in 1975.
- *Apollo Creed* is the chief antagonist in the original film, based largely on the character of Muhammad Ali. He's a superior athlete, a silky boxer-mover, and a showman to boot. So you could say that Ali existed in the Rocky universe via Apollo Creed's character.
- *Clubber Lang* is the chief antagonist in Rocky 3. He is largely based on the looming personas of Sonny Liston and George Foreman. Like Liston, Lang is an ex-con, but this shadier side of his character is never elaborated upon in the movie. His main character traits of being aloof, mean, and unapproachable are 1970s Foreman through and through. He's a no-nonsense slugger with tremendous raw power but limited stamina and ring IQ. Basically when plan A fails (as in the *Rocky 3* rematch), Lang has no Plan B. (Remember the Rumble in the Jungle, hint, hint?) So essentially you could say that Big George Foreman existed in the Rocky universe via the character of Clubber.

—October 2020

Jonathan Alexander: Am I right that in *Rocky 3,* it is revealed that Clubber Lang is also a southpaw?

J. A.: Yes, Clubber Lang is a movie southpaw in that he leads with his right side. However, in various boxing scenes, his stance is a fairly exaggerated and open southpaw stance.

In the "Eye of the Tiger" montage at the beginning of *Rocky 3,* Clubber can clearly be seen boxing from the southpaw stance—that is, right hand and right foot leading. In a different segment of the intro, he charges forward aggressively, and it is again evident that he is fighting left-handed.

Additionally, in both fights with Balboa, he boxes left-handed or from the southpaw stance. So Clubber was definitely a southpaw in *Rocky 3*.

—December 2020

Richard Guy: Who are the best Rocky Balboa opponents, ranked in order?

J.A.:

1) *Apollo Creed, "Master of Disaster"*

"I saw you beat that man like you beat no other, and the man kept coming. We don't need that kind of man in our lives—let's go after some new meat." Apollo should have listened to his trainer Tony's well-intentioned advice. Creed was a great boxer, a great mover, and a supreme athlete—he was really a cut above Rocky. However, at world level, you underestimate your opponent at your peril, especially a guy as tough, resilient, and single-mindedly determined as Balboa. In the first fight, Creed gave a motivated and fearless Balboa a tremendous beating but couldn't finish him off. He won a close points decision nonetheless. In the rematch, he carried out further butchery on the orthodox version of Rocky but again failed to finish him off. Creed's main weakness was his vulnerability to body punching, and this caught up with him in the final round of the rematch.

2) *Clubber Lang*

Lang was a very powerful and truly intimidating warrior with a serious mean streak—surely the toughest-looking onscreen boxer ever. Lang was a guy who really understood the meaning of mind games and the concept of getting under the skin of his opponents, the rationale being that an angry opponent is one who is more prone to mistakes. Lang would literally do and say anything to get a shot at the world title—including insulting Mrs Balboa. "Hey woman, I bet you stay up late every night dreaming of a real man, since your man ain't got no heart. Why don't you bring your pretty little self over to my apartment, and I'll show you what a real man is all about!" Lang's weaknesses were his stamina and predictability; he was, however, the only guy to KO Rocky.

3) *Ivan Drago, "Death from Above"*

Drago was a superhuman steroid freak who punched so hard that he could kill you, even with his eyes closed. Drago arguably gave an ageing and over-the-hill Balboa the worst beating in history, but once again somehow contrived to lose. Out of all of Balboa's championship-grade opponents, Drago had the most questionable boxing technique and heart. What percentage enhancement did the steroids give him?

4) *Tommy "the Machine" Gunn*

By *Rocky 5*, surely you'd think Balboa's opponents would have realised that it is better to box Rocky sensibly, rather than slugging it out with him! Tommy could certainly brawl, but alas, both his boxing ability and his street-fighting IQ were fairly limited. He made the cardinal mistake of slugging with the slugger and paid the price. The guys literally beat the living daylights out of each other, but ultimately Balboa's granite chin prevailed.

5) *Mason "the Line" Dixon*

Possibly a jibe at the modern manufactured heavyweight champion, Dixon was surely a pumped-up cruiserweight and had questionable punching power. Although he could definitely box, he couldn't bang. Again we saw Rocky's granite chin bailing him out.

6) *Spider Rico*

In Mickey's (Rocky's trainer) own words, "He's a bum!" Rico unfortunately didn't even make journeyman grade and surely was Rocky's weakest opponent by far. His biggest strength and signature combo was his one-two, followed by a well-disguised headbutt on the referee's blindside.

—March 2019

Michael Brett: Why did Apollo Creed lose to Ivan Drago so easily? Is it plausible in real life that a former world champion could lose so quickly to an amateur?

J. A.: He lost mainly due to accumulated ring rust caused by inactivity, which was further exacerbated by the generalised effects of Father Time. In the movie, Drago had superhuman punching power. According to the data given, he hit with an approximate force of 2,000 PSI. This effectively translated into a punching force that was three times greater than the average heavyweight. As his representative prophetically stated, "Anything he hits, he destroys."

A faded and inactive former champion became a sitting-duck target for a guy with freak-show punching power. The crude haymaker punches that Drago landed were full, clean power shots to the head which landed absolutely flush. With his punching force, Drago's punches literally exerted a bone-crushing effect. To put the force claimed for Drago into context, prime Mike Tyson was estimated to have hit with a force of around 1,200 PSI. Drago's freakish punching power, combined with Creed's age and inactivity, resulted in fatal consequences. Creed should really have listened to Rocky's words of wisdom and delayed the fight until they had more information on the unknown amateur.

It is entirely plausible that a former world champion could lose to an up-and-coming fighter—particularly an unknown. It is also possible that a former world champion could die in the ring—boxers have collapsed and died in boxing rings in real life. In the movies, the fights have simply been exaggerated for the sake of drama. However, what was fairly unbelievable was the fact that Apollo had virtually no defence against Drago's punches, particularly after the first few bombs landed. He became defenceless, immobile, and almost paralyzed. His death scene is even more implausible given that, in reality, he would surely have been knocked out long before being punched to death.

—November 2019

Darryl Morhardt: Is there some detail in the Rocky movies that you picked up that most people probably didn't?

J. A.: How long have you got? In *Rocky 1*, Balboa sustained damage to his right eye, which his cornerman cut towards the end of the fight. In the sequel, *Rocky 2*, it turned out that Balboa had some vision loss in his right eye. His trainer Mickey confirmed this by doing a quick hand-movement test on the staircase of his apartment. So we as viewers were alerted to the fact that Rocky had some vision loss in his right eye. The eye damage was effectively the motivation and main reason that Mickey gave for turning Balboa into an orthodox (right-handed) fighter instead of his natural southpaw (left-handed) stance. Mickey's explanation was that switching to orthodox would afford greater protection to Balboa's bad right eye.

Now on the surface, this probably does make some logical sense. You would think his right eye would be better shielded from Apollo's laser-gun left jab if he fights from the orthodox stance. But what is totally absurd are his actual fighting tactics, which were probably even more gung-ho and plain suicidal than in *Rocky 1.* In other words, Mickey had the common sense and tactical savvy to change Rocky's stance in order to protect his bad eye, but not the wisdom to alter his in-fight game plan? And what was that game plan? To basically get hit by everything, including the kitchen sink, and take power punches for fun, just to land a shot himself. The beating he sustained in *Rocky 2* was even worse than the *Rocky 1* beating, and yet there was no mention of any further eye damage or other repercussions in *Rocky 3*. This is clearly pure theatrical nonsense. The alleged eye damage was only included as a justification for the stance switch from lefty to righty.

—December 2018

SHAUN O'CONNOR: At the time of filming of Rocky 3, who would have actually won, Sylvester Stallone or Mr.T (Lawrence Turead)?

J.A.: Back in '82, although Mr.T looked way more fearsome, I think in a real-life regulated boxing match between the two actors, it's probably fairly even. To simplify the equation, it's *power* (Mr.T) vs *speed* (Stallone).

Believe it or not, I believe the scripted fights we saw in Rocky 3 serve as fairly accurate blueprints for what may transpire in a real life boxing match. If Stallone stands and trades with Mr.T, there's no two ways about it— he's gonna get busted up by the heavier and stronger man.

If he duplicates his more "sensible" tactics in the Rocky 3 rematch, he can frustrate Mr.T and cause him to fatigue. The two main weaknesses of Mr.T being limited ring IQ and stamina.

In a street-fight, I think Stallone literally has no chance and would be overwhelmed by Mr.T quickly. Many young fans maybe unaware but Mr.T was once rated as the toughest door-man in Chicago and actually came first in the America's toughest bouncer competition, way back in 1980.

—May 2021

CHAPTER 3

STYLES MAKE FIGHTS

David Mulata: What are some different boxing styles and what boxer most defines each one?

J.A.: Beginning with the safest style first and the riskiest last, broadly speaking we have four main classifications.

The out-fighter (paper)

The out-fighter strives to maintain a long distance from his opponent, boxing sensibly behind his jab and using the whole ring. Like Apollo's trainer Tony said in *Rocky 2*, "Just stick and move!" That is the basic premise of this style. It is largely movement based, and he boxes mostly on the back foot. It is a more passive style and is therefore more energy efficient, as the boxer is in a relaxed state. Good out-fighters have good reflexes and possess good footwork. They are fast, intelligent, and normally athletic. Their wins are mostly due to a large accumulation of punches and are often on points.

The slugger (stone)

Slugging is generally the bread-and-butter boxing style. It is characterised by fairly basic technique and overwhelming brute force. A good slugger is physically strong and heavy handed and has a good chin. His most effective punches will be crude, swinging hooks, as often depicted by Big George Foreman, the quintessential heavyweight slugger. It is a pressure-based style which is more energy intensive and inherently riskier than the out-fighter style. Cutting off the ring and cornering your opponent on the ropes are probably the most underrated slugger skills. However, the slugger is often characterised by predictability and high performance early on, fading as the fight wears on.

The boxer-puncher (all-rounder)

As the name of this boxing style suggests, the boxer-puncher is something of an all-rounder or jack of all trades. He throws a large variety of punches, both straights and hooks. He is equally comfortable boxing on the inside or on the outside, and is often quite happy to switch hit or alternate stances. As such, it is useful to be genuinely ambidextrous with this style. Of all the boxing styles, this style can be the most difficult to deal with due to the boxer-puncher's natural versatility and adaptability.

The in-fighter (scissors)

In-fighting is by far the riskiest and most off-rhythm boxing style, but potentially the most damaging and rewarding. The in-fighter wants to fight you inside a "phone booth" where your height and reach advantages are useless. This is a pressure fighting style, based on volume punching, precision power, timing, speed, and movement. It is very aggressive and energy intensive, and as such favours youth in a big way. Body punching is crucial for success, and so too is defensive head movement. Over the years, the best in-fighters or swarmers have been characterised by short, meteoric careers. The swarmer is the perfect style to deal with a good out-fighter.

The above four classifications are very broad. Any given boxer can exhibit significant crossover. Also a given boxer's style can sometimes change naturally or undergo deliberate modifications due to age and injury.

—May 2019

Kevin Hillep: What are some of the best matchups in boxing history by style— slugger versus slugger, boxer versus boxer, and swarmer versus swarmer?

J. A.*:*

Slugger versus slugger: Whenever I think of a slugger, an image of George Foreman immediately comes to mind. His classic 1970s slugfest with Ron Lyle was a pure machismo, pub brawl type of fight. Tactics and skill went out of the window, and it was simply a case of bombs away. If ever a boxing match could be summarised by the ethos of last man standing, then this was it. After a real to-and-fro battle of brawn, in the end Foreman's granite chin prevailed.

Boxer versus boxer: The classic matchup is Larry Holmes versus Michael Spinks in 1985. History has been very unkind to Michael Spinks due to the unfortunate fact he failed miserably against a rampaging Mike Tyson in 1988. There was, however, a time when Spinks was one of the silkiest boxers in the world. When he upset Larry Holmes in 1985–1986, he was probably at his skilful and crafty best. On the other hand, the legendary Larry Holmes was on the slide, Father Time having eroded some of his skills and sharpness.

Swarmer versus swarmer: I favour Julio Cesar Chavez versus Edwin Rosario in 1987. Legendary Mexican hard man Julio Caesar Chavez was the quintessential modern-day swarmer. He was a great body puncher, a great in-fighter, and a master at cutting off the ring. However, in this classic 1980s fight, Chavez didn't have it all his own way. Rosario was a dangerous banger in his own right who also brought plenty of know-how to the table. Unfortunately for Rosario, he just met the wrong guy at the wrong time in the wrong place—a guy who happened to do it all that little bit better. In the end, Chavez systematically wore his man down by switching his punches upstairs and downstairs. He put on a masterclass of in-fighting.

—December 2018

Temi Ola: It was clear after the first round that George Foreman had the perfect antidote to Joe Frazier's fighting style. Why was there no attempt to adapt?

J. A.: You can only adapt if your opponent allows you to adapt.

Fight psychology also played a huge part. From the famous pre-fight stare-down, it was already advantage to Foreman. It was by no means a foregone conclusion, but from a psychological standpoint, it appeared that he had the upper hand.

In the first round, Frazier absorbed some of the heaviest bombs in history. It is now safe to assume that he must have been both heavily concussed and confused. At the end of round 1, while sat on his stool, he clearly wasn't thinking straight. Who really knows for sure what instructions his seconds gave him?

Aside from having all of the physical advantages, Foreman also knew how to use them. Additionally his slugger style trumped Frazier's in-fighter style—stone blunts scissors!

Finally, Smokin' Joe was one of the most stubbornly resistant boxers in history. It simply wasn't in his nature to back off. He only knew how to fight in one way, and that was to seek and destroy—in many ways similar to a heat-seeking missile.

The problem was that he was up against a huge grizzly bear of a man who was also a capable boxer and simply bombed him *early on*. Frazier was barely given time to breathe, let alone adapt. If the referee hadn't intervened after the sixth and final knockdown, and if it were humanly possible, Frazier would probably have carried on through an infinite number of knockdowns.

—December 2020

Gray Summers: What adjustment could Muhammad Ali have made to get past Ken Norton's difficult style?

J. A.: Not a lot, really, as he was an ageing fighter who had become more flat-footed since his enforced three-year layoff. Additionally, both the timing of the trilogy (early 1970s) and the youth factor favoured Norton.

One of Ken Norton's boxing specialties was blocking punches with his gloves. At the time, he was the best in the business with this particular defensive technique. In some respects, he was something of a heavyweight version of Floyd Mayweather, at least from a defensive standpoint. He often employed a crab-like guard or Philly shell, which was perfectly suited to catching straight punches from a medium-punching heavyweight such as Ali. Mayweather is also famous for using the same or similar guard.

The Ali versus Norton matchup was a classic case of *styles make fights*. Norton's defence just so happened to be perfectly suited to neutralising Ali's offence. On the other hand, a slightly past-prime Ali was now a very hittable boxer due to a distinct decline in his once legendary reflexes.

Norton was a fairly slick boxer-puncher and had plenty of solid attacking options of his own. In fact, if you watch a great golden-era documentary called *Champions Forever*, Norton explained in his own words, "In my mind, I knew I could always beat Ali."

Another reason that Norton had Ali's number, so to speak, was because his trainer had Ali's number. When you're trained by a master tactician like Eddie Futch—who had an uncanny knack of seeing and exploiting an opponent's weaknesses—you're in a good place. To beat a guy as good and seasoned as Ali, you need the right game plan. Ali proved vulnerable to the left hook, and Norton hit the target, summarily breaking Ali's jaw in their first fight in 1973.

Finally, Ken Norton was known as "the black Hercules" due to his muscular physique and physical strength. In the clinches, he could more than hold his own against Ali. Ultimately, Norton could match 1970s Ali in almost all boxing departments, which was why Ali couldn't make any effective adjustments for the second or third fights. The third and final instalment in

Yankee Stadium was something of a daylight robbery, as most neutrals scored that fight either a draw or slightly in favour of Norton.

—December 2019

Piotr Gajda and John Marcus: How would you describe the boxing style of pre-exile Muhammad Ali (boxer-puncher, swarmer, etc.)?

J. A.: Muhammad Ali was always an out-fighter, pre-exile or post-exile. In general his game plan was to keep his opponent on the end of his long jab, pot-shot him at his leisure, and use athleticism to keep on the move. Any punches coming his way were dodged, largely using his feline reflexes.

The main things that changed after his enforced three-year lay-off were a decline in his abilities and a slight weight gain. This in turn led to him exhibiting increased flat-footedness and reduced mobility. Post-exile Ali could no longer "float like a butterfly". Other factors that caused a modification to his style was the increased quality of the opposition and the effects of Father Time.

His 1970s opponents (Joe Frazier and co.) were able to corner Ali more easily and apply more effective and educated pressure. This being the case, he was forced to fight inside more frequently than he would have liked during the second phase of his career. Hence the fact that 1970s Ali is sometimes referred to as "blood and guts" Ali, because he often had to rely on his toughness to get the win. But at the end of the day, he was still a slickster and an out-fighter in the 1970s. The point is that, for one reason or another, he simply wasn't as slick as he had been in his 1960s heyday.

If you like the boxing analogy of paper, stone, and scissors, then Ali was paper through and through. His career rivals, Frazier and Foreman, were scissors and stone respectively. In the case of Ali versus Foreman, the classic rule of thumb held true: paper (Ali) wrapped up stone (Foreman).

—November 2020.

Anonymous: Did Buster Douglas's fighting style neutralise Mike Tyson's head movements?

J. A.: I would say definitely no, no, no. Too many geishas and Class A drugs probably had a greater neutralising effect! But on the night (sticking with the boxing facts), Tyson's head movements were uncharacteristically poor—in fact almost non-existent. It was probably the single worst defensive performance of Tyson's whole pro career. You could, however, argue that Buster capitalised on Tyson's defensive mistakes and soundly punished him for lack of head movement. Buster landed a number of solid one-twos and threes in the early going, which set a strong precedent for the later rounds.

The notion behind Tyson's peekaboo style was to present a perpetual moving target to the taller and more rangy out-fighter. Under Rooney, his whole upper body moved from side to side in an automatic, well-drilled manner. This defensive pendulum motion had been rehearsed ad Infinitum in training with Cus and subsequently under Rooney. Against Buster, this characteristic rolling-from-the-waist movement was clearly absent, and so too was his normal head movement. Therefore he became a sitting duck for the taller fighter's standard jab and right-cross combo.

I certainly wouldn't say there was anything special in Buster's style that beat the Iron Man on that fateful and freaky night. Buster was simply the fortuitous guy who happened to be in the right place at the right time to take full advantage of a grossly distracted, poorly conditioned, and altogether underprepared Tyson.

You can ask virtually any inside-industry boxing expert and they will likely tell you that a lesser-known guy named Tony Tucker (similar style, height, and build to Douglas) was a lot better than Buster, and Mike Tyson defeated Tucker on points in 1987. Of course Tony Tucker gave Mike a stern test, but in the end Tyson prevailed handily. So a properly focused and Rooney-trained Tyson would have made light work of the normally harmless Buster Douglas. However, Buster deserves credit for his performance on the night, particularly for his use of the jab and (for a change) for being a Tyson opponent who wasn't scared stiff.

Tyson critics have a bad habit of using cause-and-effect analysis and asserting that Tyson was dominated by Douglas's style, concluding that this was the primary reason for Tyson's defeat. In my humble opinion, this is simply not true. Tyson was beaten by Douglas because of a number of freaky circumstances that intertwined and coincidentally occurred on the same night. As Tyson himself candidly commented in a post-fight interview, "Any good engine can have one bad day."

—October 2020

Rodney Chin: Does a great technical boxer usually beat the powerful brawler?

J. A.: In general, I would say yes, more often than not this rule of thumb holds true. But over the years there have been many notable exceptions. Probably the two most important and decisive questions in this classic boxer-versus-brawler matchup are "Can the boxer take a decent punch?" and "Can he avoid the brawler early on?" As long as the answers are both yes, then the boxer should have enough in his locker to outpoint the brawler. If the answer is no, then this matchup of contrasting styles can end in a hurry for the boxer.

One of the most iconic boxer-brawler matchups of the modern era was the 1980s trilogy between Sugar Ray Leonard and Roberto Duran—now the stuff of legend. In their first meeting in 1980, dubbed the "Brawl in Montreal", Sugar Ray Leonard became a victim of his own machismo. He committed one of boxing's unforgivable sins, and that was to "brawl with the brawler". He chose to slug it out with Duran at close quarters and paid the price. Roberto Duran is widely regarded by most boxing experts as the number one pound-for-pound brawler of all time. Due to Leonard's world-class chin and all-round know-how, he lasted the distance against a rampant Duran.

In the rematch later that same year, Leonard altered his tactics and put on a masterclass of out-fighting and counterpunching. During this fight, Leonard's increased mobility and slick counterpunching became a repetitive nightmare for Duran and ultimately led him to quit, uttering the now infamous Spanish words, "*No mas.*"

So what conclusions can be drawn from this classic stylistic matchup? Without doubt, at the highest level of boxing, when all other boxing ingredients and factors are equal, then tactics and strategy become crucial.

However, notable examples of brawlers obliterating better technical boxers were seen during two classic 1970s heavyweight matchups. In both fights, a world class boxer-puncher named Ken Norton (who gave Ali hell) was destroyed early on by probably the two hardest punchers in heavyweight history. In these instances, the decisive factor proved to be Norton's average chin combined with the jaw-breaking power of George Foreman and Earnie Shavers.

Apart from the obvious mistake of forgetting to duck, what other error did Norton make against Foreman in 1973? Well, according to Foreman's version of events, "Ken Norton started throwing big hooks early on." Instead of getting on his bike or simply tying his man up, Norton somehow contrived to stay at a set distance—a distance at which Foreman had maximum leverage—and was caught with huge, swinging punches. A few years later, in 1979, Earnie Shavers gave Norton a repeat dose of the same brawler medicine, only quicker.

Ultimately, I would say the technical boxer-mover has to fight smart, fight mobile, and be reasonably tough. In more recent times, Andre Ward versus Carl Froch in 2011 was a good example of a world-class technical boxer (Ward) completely controlling and easily out-pointing the tougher and cruder brawler (Froch). During this fight, on multiple occasions, Froch did land on Ward, but in this instance the boxer was more than tough enough to handle Froch's power.

—February 2019

Jovanne Rodriguez: How could George Foreman compete at such a high level in his comeback career when he looked like he was so out of shape?

J. A.: That's because he was the same mean dude, simply two to three stone fatter! Looks can also be deceiving. He was a lot wiser in his old age. He always possessed elite boxing genetics, and this didn't change with age. Given that he boxed in the division of giants, being overweight wasn't really a big deal, especially if the other guy was fat too—see a guy named Andy Ruiz Junior or another one nicknamed Butterbean. There have been numerous heavyweights over the years who have boxed successfully with more than just a layer of fat. As one gets older, the fat may well help a certain type of fighter, such as a slugger like Foreman.

An ageing Foreman realised that his contemporaries in the late 1980s and early 1990s were, on average, more bulky than the heavyweights of his original era. So he figured the extra weight would prove to be useful in the clinches. Judging by his blubbery physique, it was obvious that old Foreman was never going to win a Mr. Universe contest. But in Foreman's case, the extra blubber served a protective function—especially given his reduced mobility. Even at his best, he was always a limited defensive boxer and this wasn't going to improve with age. The extra fat was intended to provide a cushioning effect against body shots.

From a genetic standpoint, his boxing toolbox was always great. Again, this wasn't going to change much with age. Whether he was old or young, Foreman was what he was, and that was a pure slugger. He could always take a hard punch and give a hard punch, and that was it, really. The clever part was the realisation that he would tire more quickly with age and weight-gain. So, in his second coming, the punching preacher paced himself that much better.

The final reason he became the oldest heavyweight champion ever was due to the level of competition he faced. The early 1990s heavyweight division was decent but not great and lacked a great body puncher. So Foreman's vulnerability to the body wasn't fully exploited. If a certain

Iron Mike Tyson hadn't been languishing in a jail cell during the early 1990s, then there would have been a distinct possibility that Foreman never regained the title.

—November 2019

Bill Gates: Who in boxing would you say has the best brawler style?

J. A.: If you mean the best brawler ever, then a fighter once known as "Hands of Stone" would get my vote. In the boxing business, Roberto Duran virtually rewrote the manual for brawling. He is arguably the most complete and technically correct brawler in boxing history. Additionally, in a strictly pound-for-pound comparison, he may well have possessed the most rock-solid fists ever—hence the nickname. Add into the mix his rock chin, and Duran was perfectly equipped for brawling. In his finest hour, he roughed up a certain Sugar Ray Leonard in a legendary fight known as "the Brawl in Montreal". In this fight, Leonard learned a painful boxing lesson: "Never brawl with a brawler." However, even in defeat, Leonard garnered much respect and adulation for having the courage and audacity to bar fight with the master brawler.

In 1983, in a fight against the late Davey Moore, Duran was at his brutal and vicious best. He was all over Moore from the outset, literally mauling his man into submission. Apparently this Duran fight was one of Mike Tyson's favourite fights. Tyson often talked about emulating Duran's style. In particular, Tyson fondly recited the manner in which Duran stalked his prey, "cut off the runners", and surgically wore his man down.

Later on that same year, Duran was again creating headlines. This time he was throwing down the gauntlet to middleweight king Marvelous Marvin Hagler. In what turned out to be a brutal and bruising fifteen rounder, Duran came up just short and lost on a narrow split decision. Like Leonard, he still gained huge respect in defeat. In the early 1980s, Hagler had built a fearsome reputation as a physical beast and a masterful switch-hitting boxer-puncher who often wore his opponents down like a virus. Even though Duran gave away significant height and reach to Hagler, he proved once again that if you fight big, then you can more than hold your own against the naturally bigger and longer man.

Many knowledgeable boxing fans dream of a hypothetical matchup between Duran and Floyd Mayweather at 147 pounds. If there was one historical brawler who was most well-equipped to crack Floyd Mayweather's complicated defensive conundrum, then surely Duran was that guy. The outcome of this dream fight would inevitably hinge on small details, such as ring size, bout duration, and glove size. If the fight were scheduled for fifteen rounds in a smallish ring, using small gloves, then I would just about go for Duran.

—September 2019

Viktor Bondarchuk: Would you say that Mike Tyson was overrated or underrated?

J. A.: Both! Truth be told, there were some aspects of his game that were slightly overrated and others that were slightly underrated. At the time of his dominance, he was the most feared ring monster since Sonny Liston. Why? Apparently he was a very hard puncher with both hands. But he wasn't the only historical heavyweight who could punch hard. Almost all world-class heavyweights possess sufficient firepower to take each other out—that is, if they can land power punches on their opponents' chins. Believe me, this is a big if.

The media of the day droned on and on about Tyson's punching power, highlighting it as the primary driver for his stunning knockout streak. In reality, punching power was not the main reason that made prime Tyson so dangerous, dominant, and feared. It was his near-perfect boxing skills and his brilliant, textbook technique. Historically, traditional brawlers didn't fight or move like prime Tyson. He was far more advanced and skilled than the crude old-school brawlers.

Pay close attention to the phrase "angles of attack", because you better believe that Mike Tyson understood what boxing geometry is all about. Some of the angles and positions from which his power punches emerged were truly unprecedented—in particular the agility of his hooks and uppercuts was fantastic. The surprise factor associated with his attacks was very underrated. Many of his opponents were simply caught unawares. The subtle use of both body and punching feints belied his tender age; he was already boxing like a seasoned veteran.

Cus D'Amato was a true scholar of boxing and was the closest thing to a real-life boxing professor. The profound and positive influence of D'Amato on a young Tyson was very underrated and largely went unnoticed until after D'Amato's death.

So what did Cus actually do for Tyson? He provided him with the most technically advanced and bespoke boxing blueprint on how a relatively short heavyweight can capitalise on taller boxers' weaknesses. Possibly the most underrated aspect of prime Tyson's game was his uncanny ability to close the gap on taller men without taking too many counters.

This ability to close the gap quickly and efficiently was key to Tyson's early success. It relied on advanced and well-drilled defensive skills. (Just ask David Tua about the difficulties in getting close to world class opposition—he spent thirty-six minutes lumbering around after Lennox Lewis while mostly punching thin air in 2000.) As Cus himself once told a young Tyson, "You gotta be smart and not get hit—that's when you're a fighter."

In summary, I suggest that prime Tyson's punching power receives too much airtime. He was without doubt a massive puncher, but that wasn't the main factor underpinning his early success. His ability to hit *and not get hit in return* was the primary reason for his dominance. The defensive aspects of his highly aggressive style were very underrated and provided him with the "key to the lock" opportunity to knock out many taller but technically inferior opponents.

—August 2019

Michael Venturino: In boxing, Mike Tyson was absolutely mauling his opponents in the 1980s. But when he fought Tony Tucker, he basically couldn't even hurt him. Why was that?

J. A.: This was in large part due to Tucker's left jab, which was key to much of his success, particularly in the early going.

Tony Tucker kept pumping a good, solid, accurate jab in Tyson's face, which kept Mike off balance early on. When facing a massive and deadly puncher, it is imperative that you prevent him from planting his feet firmly in the canvas, particularly in the early rounds. Tucker also smothered and clinched Tyson very quickly and effectively in what was becoming known inside the industry as the "Mike Tyson kill-zone". This was a zone of canvas that extended from mid range to right up close. It was an area in which Tyson was able to time punches perfectly and unleash deadly accurate combinations. If one punch missed, the second one didn't. Tucker's jab prevented Mike from combination punching in the early rounds.

It obviously helped that Tucker was noticeably confident in his own ability and wasn't scared stiff, like so many of Tyson's opponents at the time. He, along with Bonecrusher Smith, were the two guys who fought peak Tyson with a pre-planned containment strategy and effectively executed that strategy. It revolved around the premise of not engaging Tyson in his kill-zone, where the risk of being mauled was greatest. After six rounds or eighteen minutes, it was a fairly well-known fact that Tyson's output and intensity tended to drop off.

—August 2018

Roland Diaz: Which fight showed the decline of Mike Tyson?

J. A.: I'm going to go slightly against the grain on this one. Rather than saying the obvious Buster Douglas fight, I'm going for a slightly earlier fight. Don't get me wrong; Tyson put in a dismal career-worst performance against Douglas—of that there can be no doubt. But to the trained eye, that wasn't the first fight that showed he was a fighter in decline. I do have a number of rational boxing reasons for my choice.

In the first round of Tyson versus Bruno 1, Tyson came under fire from the technically limited Frank Bruno, who surprisingly landed several clean power punches on Tyson. The masterful defensive ninja who was prime Tyson, under Rooney, would surely never have been hit cleanly by a guy like Bruno. Tyson was hit hard by Bruno more times in one round than in all of his previous championship fights combined. Underpinning all of Iron Mike's devastating displays of firepower was a watertight peekaboo defence, and against Bruno it was already in decline. An old American football adage that really summed up Tyson's decline is "Offense wins you games, but defence wins you the championship." Go figure.

At the time of the Bruno fight, in the early part of 1989, Tyson had been away from his well-intentioned trainer Kevin Rooney for a period of around six months. His last fight with Rooney in charge was the Spinks fight, in which Tyson wasn't too far off invincibility. From a boxing standpoint, the drop in his performance from Spinks to Bruno 1 was astonishing and was arguably the biggest dip of Tyson's career. On top of a now-flawed defence, Tyson's timing was also way off.

A further example of Tyson's rapid decline was his increased willingness to accept clinches. Essentially what saw him through the Bruno fight was a limited opponent and Tyson's much-vaunted punching power. Tyson's "wallpaper" was simply hiding cracks that would surface in a big way approximately a year later.

For the Bruno fight, Tyson's main cornerman was a guy named Aaron Snowell, who quite frankly didn't have a clue. Snowell had been hired by Don King, supposedly as Rooney's replacement. This was another terrible professional decision made by Don King on Tyson's behalf, which again didn't fully backfire until the Buster Douglas fight. In the Douglas fight, Tyson's corner was so poorly prepared and incompetent that they couldn't even deal with Tyson's swollen eye properly. The point is this: Can you imagine what these bozo trainers got up to during Tyson's supposed training camps, if this is what they were doing during an actual fight?

To cut a long story short, when Tyson fired Rooney, he indirectly shot himself in the foot and was always destined to fail from this point onwards. The first telltale signs of his almost inevitable failure were seen during Bruno 1.

Yet another reason that we didn't see the same stellar Tyson against Bruno was a big decline in his combination punching. Both Cus and Rooney knew that combination punching was essential for Tyson to be successful against bigger and taller men, who have correspondingly longer reaches. Peekaboo boxing works on a risk-versus-reward basis, whereby Tyson had a very narrow window of opportunity to get inside. To fully capitalise on this window, Tyson needed to use razor-sharp combos and to punch on the move, rather than simply loading up with single-shot power punches.

Against Bruno, then disastrously against Douglas, and subsequently against Razor Ruddock, Tyson developed a very bad habit of brawling willingly just to get in a single shot that would finish things. This was wrong and demonstrated a complete lack of understanding from both his later trainers and indeed himself on what his original peekaboo style was all about—*elusive aggression*. Once Tyson lost his head movement, defensive body rhythm, and combos, he became a sitting duck. All of these flaws were first evident in Bruno 1.

—March 2019

David Esposito: If you could pick any boxer from any time to fight Muhammad Ali, who would it be and why?

J. A.: Ask yourself one brutally honest question: Which other historical boxer could most easily and accurately duplicate the dominant offensive positions of Joe Frazier and execute the same left hooks? It has to be prime Tyson—who else?

Can you visualise the similarity? If you hypothetically replace Larry Holmes with Ali and keep the lethal left hook the same, then Ali's in for a rough night at the hands of the Iron Man. Good left hookers always gave Ali trouble. He was dropped on several occasions during his career with this punch. He suffered his first career knock down against a lesser-known fighter named Sonny Banks at Madison Square Garden in 1962. Same left hook, same result!

Henry's hammer also hit the mark in 1963. So it doesn't take a NASA rocket scientist to figure out that Ali was vulnerable to a fast left hook thrown from a crouch. Ali's vulnerability to the left hook did not evade Cus D'Amato's and Eddie Futch's watchful eyes. D'Amato famously predicted Ali's downfall at the hands of Joe Frazier and forewarned Ali of this possibility before "the Fight of the Century" in 1971. Not only did Ali carry his right hand habitually low, but the top trainer and tacticians had spotted characteristic mannerisms and patterns in Ali's right hand which could be exploited by a great left hooker. "Say hello to my *little friend*!"

Frazier's famous left hook landed in devastating fashion in round fifteen of his first meeting with Ali. It was pure skill, perfect timing, and repetition by Smokin' Joe. He had been smokin' all night long and had repeatedly landed this same left hook, so there was no luck involved. He knew exactly when and where to unleash this shot, precisely at the moment when Ali was about to throw his own right hand. Timing beats speed!

Something else that leads me to pick prime Tyson as my number-one hitman is his legendary ability to *close the gap* on a taller fighter. This concept is huge and is similarly crucial to beating

Ali. If Ali kept the fight long, then he was in control, as we all saw in the Rumble in the Jungle. At long range, Foreman was a sitting duck for Ali's signature one-two combination, as Foreman marched forward in straight lines without any head movement whatsoever. When Ali let him get inside, Ali simply grappled with him and performed his now-legendary "rope-a-dope" tactic. Foreman was limited on the inside and his bludgeoning power proved ineffective. On the inside and at mid range, it's all about precision power, and scissors trump stone.

On a final note, if Tyson created the opportunity to really let his hands fly, then it would be double trouble for Ali on the inside. Not only would he have to watch out for Tyson's lethal left hook, but Tyson's signature right uppercut would also await. This was arguably the most dangerous and surgical uppercut in heavyweight history. It had the power and precision to put anyone to sleep. Ali, you would have had to float like a butterfly for twelve rounds to get the decision.

—April 2019

Jonathan Sparrow: What is the best style to beat Floyd Mayweather (boxer, pusher, swarmer, etc.)?

J. A.: A hybrid style! Sugar Ray Leonard was probably the most complete boxer of the modern era, and his was the best style to beat Floyd Mayweather. He wouldn't have stopped Mayweather, but he would have done enough over the course of twelve rounds to get the decision. Mayweather was the most adaptable defensive genius in boxing history, and to beat him required a boxer who could change colours like a chameleon. Perhaps most important of all, Leonard was the most well-equipped fighter to con and impress the judges.

Leonard was the most adaptable boxer of the legendary Fab Four. He could box comfortably at the highest level using differing styles, and was the one guy who could potentially have forced Mayweather onto his front foot. Turning the tables on Mayweather would have been crucial to solving his all-time leading defensive conundrum, and Leonard was the guy most capable of taking Mayweather into unfamiliar territory.

Allow me to borrow a line or two from a legendary trainer. Ray Arcel once said he valued brains over brawn. Mayweather was clearly the most intelligent boxer of the twenty-first century. His ring IQ was off the scale. His reading of the game was the best in the business. He could read an opponent's style and then tailor his defensive movements to nullify the attacker's offensive movements, thereby creating a state of neutrality. Essentially Mayweather borrowed a page or two out of Bruce Lee's manual by "becoming like water". When the temperature in the ring rose, he turned fluid. When it got cold in there, he turned solid!

To beat such an adaptable, mouldable, and unscripted fighter requires a boxer who possesses these same qualities, and that points to Sugar Ray Leonard. Leonard put on a masterful out-fighting display against Duran in the legendary *no mas* rematch, where he forced Duran to quit. For this fight, Leonard completely changed his strategy from their first meeting, where he mistakenly brawled with the brawler. By adopting a more sensible, reserved, and long-range style, Leonard confused Duran. Once again, I believe Leonard took a page out of the Bruce Lee manual. The *no mas* fight was perhaps an example of "the art of fighting without fighting".

Another boxing facet that Leonard possessed was varying the tempo of his boxing. Varied-tempo boxing would confuse Mayweather because he was generally used to guys who came at him in the same gear. By varying the pace and intensity of his attacks, Leonard could not only conserve energy but keep Mayweather guessing. A brilliant example of Leonard's varied-tempo boxing was evident against Marvin Hagler in 1987, when he caught the judges' eyes with bursts of aggression and then intermittently got on his bike, taking a much-needed breather. This confused Hagler, who fought in a one-pace manner throughout the entire fight. The point is that Leonard was a master at controlling fight tempo and playing boxing poker. When the other guy is always kept guessing, then adaptation isn't so easy.

On a final note, boxing in an eye-catching manner was a Sugar Ray Leonard forte. He was the darling of both the boxing media and the judges. Never underestimate the concept of favouritism. To win a boxing match, you don't necessarily have to beat the other guy—you just have to beat the judges!

—April 2019

Alexandre Puissant: How did Tyson knock out so many strong opponents so instantly? Was it due to the element of surprise or his superior punch power?

J. A.: Both factors! Mike Tyson's co-manager, the late Jim Jacobs, once commented, "The specific concept of his style is to have no feeling-out time whatsoever." There was no warm-up phase, no range-finding jabs, no pitter-patter punches. When that first-round bell sounded, Kid Dynamite literally exploded like a stick of TNT. He sprang out of the blocks like Usain Bolt and came after you with a vengeance, almost as if you had stolen something from him.

Quite often, if you paid close attention, you could see Tyson visibly sweating during a pre-fight stare-down. He wasn't scared—fear was the other guy's problem. Tyson was sweating because he had been working out like a machine in the dressing room, his body already warmed up and primed for action. Quite literally when he heard that first bell, it was a cue to throw punches in bunches with bad intentions. He had a pure street-fighter mentality. He had done it for years on the streets of Brooklyn, the only difference being that he was duplicating those street fighter tactics in the pro boxing arena.

Straight after brutally knocking out an unknown boxer named Michael Johnson in 1985, Tyson gave an interesting and insightful post-fight interview along with his manager, Jim Jacobs. The fight ended in dramatic fashion with one of the hardest and most brutal right crosses I can recall. The finishing punch was an accurate, perfectly timed, unseen, and wide-open shot to the head. Johnson literally walked into the punch, thereby doubling its impact, and was laid out for a good few minutes while the doctors attended to him. It is highly likely that this punch would have stretched out any and all historical heavyweights.

"When Mike Tyson hits you, you have no choice but to go down. It's a law when Mike Tyson hits you!" said Tyson in the immediate aftermath of this most brutal of knockouts.

"We have a problem here, a marvellous problem, because when you have a kid who throws hydrogen bombs, it's very difficult calculatingly to find anyone who wants to fight him," said Jacobs. "He is the most devastating puncher of the last ten years."

From an intended-target perspective, prime Tyson was a nightmare to face. Why? "He can knock you out with either hand," said Sugar Ray Leonard. This makes a big difference, a really big difference, as you don't know when or where the killer punch is coming from.

Genady Golovkin (GGG) bears some resemblance to Tyson in this respect. He too hits very hard, and his punches carry the element of surprise. GGG often mixes up the power of his punches, so there are weaker punches intermingled with the knockout punch. This is like playing boxing poker. The opponent finds himself playing a guessing game and is often caught unawares. In crude terms, it is like a high-level sucker punch and contributes significantly to first-strike capability. He who lands the bigger punches first more often than not wins the argument.

In his first year of pro competition, this unseen, first-strike capability contributed heavily to prime Tyson's unprecedented knockout streak. The downside of this ultra-aggressive strategy was that it was very high risk and off rhythm. Tyson was open to counters. To be really successful with Mike Tyson's peekaboo style required an impregnable defence.

—May 2019

Lance Williams: Is there any boxer in history who could have penetrated and defeated Muhammad Ali's rope-a-dope tactic? What technique or techniques would you employ to do it?

J. A.: I can guarantee you that Ali's rope-a-dope tactic would prove suicidal against Iron Mike Tyson. If facing prime Tyson, I seriously doubt Ali would ever use this tactic. Why? Ali had one of the highest ring IQs of all time. He would have realised that this bespoke tactic is not suitable against a precision power puncher.

Iron Mike was a precision power puncher with an eagle eye, whose body punches were delivered with laser-guided accuracy. He would have targeted Ali's liver, solar plexus, and small rib. Rest assured that Cus D'Amato had imprinted on Tyson's brain a surgeon's map of vital body parts. If you want to see a masterclass in precision body punching, then just watch the Tyrell Biggs fight from 1987, in which Tyson was at his surgical best.

There is probably not a single reputable boxing coach in the world who would recommend that his fighter use the rope-a-dope tactic against a highly skilled brawler. It is a suicidal tactic which happened to work for Ali in 1974 because on the night, he had a dope standing in front of him, and that dope's name was George Foreman.

—May 2018

Anonymous: Why did Mike Tyson fight with his chest forward?

J. A.: This is a fairly accurate observation, as it often appeared that Tyson was fighting from a neutral and squared stance. More often than not Tyson boxed from a usual orthodox stance, but he often switch-hit from the southpaw stance. Tyson's stance switches were often nondescript and quick and were therefore hard to spot in normal-speed viewing. And, as you correctly point out, it often appeared he was throwing punches from a squared stance with his chest literally forward.

This trait largely stemmed from the fact that Iron Mike had ambidextrous knockout power. In other words, he could knock you out equally comfortably with either hand. It is precisely this reason that made him so suitable for Cus D'Amato's peekaboo style, which was all about elusive and aggressive counterpunching. The squared-up stance helped both his offense and defence and enabled Mike to ghost deep inside the guard of his taller opponents. It also helped him to dart back out of harm's way. During his prime, much of his success was to do with his positioning relative to his opponent. A squared-up, neutral stance often assisted with the attainment of positional supremacy.

Stance also assisted his combination punching. Given his ambidextrous knockout potential, a neutral stance often proved to be very effective at close quarters. A lesser-known fact about Tyson was that he was a converted southpaw who preferred hooking with his left hand and uppercutting with his right. He could therefore easily land either punch from the squared-up stance.

—*June 2018*

Alex Davies: Would Sonny Liston have been able to go twelve rounds against Joe Frazier in their respective primes?

J. A.: Remember when Smokin' Joe Frazier was forced to do a silly dance to the tune of a 1970s beast of nature named George Foreman? It turned out to be one of the most one-sided beatdowns in heavyweight championship history. It should have been a close fight—after all, both guys were true greats. Right?

Wrong! *Styles make fights*. Foreman was all wrong for Frazier, and Frazier proved to be perfect target practice for Foreman. If you hypothetically replace Foreman with Sonny Liston, you'd get the exact same result, maybe even quicker. Frazier's straight-ahead pressure and attrition style was tailor-made for the slugger style. His style was in fact suicidal against sluggers like Sonny Liston, who was the 1960s equivalent of Foreman—only more skilful and precise with his punches.

Earnie Shavers was once asked on Sky Sports how he thought he would do against Joe Frazier. He replied with great confidence that he would KO Frazier because "Joe gives you the whole square." In other words, he's right there in front of you, lacks a degree of subtlety, and brings the fight to the slugger. These are the wrong tactics to adopt when facing tremendous power men such as Liston, Foreman, or Shavers. On top of this, Joe Frazier was a well-known slow starter who usually needed a few rounds to warm up. Again, that would have been advantage Sonny.

Another major reason I fancy Liston to take care of Frazier is that Liston possessed the number-one ramrod jab in heavyweight history. He would have impaled Frazier with this punch all too easily. Coupled with his reach advantage, his jab would prove decisive.

I can't see Joe Frazier's bob-and-weave style being effective against the crushing power of Sonny Liston. It's a terrible matchup for Joe. Could Joe last even two rounds against prime-time Liston? Very doubtful.

—*December 2018*

Rodney Chin: Is it true that Mike Tyson's fighting style was so physically taxing that that was a major reason he didn't have a long reign? I also read that Joe Frazier burned himself out during training, which is why he had a short career. Is this true?

J. A.: Yes and no. Tyson's style was extremely intense and energetic, and it had a time-restricted window (around eighteen minutes at redline). There are only a few heavyweights in history who could match Tyson in terms of his intensity, output, and work-rate. To fight as Tyson did during his heyday took a tremendous degree of fitness, repetition, and conditioning. Try it yourself just for a minute—constantly bobbing and weaving, moving your head from side to side, and rolling from the waist. Then start throwing punches while on the move, and you will rapidly work up a sweat. During his peak years, in training camps, Rooney had Tyson running three six-minute miles consecutively. If this fact doesn't seriously impress you, then you either have never been for a jog yourself or are simply dismissive of the concept of being box fit. This is a sixteen-stone fighter running back-to-back six-minute miles!

It is absolutely true that Tyson's intense style was more suited to youth and aggression. But this is not why he had a short shelf life at the very top. The reason he faded so quickly was because his boxing technique faded. No other trainer understood what peekaboo boxing was all about—this was Cus D'Amato's philosophy and brainchild. When Rooney was fired, Tyson basically signed his own death warrant. He was a man-child who frankly had no idea of the degree of expertise and bespoke boxing training that he had received from Cus D'Amato.

The core principle at the heart of D'Amato's philosophy was elusive aggression. When Tyson's defensive prowess faded, which in real time took about eight months (from the Spinks fight to Bruno 1), he faded. In my humble opinion, the writing was on the wall for Tyson as early as 1989. If you watch Tyson versus Bruno 1 closely, he was caught with more power punches from a technically limited opponent than in probably all of his previous championship fights combined. Many defensive frailties were already evident, on top of which his timing was also way off in this fight.

Another big contributor to Tyson's premature demise was his personal life, which was tumultuous to say the least. "Women weaken legs", and Tyson sure as hell fulfilled this prophetic saying. Alcohol, drugs, geishas, and daily partying all took their toll. Divorces and Don King stripped him of his fighting character, and three years of prison basically finished him off. Just like Muhammad Ali, he was never the same physical specimen after his enforced three-year lay-off. Underpinning both their declines was a loss of elusiveness. Ali lost his reflexes and became more flat-footed, but his granite chin saw him through the 1970s. Tyson lost both his precision head movements and his fleet-footedness.

Ultimately, due to various reasons, Tyson never really had a chance to evolve. We will never truly know how good he could have been had he not been "seduced by the dark side". Kevin Rooney always maintained that Tyson would have broken Rocky Marciano's record of 49-0 had he remained focused on and dedicated to the very difficult task of world championship boxing.

—January 2019

Den Jackson: What are the advantages and disadvantages of using Muhammad Ali's fighting style?

J. A.: First of all, which Ali are you talking about? Broadly speaking, there were two versions of Ali. There was the almost unbeatable and unhittable 1960s "float like a butterfly, sting like a bee" prime version. It's hard to criticize a fighter as good as prime Ali but if I were to give him some advice then, "'Bad habit Cass', you keep pulling your head back from straight punches!

Lucky that you had great reflexes in your youth. Rumble, young man. Rumble and keep your hands up, sucker—you're wide open to a great left hook thrown from a crouch!"

Later came the 1970s granite-chinned, blood-and-guts Ali, who could soak up punishment like a dry sponge soaks up water.

The 1960s Ali was far better and had more strengths than weaknesses. Post-incarceration Ali had many more weaknesses, and his chronic bad habits were more soundly punished by the competition.

But what was Ali's fighting style? You will be surprised to hear that many casual boxing fans don't actually know. He was primarily an out-fighter who wanted to keep the fight as long as possible. In that situation, his height, reach, and movement were most effective. His best punches were long and straight punches, such as the jab and cross combo. In his heyday, his hand speed was almost off the scale, so he could beat 98 per cent of heavyweights to the punch. Similar to prime Mike Tyson, he was a unique heavyweight of his day, in that he was faster and more mobile than his contemporaries.

To counter a straight-punching out-fighter like Ali, you need head movement. You slip straight punches with side-to-side pendulum movements—see Frazier, see Tyson. Foreman was a sitting duck target for Ali's bread-and-butter, one-two combo because he lacked head movement. Simply put, Ali's heyday style would be great against relatively sloppy fighters who moved in straight lines and telegraphed their punches. Hence the fact that neither Sonny Liston nor George Foreman could land a meaningful headshot on Ali in fifteen rounds of combined boxing. Prime Ali beats almost any slugger—seven days a week, 365 days a year.

To exploit Ali's weaknesses, you had to get inside as quickly and as efficiently as possible. Head movement was imperative to avoid his scything jab. It goes without saying fast hands and feet were required, in conjunction with textbook body-punching. Frazier was a great body puncher, whereas Foreman wasn't. Body-punching slowed Ali down and restricted one of his biggest strengths—*movement*.

A big disadvantage of Ali's style was his punching power—he was good but not great. In the 1960s his lightning-fast hand speed more than compensated for his power. But this became a problem when he faced the big punchers of the 1970s. He landed plenty of clean leather on both Norton and Frazier, but at no point did he discourage either man. Compare Ali's punch to Foreman's, and there is no comparison. Foreman literally flattened Norton and Frazier in double-quick time. In short, in the 1970s, Ali had to work very hard for his victories. This no doubt contributed to the high mileage on his fighting clock.

Ali's biggest offensive weakness by far was the virtual absence of a decent body attack. He was almost exclusively a headhunter. Again, this was no problem in the 1960s but it sure as hell became a problem in the 1970s against guys like Frazier, who pounded Ali's body like a possessed SOB.

In summary, Ali's main advantages were his unrivalled athleticism, hand speed, and reflexes. His main weaknesses were his 1970s defence and the lack of an effective body attack. However, he still ranks as the GOAT heavyweight and deserves much credit for the grittiness of his 1970s performances, which enabled him to win ugly in many close matchups.

—February 2019

Anonymous: Lennox Lewis said that Evander Holyfield was his hardest fight, and that was after Holyfield had declined. Riddick Bowe beat Holyfield in his prime. So why do people think Lennox could have beaten Bowe when he clearly could not have done?

J. A.: Lewis is lying! In my humble opinion, his hardest fights were against Vitali Klitschko, Hasim Rahman, Zjelko Mavrovic, and Ray Mercer. Klitschko was his most dangerous opponent which is why Lewis promptly retired and didn't give Vitali a rematch.

But staying with the question, using Holyfield as a yardstick to predict who would win between Bowe and Lewis may be clouding your judgement. Although Holyfield was indeed a common opponent of Lewis and Bowe, using the common-opponent approach in this analysis is somewhat flawed. The reason is very simple: Lewis and Bowe were very different fighters, style-wise. Lewis was predominantly an out-fighter, whereas Bowe was the polar opposite and did almost all his best work at close range. Therefore their respective meetings with Holyfield were very different stylistic affairs.

Holyfield was generally at his best on the inside, so his trilogy with Bowe was mostly defined by in-fighting. On the other hand, his two meetings with Lewis were more cagey and tactical affairs, in which the action took place at various ranges. For the most part, Lewis managed to keep Holyfield on a long-range leash. Evander was too shopworn to keep sustained pressure on Lewis for the entire twelve rounds. If Holyfield had been, say, five years younger against that same version of Lewis, then he probably would have out-pointed him.

Against Bowe, I think a near-peak Holyfield was outmatched from a basic artillery standpoint. Their classic trilogy was defined by inside, machismo exchanges, whereby the bigger and denser man generally bossed the action. In the second fight with Bowe, Holyfield used lateral movement effectively, which was a key ingredient to beating an overweight and poorly conditioned Bowe. However, over the entire span of the trilogy, Bowe had the upper hand. He definitely controlled Holyfield more handily than Lewis.

In the end, we get back to the classic adage of "Styles make fights". In trying to predict the outcome of Lewis versus Bowe, I think "styles makes fights" would prove to be a far more telling yardstick for success than using the common ground of Holyfield. It is a case of out-fighter Lewis versus in-fighter Bowe. If both guys are in shape and properly motivated, then it is a fifty-fifty matchup. On the night, the outcome would depend on which guy could impose his style on the other, who got off first with the big punches, and who could sustain their respective tempo for longer. If you look at their careers overall, then Lewis clearly has the more polished CV—but at his best, Bowe was the more dominant and tougher guy. Personally, I still think on the night it's a fifty-fifty clash.

—October 2020

CHAPTER 4

MEAN STREETS

Dominik Pozder: How dangerous would Jon Jones be in a street fight?

J. A.: In his weight category, he would be seriously dangerous and it is hard to see any major weaknesses. Within the realms of UFC, he has shown that he is a complete fighter and is the real deal when it comes to all-round striking. The guy is also very effective when forced to the mat. In real life, if the fight were to end up on the ground, we know that Jones could wrestle as a contingency measure.

However, in an interdisciplinary street fight, I could see Jones struggle against a guy like peak George Foreman. I don't think he would have the power to deter a prime Foreman. It also has to be borne in mind that Foreman was a genuine heavyweight, whereas Jones is a light heavy. In a street fight, there are no weight classes, so I could see peak Foreman being way too strong for a guy like Jones. Furthermore, I can't see Jones taking Foreman down and putting him on his back, given Foreman's enormous physical strength. On top of this fact, one clean bare-knuckle punch from Foreman with serious intent and then it's all over for Jones.

Jones's style is optimal for UFC and is also very suited to street fighting, given the fact his stand-up is so good. But as with any fight, a great deal depends on the opponent. I also see him struggling against many of the other top heavyweight brawlers. I think Tyson, Liston, and Shavers would all steamroll Jones—they were too powerful, explosive, and quick. On the other hand, Jones would excel against other MMA guys because their striking capabilities would be more similar to his own. But taking on top pro boxers in a street fight would be an entirely different prospect.

Some of the high-risk moves that we see Jones pull off in the Octagon, spinning elbow etc... he wouldn't risk in a street fight, as there is way more adrenaline and much less margin for error. The fight would also most likely be over in a matter of seconds. In such a narrow time frame, there would be a high chance of Jones being countered by a fresh opponent. Many of his exotic striking manoeuvres are effective in the Octagon when the other guy is gassed. Stamina generally isn't a factor in a street fight. First-strike capability is more often the decisive factor.

—December 2018

Mestre Carlos and John Marcus: Which guard or tactic is better for a street fight or self-defence, Tyson's peekaboo or Floyd Mayweather's shell?

J. A.: Given that most street fights are over in a matter of seconds, the choice has to be Tyson's peekaboo guard. Tyson's hands were held high and to the side of his head, with his jaw virtually concealed in a defensive shield. The peekaboo guard therefore strikes a good balance between aggression and defence.

On the other hand, Mayweather's Philly shell is a much more defensive guard and is ideally suited to defensive counterpunching. It is not so much a case that this tactic can't be effective in a self-defence scenario, but it is inherently more passive and may act to motivate a bare-knuckle attacker to become even more aggressive. For a guy with Mayweather's toolbox (brittle hands and so on), the Philly shell is the most suitable style but not necessarily the more effective. Certainly his left hand, being low down, is in a great position to execute a counter-check left hook. That punch could potentially be effective in dealing with a carelessly charging fighter.

It is important to bear in mind that Mike Tyson was in reality a street fighter turned pro boxer. If given a forced choice between the two legendary styles, the peekaboo style definitely fits the street fighter template much more naturally. As well as being the more instinctive style, it inherently possesses greater first-strike potential and can therefore end the argument more quickly. On the mean streets, with no referee or rules, ending things quickly is clearly the name of the game.

—December 2019

Frederic Truong: Why do street fights often last a few seconds, like a sprint, and not in the same rhythm as MMA or boxing matches?

J. A.: First of all, it is interesting that you are comparing street fights to both boxing and MMA, which are two completely different combat sports. Of the two, MMA is clearly more similar to a street fight. You will find that many MMA fights are over in seconds. For example, in the UFC clash between Jorge Masvidal and Ben Askren from 2019, the fight was over in just five seconds!

There are various reasons that street fights and MMA fights can end quickly. The following is a breakdown of important factors contributing to a fast finish:

- A bare-knuckle punch is obviously harder and more concussive than a punch from a fist in a boxing glove. If that punch lands to the chin from a power puncher like Francis Ngannou, you know it's game over.
- There are far more random events in MMA and street fights as compared to a boxing match.
- Due to the diverse nature of MMA, the likelihood of a mismatch is far greater than in boxing. The prime example is Brock versus Overeem. Brock was an elite wrestler and Overeem an elite kickboxer. On paper you might think that this was going to be a long and drawn-out affair. In the end it was over in a hurry, largely because Brock couldn't

execute the takedown. It became a pure stand-up affair. In stand-up, a kickboxer usually beats a wrestler.

- Adrenaline is a factor. Fight-or-flight survival instinct is far greater in a street fight.
- Street fights in particular have no environmental controls. Clearly this leads to far more unknowns. Both boxing and UFC matches take place in a controlled and regulated environment.
- Whether it's Mills Lane or Big John McCarthy, the presence of a referee makes a big difference. In general, referees prolong a fight. See Kimbo versus Tank Abbott, in which the referee kept breaking up the action.
- The size of the audience and associated crowd noise serves as a distraction. This inevitably affects some fighters more than others. Boxing matches have by far the largest live audience. Professional fighters do not like to fail on a big stage, and in general will fight more cautiously in front of big crowds.
- The number of striking options is also a factor. In boxing there are two: the right and left fists. In street fights and MMA, there are an additional six striking options (not counting headbutts): two kicks, two knees, and two elbows. This will inevitably lead to a shorter fight.

—December 2020

Dominik Pozder: Who would win in a street fight, Fedor Emelianenko or Mike Tyson?

J. A.: Let's assume that both guys were complete unknowns and were involved in a completely random street encounter. In this instance, I'm going with Iron Mike by a brutal knockout. I don't think Fedor would attempt to take down Tyson in a street fight—not on a concrete floor anyway. Additionally Fedor likes to stand and bang, irrespective of the opponent. It is this kind of machismo that would prove to be his undoing against Tyson. I don't think any guy in history could match a 1988 Tyson in a bare-knuckle street fight.

If the fight went to script, then it would appear that Fedor's chin could not take a professional heavyweight boxer's firepower. If you look at the evidence to hand, both Hollywood Dan Henderson and the virtually unknown Matt Mittrione have had TKO victories over Fedor. Therefore the maths is fairly simple: if he can't handle MMA firepower, there is no chance that he could take the Iron Man's firepower. As great as Fedor was in MMA—one of the best—it wouldn't look good for him against Tyson in a random street fight in which neither guy had prior information on the other.

Breaking the fight down, Fedor's slender advantage would lie in grappling, along with ground and pound. As already stated, I don't think he would attempt to take Tyson down; it would be way too risky. I perceive this encounter to be a pure stand-up, pub-brawl type of fight, as both guys have a penchant for brawling. Tyson had superior firepower in every sense and would get off first with the power punches. This would be a bad stylistic matchup for the Russian. If he wanted to face Tyson and hoped to win, then I believe it would have to be under controlled MMA rules and not a street fight.

—January 2019

MARCUS JOHNSON: Between a professional heavyweight boxer and a professional strongman, who would win in a street fight?

J.A.: The pro boxer would win easily and most probably by a knockout with the first clean punch landed. First-strike potential is often a decisive factor in the outcome of street fights. By using this concept as a yardstick for success, there really can only be one conclusion and outcome.

The most notable example of a strongman engaging in a combat sport was when ex-world's strongest man Mariusz Pudzianowski took on Tim Sylvia in an MMA event in 2010. Right from the outset, it didn't look good for Mariusz. His strength really counted for nothing, largely because it wasn't fighting strength, it was strongman strength—good for shifting static objects but not so useful for dealing with mobile objects. Quite frankly, Mariusz looked awful and immobile. The funny thing was that, by strongman standards, he was considered very mobile!

The way pure strength becomes useful in a fight is if it is George Foreman-type strength, which is contextual strength that is specific to boxing. Obviously if the street fight turned into a grappling match, then strength would come in handy. But I would personally take technique over strength anytime—see Cain Velasquez versus Brock Lesnar as a prime example of this phenomenon.

On top of this, strongmen are not geared up for taking a strike. In a fight, at some point you're gonna get hit, and a pro boxer is much more used to being hit than a strongman. So in almost every sense, apart from pure strength, it is advantage to the pro boxer. In all likelihood, a good heavyweight boxer-mover could probably dance, stay out of range, and just wait for the strongman to gas, which would take around two minutes tops. At that point, the pro boxer could pretty much do as he pleased.

—January 2019

A. J. Kposowa: What martial arts practices are useless in a real street fight?

J. A.: I think the single most useless technique would be the crane technique as depicted in the motion picture *Karate Kid* from 1984.

According to one of the film's lead characters, Mr Miyagi, "If Daniel-san do properly, then no can defend." Apart from it looking really strange, I can't see how the crane kick made it into a karate movie, even one that is now well over thirty years old. Even more bizarre was the fact that the kick won the film's embattled hero, Daniel LaRusso, the tournament against a black-belt-rated opponent, who literally walked face-first into it. Back in the good old 1980s, you could just begin to imagine thousands of bullied teens all over the world practising the crane kick in front of their bedroom mirrors!

Other types of head kicks, such as a flying kick, would also be fairly useless, unless it was a blind-side sucker kick. I also doubt a spinning kick or punch is going to be of much use in a real-life street fight. These moves no doubt look good in the movies. In reality, the risk of performing such flashy moves far outweighs the reward.

—February 2019

Dominik Pozder: How dangerous would George Foreman be in a street fight?

J. A.: Foreman would be one of the last guys in the world that I would want to face in any type of fight, let alone a street fight. He would be seriously dangerous in any number of potential fight pathways. He was one of the absolute hardest punchers in heavyweight history, and his fearsome punches would be that much scarier in the bare-knuckle form.

If I were forced to fight Foreman, I think the most viable option would be through grappling. Indeed you could even argue that you would be forced to grapple with him through sheer fear of being hit with a massive bare-knuckle hook. Herein lies the problem: taking Foreman down would be an extremely difficult and dangerous task due to his enormous physical strength. The situation would be similar to being stuck between a rock and a hard place. If you dared to stand and bang, you'd be doomed, and if you shot for the takedown, it would be like grappling with a grizzly bear. It would be wiser just to target his knees with some fierce leg kicks to tire him out and reduce his leverage, mobility, and vertical base.

The final component of Foreman's triad of boxing strengths was his legendary chin. This guy could take a seriously heavy punch. If you landed a big headshot on Foreman in a street fight, there would be a chance it would just make him madder. In the process, you'd probably fracture your own hand. Any which way you can, it doesn't look good, but I would probably go with the grappling route via knee strikes and then hope for the best.

—February 2019

Michael Brett: Who would win a street fight between Brock Lesnar and Mike Tyson, or between Braun Strowman and Mike Tyson?

J. A.: Assuming both guys are at their respective peaks, then one thing is for sure—if either of these two pairs met in a street fight, I don't see the fight going the distance. You can visualise such a classic boxer-versus-wrestler encounter as being similar to the fictional fight in *Rocky 3* between Balboa and Thunderlips.

We've all probably seen *Rocky 3* many times. The fight between Balboa and Thunderlips made some logical sense. Clearly the wrestler has size, weight, and strength advantages; you wouldn't really expect anything different. The boxer has a big striking advantage and is usually way faster and more agile. As the commentators in the movie jokingly remarked, "What happens when that big monster gets a hold of that boxer?"

In prime Tyson, I think you have a guy who would be close to the ultimate street fighter and would excel in dirty boxing. Due to his tremendously fast hands and agility, he would have massive first-strike capability. One or two clean power shots from prime Tyson with a bare-knuckle fist would end this fight. There would be a very high probability that Tyson would get off first and hit the target. If pro boxers couldn't dodge Tyson's punches, then there would be no chance that Brock could make him miss. Also bear in mind that prime Tyson would enjoy having such a large and unmissable torso in front of him. Make no mistake: at 6 feet 3 inches and 285 pounds, Brock would be a sitting duck.

As and when Brock freight-trains towards Tyson, I see Tyson remaining very calm, as he has envisaged this scenario many times over. He knows exactly what to expect and captures Brock's every move in slow motion. Tyson patiently plays the waiting game, allowing Brock to approach just within striking distance. At the last second, Tyson sidesteps, utilising feline reflexes and ballet footwork. Brock is left in no man's land. Where he thought Tyson was gonna be, there is now a counter, check left hook to the liver waiting for Brock. Game over, similar to when Alistair Overeem finished him off with a liver kick in UFC 141. If Brock can't dodge a liver kick from Overeem, there's no chance he's dodging a body punch—not from prime Tyson anyway.

If Tyson misses and Brock gets the takedown, then Tyson is clearly entering a world of hurt. If they fight ten street fights, I think Tyson wins seven or eight and Brock wins twice. Therefore I give prime Tyson around an 80 per cent chance of success in this matchup. Against other, more regular, less powerful, and less precise heavyweight boxers, I would favour Brock way more. But because prime Tyson is such a naturally fast and highly aggressive street fighter, he is all wrong for Brock.

Against Braun Strowman, I don't see that much changing from Tyson's perspective, except the fact that Strowman is even bigger and heavier.

—October 2019

Ross Taylor: Chuck Liddell says that he would KO Mike Tyson in a street fight. Who would you back?

J. A.: In a street-fight, I would go with prime Tyson, but he would have to be at his absolute sharpest. Make no mistake: Liddell is a dangerous opponent who is capable of changing the complexion of a fight in a split second. An obstacle for Liddell is the fact that he is a light heavyweight, whereas Tyson is a heavyweight. That 10 per cent or so of extra body weight will surely give Tyson the edge. For a change, I think Tyson will have to be somewhat cautious, especially in the early going, because on this occasion his opponent also has good first-strike capabilities.

Both these guys will most likely want to stay on their feet and generally preferred stand-up fighting. If Liddell stands and bangs with prime Tyson, eventually he's gonna get hurt, maybe badly. If he lands a few leg kicks early on to Tyson's knees, then maybe he can hold him off for a while. But when Tyson closes up the range, it's game over.

Liddell stands around 6 feet 2 inches tall, which is a perfect height for Tyson's favourite punch. If Tyson's vaunted arching uppercut lands with a bare-knuckle fist, he can take anyone out. If you rewind the clock to the 1980s, you will find that Tyson loves fighting the average heavyweight who stood around 6 feet and 2 to 3 inches tall.

Also factor into the equation that Tyson will have a distinct speed and agility advantage. So barring the lucky punch factor, Tyson should overwhelm Liddell with his favourite combo: right body shot followed immediately by a right uppercut and perhaps a short left-hook finisher.

—November 2019

Daniel Spencer: What tactics do not work in street fights?

J. A.: While full power head kicks can be very concussive and certainly look spectacular, I find it hard to visualise such a kick landing in a short-lived street fight. Not impossible, mind you, but unlikely, unless of course your opponent has very slow reflexes or is a particularly sloppy mover. But in general, out of all the striking techniques on show in the UFC, I would say kicks are the least useful in street encounters (apart from leg kicks). Certainly as far as head kicks are concerned, many people would argue that the risk far outweighs the reward.

In UFC 129, Lyoto Machida landed the real-life version of the crane kick from the *Karate Kid* movie. This kick looked spectacular and was a finisher—but it landed when Couture was tired. He was also caught unawares and had slow reflexes at the best of times.

In 1998, at UFC 17, Pete Williams almost decapitated Mark Coleman in one of the most famous and brutal head kicks in UFC history. Again, it landed at a point in the fight several minutes down the line, and Coleman had gassed. It is unlikely that most street fights will last long enough for this eventuality to occur—not impossible, but unlikely.

A more practical demonstration of useful real-world kicks are *low kicks*. They are far less risky and clearly won't leave you so off balance and vulnerable to counter-strikes. Not to mention that a low kick has a much shorter distance to cover compared to a high kick, the horizontal distance being much shorter than the diagonal. In general, the best street-fighter tactics are dirty boxing mixed with grappling as a contingency measure.

—September 2019

Dominik Pozder: How dangerous would Mike Tyson have been in a street fight in his prime?

J. A.: In all honesty, I think he would be even more dangerous in a street fight than he was in the professional ring. Ask experts and casual fans alike who is the closest thing to a real-life street fighter in the world of pro boxing, and the majority will say Mike Tyson. You could even argue that Tyson was a street fighter turned pro boxer.

Peak Tyson would be a fearsome proposition in a street fight, mainly due to power, speed, and massive first-strike potential. It is a well-known fact that most street fights are over in a matter of seconds. Without a shadow of a doubt, Tyson's peekaboo style would suit the street fighting template perfectly. In fact, I don't think any other fighter during their prime years has ever recorded a higher percentage of first-round knockouts. Other factors that would make Tyson virtually unbeatable in a street fight are disguise and the throwing unseen punches. Furthermore his highly compact physique and relatively short stature would make him extremely elusive.

A real-life example of Tyson's street-fighting potential was observed when he encountered one of his old pro boxing adversaries, a guy named Mitch "Blood" Green, outside a New York shop. Green was a known rival gang member and apparently wanted a rematch with "the baddest man on the planet", so Tyson duly obliged. Tyson settled the dispute with a single bare-knuckle punch to the face, leaving Green bruised and battered. The fight was quickly broken up before any life-changing damage was done.

In my humble opinion, virtually anybody who tried stand-up with peak Tyson in a street fight would get beat up and inevitably hospitalised. The best way to deal with Tyson would be through grappling; otherwise he would overwhelm you with a quick and accurate barrage of punches. On top of these factors, Tyson had a seriously ruthless mean streak, which was ideally suited to street fighting.

—July 2018

Mark Adams: Who would win in a street fight between a judo expert and a boxer?

J. A.: By judo expert, I guess you mean a black belt, and since you haven't specified the skill level of the boxer, let's assume he is at least a pro boxer. In a street fight, literally anything can happen, and therefore they are almost impossible to predict. The only very general pattern that emerges is the fact that they end quite quickly, sometimes in seconds and at most in a minute or two.

Breaking the fight down, we have a grappling martial art versus a stand-up striking martial art. The judoka needs to be as close as possible to attempt a takedown or throw. The outcome of the fight largely depends on what happens during the first takedown attempt, as we have to assume the only possible victory path for the judoka is by takedown. We can assume this because pure judokas are not trained at all in striking. As and when the judoka shoots, the boxer will unload with counterpunches. One clean bare-knuckle shot to the head from a pro boxer ends this fight. If the judoka avoids the killer blow or combo and executes a throw onto a concrete floor, it's over for the boxer.

As much as I would like to predict a victory for the boxer, I have to go with the judoka in a street fight. My reasoning is fairly simple. In UFC, Brazilian ju-jitsu (a modern derivative of judo) has shown itself to be the most dominant martial art. A lot of data also points to the majority of street fights ending up on the ground, so once again advantage to the judoka. If we repeated this same experiment in, say, ten or even twenty street fights, the judoka is more likely to avoid a knockout blow in such a short time frame . Once or twice, of course, the judoka will get knocked out. But the majority of the time, I can see him getting the takedown, and then it's curtains for the pure boxer.

—June 2018

Tamia Boyden: Who would win in a street fight in their respective primes, Muhammad Ali or Mike Tyson?

J. A.: Tyson all the way! Back in the day, we used to have this discussion all the time. Almost everyone in my gym social circle picked Ali in a regulated boxing match, but picked Tyson in a no-holds-barred street fight. What a difference boxing gloves and a ring make!

In 1988, Tyson had an infamous street encounter with Mitch "Blood" Green which ended in a hurry. Tyson settled the argument with a swift jab to Green's face. The pattern of the street fight was all too familiar—it was over in a matter of seconds, and the guy who landed the first strike basically came out on top. This same Green had gone the distance with Tyson in a pro boxing match two years earlier in 1986.

The five main reasons I pick Tyson to conquer Ali in a street fight are these:

- *Street-fighter style*: Prime Tyson was the closest thing to a street-fighter turn pro boxer we have ever seen. Tyson's classic peekaboo style was way more suited to street fighting than Ali's out-fighter style.
- *First-strike capability*: In his heyday, Tyson was almost always first to land the big bomb. In the bare-knuckle form of the game, this first-strike capability would prove even more decisive.
- *Punching power*: Tyson was a killer, whereas Ali was primarily a finesse boxer, albeit a very tough one. On the mean streets, power trumps finesse, pure and simple.
- *Window of opportunity*: We all know that as a general rule of thumb, street fights last for a matter of seconds. The fighter who can better exploit this narrow window of opportunity will probably win. All the evidence points to a Tyson win.
- *Physique*: Prime Tyson had a pit-bull-type physique, whereas Ali had a long, slender, and athletic build. In a street fight, the pit bull generally beats the greyhound.

While Ali has a slight edge in terms of hand speed, foot-speed, and toughness, I see these advantages being less important in a short, sharp street encounter.

—October 2020

RANDY TRULIO: Realistically how would Mike Tyson do in a street fight against 6 people his size with minimal boxing experience?

J.A.: As long as the six minimally trained guys mean business, work as a team and don't pay Tyson too much respect, then they should overwhelm Tyson. Not even prime Tyson can overcome such long odds and most likely neither could the master, Bruce Lee.

Of course, Tyson may well stretch out one or two of his adversaries but not all six. Also take into consideration the criteria you have specified— we're talking six guys, each weighing around 220lbs, with some training...If it's a case of all six circling around Tyson and ideally at least three of them blindsiding him, then he is doomed fairly quickly. Other than a superhuman, no one can deal with multiple blindsiding opponents.

In such a scenario, I would humbly suggest Iron Mike could probably just about handle a max of three guys his own size and even that is a stretch of the imagination.

A graphic example of the difficulties that multiple bull rushing opponents could pose to Tyson was observed when he faced a guy named Peter McNeeley in 1995. This guy was Tyson's first opponent following his release from prison and was basically journeyman grade opposition. He literally rushed towards Tyson in a threatening, adrenaline charged way, which momentarily caused Tyson some trouble. Now imagine six Peter McNeeleys charging towards Tyson, at the same time, in a reverse starbursting formation...?

—April 2021

CHAPTER 5

CLOSE ENCOUNTERS OF THE HYPOTHETICAL KIND

ANONYMOUS: What do you think would have happened if Muhammad Ali had retired after losing to Frazier?

J. A.: Ali lost to Frazier in the "Fight of the Century" in 1971. If he had hypothetically retired, what would have transpired? Who would have filled the void left by Ali? I think the door would have been left wide open for a certain strongman by the name of George Foreman. Ali retiring would not have changed the fact that Foreman wiped out Joe Frazier and Ken Norton. So I suppose the $64,000 question is "Who would have been Foreman's main challenger instead of Ali in 1974?"

In theory, it may have brought the fight with big-punching Ron Lyle forward or possibly paved the way for a Foreman versus Shavers matchup. Either way, I think Foreman would have remained undefeated for a long time, as I can see him just about beating Shavers. It would have been a dream matchup, but Foreman had enough in his locker to KO Shavers.

In real time, Foreman's next defeat came at the hands of a slippery Jimmy Young in 1977. Do you think he would have lost to Young had he never fought Ali? I think not. Foreman went into a well-known depression following "the Rumble in the Jungle" and was never again at his brutal best. So in the alternate timeline (without Ali in the picture), I think Foreman turns the tables on Young and wins by KO.

In the alternate timeline, Foreman is still unbeaten but is now ageing. We are rapidly approaching the late 1970s, and there is a new kid on the block by the name of Larry Holmes. He isn't half bad with a pair of boxing gloves. By around 1978, a slugger like Foreman would probably have been in decline. I think a smart slickster like a young Larry Holmes would have had enough boxing skill and savvy to out-point a past-prime Foreman. In theory, you could look to the Rumble in the Jungle for the evidence-based answer. Could Holmes have repeated Ali's voodoo job on Foreman? Probably.

—December 2018

Rodney Chin: Could Larry Holmes or Rocky Marciano beat Deontay Wilder?

J. A.: Starting with Holmes, this is a fairly straightforward analysis. Essentially you are comparing a Mercedes to a Nissan (not the Skyline). Larry Holmes was arguably the number-one heavyweight technician-type fighter of all time. I would give even money that he beats Wilder on points with his right hand tied behind his back. With his left hand only, he jabs Wilder's head off all night long, and precision footwork keeps him out of harm's way. Holmes wins by a middle-round TKO as and when he gets bored of carrying Wilder.

Against Marciano, I think once again Wilder has his hands full. Marciano is too tough and rugged. He wears Wilder down through pure attrition and close-range guerrilla warfare. On the inside, the Rock feasts on Wilder's beanpole body and puts on a body-punching masterclass. The Rock wins by a middle-round TKO. No, Wilder won't catch Marciano with his trademark haymaker right, and yes, Wilder has height and reach advantages—who cares? Marciano is the vastly superior boxer.

—December 2018

Leroy Holiday: Who would win between Gennady Golovkin and prime Roy Jones Junior ?

J. A.: This is an intriguing hypothetical matchup between two legendary warriors. Since you have mentioned prime Roy Jones Junior, then there can only be one winner, and that is a fairly comfortable points win for Roy Jones. Don't get me wrong: it will be a competitive fight, but at his best, Jones will handle Golovkin's pressure. During his early- to mid-1990s heyday, Jones was one of the best boxers ever. In my opinion, he was the equal of Muhammad Ali in terms of pure athleticism. He had all the moves and then some. Anybody who has any doubts can watch the masterclass he put on against the world-class James "Lights Out" Toney in 1994. Toney was one of the best in-fighters ever, yet on that night he was pretty much left chasing Jones's shadow. He couldn't lay a meaningful glove on Jones. In a similar manner, I don't think Golovkin is able to live with a prime Jones—he is in a different class.

With the benefit of hindsight, we all know that Roy Jones had a chandelier jaw, and if Golovkin tagged him cleanly, then it would be lights out for Jones. But during his prime years, Jones was extremely elusive and had some of the best reflexes ever. For this reason, I think he avoids Golovkin's power punches.

Going off on a slight tangent, Jones made a huge career-debilitating mistake by moving up to heavyweight. He was never quite the same fighter again post-John Ruiz. But ignoring the latter part of his career, I think prime Jones beats GGG seven days a week.

—December 2018

Ali Evans: Who would win, prime George Foreman or prime Earnie Shavers?

J. A.: Foreman most probably by a middle-round TKO, but not after a war. The analysis on this classic hypothetical fight is fairly linear, in that you don't really need to worry too much about "styles make fights". Both guys were the epitome of a heavyweight slugger. When two trucks collide head on, normally the heavier truck wins. This points towards Foreman prevailing in what would inevitably be a legendary slugfest.

Shavers has a realistic chance very early on, as long as he treats the boxing match as he would a street fight and boxes in an ultra-aggressive manner. He needs to box Foreman in the same manner he boxed Norton in 1979: come out with guns blazing and jump all over Foreman while he's still cold. If Foreman warms up and they start exchanging big hooks, then Foreman will win based on superior punch resistance. Both guys have suspect stamina, but Foreman generally has a bigger gas tank. So the longer the fight goes, the more it favours Foreman.

Common opponent analysis in the form of Ron Lyle favours Foreman. In a legendary 1976 slugfest, Foreman just about beat Lyle by way of a stoppage. On the other hand, Shavers lost to Lyle by stoppage in 1975.

Common opponent analysis in the form of Ali favours Shavers. A faded Ali took a bad beating from Shavers but just about managed to win by a decision, largely because Earnie tired in the later rounds. On the other hand, a slightly past-prime Ali beat Foreman by an exhaustion-facilitated KO. One thing is for sure: Shavers has a realistic puncher's chance against any heavyweight in history, given the fact he hit so hard. Common opponent analysis in the form of Ken Norton is less informative because both of them bombed Norton out very early on.

Other 1970s data, in the form of the Foreman versus Frazier fights, paints a better picture for George. Foreman destroyed Frazier twice, whereas Frazier ducked Shavers (at least according to legend). Based on golden-era evidence, it is going to be a close fight which will hinge on small details, like who lands a bomb first. Ultimately, I think Foreman should just about get across the finishing line first, largely because of his granite chin.

—December 2019

Timothy Horton: Do you think Anthony Joshua would have been a top-ten heavyweight boxer if he competed in the 1970s?

J. A.: I think there is an outside chance that he could have made it into the top ten but definitely not the top five. You have to give him a chance in any era, simply based on his size and physicality. He is, after all, a super heavyweight boxer in the heavyweight division. Given that the average 1970s heavyweight was around fifteen stone, Joshua would have significant size and weight advantages on almost every opponent. As anyone who has boxed or wrestled even casually will tell you, a weight difference of just three kilos can prove significant.

Other factors that would have affected A. J.'s chances of success (or failure) are his 1970s management and specifically his matchmaker. In that most competitive of eras, if his matchmaker were to blunder and match him against the wrong guy, then his career could be over in a flash. Simply put, he would have had to scrupulously avoid killers like Foreman, Shavers, and Lyle. Hypothetically speaking, if he had been knocked out by Ruiz Junior in the 1970s, then A. J. would have become a marked man. Loads of tough guys would have been coming out of the woodwork, also wanting to punish him.

Other fights that would have needed to be delayed were against finesse guys such as Ali and Jimmy Young. In their respective primes, Ali and Young would have boxed rings around A. J. and made him look very stiff and cumbersome. However, if those fights had been delayed until the late 1970s, then A. J. would have stood a much better chance. This is to say that the timing of a top-level boxing match is critically important.

Ultimately, A. J.'s body weight would also have been a crucial factor in his chances of success. If he came in too heavy, I think we already know what would have happened (see Ruiz versus A. J. 1). If he came in too light, then he would have been outmuscled. If he boxed at approximately seventeen stone, then he would have optimised his chances of success. Finally, the question remains—how would his porcelain chin have stood up to the 1970s big guns?

—December 2019

Roland Diaz: How would a prime Riddick Bowe do against the top heavyweight boxers in 2019?

J. A.: I think Big Daddy in his prime would be a handful in any era. He had a lot of things going for him: size, power, good fundamentals, good chin, and know-how supplied by a great trainer, Eddie Futch. On top of these qualities, he was a world-class in-fighter, unusual for such a tall heavyweight. He could also take care of business at long range.

In his finest hour, in the fall of 1992, he looked like a genuine world-beater against an outmatched Evander Holyfield. He fulfilled one of the Holy Grail rules of heavyweight boxing: "A good big guy generally beats a good little guy." I rate this fight as his peak performance, and on this form, I would back him to probably KO all of the class of 2019.

I can see him being too much of a beast for both A. J. and Deontay Wilder. As and when he starts getting close to these guys and landing heavy, clean leather, he stops them or they quit. If A. J.'s porcelain chin can't take Ruiz's punches, there is no chance that A. J. could take Bowe's heavier artillery. In Wilder's case, I see Bowe exploiting his beanpole physique with some punishing body shots and wearing him down by "the body and then the head" route.

The slippery Tyson Fury will be his toughest opponent and can perhaps last the distance? But I still see Bowe dominating that matchup, as he hits that much harder than Fury.

—December 2019

Terry Davis: How would Mayweather have fared against the prime Hands of Stone?

J. A.: I would like to predict a victory for Duran, but unfortunately I can't see it, unless he could force Mayweather to have a brawl with him. Mayweather brawling with anyone, let alone Duran, is a highly unlikely fight scenario, given Mayweather's defensive style and ring IQ. A far more likely scenario is something along the lines of the *no mas* rematch between Duran and Sugar Ray Leonard. In the rematch, Leonard fought a very smart fight. He fought to his strengths and to Duran's weaknesses. In their first fight, the Brawl in Montreal, Ray Leonard fought the wrong fight but garnered a huge amount of respect from the boxing fraternity due to the guts he showed. He brawled on the inside with probably the best brawler in boxing history. Mayweather would not make this mistake, as machismo was never his game.

Facing Duran, Mayweather would simply duplicate Sugar Ray Leonard's *no mas* tactics and likely win a points decision. He may even frustrate Duran better and faster than Leonard did and force him to quit sooner. In the rematch with Duran, Leonard gave the boxing world a perfect blueprint of how to nullify and frustrate an elite brawler by using intelligence, mobility, and silky boxing skills. Mayweather excels in all these areas and does it all on the back foot at least as well as Leonard. Clearly he's not as versatile or attack-minded as Leonard, but that negativity would work better against Duran. I would go for Mayweather by decision after surviving some severe pressure, particularly in the early rounds. As soon as Mayweather started to read Duran, he would adapt and neutralise him.

—December 2018

Enosh Collins: Can Mike Tyson dance with the current heavyweights at age 54?

J. A.: No chance. If you want to predict the future, then look at the recent past. Tyson's last proper fight was against journeyman Kevin McBride in 2005. It turned out to be a physical mismatch; McBride was too much of a physical beast for an ageing and rusting Tyson. He towered over Tyson and outweighed him by nearly three stone. This is too much weight and height to give away, even for Tyson, and especially when you are old.

If McBride had been facing prime Tyson, it would obviously have been a very different story. Prime Tyson would have used McBride as a mobile heavy bag. But an ageing Tyson was much slower with his punches. The combination punching was gone, his balance was poor, and his footwork was sloppy. To cut a long story short, Father Time has been very unkind to Mike Tyson's peekaboo style.

Now imagine Tyson facing the current crop of heavyweights, who are all roughly the same size and weight as McBride. The outcome is going to be the same—these modern giants will lean all over an old Tyson in the clinches. Tyson will not be able to use his once-legendary hit-and-run style against today's giants because he has lost his foot speed, balance, and reflexes. Prime Tyson was always a youth and aggression type of fighter.

—November 2020

Oguz Sapanci: If Wladimir Klitsckho were in his prime, could he beat Anthony Joshua?

J. A.: Yes, I think prime Klitschko would beat Joshua by a knockout. There is a very simple reason why I make this prediction. Just rewind the clock to 2017 and watch their fight again. I think an over-the-hill Klitschko was perhaps a punch or two away from stopping Joshua in real time. The sight of Joshua being clipped became all too familiar on the night. He was caught way too easily with power punches from an old man, who made him look quite ordinary at times. Joshua had nothing more than youth on his side, which in the end was the only thing that got him over the finishing line first.

In 2015, pretty much that same version of Klitschko couldn't lay a meaningful glove on Tyson Fury. So what changed? The only thing that changed was that Klitschko had a much easier target in front of him when facing Joshua.

Since A. J. lost by KO to Ruiz Junior in 2019, it has proven beyond any reasonable doubt that Joshua will always be vulnerable to a decent puncher who comes to fight and actually lets his hands fly. In his prime, Klitschko was much more than just a decent puncher—he was a generational great.

—December 2020

Daniel Tran: Who would win in a match between Mike Tyson and Anthony Joshua if we were to put them in the ring right now, with no warmup, no advance notice, and no additional training?

J. A.: Joshua wins easily.

If Joshua had to face prime Tyson, everyone knows what would happen—prime Tyson would drop Joshua like a bad habit.

Unfortunately for Tyson, the date on the calendar reads 2020 and not 1988. So as great as Tyson was in his heyday, he cannot roll back that many years, not at the grand old age of 54.

Even if they boxed without any prior warning, the age and inactivity difference is too much. Also bear in mind the self-inflicted abuse that Tyson has incurred over the years—drugs, alcohol, and partying have inevitably added a lot of unwanted and useless mileage on his body.

As an afterthought, I suppose that you always have to give Tyson a puncher's chance. If Tyson, aged 54, were to strike it lucky and land a bomb on Joshua's suspect chin, then perhaps he could score an unlikely knockout. If I am being optimistic for Tyson, there is maybe a 10 per cent chance of that happening—that is, if he catches Joshua cold and unawares.

—December 2020

Najiur Rahman: If Muhammad Ali competed today, would he be one of the top-ten heavyweight boxers? I think modern training (boxing evolution) has improved a lot since 1967.

J. A.: Assuming that we are talking about 1966 Ali, then yes, he would definitely be in the top ten. In fact, if I were a betting man, I would bet on prime Ali to be the undisputed heavyweight champion of the world.

Way back in 1966, Ali gave a career-defining performance. He totally outclassed and beat up a guy named Cleveland "Big Cat" Williams. His performance in this fight has generally been rated as the number-one performance by any heavyweight in history. He was so talented and skilful that Williams barely laid a glove on him, while Ali landed some of the most dazzling punches ever seen. In this form, it is believed that Ali was close to unbeatable.

Now fast-forward to the twenty-first century. What has really changed in the heavyweight division? I'll tell you what has changed—skill has been traded in for size.

A prime example of this concept was observed in 2009, when David Haye dethroned the super giant Nikolai Valuev. The "Beast from the East" stood a foot taller than Haye and outweighed him by nearly a hundred pounds. Yet all that size and weight advantage counted for nothing on the night. If a former cruiserweight boxer such as David Haye can out-point Valuev, then I suggest that Ali would have gone one better and most probably have stopped him. Size literally means nothing without skill.

Tyson Fury is a much better example of an evolved giant who can also box. The 2015 version of Tyson Fury that outboxed Klitschko would surely be a handful for anyone, based on his combination of size, skill, and ring smarts. I still don't see him beating Ali, but he would give Ali a stern test.

As for your assertion that boxing has evolved, I beg to differ. Certain training methods, such as strength training, have definitely improved. But the implementation of strength in boxing only works up to a point. There is a powerful law of diminishing returns which limits the usefulness of strength. Remember, we're talking boxing here and not wrestling.

Sports science and nutrition have also evolved and improved since the 1960s. But the improvements in these areas are still not significant enough to bridge the huge gap in skill between today's lumbering giants and the superior athletes of yesteryear.

—November 2020

Nicholas Roberts: Could Frank Bruno have held on to the WBC title if he hadn't faced Tyson?

J. A.: Assume for a second that Tyson had never mauled Bruno into submission for a second time in early 1996. Bruno may have had to face Holyfield or a grudge rematch with Lewis sooner or later.

If you follow the same timeline through (assuming he avoided Tyson), then Bruno would probably have had to face his next mandatory challenger, who was Holyfield. In other words, instead of Tyson versus Holyfield in the fall of 1996, you would potentially have had a Bruno versus Holyfield matchup.

Given the fact that Holyfield (and PEDs) defeated Tyson, then you would think that the same Holyfield would beat Bruno too. It would still be a tough fight, as Bruno was always in shape, had good power, was as strong as an ox, and was always a game opponent. However, Bruno was technically limited. An all-rounder like Holyfield would surely have had enough in his locker to out-point him.

Assume for a second that Bruno ducks Holyfield and wants to take a higher-payday fight against, say, Lewis. He had already faced Lewis in 1993 and come up short. It was a competitive fight while it lasted, but Lewis eventually exploited Bruno's defensive frailties. So if there were a hypothetical rematch with Lewis in the late 1990s, then it would be likely to have a repeat result.

The main way that Bruno could have held on to his belt for as long as possible would have been to avoid Holyfield and Lewis. If he played it safe, then he could maybe have remained champion a year or so longer. But ultimately, Bruno's defence was his perennial Achilles heel. If it weren't Tyson working him over, then it would have been some other top contender doing the same.

—November 2020

Martin Asiner: If you take the Buster Douglas from the Tyson fight and put him against the Sonny Liston from 1958, who would win?

J. A.: Sticking just to the boxing, Douglas's jab was probably the key to upsetting Tyson in 1990. On the night, his jab, one-two, and one-two-three were his key combos. Essentially these were all straight punches which Tyson kept eating from the get-go. Douglas also displayed decent defensive footwork, which kept him out of harm's way.

Now take into consideration the psychological state of each boxer on the night. Douglas was on an extreme emotional high and Tyson was on a low. So would these same fight tactics from the *exact* same Douglas work against a prime Sonny Liston?

Essentially you have a matchup of a fringe contender (Douglas) against an all-time great (Liston). The slight complication is that Douglas is a *scared fighter turned brave*, which makes him that much more dangerous.

Would Douglas's jab and one-two combo work against prime Liston? Maybe for a couple of rounds, but not for an extended time period. Liston had a great jab of his own, which was better and longer than Douglas's. So Liston should win the battle of the jabs and ultimately take control of the centre of the ring—perhaps from round four onwards.

Once Liston forces Douglas to back up, it will create the space and opportunity for him to unload with some power punches. I can't see Douglas's chin taking too many clean power punches from a prime Liston. Essentially, it will be a stalking and wearing-down job for Liston, and he probably gets to Douglas somewhere in the middle rounds.

—December 2020

Kinyanjui Kamau: Who wins this heavyweight bout, 1971 Joe Frazier or 1988 Mike Tyson?

J. A.: Imagine a scenario whereby you replace 1973 George Foreman with 1988 Mike Tyson. It isn't too much of a stretch of the imagination to envisage a similar result to "the Sunshine Showdown".

At the highest level of boxing, the classic law of styles make fights more often than not holds true. Smokin' Joe was a great swarmer, and this style essentially proved suicidal against the bludgeoning "stone" power of George Foreman. To simplify Frazier versus Foreman 1, it was a gross miscalculation on the part of team Frazier. His seek-and-destroy style brought him head first into huge, swinging punches from Foreman, which essentially doubled their impact. It really was a case of boxing suicide.

So why do they do it? Why did Frazier deliberately collide with the Mack truck that was prime Foreman? Very simply, he couldn't fight in any other way. Joe was great to watch, but his style was one-dimensional. This lack of versatility sealed his fate against Foreman before a punch was ever thrown.

In addition to the styles make fights issue, peak Tyson also had the small matter of about twenty pounds of pure lean muscle mass on prime Frazier. He was also a faster and harder two-handed puncher. If this is not enough to convince you that Tyson would win by a massacre, I'll give you one more bit of evidence-based data: the fastest heavyweight in history out of the blocks was prime Tyson. To make matters worse, Joe was a well-known slow starter who took a few rounds to warm up.

However, it isn't all doom and gloom for Frazier. Joe was tougher and had more stamina than Tyson. He was the more dangerous late-rounds fighter. Unfortunately, I really don't see the fight going long enough for Frazier to make these advantages count.

The final nail in Joe's coffin is Tyson's signature punch—his deadly, arching uppercut. Tyson finished Joe's son Marvis Frazier off with the uppercut. While Marvis wasn't even half the fighter his father was, I still see the same huge vulnerability to the uppercut in Frazier senior. Foreman teed off on Joe Frazier with his own uppercut.

In general, it's not a good idea to stand right in front of tremendous power men such as Tyson, Foreman, Liston, or Shavers. To be successful against such fighters requires mobile counterpunching, good ring smarts, and a degree of caution early on.

—December 2020

Mike Harper: Who wins between 1971 Joe Frazier and 1980 Larry Holmes?

J. A.: Holmes, probably by a very narrow split decision in an action-packed fight.

Larry Holmes really laid into Joe Frazier's son Marvis in 1983. On the night, a ruthless Holmes made light work of a ridiculously overmatched Frazier.

It is safe to assume that a 1971 Joe Frazier, fresh off his victory over Ali, would be a far sterner test for Holmes. The general pattern of the fight would be very similar to Ali versus Frazier 1. Essentially, you would be replacing one out-fighter (Ali) with another (Holmes). Frazier would be his usual self, applying relentless pressure as he always did. Like Ali, Holmes would soak up that pressure, as he always did.

In any Holmes fight, his "key to the lock" punch was his legendary jab. In any Joe Frazier fight, his "key to victory" punch was his legendary left hook. If you ever wanted to see a picture-perfect left hook thrown with speed, power, timing, and disguise, then look no further than Frazier's lethal left—not to mention the fact that he could pretty much throw this punch at will all night long.

At the end of the day, I see this fight being extremely close and almost inevitably going to points. The two fighters are both Hall of Famers and very closely matched. In 1971, Frazier was at his peak and put in his career-defining performance to out-point a slightly past-prime Ali. I think a 1980 Holmes was slightly better and cagier than a 1971 Ali. Perhaps most importantly, Holmes had a better jab than the great Ali's—hard to believe, I know, but he did.

Furthermore, Holmes had defeated Ken Norton in 1978 by a narrow split decision. In terms of power-punching offense, Holmes was none too shabby himself. His right cross proved to be particularly damaging to Norton. If he could catch the slippery Ken Norton with this power punch, I think he could catch the less elusive Frazier more easily and more often.

Over the years, Norton was also trained by Frazier's long-time trainer, the legendary Eddie Futch. Although Futch was known to be a master tactician, Holmes still seemed to fare well against Futch-trained fighters. Additionally Holmes was a very smart boxer and was well-versed in spoiling tactics. In the end, I see Holmes just about being busy enough to catch the judges' eyes, particularly down the stretch, as he did against Norton.

—November 2020

Shaun Duggal: Would Tua have been too good for Tyson?

J. A.: Other way around really—Tyson would have been way too good for Tua.

If you analyse both streaming fight footage and still photos of these two, you will easily grasp the concept of a picture speaking a thousand words. Over the course of their respective careers,

Tyson's power punches were consistently more accurate and clean. They generally landed more flush than Tua's. Although Tua was a ferocious puncher in his own right, at the highest level his notoriously concussive left hooks often lacked accuracy and regularly fell short of the intended target. In a real-life fight between these two, the gulf in class would rapidly become apparent. Mike would nail Tua almost at will, whereas Tua would mostly punch thin air.

If you remember only one thing about boxing, remember this: *boxing is all about levels*, similar to the layers of an onion. Mike penetrated that boxing onion to its very core, whereas Tua perhaps peeled off the top two layers.

Comparing David Tua to Mike Tyson is almost like comparing a Nissan Skyline to a Bugatti Veyron. Yes, there are certain similarities, but there are also a lot of differences. Tyson does it all better, faster, and slicker than Tua and generally boxed at a way higher level.

If I recall correctly, prime Tyson was a unified world champion, the most dominant heavyweight champion in history, and the second-most feared boxer in history. On the other hand, Tua was a fringe contender with a very hard left hand, an interesting hairstyle, and limited boxing skills.

Tua's fight with Lewis was an anticlimax of epic proportions. Hasim Rahman once commented on this fight, "Both guys basically stunk up the joint." I couldn't agree more. Tua basically followed Lewis around the ring aimlessly for twelve boring and uneventful rounds. In the process, he barely laid a glove on a leisurely Lewis, who strolled to an inevitable points victory. And this was prime David Tua, who, as far as I could see, had no excuse for such an underwhelming display.

The point is this: if you're going to apply pressure to a world-class boxer like Lewis, it has to be a lot more subtle and educated than Tua's failed attempt in the fall of 2000.

Tua also failed against another strong opponent named Ike Ibeabuchi in 1997. On this occasion, the fight was a more action-packed affair, but again it only served to highlight Tua's limitations—the guy could bang, but he couldn't box.

In a direct comparison with Tyson, I think Tua literally has no advantages. The only positive that I can see is his left hook is comparable to Tyson's in terms of raw power. Other than this, Tyson is vastly superior in every other boxing department and would probably win by a referee's stoppage, somewhere in the middle rounds.

—October 2020

Daryl Woodard: Who would Mike Tyson have a tougher time fighting, Earnie Shavers or Mac Foster?

J. A.: In terms of danger factor, it has to be the devastating 1970s power puncher that was Earnie Shavers. Although Mac Foster was a better boxer than Shavers, Shavers was in a different league to Foster when it came to firepower. Looking at the two potential opponents through Tyson's eyes, I think it would be Shavers's superior firepower that Tyson would fear more.

In the end, I think the Iron Man will KO both guys, but against a knockout artist like Shavers he has to exercise caution in the early going. Probably the last punch in the world that you want to get nailed with in the early rounds is Shavers's legendary right haymaker. Shavers was a notoriously concussive puncher and is the one historical boxer I would back to KO a horse, let alone another pro boxer. Make no mistake: in this matchup, Tyson has to temper his own natural aggression early on. After a few rounds, Earnie should begin to gas, at which point Tyson can up the ante and finish him off with one of his patented combos.

While a fight between Tyson and Shavers would inevitably be a slugfest, I think a matchup between Tyson and Foster would be a more cagey affair, similar to Tyson's meeting with James "Quick" Tillis. Foster was a similar height and build to Tillis and had a similar skill set. I can also imagine him keeping Mike at bay with his rangy jab, at least for a while. But a big difference between Tillis and Foster was chin strength, and I can't see Foster taking too many clean headshots from prime Tyson.

In 1970, Foster was on top against Jerry Quarry, but when Quarry closed up the range and landed a few trademark short hooks, it was over in a hurry. Quarry got to Mac Foster in round six, so I guess prime Tyson gets him out of there a couple of rounds sooner.

—October 2020

Jose Gonzalez: Which heavyweight boxer in his prime would have the best chance of defeating Muhammad Ali in his prime?

J. A.: The moment I read this question, I didn't even have to think. An image of a 1988 Tyson nonchalantly stepping through the ropes to face Michael Spinks immediately came to mind. If you even asked Ali (rest in peace), off the record, "Who would have been your toughest opponent?", I think Ali would have reluctantly replied that peak Tyson presented the greatest threat.

My reasoning behind picking prime Tyson as Ali's toughest opponent is multifactorial.

- Tyson was the number-one precision power puncher of the modern heavyweight era. If there was one heavyweight who could thread the needle with power punches then that guy was surely Iron Mike. By now we have all seen a hapless and inaccurate George Foreman fail miserably against Ali in 1974. Even when he had Ali pinned on the ropes, he had little success. I believe Foreman's failures would not be repeated by Tyson.
- To beat a dancing master like Ali, you need a guy who can cut the ring off and block any escape routes in the blink of an eye. Mike Tyson was probably the most technically proficient gap closer in heavyweight history.
- Ali had most trouble seeing and blocking a fast left hook thrown from a crouch. Probably the top two exponents of a fast, well-disguised, and powerful left hook thrown from a crouch were Joe Frazier and Mike Tyson.
- Prime Tyson was the most ambidextrous knockout artist in the division's history. Ali has double trouble as he also has to look out for Tyson's nightmare right uppercut.
- The uppercut was a Mike Tyson specialty and is generally rated as the most dangerous unseen punch in heavyweight history—a perfect shot to throw on the inside against a taller fighter.
- Tyson also had body punching expertise. To restrict the mobility of an out-fighter, you need to take away his legs. Tyson and Frazier were elite body punchers who pursued opponents relentlessly, gradually taking away their mobility with accurately placed body

shots. On the other hand, George Foreman wasn't a particularly good or accurate body puncher, hence the fact Ali dealt with him so comfortably. In other words, Ali knew from Foreman's previous fights that he was predominantly a headhunter.

- To get the job done at the highest level of boxing, it normally takes more than one punch. More often than not, a series of punches or a combination settles the argument. In terms of throwing deadly "punches in bunches", I think prime Tyson had no historical peer.
- Out of all the great historical heavyweight brawlers, Iron Mike probably had the most effective defence. In his peak years (1985 to 1988 inclusive), he possessed great upper body movement, even more so given the nature of his robust and well-muscled physique. These facts coupled with his ultra-aggressive style meant that he took very few hard shots during his heyday.
- Again like Joe Frazier before him, Mike could close the gap efficiently by punching while on the move. Quite often this was evident through his use of Dempsey-like leaping hooks. Doing two things simultaneously—moving and punching—effectively negated the taller fighter's natural physical advantages.
- Peak Tyson was arguably subjected to the most comprehensive and bespoke training regimen in heavyweight history, thanks largely to Cus D'Amato. This legendary boxing guru developed a highly scientific system of boxing, later to be known as peekaboo, which happened to be ideally suited to the boxing genetics of a juvenile Tyson.
- Make no mistake, during his prime years Mike meant business both in and out of the ring. He was a consummate professional. When he was with his original team, right in the head, and properly focused strictly on boxing, he was a world-beater. With this kind of single-minded "eye of the tiger" attitude, prime Tyson would unquestionably have been Ali's acid test.

—October 2020

SHINO REID: How long do you think it would take a prime Mike Tyson to knock out a prime Lennox Lewis? One round? Two?

J. A.: I think the highly skilled, almost unbeatable, and properly motivated beast of nature that was 1988 prime Tyson would take four to seven rounds to get the job done. I if I were a betting man and had to pick a specific round, I'd go for round five. My main reason for picking round five for Lewis's demise is because that is the same round in which Hasim "The Rock" Rahman turned his lights off.

Generally boxing from a crouch, Rahman consistently threw aggressive and solid punches in an upward trajectory at his taller opponent. Prime Tyson would throw dozens of similar "punches in bunches with bad intentions". If prime Lewis couldn't avoid Rahman's punches, there is no chance he could deal with the premier heavyweight brawler in boxing history.

Lewis's one-punch knockout defeat to essentially a journeyman-grade opponent was very damaging to his legacy. Thankfully for his sake, Lewis limited the long-term damage by avenging the loss to Rahman in the rematch. But ultimately, all these years on, glaring question marks still remain over Lewis's ability to hold a punch. Most neutral fans are left pondering, "Do truly great fighters really lose by knockout to journeymen?"

Ultimately, I feel the "prime Tyson versus prime Lewis" analysis is fairly straightforward and linear. Hasim Rahman, Ray Mercer, and Vitali Klitschko can all be used as fairly accurate yardsticks to gauge Lewis's hypothetical performance against prime Tyson. We know that Lewis didn't like to be pressured and was always at his best when boxing at his own tempo in his comfort zone. Rahman, Mercer, and Klitschko applied a little pressure, and he almost fell to pieces.

Amplify that pressure tenfold and imagine he's got the Tasmanian devil that was prime Tyson in his face. You already know what's going down.

—October 2020

Najiur Rahman: What is the chance that Deontay Wilder could make it to the third round against prime Muhammad Ali? Since modern training (boxing evolution) has improved a lot since 1967.

J. A.: Quite high, really, since Ali was never a particularly hard puncher. Punching hard was never Ali's game. He was primarily a finesse boxer who wore opponents down with an accumulation of punches. I think most experts would classify Ali as a medium-power puncher at best. He could still obviously knock the average Joe into tomorrow, but by pro heavyweight standards, his power was probably medium.

Staying with the question, Ali will still dominate Wilder and outbox him in cruise control.

I can see Wilder eating Ali's signature right cross all night long. If I were a betting man, I would put money on Wilder just about making it to the second half of the fight. He will become demoralised as Ali shows him angles and movement that he has never even dreamed of. By round seven, his trainer Mark Breland will likely do him a favour by throwing in the towel, similar to when Tyson Fury opened up a can of whoop-ass on him.

As for boxing evolution favouring Wilder, I'm not so sure. Yes, there have inevitably been improvements in sports science, better implementation of strength training into boxing, and so on. Some of this will no doubt help Wilder survive a few rounds longer. But it won't help him bridge the huge gulf in class between him and a prime Ali.

Boxing technique hasn't improved or evolved all that much since the 1960s. Some would even argue that the skill factor found in today's lumbering giants is a lot lower than in the golden era of boxing. You could easily argue that today's heavyweights are resorting to gigantism because they have no skill. Remember that boxing is both a physical and a skill sport. You need both ingredients to beat the top guy in history. When Wilder is right, he has plenty of physicality and power—but almost no skill.

—November 2020

Gray Summers: What if Muhammad Ali had also had Joe Louis-like punching power—would he have gone undefeated in his career?

J. A.: There is a good chance that he may have gone undefeated for longer and could perhaps have joked about his own "bum of the month club". But to go undefeated his whole career is too hard to predict. Bear in mind that in your question, you are hypothetically giving him all-time great firepower. On paper, this looks fantastic and clearly turns Ali Into a lethal weapon.

But rewind the clock to the 1960s and match him against all those same guys. Do you think Ali's pre-exile boxing record would look different? Of course it would. Because Ali would now be leaving a trail of KO victims in his wake. So by 1971, when Smokin' Joe was on his radar, what do you think Joe's approach would have been if he knew he was up against a great slickster who possessed a genuine KO punch?

The point is this: Ali was at his brilliant best when guys like Frazier and Foreman brought the heat, thereby giving him opportunities to counterpunch off the back foot. Guys like Frazier and Foreman would not pressure Ali in the same way if they knew he could hit twice as hard. Simply put, when you're up against a huge puncher, you can no longer afford to take a punch to land a punch. This changes everything.

Ask most boxing experts who was Ali's number-one bogeyman, and most will tell you that, style-wise, it was Ken Norton. Ali hated boxing Norton. One of the main reasons for his dislike was that Norton was far less aggressive in his approach towards Ali. He didn't try for an all-out KO, but instead boxed the great boxer. This somewhat negative tactic worked a treat in their classic trilogy. If you suddenly increased Ali's punching power, then many of his career rivals would adopt Norton's more cagey and tactical approach.

Increasing Ali's punching power would probably have helped him more in the mid- to late 1970s, when he became more flat-footed and stood in the pocket for longer. The "blood and guts" Ali took a lot of beatings from some heavy hitters in the 1970s and extra firepower would definitely have come in handy. Also, lesser boxers such as Leon Spinks would have been brushed aside way more easily.

—January 2020

Martin Conlon: Would a pre-Emmanuel Steward Lennox Lewis beat Mike Tyson of 1987–1988?

J. A.: If you replace Tyrell Biggs with Lewis and keep prime Tyson's punishing left hook the same, then in 1987–1988, Lewis is in for a very rough ride and a seriously rude awakening.

I believe that no version of Lewis could ever match prime Tyson. Would he give Tyson a good fight? Yes, of course he would. But in the end, prime Tyson would cut the runners off and wear him down, similar to how one of Mike's heroes, the legendary Roberto Duran, used to do. Obviously Duran wasn't a heavyweight, but his pure brawler style would be a bad matchup for a long-range strategic boxer like Lewis.

The main reason that 1987 Tyson is a bad stylistic matchup for Lewis can be summarised in one word: *pressure*. Lewis never dealt with pressure well. Facing the Tasmanian devil that was heyday Tyson, then and only then will he fully comprehend the meaning of pressure as applied to a heavyweight boxing match. Tyson will come out of the blocks with a vengeance and floor the gas pedal in a manner that Lewis has never before seen. This fact alone doesn't bode well for Lewis, who always likes to operate out of a comfort zone. Against prime Tyson, there is no such thing as a comfort zone. Don't believe me? Ask any of his 1980s opponents if they had ever been exposed to that level of pressure before.

A pre-Emmanuel Steward Lennox Lewis was nothing special. Lewis was a fundamentally flawed boxer. Manny Steward was a legendary trainer who worked wonders on his style and ironed out many of his flaws. By the late 1990s, Steward had transformed Lewis into a vastly improved boxer who fully utilised his physical advantages and therefore fought big. Additionally, under Steward's tutelage, Lewis was transformed into a much more intimidating physical specimen.

—January 2020

Gabe Zephier: What if Mike Tyson had fought Evander Holyfield in 1990?

J. A.: The year 1990 was a bad one for Tyson, full stop. It would still have been a bad year had his opponent been Holyfield instead of Douglas. Holyfield's style matches up well with Tyson's, and Tyson would have had to be at his best to beat Holyfield (even minus the performance-enhancing drugs).

Tyson's best year was 1988. That version of Tyson would probably beat Holyfield by TKO in a war. Ex-world featherweight champion Barry McGuigan carried out an analysis on this very point in one of his newspaper columns years and years ago, and he addressed this tantalising "what if" scenario. He felt that prime versus prime, Tyson would be too fast and powerful for Holyfield. McGuigan reiterated that the fight would no doubt be competitive, but ultimately Tyson's superior firepower would get the job done.

In 1996, if you looked at the first fight closely, there wasn't too much between the two fighters until the finish—at which time Tyson had clearly gassed. In 1990, Tyson was two years past his prime and was already in premature and steep decline. As we now all know, a ton of personal problems had taken their toll. Without Rooney guiding him, Tyson was just another 5 feet 11 inch, 220-pound guy who was no longer elusive or fleet-footed. As we all saw against Buster Douglas, he was uncharacteristically caught by all manner of power punches that a Rooney-trained Tyson would have avoided. Rooney was a big proponent of proper head movement, and it was exactly this lack of head movement that cost Tyson against Douglas.

Hypothetically speaking, if they had fought in 1990, I would pick Holyfield to win on points. If they had boxed in 1988, I would pick Tyson by TKO. Timing is everything in boxing.

—January 2019

Michael Brett and Brian Birdsall: Who would win in the Octagon with no rules or time limits—a prime Iron Mike or a prime Brock Lesnar?

J. A.: This encounter almost encapsulates that age-old fighting conundrum, "What happens when that wrestler grabs hold of that boxer?" It is a very dangerous fight for both guys and would no doubt be a seriously exciting encounter. In prime Tyson, you have arguably the most capable street- fighter in heavyweight history. In Brock, you have a very physically intimidating and world-class grappler. Can Tyson's speed and technique overcome Brock's horsepower? Yes, I think so—but it won't be easy.

Breaking the fight down, Brock's main advantages are strength and weight. To make his

50-pound weight advantage count, he has to grab Tyson, take him down, and exercise ground control. Against prime Tyson, this is a very difficult task. It would be like trying to control a fully grown panther without claws.

At his peak, prime Tyson did indeed move around the boxing ring like a 220-pound panther. He would evade Brock's clumsy lunges and make him pay the price with some lethal body punches. When Brock shoots, Tyson isn't there. Instead there is a beautiful check hook waiting for Lesnar. Given Tyson's ambidextrous punching ability, he would easily target Brock's liver, as Alistair Overeem did in UFC 141. On that occasion, one kick to the liver from Overeem settled the argument.

Ultimately, I think prime Tyson would be too fast, agile, and precise for a game Brock, who would simply present a much too static target for prime Tyson.

—January 2019

Michael Rebovich: What do you think a Jack Johnson versus Mike Tyson fight would look like?

J. A.: Most probably a one-sided beatdown. As Stone Cold Steve Austin would say, "Tyson's gonna open up a can of whoop-ass on Johnson and that's the bottom line!"

In all seriousness, it would be a mismatch of epic proportions. Tyson could probably drop Johnson in the first round if he wanted to. Alternatively, if he wanted to play with Johnson and use him in order to practice certain combinations, then so be it. Tyson would have the skill, means, and firepower to carry out whichever type of beatdown took his fancy.

In my humble opinion, Jack Johnson is one legendary name from a bygone era who has been somewhat overrated because of the extracurricular racial and political issues of the time. The phrase "famous for being famous" comes to mind. I personally think, based on old footage, that Sam Langford would be a much tougher test than Jack Johnson. I can't see a single boxing advantage that Johnson has over prime Tyson, apart from posing.

—January 2019

Anonymous: Which of the Fab Four boxers from the 1980s (Hagler, Hearns, Leonard, and Duran) could have beaten Floyd Mayweather Junior in their prime?

J. A.: Hagler would definitely have beaten Floyd Mayweather; he would have been too tough, rugged, and durable. With a chin as strong as Hagler's he would have literally walked through Mayweather's punches to deliver his own blows. On top of this, being a natural middleweight, Hagler would have been way too strong for Mayweather in the clinches. I favour Hagler in a middle-rounds TKO.

With the Hitman Thomas Hearns, I think Mayweather again has his hands full in the early rounds. In the early going, Hearns was as lethal as any boxer in history. There is a danger he can do Mayweather some serious damage—that is, if he catches him clean. The right hand that almost decapitated an unsuspecting Roberto Duran was a prime example of a punch that can kill. If Hearns detonates that same right hand on Mayweather, it could end Mayweather's career. This appears to be a bad matchup for Mayweather, as it normally takes him a few rounds to warm up and read his opponent's offense. Twelve minutes is an eternity against prime Hitman. Therefore Hearns should win in an early-rounds blowout.

Moving on to Sugar Ray Leonard, this fight is going to be a cat-and-mouse affair between two of the slickest boxers of the modern era. It is very difficult to call this one, as both fighters on paper are evenly matched and well rounded. It has a points decision written all over it. In this case, you may as well toss a coin, as the three judges will most likely see the fight in three different ways. Cue the rematch clause!

That leaves Roberto Duran, who I think Mayweather would most probably out-point. Mayweather will be extremely cautious with the Hands of Stone, as Duran can hurt you at any time in the fight. But I think Mayweather's defensive wizardry will frustrate Duran and see him through the twelve rounds. If I were Duran, I would demand a fifteen-round duration and a small ring to improve my chances.

—January 2019

Rodney Chin: Could Riddick Bowe beat Tyson or Foreman?

J.A.: I know for a fact that Riddick Bowe was scared of Tyson. Both guys grew up in New York and were apparently aware of each other during adolescence. Based on this fact, it is extremely unlikely that Bowe would step into the ring with a peak Tyson. Obviously the post-incarceration Tyson was a shell of his former self, and Bowe most likely could have beaten him.

Comparing prime for prime, Bowe has all the physical advantages of height, weight, and reach. But that's exactly where his advantages start and end. The fact that he is taller and longer than Tyson is a moot statistic because all of Tyson's opponents had height and reach over him. So what's different about Bowe? Tyson would be too fast and precise for Bowe, and on the inside would pound Bowe's body. Bowe being Bowe, he would definitely fire back but would probably quit when the brutal realisation strikes home that he is outmatched. Tyson wins by a middle-rounds TKO.

Against prime Foreman, Bowe would never take the fight. Lennox Lewis was always adamant that Bowe avoided him, and Bowe would surely do the same against Foreman. Big George was too strong and tough for Bowe.

—January 2019

Anonymous: How would Sonny Liston have done in the 1990s? Would those boxers be able to handle him?

J. A.: Prime Liston would have been a beast in any era, based on his superior boxing genetics, the intimidation factor, and one of the absolute strongest jabs in heavyweight history. At his best, Liston was probably the second most destructive heavyweight ever, one of the strongest heavyweights ever, and had one of the best precision left hooks ever.

His three main competitors in the 1990s would obviously have been Holyfield, Bowe, and Lewis, all of whom he could potentially beat by knockout.

Starting with Holyfield, I think his style would play into Liston's hands, as Holyfield likes an inside tear-up. Liston was way too powerful and heavy handed. It could potentially be similar to the fight that Holyfield had with James Toney, in which Toney overwhelmed Holyfield on the inside. I think Liston beats Holyfield by middle- to late-rounds TKO, after a war.

Chicken Bowe would be fearful of Liston and would simply avoid him in the same way he ducked Lewis. Bowe was never great in the gym and had suspect conditioning at the best of times. Supposedly at his peak, in between his first two meetings with Holyfield, he gained around a stone of fat. Holyfield gained a stone of muscle in the same time frame. Liston would no doubt feast on such a large and blubbery target—that is, if Bowe had the guts to face him.

Lennox Lewis would probably give Liston the best fight and a danger of out-pointing him. Lewis has a comparable reach and would fight Liston at very long range—the only way to do it, really. Always the smart boxer, Lewis would also avoid Liston in the early rounds. If at any time Lewis gets even slightly careless, then he could have his lights turned out in the blink of an eye. If a journeyman like Hasim Rahman can spark Lewis, then imagine what Liston could do. The difference obviously is that Lewis would prepare much more meticulously for a fighter of Liston's calibre. Nonetheless Lewis was always vulnerable, even at the best of times.

If I were training Liston, the main improvement I would make would be to his mobility. Looking at the old and grainy 1960s footage, he appears to be somewhat cumbersome in his movements, although a prime Ali would make almost any heavyweight look cumbersome!

—February 2019

Manny Apea: You have to fight Mike Tyson in his prime. Who are you taking with you into the ring?

J. A.: How about Jon "Bones" Jones?

Fighting prime Tyson could turn out to be a nightmarish experience and would surely be an exercise in containment and back-foot countering. I think Bones Jones would probably be the best all-round fighter to attempt such a risky exercise. Ultimately, you want a guy who is technically proficient both on the ground and in stand-up. Jones's vaunted leg kicks would prove invaluable for limiting prime Tyson's movements. Jones also has good reach, which will help to keep Tyson at arm's length and deny Tyson the leverage he needs to really let fly with his patented combos.

The ultimate objective is to wear Tyson out and then put him on his back as soon as it is safe to do so. Jones appears to be the one MMA fighter most suited to this containment task, as he possesses the right blend of cardio, stamina, striking ability, and grappling skills. Trying to wrap up a fresh Tyson would be way too dangerous. It is imperative to cause him to fatigue first. The main wearing-out tactic will be leg kicks to upset Tyson's balance. Then each guy will work in tandem to systematically blindside him . If Tyson clips you with a bare-knuckle punch, even a glancing blow, then it's game over; so it is absolutely imperative to prevent him from getting too close. After a period of time, you hope that Tyson tires from the accumulated leg kicks and the fact he is chasing two guys instead of one.

—February 2019

Rodney Chin: If there was one middleweight person who had a chance to beat Tyson in his prime, who would it be?

J. A.: I don't think any middleweight would have a realistic chance of beating prime Tyson. Possibly one or two guys down the years would have had a theoretical chance of maybe outpointing him? It is highly unlikely that any middleweight boxer would have the firepower to discourage a rampaging Tyson. As soon as Tyson cornered the middleweight and unloaded with his trademark power combos, it would be game over. The harsh reality for the middleweight boxer is that he is outmatched in most decisive boxing traits: punching power, chin strength, physical strength, and so on. What makes matters worse is that against almost any other heavyweight boxer, you could assume that the middleweight has a speed advantage, but against prime Tyson this would not necessarily hold true.

Since you've mentioned a chance, then I suppose there is a very slim chance of Roy Jones Junior going the distance and receiving a generous points decision from friendly judges. When you asked this question, you were probably thinking of Roy Jones Junior facing John Ruiz in 2003, right? But believe me, John Ruiz was a poor heavyweight champion at the best of times. Against a killer like Tyson, Jones would risk being hospitalised. Remember what Antonio Tarver did to him? Imagine that same left hook coming from Tyson. It would probably be 100 per cent more solid and powerful.

Let's assume that Jones was at his mid 1990s brilliant and athletic best. He could prove to be a very elusive target, but at some point over the course of a twelve rounder, you would think that Tyson would corner him. Being very optimistic for Jones, maybe a below-par Tyson (similar to his career-worst showing against Buster Douglas) would lack motivation and tire in the later rounds. It isn't inconceivable. But we inevitably get back to the subject of punching power, and even a below-par Tyson dropped Douglas with a vicious uppercut in round eight. So Jones would have to stay on his bike continuously and hope for a friendly and biased referee who also doesn't allow Tyson to rough him up on the inside. I give Jones a 5 per cent chance of success. In other words, if he faced Tyson twenty times, then on one occasion he may pull off this miracle.

—February 2019

Anonymous: What if Ali had lost to George Foreman? Would he still be remembered the way he is now?

J. A.: Absolutely not! That victory was pivotal in securing him the GOAT title. In Angelo Dundee's words about his fighter, "I have always believed he is the best heavyweight ever. He has to lick Foreman to make the press admit this." The Rumble in the Jungle was arguably the most important boxing match in history, and the outcome was even more important in terms of shaping the all-time heavyweight pecking order. If Ali had lost, he may have been demoted to an also-ran. If he had been knocked out, that would have made matters even worse.

The effect of losing to Foreman would have been a double whammy. Foreman may have gone on to dominate the rest of the 1970s, and it isn't inconceivable that he could have gone undefeated for his whole career. Losing to Foreman would have been nothing short of catastrophic for Ali, especially so as Foreman had annihilated two of Ali's conquerors in Norton and Frazier. So, effectively, it would have been Foreman who emerged as the dominant heavyweight from the golden era of heavyweight boxing.

Foreman once jokingly remarked that "losing that sweaty old boxing match cost me a year's worth of sleep!" Believe me, he wasn't exaggerating. Some would argue he was never the same fighter again. Ali effectively derailed the freight train that was 1970s Foreman. This victory most definitely secured Ali the GOAT status—apologies to all Joe Louis fans!

—February 2019

Leroy Holiday: Who would win between Jack Dempsey and Wladimir Klitschko?

J. A.: As long as Jack Dempsey was an unknown entity, I would fancy him to take care of Wladimir Klitschko. My reasoning is fairly simple. Dempsey was as aggressive as hell and had the skill and agility to close up the range on Klitschko before eating too many counters. Dempsey was a great two-handed puncher who punched effectively while on the move, thereby achieving two simultaneous goals. Once inside, his fists of steel would punish Klitschko to the head and body. It would potentially be similar to the beatdown inflicted on Klitschko by the late South African heavyweight Corrie Sanders in 2003. But in Dempsey, you have a much more explosive and dangerous early-rounds puncher.

In the possible rematch, it is entirely possible that Klitschko could reverse the outcome and grind out either a points victory or stop Dempsey late on. My reasoning again is fairly simple. Once Klitschko boxed Dempsey and had a chance to analyse the footage of their first fight, he could prepare more thoroughly for the rematch, which is incredibly important to a tactical fighter. In short, he simply wouldn't engage with Dempsey on the inside. At the highest level of boxing, small details make big differences, and I see Klitschko just about making the necessary adjustments to neutralise Dempsey in the rematch.

A prime example of this adjustment phenomenon was seen in Froch versus Groves in 2013 and 2014. Groves was a relative unknown and jumped all over an unsuspecting Froch in the very first round. In the rematch, Froch was better prepared and raised his game, while Groves fought too cautiously and paid the price. Having already boxed Groves, Froch had information and could better target his opponent's weaknesses.

—February 2019

Julian Brown: How would a boxing match between Sonny Liston and Rocky Marciano have gone?

J. A.: I would favour Liston in a big way. The cynical boxing historians may suggest that Marciano retired just in time to avoid prime Liston. I can't say that I blame him—I would have done exactly the same thing!

Liston won't have it all his own way, as Marciano is a genuine tough guy with a great right-hand punch and an all-action style that is very pleasing to the eye. However, his style will likely play into Liston's hands and potentially violate one of boxing's central rules: "Never brawl with a brawler." Especially when that brawler's name is Sonny Liston. Simply put, Liston does it all better than Marciano and also has height, weight, and reach advantages.

In this matchup, Liston's jab will be a formidable weapon, given the fact he won't have to go looking for Marciano. To put the concept of Liston's jab and reach advantage into perspective, you have Liston with a monster 84-inch reach compared to Marciano's paltry 68-inch reach. This difference will likely prove decisive.

It will no doubt be a competitive fight while it lasts. Rocky's legendary chin will keep him in the fight, probably, until the middle rounds. After a game show from the Rock, either his cornermen or the referee will pull him out before he gets himself KO'd.

—February 2019

Alyn Jones: If a 21-year-old Mike Tyson were competing in today's heavyweight division, how do you think he would do, and would any current heavyweights actually pose a threat to him?

J. A.: Tyson was a master at what the old-timers used to call "snarling and punching". Often when laying into his opponents, Tyson's facial expressions told a dark story and were reflective of what Big George Foreman used to called "boxing with intent". Replace Frank Bruno with Deontay Wilder or Anthony Joshua, and you will get the same result. Tyson mauled Bruno into submission in round five in 1989 and subsequently in round three in 1996. Joshua isn't quite as stiff and cumbersome as Bruno, but not too far out.

If I were a bookmaker, I would give even-money odds that prime Tyson could knock out Wilder and Joshua on the same night, as long as Tyson got a short rest in between fights.

The face of fear that Michael Spinks exhibited on his ring walk to fight a 21-year-old Tyson in 1988 has become the stuff of legend. Few professional boxers can claim the infamy of being more scared than Spinks—he really was like a deer caught in the headlights. I can't say that I blame him. Spinks's manager was a guy named Butch Lewis. Shortly before the stare-down, Lewis observed Tyson punching holes in the plasterboard walls of his dressing room! It isn't a stretch of the imagination that Joshua and Wilder would be equally as scared as Spinks was. This intimidation factor would surely seal both their fates before a punch was thrown.

Tyson Fury is the one current world-class heavyweight who would post a modest threat. I would back him to go the distance with Iron Mike. My reasoning is fairly straightforward. Fury has the size, skill, intelligence, and know-how to do a spoiling job on Tyson. He is at least as capable as James Smith, James Tillis, and Mitch Green were of carrying out containment jobs on Tyson. Ultimately, Fury would still lose a clear points decision, and there is an outside chance that Tyson mauls Fury early on—that is, if Fury gets careless and deviates from his fight plan.

Other than these three heavyweights, prime Tyson would simply annihilate everybody else in a matter of seconds, as he did in his classic mid 1980s one-round massacres. The modern heavyweight division has never seen anybody of the ilk, the ultra-aggressive style, and the sheer ferocity of a prime Tyson. In 1986, British commentator Reg Gutteridge summed up Tyson best: "Mike Tyson is a twentieth-century caveman—this really is a black version of a Rocky Marciano, and two stone heavier!"

—February 2019

Anonymous: Who are some boxers who could have beaten Ali in his prime—or at least got close?

J. A.: If I were prime Ali, the three boxers I want most to avoid are Iron Mike Tyson, Larry

Holmes, and Ken Norton. These three guys would pose the greatest threat to Ali's out-fighting style, and in Tyson we surely have Ali's worst nightmare come true. Tyson is the one historical heavyweight who could turn anybody's lights out with a 10-second barrage of punches, such as his legendary seventeen-punch "avalanche of leather" finish on Pinklon Thomas in the spring of 1987.

Back in the day, Tyson's body-punching was somewhat underrated, and against Thomas, he pounded the midsection with a vengeance. Similarly, if Tyson lands his trademark precision left hook to Ali's liver, it's all over. Furthermore, it is hard to envisage many historical heavyweights (not even granite-chinned George Foreman) who could take seventeen clean headshots in a row from Tyson and remain standing.

After Tyson, I think a peak Larry Holmes would be Ali's other nemesis. He had an out-fighting style similar to Ali's, which had been fine-tuned through years of being Ali's sparring partner in the early 1970s. So Holmes would be the one fighter perhaps most capable of reading and adapting to Ali's style. He also possessed a fast, ramrod jab which was comparable to Ali's.

Against Ali, Holmes was well capable of winning the battle of the jabs. If this eventuality transpired, it would mean that he controlled the centre of the ring. This would be a big problem, as most of Ali's best work generally flowed off his jab. Holmes was also a very underrated boxer and was a supreme ring technician—dare I say it, even better than Ali. But because nobody really liked him, the history writers have been somewhat unkind to him.

Finally on to Ali's real-time nemesis, Ken Norton: Ali hated fighting Norton. Norton's cross-armed defence and jab thrown from low down were nightmares for Ali to deal with.

Anybody who thinks that Floyd Mayweather invented the Philly shell, think again. Imagine fighting a heavyweight who was almost as defensively crafty as Floyd Mayweather and nearly as strong as George Foreman—Kenny Norton was your man. Norton struggled with big punchers and good body-punchers, but since Ali was neither, some would say that Ali's style was tailor-made for Norton.

In their final encounter in Yankee Stadium in 1975, many onlookers believed that Norton won. Alas, questionable boxing decisions are nothing new and have been around since the dawn of the gloved sport. Still to this day, many Norton fans believe it is actually 2–1 in favour of Norton in this classic stylistic trilogy. So even in Ali's prime, I believe he hated fighting Norton, who was a great boxer-puncher.

In general, you will find that boxer-punchers and all-rounders do well against out-fighters like Ali. According to George Foreman, Norton was one of the greatest physical specimens in heavyweight history, who could more than hold his own with Ali in the clinches. In other words, Norton was the equal of 1970s Ali in most boxing departments.

Having said all of the above, I still think 1966 Ali beats all three guys—but only just.

—February 2019

Jose Gonzalez: How would Lennox Lewis in his prime have fared in the 1960s and 1970s?

J. A.: It's gonna be tough for him. A lot depends on his matchmaker and the timing of key fights. His three toughest opponents would obviously be Ali, Foreman, and Frazier.

I can't see him out-boxing any version of Ali, although he may be capable of out-muscling an old and shopworn Ali. But if he steps in the ring with a pre-1975 Ali, then he will lose on points. Other than punching power, he has no real advantages over Ali. Additionally, Ali does everything better and slicker than Lewis and is also a lot tougher.

Although Ali pulled the rug out from under Foreman, I seriously doubt Lewis can imitate the master. Therefore I feel Lewis versus 1970s Foreman is a bad matchup for Lewis. It is difficult to see a feasible route to victory for him. He clearly has to keep the fight as long and as strategic as possible and hope that Foreman gasses. While 1970s Foreman has limited ring smarts, he more than makes up for this deficiency with overwhelming brute force, strength, and a granite chin. At some point over the course of a fifteen-rounder, I think Foreman corners Lewis and lands the inevitable bomb. Based on the evidence to hand, Lewis's chin isn't durable enough to absorb Foreman's punching power.

Even at his best, Lewis hates pressure fighters, and when he faces Joe Frazier, he is up against a guy who will bring the heat and apply that pressure for the entire fifteen rounds. I can see Lewis taking the early rounds as long as he boxes sensibly behind his jab. But as the fight wears on, Lewis will wear down, whereas Frazier will grow stronger. I think Frazier beats Lewis in a very competitive fight by a late-round TKO based on his superior engine, work rate, and toughness.

Other seriously dangerous fighters that Lewis needs to duck are Earnie Shavers, Ron Lyle, and Ken Norton. On their special day, any of these three guys are capable of putting Lewis to sleep.

—December 2020

Sungur Tekin: How would Anthony Joshua do in one-on-one boxing matches against George Foreman, Mike Tyson, and Muhammad Ali in their primes?

J. A.: Boxing matches are always one on one! There is no such thing as a tag-team boxing match or a handicap match. But never mind—on to the nitty gritty of the question.

Foreman versus A. J.

Foreman, prime or un-prime, I fancy to beat Joshua easily. My reasoning is fairly straightforward. Foreman possesses one of the strongest chins in heavyweight history and also has a very high pain tolerance. I can see even old Foreman taking Joshua's best shots and continuing to march forward unfazed. As and when he gets close to Joshua and lands some heavy, clean leather, it's game over. Joshua's chin can't take medium firepower, let alone all-time leading heavyweight firepower. Foreman should win by knockout as and when he gets close. Prime Foreman probably flattens Joshua in the third round, whereas old Foreman takes longer but nonetheless eventually gets to him in the later rounds.

Mike Tyson versus A. J.

Joshua is apparently a big Mike Tyson fan, so Tyson may take it easy on him. Of the three guys in your question, I think Tyson is by far the worst matchup for Joshua. Simply rewind the clock and watch Ruiz versus A. J. 1 again. Anything that Ruiz Junior can do, Tyson can do faster and better. Joshua is too statuesque and predictable in his movements. Prime Tyson will surgically dissect him, particularly to the body. I seriously doubt Joshua hears the bell for the third round.

Ali versus A. J.

Believe it or not, I think Ali would be a better matchup for Joshua than the other two killers on your list. Ali is the best boxer of the three, but the softest puncher, and this suits Joshua. If you watch the vast majority of Ali's fights, he generally got the job done by an accumulation of punches over a number of rounds. So there is an outside chance Joshua lasts the distance. But simply replace a 1960s six-feet six-inch strongman named Ernie Terrell with Joshua, and I think a similar fight will transpire. Ali bosses the majority of the action and wins either by late-rounds stoppage (A. J. quits or the ref intervenes) or by unanimous points decision.

Make no mistake: boxing is all about levels, and the three guys in your question are legitimate all-time greats. They are at least one, maybe even two levels above Joshua. Based on the evidence to hand, over the last five years or so, Joshua has been something of a flat-track bully. When Andy Ruiz introduced Joshua to jumps, he unfortunately fell at the first hurdle.

—December 2019

Lance Williams: In the absence of Cassius Clay (Muhammad Ali), how long would Sonny Liston have been champ, who would eventually beat him, and when? Also, under those circumstances, would he have been regarded as the greatest of all time?

J. A.: I think Liston would eventually have been dethroned by a solid and strong guy named George Foreman, sometime during the early 1970s. Foreman was Liston's one-time training and sparring partner, quite similar to how Larry Holmes was Muhammad Ali's . A sparring session is simply a less intense boxing match with head guards on, and you no doubt learn a lot from those sessions. Eventually the young and upcoming boxer will overwhelm the old warhorse.

It's not that I think Foreman was a better boxer than Liston—he wasn't. Liston was comfortably a better boxer than Foreman, but Father Time catches up to everyone. So by the late 1960s, Liston would have been too old and just about ripe for retirement. Around that time, Foreman and Frazier were the top young guns who possessed the firepower and means to retire Liston. I would still, however, back an old Liston to match a young Frazier, because styles make fights and Liston is all wrong for Frazier.

Let's assume for a moment that Liston didn't lose to Ali in 1964. I could see him remaining as heavyweight champion until around 1970. This would have extended his reign by another five or six years. It is then possible that his boxing resumé would have rivalled that of another GOAT candidate, Joe Louis.

So it is theoretically possible that Liston could have replaced Ali as the GOAT, but it is a real stretch of the imagination. In reality, he was already well past his best days when Ali beat him in 1964.

—November 2019

Anonymous: Say you had to fight Mike Tyson in one year. If you could have any person train you, who would it be?

J. A.: I would probably opt for Muhammad Ali's old trainer Angelo Dundee. Well known as a great boxing trainer and a master tactician, Dundee was one of the greatest trainers in boxing history.

Dundee was obviously most well known for his collaboration with Ali, but his priceless knowledge was well utilised by many other great fighters. It was a fairly well-known fact that in the 1970s and 1980s boxing industry, this guy knew every trick in the book and then some. His masterstroke was plotting the downfall of the 1974 heavyweight beast that was prime George Foreman. In reality, Dundee is one of the main reasons that Ali still gets the nod as the GOAT heavyweight. It's due in large part to his influence and tactical savvy in the Rumble in the Jungle.

Leaving all opinion aside, this question is almost a no-brainer. Why? We can use a bit of historical boxing knowledge and wind the clock back to 22 November 1986, when Tyson challenged Berbick for the heavyweight title. Trevor Berbick hired Dundee to train him. In this instance, Dundee's knowledge and influence made no difference to the outcome of the fight, as Berbick was knocked out in brutal fashion.

Six months after Tyson demolished Berbick, he faced Pinklon Thomas. Who did Thomas hire to train him? It was Angelo Dundee again! Yet again, it made no difference to the result; an unstoppable Tyson mauled Pinklon Thomas.

Although his results against prime Tyson were patchy at best, I would still go with Dundee as the guy who was most capable of plotting the downfall of prime Tyson.

—November 2019

Mike Shaner: If Tyson had fought in the 1960s and 1970s, would he have ever won a world title?

J.A.: It's gonna be difficult. One thing is for sure: the Iron Man better watch his back!

In the 1960s and 1970s, two solid and scary guys named Sonny Liston and George Foreman would be stalking Tyson with some dangerous intent. Back in the day, Sonny Liston was the most feared boxer in the world, inside and outside the ring. A well-known extract from a tabloid article read, "Men like Liston should not be fought in a boxing ring—instead they should be hunted down." If they had faced off, it would have been very interesting to see whether Liston or Tyson would have won the pre-fight psychological war games.

The 1960s and 1970s were arguably the most competitive decades in heavyweight history, and Tyson would therefore have to be at his sharpest and most elusive to thrive. Besides Liston and Foreman, two legendary warhorses named Ali and Frazier would also be waiting in the wings.

If that weren't bad enough, there were many other world-class heavyweights in the mix, such as Earnie Shavers, Ken Norton, Larry Holmes, George Chuvalo, Zora Folley, Jerry Quarry, Oscar Bonavena, and Ron Lyle. This is why that era has justifiably been called the golden era of heavyweights.

As long as Tyson remained 100 per cent focused on and dedicated to boxing, without any external distractions whatsoever, I think he could just about have been a world champion in that era. But he would have to have been guided very carefully by his original mentor and trainer, Cus D'Amato, and his opponents would have to be cherry-picked, at least to a certain extent. Specifically, he would have to avoid Ali and Foreman pre-1974; this would be absolutely imperative to maximise his chances of success. Those two matchups prior to 1974 would be very, very risky and are real fifty-fifies. Boxing is all about timing. When you fight a certain opponent is as important as who you fight.

I think Tyson takes Liston because by the mid 1960s, Liston is getting old anyway. Tyson takes Frazier because I think that particular matchup suits Tyson down to the ground. The other background guys in that era will be tough competition, but I think prime Tyson (under Cus) has enough in his locker to beat them. It is Ali and Foreman who will be the acid tests. In all honesty, if Foreman were a normal heavyweight with a normal chin, then Tyson could potentially beat him to a pulp with his patented combos. But the fact of the matter is that Foreman has a pure granite chin, a high pain tolerance, and the strength of an ox. Therefore, Foreman can take a serious beating and then keep coming. This changes everything. It can be the case that Tyson's superior firepower will not be enough to stop Foreman.

In this instance, it comes down to Cus D'Amato. How exactly will he modify Tyson's normal tactics for the Foreman fight? If D'Amato concludes that Tyson can't KO Foreman, then perhaps for this one fight, Tyson will need to adopt a more cautious and reserved approach—particularly in the early going.

—August 2019

Leroy Holiday: Who would win between prime George Foreman and Buster Douglas?

J. A.: I don't think this one's even close. As long as, this time around, Buster doesn't suffer a family bereavement two weeks before the fight, then Foreman should spectacularly destroy the greatest one-hit wonder in heavyweight history.

Replace "the black Hercules" Ken Norton with Douglas, and heyday Foreman should carry out a similar beatdown. I very much doubt Douglas gets by the second round as long as Foreman's mind is on the task at hand.

In February 1990, Mike Tyson's mind was not on the job. An emotionally empowered Douglas put in a career-best performance and handed the distracted Tyson his first pro defeat. Due to the sheer magnitude of his victory over Tyson, Douglas's boxing abilities have been grossly exaggerated. In reality it was nothing more than a freak occurrence.

As Tyson remarked about his career-worst performance, "Any good engine can have one bad day." At world level, this is very true. The opposite also holds true—any average engine can sometimes have a special day. That night in the Tokyo Dome in 1990, Douglas was that mediocre and average engine who simply performed way, way above everyone's expectations, largely due to the untimely passing of his mother shortly before the fight. If you don't believe me, then just look at his own cornermen going crazy with emotion after the finale. Like everyone else, they couldn't believe their eyes. Miracles do sometimes happen.

But staying with the matchup in the question, I think Foreman would be too powerful in the early rounds. I can't really see Douglas's jab and cross (one-two combo) keeping Foreman at bay for any length of time. If he somehow scrounges his way through the early rounds, then maybe he has the remote potential to do a sniper-fighter type of job, similar to Jimmy Young versus Foreman. In the late 1970s, prime Foreman could be confused by a good boxer-mover, but I don't think Buster Douglas was ever that guy. There isn't much evidence in Douglas's resumé that suggests he could cope with an all-time leading physical specimen like Foreman. I very much doubt he has the firepower to discourage the granite-chinned Foreman either. Other than beating a below-par and distracted Mike Tyson, Douglas did nothing else in his whole career. If you look at his pro record, mediocre guys such as Lou Savarese, David Bey, and Jesse Ferguson beat Douglas. Tony Tucker also has a knockout victory over Douglas.

—August 2019

Gabe Zephier: What if Buster Douglas hadn't knocked out Mike Tyson in 1990? What if Tyson had won their fight?

J. A.: Interesting point. It would be a *Back to the Future* moment whereby the heavyweight landscape was shifted to a new timeline and reality. In all honesty, Tyson winning that fight would only have served to delay the inevitable. On that particular night in February 1990 in the Tokyo Dome, Iron Mike Tyson literally self-imploded due to a number of insurmountable personal and professional problems. Nothing against Buster Douglas, but ask any top boxing expert—he was a nobody figure whose own emotional high conveniently coincided with Tyson's career low point. Had Douglas failed to KO Tyson, then some other wannabe wise guy would surely have crawled out of the woodwork sooner or later. By 1990 Tyson was a spent force, already in premature decline and asking to be knocked out.

There is an outside chance that Tyson may have got his act together and gone back to basics, meaning that he rehired Kevin Rooney. But under Don King's tutelage, Tyson was out of control and simply wasn't concentrating on the very difficult task of heavyweight boxing. He had forgotten about the hard side—namely the twelve weeks of intense pre-fight training and sparring that goes hand in hand with being a world champion. In the run-up to the Douglas fight, his training camp was a joke. It was a fairly well-known fact that he had become much more interested in geishas than he was in training. He was said to be "in and out of them faster than a Time Square pickpocket". This kind of carefree, sex-addicted, alcoholic, and partying lifestyle caught up with him in early 1990. It was that simple. So had Douglas not knocked out Tyson, then some other unknown journeyman would have done so very soon after.

—November 2018

Roland Diaz: Could the George Foreman who beat Frazier destroy a prime Tyson?

J. A.: No way, Jose!

In the good old 1980s, Mike Tyson was always in the mood to do serious damage; after all, that was what prime Tyson was all about. He created a media frenzy. The cameras were glued to him, and he gave the fight public of the day exactly what it wanted—knockouts. He was described by sports journalists as "the most exciting and incredible specimen of heavyweight boxing talent since a young Cassius Clay took the world by storm".

I don't think any other heavyweight in history—not prime Foreman, not prime Ali, not prime Liston, no one—could ever contemplate destroying prime Tyson. Could any of these guys beat Tyson? Yes, of course they could. But by the same token, Tyson could also beat them.

From a purely physical standpoint, if you compare prime Joe Frazier to prime Tyson, you tell me—who looks rougher and tougher? The answer is debatable. Many casual boxing fans make the common mistake of comparing two fighters of approximately the same height, failing to realise that Tyson was nearly twenty pounds heavier, due to pure, lean muscle mass. Believe me, this makes a massive difference. In terms of body weight, prime Foreman outweighs Tyson by only 2 kilograms, rather than the 9 kilograms he had on Frazier.

Consider the fact that Tyson was not a pure swarmer like Frazier. Tyson was a peekaboo street fighter, a different style to Frazier's "seek and destroy". Frazier's style proved suicidal against Foreman; Tyson was much more elusive. His hit-and-run style would be much more effective against a relatively cumbersome Foreman. Tyson would home in on Foreman's weaker left side and use blindside attacks to weaken him. The key to beating Foreman is movement—see Jimmy Young's and Evander Holyfield's performances versus Foreman. Both Holyfield and Young boxed well on the fly and used movement to confuse the big fella. On ESPN Classic, Foreman was very complimentary about Tyson's ring movements. He said, "Tyson was knocking guys out left and right, not unlike Joe Louis and George Foreman, and he'd move around the ring. He's gonna be remembered for a long time!" That was Foreman's own insight regarding what made prime Tyson so effective.

Breaking the fight down, Foreman is the harder long-range puncher, is physically stronger, and has the better chin. Tyson is the harder short-range puncher, has a better combo punch, is faster, and has the better defence. In my humble opinion, this fight is balanced on a knife edge and could swing either way—but believe me, neither guy is getting destroyed.

As for all this nonsense about Tyson being scared of Foreman, then yes, he is scared. He's a smart guy, and anyone who wasn't scared of Foreman must be dumb, lacking in common sense, or just plain stupid. Tyson feared *all* his opponents. "I use fear as my friend. I reflect it back on my opponent. If I don't have fear, then I don't fight."

—March 2019

ANONYMOUS: Who would win between a prime Evander Holyfield (Foreman fight) and a prime Lennox Lewis (Rahman 2) fight?

J. A.: A prime Holyfield was once described as being "bombproof". Could any normal, un-enhanced human hurt him? Holyfield's prime is debatable and open to all kinds of realistic as well as outlandish speculations. One thing is for sure: the timelines of his technical and physical primes are widely skewed and occur as entirely separate chronological entities. Therefore, answering this question isn't straightforward. His physical attributes have clearly followed a non-linear progression and have been subject to large fluctuations in performance, whereas his technical attributes have remained relatively stable.

In 1999, Lewis landed his signature, wicked right cross on the supposedly bombproof Holyfield on a number of occasions, often sending the spray flying from Holyfield's shaven head. This punch had a limited concussive effect; Holyfield simply sucked up the impact like a bone-dry sponge. Their two 1999 meetings were accurate blueprints for a prime Holyfield versus a prime Lewis matchup. Lewis peaked naturally late in his career. Holyfield was past his biological peak for the Lewis fights but was probably at his enhanced peak, being almost superhuman in terms of his punch resistance. Go figure.

Breaking the fight down, it is a case of Holyfield's in-fighter style versus Lewis's strategic out-fighter style. Can prime Holyfield keep the pressure on Lewis long enough to wear Lewis down? The flip side of the coin is can Lewis keep Holyfield on a long-range leash, where he can pot-shot him at his leisure? Height, reach, weight, and power all favour Lewis in a big way. Stamina, all-round ring craft, and toughness favour Holyfield. Speed is fairly even. I say prime Lewis would win a points decision, as he did in real time in 1999. If prime Holyfield has a knockout punch, it will change the complexion of this fight.

—March 2019

Jovanne Rodriguez: Is Deontay Wilder overrated? Would he have fared well in any areas with significant challenges, such as the 1970s with Joe Frazier, Muhammad Ali, and George Foreman? Is this era easiest for him to find success in?

J. A.: One hundred per cent yes! But Wilder is only overrated by casual fans; knowledgeable and savvy boxing observers recognise him to be a poor technical fighter who only really possesses the equaliser of one-hit power.

Even when he was in action against a poorly conditioned and inactive Tyson Fury, Wilder regularly missed the target, as per usual. In terms of technique, his signature and clumsy-looking power punches resemble slap-punches. His return on these punches is poor at the best of times, but against Fury, his power punch accuracy was a meagre 17 per cent—in other words, less than one in five of his power punches landed. Give Fury some of the credit—he is a slippery customer. Nonetheless, 17 per cent is a very poor return for a world champion. Compare this to a genuine top of the food chain predator, such as Mayweather. His success rate with power punches against Pacquiao was a whopping 48 per cent! In simple terms, Mayweather is three times more accurate than Wilder. In my humble opinion, this is more of a damning indictment of how poor Wilder is than of how good Mayweather is.

If Wilder were facing Muhammad Ali, not only would he be chasing shadows, but he would be made to pay a much heavier price when he missed. Ali would sicken him with precision counters. I can see Wilder quitting as and when the going gets too tough (probably somewhere in the middle rounds—that is, if Ali wants to play with him). I give even money that Ali beats Wilder without even utilising a proper defensive head guard. Ali will be up on his toes, leaning back and enjoying himself, letting his reflexes and feet do the work.

Against Joe Frazier's bob-and-weave style, Wilder will again miss the target on a regular basis. Frazier will get under Wilder's defence all too easily. When Joe closes up the range and takes Wilder into the phone booth, then it will be double trouble for Wilder—to head and to body. The best left hook in heavyweight history will chop him down like a lumberjack taking down an oak tree.

And against Foreman, just forget about it. Don't even go there. In the face of maybe the biggest cannon in heavyweight history, Wilder's power will seem like peashooter power. If Foreman is really in the mood and at his fearsome best, he is capable of launching Wilder out of the ring.

If I were Wilder, I would stick to fighting old George—that way at least Wilder stands a chance.

On a final note, as you suggest in your question, this is without doubt a very weak era for heavyweight boxing. The lack of variety and the strength in depth is a shambles. In my humble opinion, it is the weakest heavyweight division for the past hundred years. This is exactly why a guy like Wilder, who essentially should be playing basketball, is a boxing world champion. In the legendary 1970s golden era, I don't see Wilder making it to gatekeeper grade. In fact, his boxing technique would probably just about make it to journeyman grade. Boxing is all about levels, and right now Wilder's contemporaries are boxing at a relatively low level.

—March 2019

Bradley Johnson and David Esposito: Who would win in a boxing match: Joe Frazier or Mike Tyson?

J. A.: Like father, like son! Replace Marvis Frazier with his father Joe and you'll probably get the same result. Tyson is all wrong for Smokin' Joe, and Joe is perfect target practice for Tyson. I do have a number of rational boxing reasons for picking Tyson over Joe, who himself was a legend.

- At the highest level of boxing, the concept of "styles make fights" is huge. Joe's legendary runaway freight train style will bring him to Tyson. This is boxing suicide. Joe will effectively find himself stuck between a rock and a hard place. Simply put, he can't fight on the back foot; he never did. It will be the same story as when he ran into Foreman.
- Speed kills! Joe is a very good and fast puncher. Tyson is faster.
- Joe has a great left-hand punch. Tyson had great left- and right-hand punches. It's double trouble for Joe. Tyson's ambidextrous knockout punching advantage will prove to be decisive.
- Joe's diesel-powered engine takes a few rounds to warm up. Tyson's high-octane, V-12, twin-turbocharged engine is the fastest out of the blocks ever seen in the heavyweight division. It doesn't look good for Joe in the early rounds.
- Like his son Marvis, Joe is distinctly vulnerable to the right uppercut. Bad habits and family traits die hard. Do you remember in 1973 when George Foreman nearly lifted Joe Frazier off his feet with the right uppercut in their first fight? As we all know, the all-time heavyweight master of this dangerous punch is a certain Michael Gerard Tyson. If Joe couldn't evade Foreman's uppercut, there isn't a chance in hell he's dodging Tyson's favourite punch.
- Joe has a good bob-and-weave defence. Tyson's upper-body pendulum motion is better and technically more advanced.
- Tyson has the lean muscle weight advantage—around 7 kilograms of useful lean mass on Joe, without any noticeable loss in speed, agility, or flexibility.
- Tyson has the advantage in agility and movement. Both guys move around the ring very well and are skilled at closing the gap on their taller opponents. Given that Tyson is the heavier fighter, his footwork and movement are slightly better and slicker than Joe's.

Without doubt, Joe Frazier is more durable, tougher, and braver. He also has greater stamina than Tyson. If he gets through the early rounds, the momentum swings to Joe. As much as we all rate Smokin' Joe, I don't see him making it past round four to give his stamina and character advantages a chance to take hold.

—April 2019

Sameer Husain: Who would win in a fight, Anthony Joshua or Muhammad Ali, taking into account the improvements of boxing as a sport?

J. A.: Don't believe the hype just because some A. J. fanboy has made the comparison that on some occasions A. J. bears a resemblance to Ali. That is where the comparison starts and ends.

Making a prime Muhammad Ali mad is a dangerous game to play. A wise man once wrote, "if you fuck with the bull, then sooner or later you get the horns." A ponderous, 6-feet 6-inch 1960s strongman with an 82-inch reach, named Ernie Terrell, refused to call Ali by his new name, instead referring to him as Clay. For this reason and this reason alone, Ali tortured Terrell over fifteen savage rounds, repeatedly screaming, "What's my name?" every time he pounded on him. This was the nasty and cruel side of Ali. not many casuals know about. Ali punished Terrell in the same way he would punish the 6-feet 6-inch Joshua. In this hypothetical fight, I imagine Ali staring A. J. down and whispering in his ear, "Son, you do know that you're out of your league? Don't you know that your hands can't hit what your eyes can't see?"

Nothing against A. J.—he's a big, friendly giant type of guy. But against Ali, he's outmatched in almost every way I can think of, apart from strength. I think Ali's movements will be way too hot to handle. If you think A. J. looked a bit confused and cumbersome against Joseph Parker, then you ain't seen nothing yet. He will be chasing Ali's shadow while Ali takes potshots all night long. Joshua will have periods of success, largely when Ali takes the occasional breather.

As for your suggestion that boxing has improved, and we need to adjust Ali's performance in line with inflation? Well, I suggest we need to do the exact opposite. Boxing has not improved since Ali's era. We need to handicap Ali in some way in order to give Joshua a better chance. Sport science, training methods, and nutrition have improved—but that won't do Joshua much good against the Greatest. Ali faced the toughest competition in heavyweight history and just about emerged as the top dog. The gold standard competition that he faced is the main reason he is called the GOAT. So make no mistake: Ali has faced plenty of strongman heavyweights like Joshua, whereas AJ has never faced anyone as talented, unorthodox, athletic, technical, and well-schooled as Ali. "If A. J. even dreams he can beat me, he better wake up and apologize." Ali should get the job done in the later rounds, probably by a referee's stoppage.

—April 2019

Anonymous: In their respective primes, who would win a matchup between Marvin Hagler and Sugar Ray Leonard?

J. A.: In 1987, *Sports Illustrated* described the result of this fight as a shocker. The headline was no doubt referring to the scorecards. One scorecard in particular stood out and took almost all experts by surprise. Two of the sensible judges scored the fight 115 to 113, one for Leonard and the other for Hagler. These were fair and understandable scores. The third judge—who deserved to be investigated—scored the fight 118 to 110 in favour of Leonard! This was shockingly biased judging and stunk of a setup. If we were to believe this clown of a judge, it would mean he saw at least ten rounds differently to one judge and six rounds differently to the other. Go figure.

Hypothetically speaking, in their primes at middleweight, I believe the fight would never have happened. Why? Hagler wanted a piece of Leonard as early as 1983. The fight with Leonard loomed larger on Hagler's radar than the Hearns fight, but Leonard was temporarily retired at this juncture. Leonard has gone on record as saying that he believed he could only have beaten Hagler after the Mugabi fight—in other words, post-1986. He was a ringside commentator on the Hagler versus Mugabi fight and claims that he saw definite chinks surfacing in Hagler's armour that he too could exploit. In reality, those chinks were boxing mileage and the accumulated effects of Father Time. Leonard had a couple of years of youth on Hagler and far less mileage on his clock. In 1987 both these factors worked in his favour.

If Hagler and Leonard fight in their primes, I go for Hagler—as long as Las Vegas judges aren't used. At middleweight, Hagler can do everything that Leonard can, just not quite as slick or as fast. Boxing ability slightly favours Leonard but is offset by Hagler's legendary toughness and work rate. At 160 pounds, Hagler is too much of a physical beast for Leonard and will end up taking a points verdict—as long as the judges haven't filled in their scorecards prior to a punch being thrown.

—June 2019

Gustavo Carrillo: Would Mike Tyson have beaten Evander Holyfield when Tyson was in his prime?

J. A.: Like the Iron Man said to Holy's face at the press conference in 1996, "You're out of your league, son." In 1991, Holyfield would indeed have been out of his league, and Tyson's fists would have wiped those smug and fake smiles off his face. Alas, much water passed under the bridge before they met. Many years and PEDs later, poor old Mike had to deal with a steroid-skulled chemical freak who had become deceptively strong and impervious to pain, and who hit way harder than he used to. A real-life Dr Jekyll to Mr Hyde transformation had occurred before our very eyes. Many a fan and expert pundit alike were completely unaware of the dark, driving force behind Holyfield's astonishing physical transformation.

Getting back to the question of prime Tyson versus Holyfield (sans PEDs), I can honestly see only one winner—Tyson by a technical knockout, but not after a serious argument and a firefight. It will be similar to the war they had when they sparred as amateurs. In the end, Tyson's superior speed and power will prevail. However, Holyfield's highly competitive nature and warrior spirit will give Tyson plenty to think about.

I do have some rational boxing logic backing up my bias towards Tyson.

Holyfield boxed a journeyman named Bert Cooper in the fall of 1991. At one point in the fight, Holyfield came under heavy fire and was out on his feet, the ropes literally intervening and keeping him upright. Cooper was a keeping-busy opponent for Holyfield, because his originally scheduled 1991 meeting with Tyson had been postponed due to a freak training injury. Holyfield just about survived the Cooper scare to go on to bigger and better things.

The Cooper fight is particularly relevant as Cooper had been described as the poor man's

Tyson. Ex-professional boxer and former Tyson sparring partner Glenn McCrory of Sky Sports described Cooper as being physically similar to Tyson, but lacking Tyson's skills. The conclusion is simple and linear: if Holyfield struggled with Cooper in the fall of 1991, then he would have struggled even more against Tyson.

—June 2019

Anonymous: How would a bodybuilder do against Mike Tyson in his prime?

J. A.: Not too well, really, and it could prove to be a career-ending fight for the bodybuilder. Depending on Iron Mike's mood, it could turn into a long and painful night. In all honesty, Tyson would probably use such an opportunity to practice his body punching on a mobile heavy bag. It would perhaps be similar to the two demolition jobs he carried out on the hapless and heavily muscle-bound Frank Bruno, where both fights turned out to be nothing more than intense sparring sessions for Tyson.

I doubt if the bodybuilder would have the skill or capacity to land a single glove on Tyson or even be in a position to throw a meaningful punch. In his prime, Tyson was perpetual motion in the ring, and his footwork was right up there with the heavyweight greats. He would be in and out of range before the bodybuilder could react. Tyson would win by brutal knockout as and when he felt like it, with the bodybuilder visiting the hospital as a bare minimum.

—July 2018

Jose Gonzalez: How would Rocky Marciano fare if he competed in 1960s, 1970s, 1980s, 1990s, and present-day heavyweight pro boxing?

J. A.: Beginning with the 1960s, I think a prime Marciano would be comfortably out-pointed by a sublime Ali. Ali would have too much finesse, footwork, and speed for Marciano. I can see Marciano taking a worse head-beating than Ali gave Sonny Liston. What would keep Marciano in the fight would be his granite chin and legendary stamina. But I can't see him mounting any serious offense other than the odd body attack here and there, when Ali is taking a breather. It's a bad matchup for the Rock.

Moving on to the 1970s, Marciano's nemesis would be the slugger of all sluggers, Big George Foreman. This would be a legendary slugfest, with both fighters throwing caution to the wind and throwing bombs. Since neither fighter ever understood the concept of defence, it would boil down to who could hit harder—advantage to Foreman, but not after a serious argument from Marciano. Surely no man in history could take too much of Foreman's natural freak-show power. He is arguably the hardest natural puncher ever. The contest goes to Foreman by a middle-rounds TKO.

The 1980s will also unfortunately be a bleak hunting ground for Rocky, as initially he will have to deal with the number-one heavyweight technician all time, Larry Holmes. His straight-ahead machismo and swarmer style is unfortunately tailor-made for one of the best jabs in heavyweight history. Holmes sticks and moves all night long and lands the odd power right cross here and there. It's an easy points win for Larry.

After facing Larry, Marciano has to deal with Kid Dynamite from 1985 onwards. The late British commentator Reg Gutteridge once famously described Tyson as "a black version of Rocky

Marciano and two stone heavier". This statement summarises the Tyson versus Marciano matchup quite succinctly. On top of this, Tyson is faster and has superior timing and way better defence. Tyson wins by an early-rounds blowout—a bad matchup for Rocky.

The 1990s will be Marciano's best decade by far. The three standout heavyweights are Bowe, Holyfield, and Lewis. Marciano is too tough, rugged, and downright dirty for Bowe, who has a suspect heart at the best of times. Obviously Marciano is giving away a lot of weight and size to Bowe, but I think he can just about overcome the weight differential. Conditioning is never Bowe's strong point. I see Rocky overwhelming an unmotivated Bowe late—Rocky by a late-rounds TKO.

Marciano against Holyfield will be an all-out, toe-to-toe war. Neither Holyfield nor Marciano are ever that elusive, and both guys will hit and hurt each other plenty. Both guys have granite chins and tremendous conditioning. Rocky is pound for pound the harder puncher, and I see him bossing the fight down the stretch, largely due to accumulated damage on Holyfield. Marciano wins on points.

This leaves Lewis. Marciano's old-school brawler style is quite suited to Lewis's safety first, strategic, out-fighter style. Lewis hates facing pressure fighters and as such is often found wanting in high-pressure situations. This is the type of matchup in which Rocky's bread and butter tactic of taking a punch to land a punch will work quite well. He has comfortably the better chin, greater stamina, and pound for pound more power. He has physical advantages to overcome, with Lewis being much the bigger man, but I think he can deal with these. Marciano is at least as capable as Ray Mercer was in 1996 against Lewis and probably can go one better. Marciano wins by decision.

In the really modern era, I don't think Marciano has much to fear other than the sheer size of the modern heavyweights. But who is to say that Marciano himself can't bulk up in readiness for dealing with the modern giants? He is well known to be super fit, very tough, and a genuine fighting man. I don't think the modern era has seen a guy as tough as a prime Marciano. If he can do a Holyfield and gain about a stone of lean muscle without any corresponding loss of speed and technique, he can still be a world-beater.

—July 2018

Edmund Ko: Who would have won in their matchup, Lennox Lewis or Riddick Bowe?

J. A.: This is probably the biggest heavyweight clash that never happened in the modern era. On paper it appears to be a fifty-fifty fight, with the outcome hinging on small details. It is a matchup of two big, athletic, Olympic-standard boxers who have a genuine score to settle. For Lewis it will be his defining fight, and for Bowe it will be a chance for redemption. It's an opportunity to avenge his loss to Lewis in the Olympic super heavyweight final of 1988.

Breaking the fight down, I think Lewis has to keep the fight long and box sensibly behind his jab, peppering Bowe with his huge right cross. At distance, I think Lewis is comfortably the better boxer. But at close range, it is advantage to Big Daddy Bowe in a big way.

Bowe is very different to most really big men, in that he is most often comfortable in the trenches. He is a great in-fighter, as we saw in the epic trilogy with Evander Holyfield. On the inside, there is a danger that Bowe can overwhelm Lewis with vicious hooks and overhand rights.

Prime Bowe is a better two-handed puncher than Lewis and also a much better body-puncher. Lewis throughout his career was a headhunter and was never really renowned for body attacks.

In terms of defence, Lewis probably has the tighter defence, in large part due to his negative, long-range, and safety-first approach. Bowe has comfortably the better chin and is probably the better twelve-round fighter, if in shape. Lewis is the smarter boxer and far better conditioned over the course of his whole career. Both fighters blow hot and cold and never string together a series of really impressive performances. However, at their best, each guy is undoubtedly a world-beater.

Using common-opponent analysis, it is advantage to Bowe, given the fact he dealt with Holyfield in a more decisive manner than did Lewis. But, as always at the top level of boxing, styles make fights. This concept is probably more significant than the common-opponent approach. In terms of longevity and versatility, Lewis has much the more polished CV. But on any given day, literally anything can happen. The CV is often rendered meaningless—remember a guy named Buster Douglas?

Ultimately, this fight probably boils down to who can avoid the other guy's knockout punch better. Based on the evidence to hand, Lewis probably accomplishes this task better than Bowe, but only just. Therefore I go for Lewis on points after surviving some roller-coaster moments.

—November 2018

James Short: Could Mike Tyson in his prime beat even the weakest modern professional boxer, given that no modern heavyweight is as short as 5 feet 10 inches?

J. A.: It's not the size of the dog in the fight but the size of the fight in the dog that matters most.

Prime Tyson made up for his apparent lack of height and reach with an abundance of boxing talent. He was both a physical beast and a technical master, who in his heyday also possessed an obsessive will to win. Not to mention the fact that back in the day, he loved the game and enjoyed what he was doing.

I believe that out of the big three, Joshua and Wilder would heed their worst nightmares and duck prime Tyson, fully realising that they are totally outmatched. Tyson is apparently Joshua's favourite historical heavyweight and he respects him hugely, so this is another valid reason for ducking him. After all, no one wants to fight their hero.

I can see Tyson Fury having the intestinal fortitude to step into the ring with his namesake. Fury is an intelligent giant who can also box, and he normally prepares meticulously for his fights. This being the case, he is the most well equipped to do a containment job on prime Tyson. Even so, Tyson should win handily on points or by a late-rounds technical knockout.

This leaves Andy Ruiz Junior as the remaining threat. I can also see him having the guts to take on Tyson. If he comes to the fight in better shape, he is capable of giving Tyson a decent argument. If he tips the scales at the wrong end of 19 stone, then I see him being target practice for Tyson. The wording of your question indicates to me that you think physical dimensions are what wins a boxing match. In reality, height, reach, and weight are small pieces in a large jigsaw puzzle.

—January 2021

CHAPTER 6

I'VE GOT THE POWER

Max Sundram: How can people say Mike Tyson is the hardest hitter ever?

J. A.: A more accurate description of Tyson's vaunted punching power is maybe that he was the most dangerous hitter ever. Back in the day, he put guys to sleep with some of the most accurate punches ever seen. When you can throw power punches with pinpoint precision to a vital area, the intrinsic power or force of the punch is almost a moot point. Not that Tyson didn't hit hard; on the contrary, he hit like a mule. But the accuracy and timing of his hits are what made him really stand out from the 1980s heavyweight crowd. All heavyweights have the firepower to knock each other out, but having the means and methodology to land the KO punch in a high-pressure situation is a more complex task.

A large body of expert opinion points to the fact that Tyson was the best precision power-puncher in the heavyweight division since heyday Sonny Liston. In terms of pure one-hit power, Tyson is probably the joint third-hardest hitter ever, tied with Liston. Earnie Shavers and George Foreman are the top two for absolute power.

Another reason that Tyson sometimes gets rated as the hardest hitter ever is because of his outstanding two-handed punching power. If you analyse his knockout record during his prime years, he was landing a virtually dead-even split of power punches with either hand. In my humble opinion, this makes him the most ambidextrous knockout artist of the modern era.

Tyson was quite often observed boxing from a neutral, squared stance. In that situation, which hand was the power shot? If you were the intended target during his heyday, reading Tyson's moves was almost like playing a game of poker. As Sugar Ray Leonard once commented, "Mike Tyson can knock you out with either hand, from any angle or position." So his actual punching power was often confused with his punching effectiveness.

—November 2019

Jaehoon Kim: Who in boxing history could deliver the fastest punches that were equally devastating?

J. A.: In this category, I can see a very close race among the five top guys. We're looking for a perfect blend of hand speed, pound-for-pound power, timing, and accuracy. In chronological order:

1. *The Brown Bomber Joe Louis*: Joe Louis was a textbook precision power-puncher personified. Once described as "a machine of destruction", he was rated by *Ring* magazine as the greatest puncher in heavyweight history. If you ever want to see a boxer with the most precise footwork and optimum balance to deliver fast, powerful, and accurate combos, then Louis is your man. He could deliver instinctive knock-out punches with either hand from almost any angle. His 87 per cent knockout-to-wins ratio speaks for itself.
2. *Sugar Ray Robinson*: Pound for pound king, Sugar Ray Robinson could unleash the hurt from either hand and from any stance. He was surely the number-one boxer-puncher in history, a great athlete who was very tough and got the punch there pretty fast too. Unfortunately, he also had the notoriety of having tragically killed one of his opponents in the ring.
3. *Sugar Ray Leonard*: Sugar Ray Leonard is certainly a strong candidate for the best all-round boxer in history. He was without doubt more renowned for his hand speed than his power, but on occasion could be a very hard puncher and could easily get you out of there with one punch. He was also one of the best finishers in boxing history. and when he smelt blood, he really put his punches together, combining speed, power, and accuracy to devastating effect. His most notorious knockout victim was a guy named Dave Green, whom Leonard knocked out with a very fast, precise, and powerful left hook. It has drawn comparisons to Sugar Ray Robinson's gold-standard left hook.
4. *The Hitman Thomas Hearns*: Simply put, you didn't want to mess around with the Hitman in the early rounds—he would take you out. Some observers described his punches as exhibiting an electric shock effect. What this description may be attempting to convey is that if the initial punch didn't knock you out, the inevitable follow-up punches would keep you awake and electrified, similar to an alternating current! His vaunted right cross was arguably the most potent right-hand punch of the modern era and literally had everything you could want from a power punch. Thomas Hearns was probably the most complete attacking boxer ever. Don't believe me? Just ask Roberto Duran. Who else on the planet could have annihilated him in the same manner as Hearns?
5. *Iron Mike Tyson*: George Foreman said of Mike Tyson, "He was knocking guys out left and right, not unlike me and Joe Louis, and he'd move around the ring. He's gonna be remembered for a long time." Arguably the most ferocious puncher of the modern heavyweight era, Tyson surely possessed the most varied and dangerous offensive arsenal in heavyweight history. His one-time co-manager Jim Jacobs once said, "We have a problem here, a marvelous problem. When you have a kid who throws hydrogen bombs, it's very difficult finding guys who want to fight him." Not only did he throw hydrogen bombs, he threw pinpoint bombs with unprecedented first-strike capability. He could knock you out with either hand from any angle or position, and he was none too shabby in the hand-speed stakes either.

—April 2019

ANONYMOUS: What were some of Earnie Shavers's flaws as a boxer?

J. A.: No, it's not Jason Voorhees! It's the Acorn Earnie Shavers. But given Earnie's build and his penchant for chopping wood with an axe, he'd certainly have made a good stunt double for the horror movie character. One thing is for sure: punching power was not one of Earnie's flaws. Shavers was another member of that vintage crop of legendary 1970s heavyweights who swore by chopping wood as a staple part of their training regimen. Foreman and Shavers weren't half bad with an axe and got through loads of timber during their training camps. And guess what? These guys generally rank one and two on the list of hardest punchers in boxing history. Is there a direct connection between chopping wood and punching power?

According to my observations, Shavers's main flaw was that he truly was a one-hit specialist. He didn't use combinations of punches, and his all-time great leverage was only good for one hit. This flaw limited his destructive capabilities, since a combination puncher is far more dangerous than a one-shot hitter. To simplify matters, in this instance we are simply comparing an old-fashioned cannon to a machine gun. If the cannon hits its target, it is devastating; if it misses, it is a waste of time, energy, and stamina. After loading up with a huge haymaker and missing, Shavers often appeared off balance and wide open to counters. Had he been a good combination puncher, he most probably would have rewritten the history books by replacing Larry Holmes as the top dog during the late 1970s. Shavers could have given a young Larry Holmes the same type of beating that Tyson gave an old Larry Holmes. What was the main attacking difference between Shavers and Tyson? Combination punching!

If there ever was a dictionary definition of jaw-breaking power, then Shavers's picture would surely be next to the definition. If only his skill level had matched his power, then there was every chance he could have changed heavyweight history.

His next biggest flaw was stamina. He was quite similar to George Foreman in this respect. Poor stamina appears to be a fairly common weakness among heavyweight sluggers—they train for power rather than endurance. In Shavers's case, his stamina was particularly lacking. He would gas quite quickly even at moderate fight intensity. If you got through the first few rounds with him—which was a big if—your chances of winning improved dramatically.

Shavers's final weakness was his chin. Though not a glass jaw, his chin wasn't world class either—he was something of a heavyweight version of Julian Jackson. He looked like a million dollars when dishing out the hurt, but like an old and well-used ten-dollar bill when taking it. In an ideal world, slugger-type fighters should have granite chins like George Foreman, which is one of the main reasons that Foreman gets rated higher than Shavers.

Another well-known blast from the past was the late Jerry Quarry. He faced off against Shavers in a great 1970s matchup. In what turned out to be a first-round blowout, Shavers was on the receiving end of a quick and explosive barrage of punches. Against Quarry, his chin, defence, and fighting instincts were lacking.

It has been speculated that prime Foreman would probably have knocked out prime Shavers based mostly on Foreman's superior punch resistance. Indeed it was probably Shavers's suspect stamina and chin that cost him against Ron Lyle in yet another classic mid 1970s slugfest. Both

Lyle and Shavers landed home-run shots on each other, but Lyle prevailed based largely on a superior chin and better conditioning.

—March 2019

Sittie Nakan: Which boxer who isn't in the heavyweight division hit the hardest?

J. A.: The Hitman Thomas Hearns. During his heyday, Hearns's right cross was described as "the most potent right-hand punch in the business". It was a near-perfect punch which had everything—speed, power, timing, torque, and disguise. In 1984, he stretched out the legendary Roberto Duran in devastating fashion with a perfect, unseen right cross. *No one* knocked out the Hands of Stone. Not only did Hearns knock him out, but he knocked him unconscious. This in fact was the only knockout defeat on Duran's record during his prime years.

Thomas Hearns was one of those boxers who hit too hard for his own good, and he suffered chronic hand injuries as a result. He detonated bomb after bomb on Hagler in their classic 1985 meeting. In arguably the most action-packed and nail-biting first round in boxing history, he hit Hagler so hard that he fractured his own right hand.

Former heavyweight champion David Haye once described Hearns as having "freak-show" power. Other knowledgeable observers described Hearns's punches as exhibiting an electric shock effect. The first power punch put the guy to sleep, with the follow-up punches waking him back up, similar to an alternating current.

—February 2021

Dillon Price: Why do heavyweight boxers have fewer boxing skills than lighter boxers?

J. A.: It comes down to punching power, pure and simple. In a very general sense, increasing punching power results in a corresponding decrease in skill.

First let's check out a skilful guy named Muhammad Ali. Without doubt, he is the exception to the rule. It's difficult to think of a more skilful heavyweight. When Ali hit the heavy bag, he hit it "nicely". He didn't want to fork out for a new bag; rather, he wanted to finesse the same bag for his entire boxing career!

Now compare Ali's heavy-bag work to that of a certain powerhouse named George Foreman. Watching Foreman destroy the heavy bag was an awesome sight. Onlookers often remarked on the huge, pumpkin-sized dent in the heavy bag and the fact that Foreman had his trainer holding the bag steady. Foreman wanted to rip that bag apart with a devastating display of firepower. He didn't care about skill or technique.

Foreman brought a pure brute-force approach to heavyweight boxing, whereas Ali brought a skilled approach. Foreman could afford to cut corners in technique, whereas Ali couldn't. Look at it this way—one guy knows he has to punch his opponent around 500 times to get the win, and the other guy knows he only has to connect once cleanly and it's game over.

Comparing these contrasting heavyweight greats doesn't completely answer the question of course. The point is that boxers from lighter divisions cannot rely on equalising punching power, because in general they do not possess one-hit punch power. One-punch knockouts become increasingly less frequent in the lower divisions. Lighter boxers simply do not possess the same concussive power as heavyweights. Additionally, it is likely that lighter boxers possess greater pound-for-pound punch resistance than their heavier counterparts. To simplify this point, increasing the body weight of a specific boxer will increase his punching power but not his punch resistance.

The massive and clinically obese heavyweight nicknamed Butterbean is an extreme example of this concept. Butterbean has tremendous punching power, as long as he can implement the fat weight into the punch through leverage. But over the years his weight gain has not altered his chin strength. In other words, chin strength is largely genetic and cannot be altered much by environment, whereas punching power can be changed.

In summary, lighter boxers are generally more skilled than their heavier counterparts because they have to be. It has always been this way. They do not have the luxury of punching power to equalise the argument and therefore have to resort to the many other facets of boxing to achieve success, e.g., speed, timing, and footwork.

—April 2019

Jeffrey Dog: Where did Rocky Marciano get his amazing power from? He wasn't ripped or huge like Anthony Joshua, but he still hit like a sledgehammer. How so?

J. A.: Way back in 1952, Marciano scored one of the most famous and iconic knockouts in boxing history against a guy named Jersey Joe Walcott. The finishing punch was a perfectly executed right cross, which had everything you would want from a knockout punch. In particular, the timing and delivery of the punch were picture perfect. Perhaps most importantly, Jersey Joe knew nothing about the punch until it was too late. The punch you don't see is the one that really nails you.

Although Marciano weighed less than 200 pounds (modern cruiserweight), he made terrific use of his body weight. I suspect he was also a lot faster in real life then he appears on old black-and-white, slow frame rate footage. Speed is power, and while he wasn't the fastest, I think he was a lot faster than he appeared.

Another facet of his punching power was body-weight momentum. He was constantly moving forward into the punch, which meant he had good leverage and momentum. If you watch him on the inside, those short, clubbing punches were heavier than they appear.

Additionally, if you analyse his career overall, you will find that at world level, his knockouts often came in the middle to later rounds. This was testament to his undying stamina, which meant he retained his power until the final bell.

Finally, Marciano was a genuine old-school tough guy. He could take a punch better than the other fellow, which afforded him the luxury of brawling and trading power punches. Simply put, he often took a punch to land a punch—that's what inside fighters do. Since Marciano was tougher than almost all his opponents, they inevitably wore down faster than him. Eventually he'd get the KO or TKO. There are a number of TKOs on his record, which indicate he had good cumulative power.

—January 2021

Axel Henriksen: What is the hardest shot anyone has gotten up from in boxing history?

J. A.: My money's on the huge right hand that Shavers landed flush on Larry Holmes in their second meeting in 1979.

Earnie Shavers possessed freak-show punching power. His lethal right hand earned him the nickname "Puncher of the Century". A notable 1970s boxing journalist once described Shavers as having the power to "take down the walls of a city". Simply put, if this guy clipped you, there was a very high probability you were going to sleep.

Larry Holmes had a world-class elastic chin which somehow absorbed the impact of this bomb. He went down heavy but managed to beat the count. It was also fortunate for Larry that the punch didn't land right on the point of the chin; otherwise he may have been stretched out cold. But either way, Holmes had probably the best recuperative powers in heavyweight history.

A close second would be the huge right cross that Tyson dropped Holmes with for the first knock-down in the fourth round of their 1988 meeting. This was a very dangerous shot, because Holmes clearly didn't see the punch and so caught the full force of the blow. Again, somewhat fortuitously, it appears that the punch didn't land on the chin. Otherwise Holmes would surely have been knocked out. But huge credit to Larry, a true legend of the sport and as brave as they come. Any guy who stepped between the ropes with prime Tyson was a seriously courageous guy.

—December 2019

Mike Cosseva and Jeff Fernandez: Did you know that Mike Tyson actually knocked Lennox Lewis out cold when they sparred in the 1980s?

J. A.: Yes, I was aware of this fact. Apparently Lewis had the upper hand early on and was boxing well behind his jab. As soon as Tyson closed up the range and landed some of his patented combos, it was a different story altogether. In one interview that Tyson gave about this notorious 1980s sparring session, he said, "I knocked Lennox out of the ring!"

The closest real-time blueprint of a prime Tyson versus Lewis matchup can be found by watching the 1996 meeting between Lewis and Merciless Ray Mercer. Mercer was a similar size, weight, and build to Tyson, and he gave Lewis all the trouble he could handle. It was a real fifty-fifty fight. Mercer always had a limited toolbox but still managed to land plenty of clean leather on a very hittable Lewis.

So if Lewis faced heyday Tyson, then make no mistake: he is in for a very rough ride. Lewis hates facing pressure fighters, and in prime Tyson, he is up against a Tasmanian Devil of a pressure fighter who would have knocked him out cold!

—December 2020

Michael Rebovich: How have some of Mike Tyson's opponents described getting hit by him?

J. A.: Tyson boxed a British journeyman named Julius Francis in 2000. At the time, Tyson was more than a decade past his prime, but he still made light work of the outmatched Francis. In one post-fight interview, Francis described Tyson's vaunted punch in the following way: "Every punch he threw felt like a kick from a horse."

In Tyson's very early career, he fought an unknown guy named Sterling Benjamin. Tyson bombed Benjamin early in the first round. In the immediate post-fight interview, Benjamin said in disbelief, "He have a sledgehammer, man. That's the hardest I ever been hit in my whole career."

After one of Tyson's most famous demolition jobs—on the WBC champion Trevor Berbick in 1986—Berbick described Tyson as having "a funny kind of punch".

—December 2020

Lance Dillinger: Is it true like Mike Tyson said, "It's not the hardest punch that always knocks you out, it's the one that you don't see coming"? Can that be applied to life in general?

J.A.: This is 100 per cent true. Mike Tyson's arching uppercut on Jose Ribalta in round two of their 1986 clash has been described as the scariest unseen punch in boxing history. Tyson set this deadly punch up by preoccupying Ribalta's mind with a right-body shot. Before Ribalta knew what had happened, he was hit almost instantaneously by the more damaging follow-up power punch.

The punch that you don't see is essentially very similar to a sucker punch. You don't expect it or see it, so you cannot brace yourself, roll with it, or block it. This gives the unseen punch much greater shock power.

In a real-life situation, the unseen punch can be applied perfectly to a self-defence scenario, such as taking on multiple opponents or muggers in a closed-off space.

—November 2020

John Johansson: Considering that Deontay Wilder has fought journeymen his entire career, is his power overrated?

J. A.: I think his power is only overrated by the casual fan who pays too much attention to tabloid headlines and modern statistical analysis. Don't get me wrong: Wilder is a huge one-hit puncher but nowhere near the hardest in history—not even close. Anyone who really knows boxing knows that Wilder would never catch the best historical heavyweights with his crude and telegraphed haymakers. If you look closely at Wilder's power punches, they are more often than not wild, hard punches.

So yes, perception of his power has clearly been inflated because of the weak opposition he has faced. He reminds me of the sort of fighter who looks devastating against a journeyman but clueless against a top-class opponent. In the rematch with Fury, he literally looked clueless. Say for a second that you were unaware of Wilder's previous KO-to-wins ratio, and you were seeing him for the first time against Fury. In Fury 2, you could easily be forgiven for thinking that this guy was a bum. Tyson Fury was a top-class opponent who made the necessary adjustments for the rematch, and in doing so completely nullified Wilder's power.

As Fury himself commented, "If you stand still in front of Wilder at a certain distance, he'll take you out." In the rematch, Fury clearly had the benefit of hindsight and this time stayed much closer to Wilder. His inside mauling tactics worked a treat and denied Wilder the leverage he is used to. To summarise, I think Wilder has terrific long-range power but relatively weak short-range power.

If I had to guesstimate, then I would suggest that Wilder's intrinsic punching force is comparable to that of Wladimir Klitschko and Lennox Lewis. Those guys were of similar size to Wilder but had better punching form. However, where Wilder scores above those guys is in terms of the surprise and unpredictability factors of his punches. The surprise factor gives his punches more shock power than Lewis's or Klitschko's, which is probably why he scores more one-punch knockouts. It is exactly these sorts of spectacular one-punch finishes against journeymen that hype up his power.

—November 2020

Shaun Duggal: Comparing "Henry's hammer", which Ali said knocked him back in time to his ancestors, and Frazier's left that knocked him down in fight one in the fifteenth round, who had the best left—Cooper or Frazier?

J. A.: Both of those left hooks were unseen punches which Ali clearly didn't see. Therefore he couldn't react, and they landed flush. Both punches were concussive and resulted in heavy knockdowns. Specifically comparing just those two punches, within the context of each fight I would say they were equally good. Cooper's left hook may have caused a bigger concussion, and it was lucky for Ali that it came right at the end of round four. Frazier dropped Ali in the fifteenth round, when Ali was heavily fatigued. Also bear in mind the variable of age-related toughness; Ali had become a tougher guy by the time he faced Frazier.

But overall, comparing each guy's left hook over the course of their respective careers, I say Joe had the more dangerous left hook. He could throw that punch all night long with minimal backlift. The punch was fast, thrown from a crouch, and well disguised. In fact, it was probably the perfect shot to throw at a taller out-fighter who coincidentally had a bad habit of carrying his right hand low.

In fact, you will find that Joe Frazier generally gets rated as the best left hooker in the heavyweight division's history.

—November 2020

Efrayim Bulka: How strong was Muhammad Ali's punch?

J. A.: His power was medium when compared to other heavyweights of his era. Straight from the horse's mouth: "I'm not known as a hard puncher. I fought many men—George Chuvalo, Floyd Patterson and Zora Folley—who were stronger than me and hit harder. I am a scientific fighter." Ali said this in an interview he gave at ringside straight after George Foreman demolished Ken Norton in 1973. He was responding to the commentator asking him, "How come Ken Norton went twenty-four rounds with you but only two rounds with Foreman?"

To simplify punching power, broadly speaking you can classify a boxer as having a hard, medium, or soft punch. In my humble opinion, Ali's power fell into the medium category. He hit in line with his body weight of approximately 217 pounds. If you look at his career overall, then the majority of his victories came on points or late-rounds knockouts, when his opponents were tired. He hardly ever took care of business in the opening third of a fight.

If you compare Ali's knockout resumé to the Tysons and Foremans of this world, you see a distinct difference in the manner of their respective victories and specifically in the timing of their knockout wins. Hard punchers can end a fight at any time. They often take their opponents out early on and are described as punching *above* their body weight.

Another method of gauging punching power is to look at the total number of rounds boxed during their respective victories. You will inevitably find that killers like Tyson and Foreman have boxed far fewer rounds cumulatively when compared to Ali.

If you are looking for a number in order to quantify Ali's power and compare it to, say, a harder-hitting heavyweight, then I would guesstimate that he hit with around 700 PSI—the average heavyweight. Incidentally, former British and world heavyweight champion Frank Bruno had been measured with a punching power of around 1300 PSI.

—December 2020

Emilio Zaccardo: What are the steps and technique to get maximum power in your knockout punch?

J. A.: Check out Earnie Shavers and pay close attention to his fights with Ali, Norton, and Holmes. It is a fairly well-known fact that Shavers was the hardest puncher in boxing history. This fact was pretty much unanimously confirmed by most of Shavers's opponents. Shavers literally possessed sledgehammer power. Ali once jokingly remarked, "Earnie hit me so hard that my kinfolk in Africa felt the aftershock." To simplify matters, if you want to generate max power from your body weight, then copy Shavers. He wasn't the biggest heavyweight, but he was more than big enough to get the job done. In those days, all the top boxers feared this guy. He was perhaps the most avoided heavyweight of the 1970s. Ali's physician, Ferdie Pacheco, believes that Earnie did the most damage to Ali.

A favourite old-time exercise used by many of the golden era boxers was chopping wood. Both Shavers and Foreman were known to have gotten through "tons" of timber during training camps. There surely has to be a common link there. If you think about it logically, chopping wood does kind of mimic a punching motion and serves to develop the boxing-specific muscles required to generate power . Both Foreman and Shavers had renowned grip strength, possibly enhanced by arduous hours spent chopping wood. The stronger your hand grip, the stronger your clenched fist. Having powerful legs and a firm base are also big factors in power punching, especially for leverage punching. Shavers in particular had renowned lower-body strength, which he very effectively channelled into his power punches through leverage.

Probably the top heavy-bag destroyer in heavyweight history was Big George Foreman. Watching Foreman hit the heavy bag was an intimidating sight. It has been speculated that one full-power body shot from Foreman was capable of cracking the spine of an untrained human. So copy Foreman's technique on the heavy bag, specifically his hooks. Hitting a static target such as a heavy bag will clearly translate eventually into enhanced power.

The other major ingredient is timing. To maximise punching power on a live, moving target, it is all about timing. Knowing when to punch and how to implement your body weight into the punch at the point of contact—this is timing. It take lots and lots of skill, practice, and hand-eye coordination. Simply put, watch a heavyweight named Mike Tyson or another one named Joe

Louis. In their respective primes, these two probably had the best timing of any heavyweights in history.

—January 2019

Anonymous: Is punching power something that you are born with, like Mike Tyson?

J. A.: Yes and no. Imagine if you saw a random guy doing full body-weight neck rolls like Tyson. Would you say that he looked naturally tough? Although Tyson doing neck rolls has no direct link to punching power, the exercise showcases Tyson's natural genetic traits. I don't think any amount of neck rolls will get you to a 20-inch neck or have you balancing 16 stone of body weight on your neck. Much of Iron Mike was indeed God-given talent, but this natural talent still had to be fine-tuned and improved through proper training, coaching, and diet.

As for punching power, Cus D'Amato once said, "There is no such thing as a natural puncher, but rather some fighters have a natural aptitude for punching." This implies that punching power is a combination of nature and nurture, but certain fighters are indeed genetically predisposed to having a harder punch.

A prime example of a phenomenal natural puncher based on his genetics was Sonny Liston, who had huge, dense hands and the most rock-solid fists in heavyweight history. His punches were described by boxing writers of the day as exhibiting crushing power. It was literally like being hit by a hammer made of hyper-dense bone. But even Sonny maximised his punching power through hours and hours of arduous heavy-bag work.

One boxer who wasn't a natural puncher was Lennox Lewis. If you look at his punching power before he hooked up with the late, great trainer of champions, Manny Steward, he was nothing special. Steward, being a master trainer, literally taught Lennox how to punch hard and transformed him into one of the best right-hand hitters in the heavyweight division's history. In Lewis's case, it was all about training, fine-tuning, and sharpening up his tools—he wasn't a natural.

—January 2019

Josiah Landrom: Would you say George Foreman had stronger but slower punches than Mike Tyson?

J. A.: Foreman was on average a harder long-range puncher than Tyson, because he had longer arms which produced greater leverage for his long-range bombs. However, his punches were slow as hell compared to Tyson's bullets. At close range, there is no comparison; Tyson hit way harder with short, explosive punches and greater short-range leverage. Hence he earned the nickname Kid Dynamite.

A simple analogy that helps to visualise and describe these two guys' punching power and technique is that of a cannon versus a machine gun. Foreman's power was like an old-fashioned cannon, where you lit the fuse and waited for it to fire. If the cannonball hits you, then you're dead. If it misses, then he's wasted energy and he's wide open to counters from a slick boxer. Tyson's power was all about positional supremacy, which created the opportunity for rapid-fire combos, similar to a machine gun volley of bullets. You may dodge or block the first bullet but not the second or third. This made prime Tyson way more dangerous than Foreman, because a machine gun is clearly more technologically advanced than a cannon.

Another analogy that has been used is a Mack truck versus a Ferrari, Foreman being the truck and Tyson the Ferrari. The truck has more momentum once it gets going, but the Ferrari has way more acceleration from a standing start.

In terms of stronger punches, I personally don't think you can measure how strong a punch is. Punches are normally described as soft, medium, or hard and are measured in units of pounds per square inch (PSI). Certainly Foreman was physically stronger than Tyson and excelled at implementing his physical strength in boxing matches. But pure strength on its own is not really a measure of punching power; otherwise guys who compete in world's strongest man competitions would easily beat heavyweight boxers. You can certainly argue that physical strength *contributes* to a punch, but from a technical standpoint, punching power is derived mainly from leverage, speed, timing, and torque.

—October 2019

Leonnius Herbalies: Do all muscular guys punch hard?

J. A.: No, not necessarily, but some clearly do. Compare a monster like Bob Sapp to a lean, mean fighting machine such as Thomas Hearns. Which guy hits harder? I know which guy *looks like* he hits harder, but remember, "Never judge a book by its cover." Bob Sapp was a massive guy with an overwhelmingly dominant physique, but I am willing to place a small wager that the Hitman Thomas Hearns hit harder, both in absolute terms and even more so in a pound-for-pound comparison.

Casual fans may be thinking, "No way—the big, massive, muscular guy would hit harder." But punching hard doesn't have all that much to do with big muscles. Punching power is derived mainly from four drivers: speed, timing, leverage, and torque. None of these factors are directly linked to muscle mass. If muscle mass were decisive, then Ronnie Coleman, Arnold Schwarzenegger, and company would be the hardest punchers in history.

Some readers may be raising an eyebrow and asking, "Well, how come heavyweights hit harder than middleweights then?" In general this is obviously true—a heavyweight boxer does hit harder than a middleweight. But that is because the heavyweight is heavier, not necessarily more muscular. A heavyweight will have greater intrinsic leverage for a given technique. After all, it is leverage that enables body weight to be implemented into a punch.

So why does a lean heavyweight weigh more than a lean middleweight? No doubt some of this is indeed due to greater lean muscle mass. But the heavyweight inevitably will have a larger frame and therefore a larger skeleton, which weighs more. Also heavyweights are on average at least 6 inches taller than middleweights, and each extra inch of height can correlate with anything up to ten pounds of extra weight. Also a heavyweight will probably have a higher wet weight than the middleweight.

Now some of you are probably thinking, "Mike Tyson was muscular, and he hit like a mule." No doubt some of his power came from lean muscle, but the vast majority of his power was from the aforementioned drivers. Certainly his freakish, unprecedented short-range power was primarily from leverage. In simple terms, Tyson punched well above his body weight; this is called leverage punching. He just so happened to be a muscular guy who had great genetics and even greater technique.

—January 2019

Viktor Bondarchuk: Which boxers were powerful but had poor stamina? How did this affect their performance?

J. A.: Always pay close attention to the small details and fine print! Do you think a guy as powerful as Earnie Shavers could afford to cut corners in his cardio workouts? Do you think stamina was one of his main priorities? We can only speculate, but when you have a right-hand punch that can shake a building, I guess this gives you a valid excuse to skip that 5:00 a.m. run.

Remember when Ali shocked the whole world by knocking out George Foreman? On that October day in 1974 in Kinshasa, Zaire, the heavyweight champion of the world ran out of gas in the eighth round of a scheduled fifteen-round fight. Foreman didn't even have sufficient stamina to get to the halfway point of the race! Of course, receiving a perfectly timed one-two combo on the point of the chin from Ali probably didn't help his fitness status. But why didn't Ali gas? He fought in the same heat and humidity as Foreman, didn't he? Ali also took a tremendous body beating, yet by the end of the fight, he looked almost as fresh as a daisy.

Earnie Shavers regularly gets rated as the hardest hitter in boxing history, an opinion which has been consistently corroborated by his opponents. Back in the day, Shavers's boxing traits were largely characterised by his vaunted punching power and his limited stamina. He was notorious for gassing early in fights. This was particularly evident in his classic mid 1970s slugfest with Ron Lyle. Why? Why would a professional boxer not have the required fuel to finish a full fight? Is this a random oversight?

My powers of detection are seeing a common weak link between Shavers and Foreman. Two of the heaviest hitters in boxing history were also characterised by limitations in stamina during big fights. In Shavers's case, his trainers and specifically his training regimen have been criticised, with his cardio simply not up to scratch for world level. In Foreman's case, he was better conditioned but got his tactics all wrong against Ali. I still suggest that cardio probably wasn't one of Foreman's priorities, even in his "second coming".

When you are blessed with overwhelming firepower, there is a tendency to resort to brutality as the primary option. In general, slugger-type fighters are most effective when their fast-twitch muscle fibres are most effective, and that is early in the fight. Get through the early rounds, and your chances of success improve dramatically against such fighters.

Foreman boxed a very slippery boxer named Jimmy Young in a late-1970s heavyweight clash. While Foreman lasted the distance, once again his conditioning was suspect. It was evident that his waistline was slightly blubbery. Young was physically outmatched but still managed to control Foreman with an intelligent and mobile boxing approach. Following this upset defeat, Foreman retired prematurely while still in his physical prime. Stamina is very important, particularly in the championship rounds!

—April 2019

Emil Goubasarian: Do people underestimate how hard pro boxers hit?

J. A.: By "people", who do you mean? I think a random Joe Public who has no interest in or knowledge of boxing would certainly struggle to visualise what kind of force a guy like George Foreman could generate. Foreman hit the heavy bag so hard that onlookers would jokingly comment, "He's kicking his own trainer's ass through the heavy bag!"

Even if you gave a casual fan an approximate figure of half a metric tonne of force, the first thing he would think about is relating this figure to some kind of real-world object, e.g., a car or a barbell—in other words, something tangible. He would probably shake his head in disbelief and say, "No way. A heavyweight boxer can't generate 500 kilograms of force. If that is the case, then why isn't somebody killed every time there is a heavyweight boxing match?" This is precisely why boxing gloves are worn (and of course to protect those delicate hands).

When casual fans watch a professional boxing match, I sometimes get the impression that they think anybody can do this. "It's just a couple of guys beating the hell out of one another—what's skilful about that?" When someone gets knocked out clean by a blinding punch, the first thing a casual says is "That guy can't take a punch." I had an argument with a bodybuilder I knew regarding this very issue—specifically about Hasim Rahman sparking Lewis in 2001. The bodybuilder called Lewis "a bum with a glass jaw" and described Rahman's lethal right cross as a "little tap on the chin". His naive rhetoric had me shaking my head. I could only surmise that this guy had maybe watched *Rocky 4* one too many times. He had been brainwashed by the movies.

Another big misconception that Joe Public has about pro boxers and punching power relates to the technique that is involved in generating that knockout power. They simply don't have a clue. When you punch, they think, "you just swing your arm, don't you?" The casual fan doesn't understand leverage, timing, or torque. Some may just about grasp the concept that speed is power, but many struggle even with this. They more often than not relate punching power to strength. Some casuals believe that bodybuilders like Arnold Schwarzenegger are devastating punchers. This is psychology: you see a big muscle and think this means power.

Finally, I think certain people underestimate just how damn tough professional boxers are. They are the hardest of the hard. Casuals don't see this. They often fail to understand the genetics of boxing and the fact that boxers train to take a hit. Boxers practise all kinds of defensive techniques to prepare their bodies. As Amir Khan liked to say, "When you get in the shower, you're gonna get wet!"

So I think the casual fan certainly doesn't realise how much more deadly a professional boxer's punch would be if it landed on an untrained member of the public. We are all conditioned by environment. As such, we are used to seeing pros hit pros and not pros beating up on innocents.

—February 2019

Anonymous: How hard, in pounds per square inch (PSI), can the average person punch with no training?

J. A.: Certainly nowhere near as hard as Ivan Drago! Ivan Drago's fictional punching power was approximately 2,000 PSI, according to the fictional lab testing in *Rocky 4*.

Let's assume the average guy weighs around 70 kilograms—roughly a middleweight. A person without any kind of training will have fairly mediocre leverage but let's just assume he can get half his body weight into the punch. Now assume his fist is moving at 7 metres per second at impact. This is approximately the hand speed of the average heavyweight boxer. Assume our Joe Public's punch is clocked at 0.5 seconds—the blink of an eye.

Force in Newtons (N) = mass x acceleration

Mass = half his bodyweight = 35 kg

Acceleration = 7/0.5 = 14m/s/s

Therefore force = 35 x 14 = 490 N

Force in kg = 490/g where g = 9.81

490/9.81 = 50 kg

Force in lbs = 50 x 2.2 = 120 lbs

Assume this force is applied as evenly as possible across the two main knuckles.

The approximate area of a human knuckle is a quarter of a square inch; therefore contact area = 2 x 0.25 = 0.5 square inches

Therefore in PSI this force = 120/0.5 = 240 PSI, which is around ten times weaker than Drago's punch.

—*February 2019*

Anonymous: Who hit harder, Earnie Shavers or George Foreman?

J. A.: Shavers hit harder, but only just. If you ask the old-timers who were around in the 1970s, they will mostly tell you that it was a fairly well-known inside-industry fact that Shavers was the hardest puncher ever. I know for a fact if you asked notable trainers of the day, such as Angelo Dundee, Eddie Futch, and Ray Arcel, they would tell you that Shavers hit harder. Just for the record, *Ring* magazine rates Foreman as the most fearsome puncher ever. I think we now need different categories to describe punching prowess, such as deadly, destructive, and lethal!

If you like stats, then Shavers has the edge, boasting a 92 per cent knockout-to-wins ratio. Foreman's knockout-to-wins ratio isn't too shabby either, with 90 per cent of his wins coming by way of knockout.

Perhaps the best and most informative way of comparing the punching power of these two killers is to use the common opponent approach. High-profile opponents who faced off against both prime Shavers and prime Foreman include Ali, Norton, Jimmy Young, and Ron Lyle. Based on the verbal testimony of these notable boxing authorities, there is a unanimous consensus that indicates Shavers was indeed the harder puncher. I see no reason why any of these guys would mendaciously all pick Shavers over Foreman.

Finally, if you look at one last bit of scientific data, you will find that it too points to Shavers being marginally the harder puncher. Prime Foreman generally outweighed prime Shavers by around a stone of lean mass, which equates to around 7 per cent of body weight. So in a strictly pound-for-pound comparison, it is once again advantage to the Acorn.

If you received a clean and flush right hand to the jaw from either of these two, I doubt if the average Joe Public could tell the difference. But professional boxers apparently can, since they are far more used to being hit.

—February 2019

Ali Raza: What was the strongest punch delivered by Muhammad Ali?

J. A.: It may have been one of the many hard right crosses that he landed on Joe Frazier in the final instalment of their trilogy, the Thrilla in Manila. There was one particularly hard right cross in the later rounds where Ali sent Joe's mouthpiece flying into the crowd; I don't recall Ali ever knocking out anybody else's mouthpiece. Their third meeting in 1975 was probably the toughest and most brutal heavyweight bout of the modern era. Ali's personal fight physician was a guy named Ferdie Pacheco, and in a post-fight interview he said, "Ali was half dead and Frazier was more than half dead." So you can just begin to imagine how fierce some of those punching exchanges must have been between these two bitter rivals.

Ali also punched with bad intentions against a guy named Cleveland "Big Cat" Williams. Ali landed some heavy and accurate artillery on this guy, and these were again some of the hardest punches I can recall him throwing. This fight took place at the Houston Astrodome in 1966 and is generally regarded as Ali's peak performance. For a guy who once modestly described himself as "not being known as a hard puncher", well, in the Williams fight he sure fooled me.

Another fight where Ali showcased his punching power was against Sonny Liston in their first meeting. It was more an accumulation of headshots over a series of rounds, but some of those individual punches were nonetheless very hard.

In general, Ali was never famous for his punching power. By heavyweight standards, he was a medium puncher. He made his bones from unmatched hand speed, footwork, reflexes, ring smarts, and athleticism.

—October 2019

Ross Taylor: How did Deontay Wilder obtain such a devastatingly hard punch?

J. A.: His punching technique in some ways is similar to that of a middleweight knockout artist of yesteryear, Julian Jackson. If you analyse Wilder's knockout of Dominic Breazeale, you will notice him moving forward into the punch, thereby ensuring almost full body-weight momentum was delivered into the shot. He has a lot of snap in his one-two, and his right haymaker mimics a whipping motion. It was also evident that he was punching right through the target, which means he was essentially aiming slightly behind the impact point. This technique is common to many big punchers. Mike Tyson, Thomas Hearns, and more recently David Haye have also used this technique very successfully.

If you want to see a perfect example of punching through a target, then check out Thomas Hearns' chilling knockout of Roberto Duran in 1984. This was possibly the hardest and most dangerous right cross of the modern boxing era. Roberto Duran knew nothing about it, other than waking up from unconsciousness about twenty seconds later.

Although Wilder doesn't have the technique of a Thomas Hearns, he shares certain similarities to the Hitman, in that he is very tall at the weight. Like Hearns, he also has a lanky, gangling build. The physical length of his limbs no doubt helps to generate that whip-like action.

Punching power is generally derived from four main drivers, and those are speed, leverage, timing, and torque. In the case of Wilder's haymaker punch, much of its power is derived from leverage and torque. His long arms are effectively long levers which mimic a whipping motion. The punch is also reasonably fast, and speed is power. But you will find that most big punchers generate power primarily through the incorporation of maximum body weight into the punch, which is known as leverage. Due to Wilder's height and reach, he has significant long-range leverage.

An additional factor that may be at work in Wilder's case is his training regimen. I doubt that any trainer or fighter fully discloses all their secrets. Wilder is well known to be a limited boxer, and his trainer Mark Breland freely admits this fact. Therefore, to maximise his boxing return, they concentrate a disproportionate amount of training time into his main asset—punching power. For Wilder, power is the name of the game, because at his age, it is unlikely that his boxing skills will improve all that much.

—October 2019

Stevie Van Zandt: What punch thrown by boxers is responsible for the most knockouts?

J. A.: I think it is a toss-up between the *left hook* and the *right cross*. Given the fact that around 85 to 90 per cent of pro boxers fight from the classical orthodox stance, then the two most frequently thrown power punches are the left hook and right cross.

Joe Frazier possessed the most dangerous left hook in heavyweight history and could throw this punch all night long with minimum backlift and load-up time. Believe me, to score a heavy knockdown on a guy as tough, seasoned, and skilful as Ali would take a special punch from a special fighter. Certainly, over the course of most of Ali's career, the left hook came to haunt him time and time again. A lesser-known fighter named Sonny Banks dropped Ali, and so too did Henry Cooper, on both occasions with well-timed, fast left hooks.

Prime Tyson also laid into many of his 1980s opponents with his own peach of a left hook. A very brave and game Pinklon Thomas was caught by many left hooks from Tyson in their 1987 meeting. In one round, Tyson caught Thomas with a picture-perfect left hook which was, interestingly, thrown from the southpaw stance. In many of heyday Tyson's fights, he got his feet mixed up and threw crazy hooks from the wrong stance, as well as quite often from a neutral, squared-up stance.

Earnie Shavers's right cross, come haymaker was probably the closest equivalent to a mule kick ever seen in the pro game. He wasn't a pretty, textbook fighter; he was never that good. But as a sporting journalist of the day once wrote, "He had power that could take down the walls of a city." In the build-up to his demolition job on Ken Norton, Shavers casually described his punching power as follows: "Anything I hit, I can take out."

Ali landed many well-timed, mean, and nasty right crosses on Foreman in their 1974 meeting. Ali had a great right cross which was as accurate as an arrow. Lucky for Foreman, he had a rock chin. If Ali were to tag someone like Anthony Joshua with this punch, no doubt he would put him to sleep.

Other fighters with notable right crosses over the years were Lennox Lewis, Wladimir Klitschko, and of course Big George Foreman. Mike Tyson, Jack Dempsey, Rocky Marciano, and Sonny Liston too had deadly right crosses—but then again, all their punches were very dangerous.

If you want a glimpse of the gold-standard left hook, then check out Sugar Ray Robinson's perfect knockout of Gene Fullmer way back in 1957. In terms of textbook form and precision, this left hook was literally as good as it gets. Robinson's body shape exhibited a perfect blend of twist, snap, and torque.

On a final note, it is interesting to observe that a strong pattern emerges over the years. Various great fighters noticed and capitalised on their opponents' weakness to left hooks—but not to the right hook. This is most probably to do with the fact that the left hook is a lead hook when thrown from the orthodox stance, and great fighters can time their opponents with this power punch. Typically, a great fighter like Sugar Ray Robinson will wait until his opponent is loading up with a right cross and delay his counter left hook until the last split second, when the other guy is most vulnerable. Timing beats speed.

—August 2019

Sudi Narasimhan: Is it true that Mike Tyson could throw a punch harder than anyone else?

J. A.: If you mean short-range precision punches, then 100 per cent yes. The late, great trainer of world champions, Emmanuel Steward, admitted this—though he never trained Tyson. Tyson's short-range punches could go from nought to sixty in less than half a second with huge amounts of velocity, torque, and snap.

Mike Tyson's own version of Bruce Lee's famous one-inch punch was observed when he nailed "the White Buffalo" Francois Botha with a peach of a right cross that barely travelled six inches in space and yet had a truly devastating effect. The accuracy and power of this punch was fantastic and was almost reminiscent of a laser-pointed gunshot. From this kind of close range, Mike was surely in a league of his own. Botha commented on his demise in this fight that he had unwittingly drifted into the Mike Tyson "kill-zone".

Tyson boxed an unknown guy named Alfonso Ratliff in 1986. Ratliff fully understood the concept of the Tyson kill-zone but nonetheless could do nothing about it. Tyson bombed this guy just as he started to run, and the power in Tyson's short-range punches was gobsmacking. The fight with Ratliff was a final tune-up for his eagerly anticipated challenge for the WBC heavyweight title against Trevor Berbick.

One of the main reasons prime Tyson generated unprecedented levels of short-range power was due to his quad and ham muscles, which were freakishly strong. Additionally, his superior technique enabled him to implement those muscles into an upward punching motion, whereby his whole body was incorporated like an express elevator moving upward and forward.

The hardest overall punchers in heavyweight history were probably Earnie Shavers and George Foreman, but their hardest punches were generally long-range haymakers. Those long punches could mostly be seen coming from a mile away and were easily dodged by skilful fighters. Shavers's and Foreman's hardest shots were similar to cannon blasts—delivered one at a time, but nonetheless truly devastating.

For precision power, the top guys in heavyweight history were probably Mike Tyson, Joe Louis, Sonny Liston, Jack Dempsey, Rocky Marciano, and Joe Frazier. These six guys could thread the eye of a needle with power punches from *economic* punching motions.

—August 2019

Cameron Mccall: How much force does it take to knock someone out with one punch?

J. A.: As little as ten newtons or around one kilogram of force can get the job done, as long as it hits the bullseye!

The notorious, finishing right cross from Foreman on Moorer was allegedly one of the weakest punches ever to score a knockout on a reigning heavyweight champion, and has been described by some notable authorities as a "little tap". Yet Moorer went down heavily, possibly as much through exhaustion as concussion. He also had a notorious glass jaw, and Foreman was famously heavy-handed, with the punch landing perfectly on the point of the chin.

According to my calculations, the minimum force required to knock someone out is very low and may surprise a lot of readers. If a completely untrained person is punched accurately on the point of the chin with a bare-knuckle punch, then a force as low as 5 PSI can potentially cause a concussion. Many of you may be laughing out loud or raising an eyebrow or even scratching your heads. Yes, 5 pounds per square inch—this isn't a typing mistake. Five PSI can indeed potentially knock out a random, untrained skinny guy. Another way to visualise this question is by considering "What's the minimum force required to make your brain collide with the inside of your skull?"

This is why anybody with even a little boxing knowledge or training will be laughing their heads off after watching *Rocky 4*, in which it's claimed that Drago generated 2,000 PSI—with boxing gloves on! He would have broken his own hand and probably his wrist with that kind of force. If someone were hit with that kind of power to the head, one such punch would kill even a professionally trained boxer with a granite chin.

Now the figure of 5 pounds per square inch is a minimum threshold figure and will increase markedly with a corresponding increase in the recipient's body weight. Simply put, it takes more force to knock out a heavyweight boxer compared to, say, a middleweight. Other factors, such as neck thickness, head structure, and location of impact point, will cause variations in the required knockout force. This is exactly why chin strikes are so effective in terms of causing knockouts. What at first sight may appear to be a little tap can in reality be a finishing blow even if minimum body weight is behind the punch. Sometimes the mere weight of an arm punch is enough to cause a knockout—particularly if that arm belongs to Big George Foreman and the recipient is a palooka.

Now if the puncher is wearing boxing gloves, the figures will change. A gloved punch exerts much less pressure, since the contact area of a boxing glove is considerably greater than that of a naked fist. The reduced contact pressure exerted by boxing gloves is, however, slightly offset by the fact that a boxer can use more punching force without worrying about hand fractures. Also, wearing boxing gloves obviously adds some weight to the punching hand.

—March 2019

Anonymous: Why is it that the hardest punchers in boxing usually have big, muscular legs?

J. A.: I agree and disagree with the wording of your question. The hardest *short-range* punchers in boxing do appear to have big, muscular legs.

According to my own observations, the two hardest-hitting heavyweights of the last thirty years were Mike Tyson and David Tua, both of whom had well-known and documented thunder thighs. Both guys were also relatively short heavyweights, standing below six feet tall, and therefore had low centres of gravity. This meant they had very firm bases. Their feet were firmly planted on the canvas, much like a building with a solid foundation or a tree with deep roots.

Now imagine a strong wind acting on a house or a tree. The firmer the base of the structure, the stronger the wind required to blow it down. In boxing terminology, one word summarises this phenomenon, and it is *leverage*. For casual fans, another way to visualise leverage is to imagine punching while standing on ice—you will have virtually zero leverage.

Generating knockout power in short punches is mostly to do with leverage. A short punch that travels only six inches in space will incorporate minimal backlift and have less shoulder snap and velocity than a longer punch, as its travel time and distance are so short. So where did Tyson's unprecedented short-range power come from? He was the quintessential heavyweight leverage puncher. Leg strength, core strength, and lower back strength provided him with the leverage and torque to implement as much of his 220 pounds as was possible into short punches. An abundance of fast-twitch muscle fibres also facilitated his explosiveness from a standing start, similar to a sprinter exploding out of the blocks. Simply put, he could go from nought to sixty in half a second because of his explosive upper leg muscles.

Tyson's lethal finishing right cross on "the White Buffalo" Francois Botha was a punch that barely travelled six inches in space, had minimal load-up and backlift, and yet had a devastating effect on a durable boxer. Former light heavyweight world champion Bobby Czyz was a colour commentator on this fight and was in awe of Tyson's power—and this was an old and washed-up Tyson. This knockout punch was all about momentum and leverage, which were underpinned by Tyson's leg strength, providing a very firm base. The solid base and low centre of gravity essentially counterbalanced and stabilised the upper body punching weight.

David Tua boxed a guy named Ike Ibeabuchi in 1997, in what turned out to be a classic late-1990s slugfest. Tua also had massive thigh development, which gave him a very firm base and also enabled him to leap into his hooks.

His brutal first-round knockout of "the Quiet Man" John Ruiz was very reminiscent of a young Tyson, in that he simply jumped all over his man and didn't give Ruiz any chance to recover once he had him stunned. Inside, Tua finished Ruiz off with some deadly close-range hooks, which had Ruiz badly concussed.

If you compare George Foreman to Tua and Tyson, you will see that his body shape is different. Specifically, his legs are not so well built and thick, but his upper body is huge. Therefore his centre of gravity is significantly higher up than that of Tyson and Tua. Foreman was a massive long-range puncher and in general was not considered to be a leverage puncher. His power was more from strength and huge tree-trunk arms, which were very heavy. His punches were often telegraphed with a long load-up time, but no less devastating. No doubt the length of a boxer's arms and legs appears to strongly influence the specific distance at which he has greatest power.

—March 2019

Mahesh: How do boxers like George Foreman and Charles "Sonny" Liston exert so much power without making a big swing?

J. A.: If you don't mind, let me correct you on one point. Your question is good but flawed. Why? One of your two chosen fighters exhibits this quality, but the other one doesn't. By rights Mike Tyson should replace George Foreman in your question.

Liston and Tyson generated all-time great firepower with economic punching movements. Foreman didn't. It is a fairly well-known fact within the boxing fraternity that out of all of the really big-hitting heavyweights, Foreman had the most basic punching technique. His punches were more often than not huge, swinging home-run shots that could be seen coming from a mile away. He was still a lethal puncher, but Foreman was never a precision puncher. He was rather the epitome of pure brute force.

Sonny Liston, on the other hand, could thread the eye of a needle with a punch that barely travelled twelve inches in space but still had the power to take you out cold. He was probably the only guy in history who could knock a pro boxer out with a jab!

How exactly did he generate so much power with short punching movements? It was primarily due to freak genetics, accurate timing, and near-perfect punching technique. What made him so good was that he was a slugger by nature, but, for a change, this heavyweight slugger could actually box! Liston was very similar to Tyson in this respect. Both guys' boxing skills were underrated and overshadowed by their punching power.

Along with Jack Dempsey, Liston is one of two historical boxers whose fists have attracted more than their fair share of media attention. They were huge, in your face, and—relative to body size—the largest fists in boxing history. Sonny Liston's fists gave the term *punching above your weight* a whole new meaning. Big hands mean heavy fists, which simply carry more weight.

The formula for momentum is *mass x velocity*. The same laws of physics apply to a heavy fist compared to a light fist. As long as the fists are travelling at the same speed, the heavy fist will have more momentum and therefore do more damage. All three guys—Dempsey, Liston, and Tyson—had legendary heavy-handedness and so could do masses of damage with short punches.

Without belabouring the point, Foreman too exhibited heavy-handedness; of this there is no doubt. But his punches were never compact. The one time he did knock someone out with a tap punch was when he knocked out Michael Moorer. Moorer was, however, notoriously glass-jawed. Regardless, unless you were crazy brave, you didn't wanna mess around with prime Foreman.

—May 2019

Justin Outlaw: Is Deontay Wilder the hardest-hitting heavyweight of all time?

J. A.: Not just yet! With his impressive first-round knockout of Dominic Breazeale, Wilder may have been sending Joshua a message along the lines of "anything you can do then I can do better". It took A. J. seven rounds and a lot more punches to dispatch Dominic Breazeale, so Wilder once again proved his right hand is probably the hardest punch in boxing right now.

For sure, Wilder can bang. No one is arguing about his world-class punching power. But remember that Dominic Breazeale is a journeyman-grade boxer with a journeyman-grade defence. He literally caught the full force of that deadly right hand. The fight turned out to be a case of a huge puncher versus a slow starter. Like Tyson Fury said, if you stand still in front of Wilder, he will take you out. Exchanging punches early with Wilder in this form was boxing suicide.

The finishing punch would probably have put most historical heavyweights down. Whether or not that same punch would have knocked them out clean is hard to say. Without belabouring the point there has never been any doubt about Wilder's punching power. Ask yourself an honest question: Do you think he would have landed that same punch on the greats? Doubtful, really. But in terms of punching power, at this juncture Wilder hits as hard as a peak Lennox Lewis or Riddick Bowe. I can easily see Lewis or Bowe taking Breazeale out in a similar fashion. But as dangerous as Wilder is right now, his concussive punching power does not match that of George Foreman, Earnie Shavers, Sonny Liston, or Mike Tyson. One thing you can be certain of: A. J. will probably want to delay the Wilder fight even more now.

—May 2019

Anonymous: Who is the hardest puncher in boxing history in the heavyweight division?

J. A.: It is a well-known inside-industry fact that the hardest single-shot puncher was a fringe contender from the 1970s named Earnie Shavers. He wasn't all that famous; hence a lot of young boxing fans have never heard of him. But many top heavyweights who fought him confirmed that he was indeed the hardest puncher, including such notable authorities as Muhammad Ali, Ken Norton, and Larry Holmes. His overhand right was truly lethal and the hardest single-shot punch in the business. He wasn't all that skilful. He lacked combination punches and stamina. So he was not as successful as he could potentially have been. Neither was he the best knockout artist or the most destructive heavyweight. Tyson, Foreman, and Liston were all better punchers, but Shavers was the hardest single-shot specialist.

—February 2018

Anonymous: How hard did boxer Mike Tyson punch in his prime?

J. A.: There is a precise and objective way to gauge Tyson's lethal punching power and, more exactly, his punching effectivity. If you look at the career records of two of peak Tyson's opponents, you will see an interesting pattern emerge.

Tyson knocked out Trevor Berbick in two brutal rounds to become champion. Berbick is an important yardstick because he had a known solid chin, was very durable, and had only suffered one other knockout loss in a pro career spanning twenty-four years. He fought on for fourteen years after the Tyson demolition, and no one else managed to knock him out.

Secondly, "the Easton Assassin" Larry Holmes, who possessed a known granite chin, was still overwhelmed by peak Tyson in round four of their championship fight in 1988. This was Tyson perhaps at his most lethal, throwing deadly accurate punches driven by an obsessive will and a commitment to nail Holmes to the canvas. Tyson managed to succeed where Earnie Shavers failed. I mention Shavers specifically because he was well known to be the hardest single-shot puncher in boxing history. Holmes fought on for another fourteen years after the Tyson knockout, and nobody else managed to KO him.

In my humble opinion, these two Tyson knockout victories were his most impressive contextual wins. They were unique examples of precision punching power that achieved something that no other opponents of either Berbick or Holmes managed to replicate.

—May 2018

CHAPTER 7

IT'S ALL IN THE NAME—PEEKABOO!

Alexandre Puissant: Why was the "peekaboo" boxing style named so?

J. A.: It is so named after the game that parents play with babies. The parent conceals their face with their hands. The high position of the parent's hands are similar to where Mike Tyson's boxing gloves would be. Tyson's boxing gloves were held high and to the side of his head, forming a defensive screen in front of his chin.

The parent then moves their hands to the side and reveals their face, saying "Peekaboo!" and the baby normally laughs. There is an element of surprise to the game, and this was also reflective of Tyson's surprise attacks.

So essentially the late, great Cus D'Amato's boxing style was named after a parent and baby's game.

—December 2020

Anonymous: What is Mike Tyson's peekaboo style?

J. A.: It is a style of boxing developed by the late, great trainer of champions, Cus D'Amato. The hands are held high and to the side of the head, and the fighter generally fights out of a crouch. The concept of the style revolves around bobbing, weaving, and slipping the opponent's punches while timing your own punches. It favours relatively shorter fighters who are ambidextrous and do not prefer a particular stance. In the case of this style's most successful practitioner, the one and only Iron Mike Tyson, he started out as a southpaw but was converted to orthodox.

The style can sometimes be regarded as an aggressive counterpunching style, as it encourages your opponent to attack. Then you capitalise on the gaps created in your opponent's guard. You time your own punches to be virtually simultaneous with the other guy's punching.

As you can imagine, this style requires a very high degree of skill, and there is a fine margin between success and failure. When Floyd Patterson used these tactics against Sonny Liston, he was carried out of the ring on a stretcher. Hand-eye coordination, speed, and especially timing are keys to success. Peekaboo is high risk, as the fighter generally remains in the pocket. Nonetheless, if performed properly, it is probably the most dominant style of boxing.

—March 2018

Jose Gonzalez and Jeff Fernandez: Why don't a lot of boxers use the peekaboo style?

J. A.: The peekaboo boxing style is high risk, requires a very specific skill set, and is very energy intensive. This being the case, it favours youth and aggression. It clearly isn't suited to many boxers, who do not possess the prerequisite toolbox. If you can't stand the heat, then stay out of the kitchen!

The most famous and successful practitioner of this legendary style was "Iron" Mike Tyson. Most true boxing fans who closely followed the Iron Man's career realise that his peekaboo style eroded badly with age. After prison, he got into bad habits and no longer stuck to the strong fundamentals of peekaboo, e.g., elusive aggression.

Another way to answer this question is as follows—how many boxing trainers were on Cus D'Amato's level? He is generally rated as the number-one boxing guru in history, and was the boxing genius who devised the number system which underpins peekaboo. To make a long story short, when prime Tyson threw pre-planned punches in bunches to a vital area at the right time, he was almost untouchable.

In his later career, when he started loading up with single-shot knockout punches, he faltered. Make no mistake: with this high-risk style, if you don't stick to the fundamentals, you will fail. The margins between success and failure are very fine.

—November 2020

Anonymous: How was Mike Tyson good even though he was so short?

J. A.: This was because he was taught and trained in the peekaboo style, which is geared for relatively short heavyweights. The common misconception that casual boxing fans have is that the shorter man is always at a disadvantage. This simply isn't true. The shorter guy is only at a disadvantage from long range. At mid-range, the fight is virtually fifty-fifty, and on the inside, it is advantage to the shorter guy. In crude terms, it is like comparing a sniper rifle to a submachine gun. At long range, Muhammad Ali's sniper jabs or George Foreman's cannon are the weapons of choice. However, on the inside, Joe Frazier's short, chopping hooks and Mike Tyson's arching uppercuts are preferable.

But sticking to the subject of Tyson's height or lack thereof, as the case may be, being under six feet tall made him more elusive and enabled him to better utilise the concept of stealth movement. Crouching down even lower enabled him to evade the taller guy's radar, so to speak. This was one of the main reasons prime Tyson was very popular with Far Eastern boxing enthusiasts, because his style made them think of a heavyweight ninja. He consistently managed to ghost inside against taller and bigger men, put them in his meat grinder where only he could land punches, get off a barrage of deadly punches, and dart back out of range before the other fellow knew what had hit him.

In 1986, against a guy named James Tillis, he provided a perfect example of his brilliant peekaboo defence. He was observed slipping and ducking punches at almost knee height. This kind of dominant defensive position is only possible for a shorter heavyweight and was the perfect position for launching devastating counterpunches. Ultimately, if you fight smart, quick, and aggressive, your apparent height disadvantage can be quickly turned into an advantage—but you do need to be fleet-footed.

—January 2019

MOHAMMED: Why is the peekaboo boxing style so rare? Why didn't Kevin Rooney and Teddy Atlas pass it to other trainers so they could teach it to short fighters? Are there any boxing gyms that still teach it?

J. A.: The streaming footage and stills of prime Tyson in the classic peekaboo stance with his proper trainer, Kevin Rooney, have become the stuff of legend. If you haven't seen this one particular peekaboo drills clip on YouTube from the late 1980s, then you need to check it out, and you will have answered your own question. Rooney jabs at high speed, with Tyson slipping jabs side to side like a high-speed pendulum. Keep watching Tyson's aggressive footwork closing up the range while he's slipping jabs. Then watch Tyson throw a powerful counter at the end of the motion. Ask yourself: How many things was Tyson doing at the same time? Dodging punches from a crouch, closing up the range, and punching with bad intentions—that's three things at the same time, in one fluid motion. If you know anything about how human beings work, you will realise that multitasking is very difficult and requires much practice. Practice makes perfect, and under Cus, Teddy Atlas, and Kevin Rooney, Tyson practiced defensive boxing drills like there was no tomorrow.

The other reason peekaboo is so rare is because it is a very high-risk style which requires a very specific skill set. Imagine a cheap suit and compare it to a bespoke, high-end suit. The bespoke suit only fits the individual for whom it was tailored, whereas the cheap, baggy suit can be worn by anyone.

In simple terms, Tyson had one-in-a-million genetics and physicality which naturally fitted the peekaboo template perfectly. The rest was down to Cus D'Amato, who was the best "tailor" in boxing history. As Rooney candidly commented in the documentary *Mike Tyson, Fallen Champ*, "The Mike Tyson story was more the Cus D'Amato story." Without Cus D'Amato guiding a juvenile Tyson, it is highly unlikely that Tyson would have made it to second base, let alone hit the home-run shots that he hit.

To cut a long story short, the style was invented by the best trainer in boxing history, who in real time knew how to exploit weaknesses in a taller fighter's defence. The flip side of the coin was that Cus D'Amato had waited his whole life for "his Liston, his Dempsey". So when Bobby Stewart first brought a certain juvenile delinquent to the attention of D'Amato, you better believe his eyes lit up like a Christmas tree. When Cus, Atlas, and Rooney first saw Tyson shadow-box, they saw right there and then an opportunity knocking.

As for why Rooney and Atlas didn't pass on the peekaboo style to other gyms, no top trainer in their right mind passes on trade secrets to the competition. In a documentary called *Mike Tyson's Greatest Hits*, Rooney explained the purpose of the slip bag. Someone (maybe paparazzi) had photographed Tyson using the slip bag in Cus's house, and therefore Rooney was almost forced to explain what that contraption was all about. He reluctantly said, "The purpose of the slip bag is to get the fighter moving their head correctly—this is one of the things that we've got over everybody else."

—September 2019

Peter Thanas: Most of Mike Tyson's opponents were much taller than he was. Would Tyson have been untouchable if he were 6 feet 3 inches or 6 feet 4 inches and fought with the same peekaboo style?

J. A.: If I may slightly correct you on one point—*all* of his opponents were taller than him. Tyson's most accurately measured height was 1.78 metres, which converts to slightly more than 5 feet 10 inches. Over the years, the height of the average heavyweight has been approximately 6 feet 3 inches, which gives the average heavyweight an approximate 5-inch height advantage on Tyson. Bear in mind this so-called advantage is only an advantage to the taller man at long range—that is, on the outside. On the inside or at mid-range, it has consistently been shown that being taller may actually be a disadvantage.

For argument's sake, let's assume we kept Tyson's build and muscularity exactly the same and simply scaled him up to 6 feet 3 inches, thereby making him five inches taller. Like for like, each inch of extra height can easily accommodate an extra seven pounds of body weight, so in theory, he would perhaps be 35 pounds heavier. The taller version of Tyson would therefore tip the scales at around the 255-pound mark—quite a monster.

About now, everyone in the know is probably raising an eyebrow. Why? There is no way on God's green earth that Tyson could execute his legendary peekaboo style with the same intensity and output at 250 pounds plus. His heart would not be able to cope with the extra load. Of course, if he took PEDs, then that would change everything. But adding 35 pounds of pure lean mass would upset his balance, cardio, and general dynamics completely. It is also highly probable that his legendary spartan training sessions would be severely compromised.

Imagine prime Tyson standing at close quarters with the average 6 feet 3 inch heavyweight and consider the natural position and height of his gloves. Eagle-eyed observers of 1980s footage of Tyson will have noticed that Tyson's punching hand was roughly at the same height as the intended target—specifically the taller fighter's ribcage. This meant that the punch had a shorter distance to travel and could be executed with greater accuracy, twist, and snap, incorporating as much body weight as possible. Simply put, at his real-life height of 5 feet 10 inches, Tyson's hands were naturally at the perfect height to pound the taller guy's body.

Over the years, Tyson gave various short training montages demonstrating how to throw powerful body shots with the proper snap and twist. It was evident that his whole body was well synchronised and moved upward and forward uniformly into the punch. The phrase "the whole is greater than the sum of its parts" comes to mind. Scaling him up to 6 feet 3 inches would again probably detract from the natural synchronicity of his body.

Without belabouring the point, consider some science. When you increase someone's height, their weight increases as a function of volume. Muscular strength increases as a function of surface area. So Tyson's legs in particular would be weaker if he were taller.

Finally, we have to address the issue of his legendary defence and the ninja elements of peekaboo. Without a shadow of a doubt, being naturally below 6 feet tall assisted his defensive stealth movements. When prime Tyson boxed from an extreme defensive crouch, it has been speculated that he was almost invincible and unhittable. It is very difficult for a taller fighter to land effective punches when a shorter fighter is crouching and slipping. Essentially, the extreme crouch underpins the concept of getting underneath the taller fighter's radar. I think most knowledgeable people would agree that a taller Tyson would be far less elusive, and therefore one of the basic fundamentals of peekaboo boxing, elusive aggression, would be compromised.

—July 2019

James Posh: Is it recommended for a 5-feet 10-inch person to use the peekaboo style in boxing?

J. A.: I would say it largely depends on whether the person in question has ambidextrous punching ability. This is a crucial factor in achieving success with the peekaboo boxing style. By now, even casual boxing fans probably realise that prime Mike Tyson was a master of peekaboo boxing and surely pushed this style right to the edge of the envelope.

For true boxing fans, watching a teenage Tyson in the classic peekaboo stance—hands held high and to the side of the head, waiting to pounce—was an exciting sight. Which hand was he coming after you with? For the intended target, it was confusing. It was almost like playing a game of poker. Just because Tyson was in the orthodox stance didn't necessarily mean he was going to throw the left jab or a lead left hook. Tyson would often feint with the jab and come over the top with a right-hand laser cannon to the head. Who knows? He may well throw a lead left hook. This game of poker was an example of street-fighter tactics being brought into the professional boxing arena. In Tyson's fights, the element of surprise often proved decisive.

At the time, many boxing fans, even experienced and knowledgeable ones, failed to see the science behind Cus D'Amato's genius invention. When performed properly, the peekaboo style uses the number system. This largely remained hidden to the competition until Tyson's bouts were covered on a national level. In nationally televised fights, microphones were present in the corners during the intervals between rounds. Then Kevin Rooney could be heard calling out combinations of numbers e.g., 6351 or 63251. Each numeric combination represented a four- or five-punch barrage which had been memorised by Tyson. He therefore knew exactly when and where to throw a particular set of punches, specifically targeting his opponent's weaker side. As Tyson was ambidextrous, he himself had no weaker side and could therefore knock you out with either hand from any stance (including a neutral, squared stance). You cannot begin to imagine how doubly dangerous a fast, ambidextrous, precise power puncher like Tyson became when potentially blindsiding an opponent on his weaker side.

This, in essence, was what D'Amato meant by "throwing the punch where you can hit him but he can't hit you". By the time the opponent responded to one of Tyson's devastating blindside combos, Tyson was back out of harm's way, his opponent was knocked out, or his opponent was badly dazed. It was pure apex-predator boxing, in many ways very similar to a great white shark torpedoing a much larger and sloppier elephant seal and circling around it after the incapacitating first strike. Frank Bruno described his two fights with Tyson as the equivalent of a harbour shark experience.

In terms of height, I think slightly under six feet tall is optimal for a heavyweight peekaboo practitioner. Any taller and you may not be as effective when boxing from the crouch. Part of the trick is to get under the taller fighter's defences. First and foremost, this means evading the defensive jab.

In 2000, Tyson boxed a decent professional named Lou Savarese, who stood a full six inches taller than Tyson. During this very short fight, what really struck me was the manner in which a well-past-prime Tyson still managed to circumvent Savarese's height and reach advantages. In this instance, Tyson overcame his opponent's physical advantages by the stunning use of his gazelle punch. The point is that to use the peekaboo style successfully means possessing the right tools for the job.

In summary, I suggest it depends on what type of fighter you want to be and what gym you attend. Being ambidextrous is vital if you want to use the peekaboo style to Tyson's level. In simple terms, it makes you a minimum of 100 per cent more deadly, compared to a normal fighter. Other factors to take into consideration are your leg strength. Prime Tyson had some serious strength in his upper legs. If you watch him closely in his youth, you will see that much of his short-range punching power came from his explosive leg strength. He would bend his knees and literally spring forward with full body weight into those close-range punches.

Finally, I suggest doing some research on how good the defensive boxing coach is at the particular gym you attend.

Believe me, even in this day and age, a massive misconception about Tyson and peekaboo boxing is that it is all about brutal first-round knockouts. The knockout used to come so easily primarily because of prime Tyson's watertight defence. He just so happened to be a very hard puncher with both hands, and later became a master at closing the gap on taller and rangier boxers. Bear in mind that peekaboo boxing is all about elusive aggression and aggressive counterpunching.

—March 2019

Gregory Bolden: What if Mike Tyson were 6 feet 3 inches tall with the same power? Would he have been even better?

J. A.: Mike Tyson had a very good jab, which was one of his most underrated punches. In the late 1980s, he was often out-jabbing taller and more rangy fighters, such as Tony Tucker, due to his superior timing. Now Tyson is 5 feet 10 inches tall and Tucker 6 feet 5 inches. Tyson has a 72-inch reach and Tucker an 82-inch reach. So Tyson was effectively giving away seven inches in height and ten inches in reach, but he was still competitive in a battle of the jabs against a very capable boxer. Can you imagine how much more effective Tyson's jab would have been with 6 inches of added reach?

But in all honesty, what Tyson would have gained in his out-fighting would surely have been lost from his all-time leading mid-range and short-range games. The peekaboo style revolves around elusive aggression, and a taller Tyson would have been far less elusive.

He would also have lost his novelty factor. Believe it or not, being shorter in a division of giants did carry certain benefits, with the main one being stealth. Boxing from the crouch and being low to the ground made Tyson that much more elusive.

Often Tyson employed an extreme crouch—a defensive position that probably only Mike Tyson could attain—courtesy of some of the most powerful leg muscles ever seen on a heavyweight boxer. In these dominant defensive positions, he was almost unhittable and could easily leap upward with his trademark hooks and uppercuts. These punches had far more leverage and surprise factor when they were thrown from low down. So it was more suited to Tyson's peekaboo style to be less than 6 feet tall, particularly at mid-range and on the inside, where he could ghost into the Tyson kill-zone and wreak havoc on his larger and unsuspecting prey.

One of peak Tyson's biggest weapons against taller fighters was his legendary body punching. He was a surgical body snatcher in there, and part of his natural skill was that his hands were at the perfect height to punish a taller fighter's body. Scaling him up to 6 feet 3 inches would surely have detracted from his body-punching prowess and his close-range power. Having shorter arms was actually a big advantage on the inside, as it gave him more room for his legendary combination punching.

On a final note, I think a taller Tyson would also have inferior balance. This is because his centre of gravity would be further up his body, changing his biomechanics and overall dynamics in a negative way. In summary, scaling Tyson up would have made him less effective. The only improvement would possibly have been to his long-range game, but even this is debatable.

—April 2019

CHAPTER 8

WHO'S A CLEVER BOY?

Anthony Andranik Moumjain: Which UFC fighter or boxer has the highest fight IQ and why?

J. A.: Love him or hate him, but when it comes to fight IQ, there is only one winner, and it isn't even close. Floyd Mayweather has probably the highest boxing IQ ever. If legendary trainer Ray Arcel were still alive, he would no doubt be Mayweather's biggest fan. One of Arcel's favourite boxing catchphrases was that he would take brains over brawn any day. "Brains over brawn" summarises Mayweather's style perfectly. Essentially, at the highest level of boxing, remaining injury-free and maximising your longevity is what it's all about. I mean, literally anybody can have a drunken pub brawl and beat the living shit out of one another, right?

Mayweather's judgement of distance is sublime; it's almost as if he has an in-built slide rule. When in the centre of the ring, he always appears to be just slightly out of range of the attacker, but in range to land his own punches. This is pure skill, pure judgement, pure ring IQ. His timing is second to none. Legendary chess master Bobby Fischer once drew an analogy between boxing and chess. He said chess, like boxing, is all about "knowing when to punch and how to duck". Again, doesn't this statement summarise Mayweather very succinctly? Not only does he time his own punches to perfection, but he has also mastered the defensive art of evading power punches.

Finally, his adaptability in the midst of a match has become the stuff of legend. Nobody reads their opponent's offense better than Floyd Mayweather, and certainly nobody makes the appropriate adjustments to neutralise their opponent better than him. Believe me, this is extremely difficult to do in the heat of battle and demonstrates an extremely deep understanding of boxing fundamentals. Floyd, "thou art the smartest"!

—February 2019

Anthony Andranik Moumjain: What makes Floyd Mayweather so successful where so many other boxers have failed?

J. A.: Sticking just to the boxing facts, the primary reason is his genius-level defence, and specifically his masterful use of the shoulder roll.

Do you think Floyd Mayweather understands the concept of boxing anatomy and the weak points of a fighter's armour? I think most knowledgeable people would agree that he does. Just look at the masterful way in which his chin is often tucked in behind his lead shoulder in a position of lockdown. Many top boxers, including Oscar De La Hoya, Ricky Hatton, Arturo Gatti, and Manny Pacquiao, have tried nailing him cleanly with power shots. All of them failed. His defence was always watertight and arguably the best in history. In terms of body shape, blocking, parrying, and neutralising, I doubt Mayweather has any historical peers.

His defensive display against a very dangerous and world-class Ricky Hatton surely ranks as one of the all-time best defensive performances. At the time, Hatton was one of the best pressure fighters in the world. He was an outstanding body puncher who garnered the respect of one or two legendary Mexican swarmers. On the night, Floyd Mayweather was right there in front of Hatton—and yet he wasn't there. Punches which had flattened Hatton's previous opponents were either catching thin air or were being blocked. And then there was the decisive check hook which virtually finished Hatton off, straight out of the coaching manual of the old-time Michigan greats. The late, great Emanuel Steward was in awe of Floyd Mayweather, and when Manny praises a boxer that he didn't train, rest assured this kid's got the X factor.

The second purely boxing reason for Mayweather's success was his ring IQ, which was also second to none. Without doubt he consistently proved himself to be one of the most versatile and adaptable boxers in history. He could read his opponent's style and adapt his defence to counter his opponent's offense. Sounds easy, right? So why don't other fighters just do the same? Look at your opponent, carry out a scouting report for three rounds or so, and then just adapt. In practice, in the heat of battle, it is very difficult to do. In this regard, Floyd is right at the top of the food chain.

The third purely boxing reason for Mayweather's success is his punching accuracy, which is number one all-time. Statistically speaking, he is the most accurate puncher in boxing history, according to CompuBox stats. When Mayweather throws a punch, it is not a random event. It is a calculated, precise event based on risk and probability. That's how you become the most accurate puncher in history, precision personified. That's exactly why a statistical website such as BoxRec ranks him as the number-one boxer all-time.

—January 2019

BIZZ TADLOCK: What are some of the hidden nuances that go unseen when the average person watches a boxing match?

J. A.: How long have you got? The simplest analogy I can think of is to a good old-fashioned game of chess. You can train a chimpanzee to move chess pieces around the board, but it will have no understanding of the bigger picture or tactical concepts. The fact of the matter is that the chimp can "play" the most complex of board games without knowing what it's doing.

When grandmasters play chess, they see moves and recognise patterns that the average player can't even dream of. Most importantly, perhaps, grandmasters don't make mistakes.

In boxing, when a casual fan watches a higher-level boxing match, they have little or no understanding of the skill and technical aspects of boxing. They see the end product—the brutality, the punching power, and the knockout. But they will have little or no intuition as to how that knockout was achieved. They will have little insight—or interest, for that matter—into the small details that accumulate and become very significant at the highest level of boxing.

Thomas Hearns's knockout of Roberto Duran is one of the most famous, iconic, downright brutal, and technically scrutinised knockouts in the modern era of boxing. Literally in the blink of an eye, one Hall of Fame boxer flattened another Hall of Fame boxer.

If you asked a casual fan, "How exactly did Hearns knock out the great Roberto Duran so easily?", the response would be along the lines of "Uh, duh, he punched him in the face, ain't it?" Well, yes, Hearns did indeed punch Duran in the face, and the concussive force was enough to temporarily detach him from his senses.

Then ask, "But how did he set up the knockout punch?" I'm pretty sure the vast majority of average fans will have no understanding of how Hearns set up that classic right cross. The main reason Duran was flattened in such devastating fashion was because he didn't *see* the punch. You have to watch the footage in slow motion several times over. You will see Hearns's "flicker jabs" to the body. The flicker jabs were nothing more than pure distraction. Then he went upstairs with the finishing, unseen power shot. Duran had a great chin and was very durable, but in this instance it made no difference whatsoever. The punch caught him completely unawares and landed 100 per cent flush as Duran rebounded off the ropes into the shot. So *distraction techniques* are one subtle nuance that only seasoned boxing observers can see.

The concept of footwork is huge at the highest level of boxing. Once again, watch the Hearns versus Duran fight and you'll see how Hearns's aggressive footwork kept Duran on the back-foot. This was a pre-planned strategy concocted by Emmanuel Steward, who had specifically told Hearns, "Duran can't fight going backwards." Therefore, one of Hearns's main objectives in this matchup was to make Duran box on the back foot, taking Duran into new and hitherto uncharted waters. When you introduce an elite fighter to an unknown, he's rendered just the same as everyone else.

Everyone has surely heard of Lionel Messi. What does he have to do with boxing? Well, his body-feinting technique is just out of this world and has been responsible for wrong-footing many a world-class defender. In high-level boxing, the use of body feints can also be a major ingredient for success. Ask none other than the great Diego Maradona (RIP) who his favourite heavyweight boxer was, and I can guarantee you that he would have said Mike Tyson. Maradona too was a master of the football feint, and similarly Mike Tyson was a master of the boxing feint. No heavyweight in the modern era used body feints more effectively than Tyson. It was definitely a hidden nuance that kept his opponents guessing.

—October 2019

ANONYMOUS: What is the most useful technique in boxing?

J. A.: In my humble opinion, the single most useful boxing technique is slipping punches. If you were to analyse many of the top fighters in history, the one trait they share is the ability to avoid heavy punishment. Prime examples of such fighters are 1960s Ali, Mike Tyson, Roy Jones Junior, and the best defensive wizard of all time, Floyd Mayweather. Great defence is more important than great offense. As they say in American football, "Offense wins games but defence wins the championship." Avoiding punches not only increases your longevity in boxing but clearly increases the probability of you leaving the sport in the same physical condition you entered it. As good referees often say at the start of a fight, "Protect yourself at all times."

—April 2018

Piotr Gajda: Which heavyweight boxer in history had the best defence?

J. A.: It has to be a skilful dude named Muhammad Ali. Way back in 1964, when Cassius Clay challenged Sonny Liston for the heavyweight title, onlookers were enthralled by the all-too-familiar sight of an almost unhittable Clay making the meanest cat in the heavyweight division, Sonny Liston, punch thin air. Liston was a very capable boxer, but on the night he barely laid a glove on a razor-sharp Clay, whose ring movements and defensive reflexes kept him well out of harm's way.

In most of Ali's fights during the 1960s, a common defensive pattern emerged whereby Ali was generally *out* of punching range but his opponents were *in* punching range. This being the case, Ali could jab and one-two them all night long while taking almost zero headshots in return. This is exactly what transpired against Liston, who understandably became demoralised and wound up taking a terrible head-beating from Clay.

However, it is fair to say that Ali's defensive brilliance only lasted for about three years, from 1964 to 1967 inclusive. After his enforced exile from boxing ended in 1970, his feline reflexes and defensive footwork were never the same. He was already a fighter in sharp decline.

This rapid decline was clearly evident in his first meeting with Joe Frazier in 1971, when he probably took more clean headshots in one fight than in all his previous fights combined. Perhaps the most elusive heavyweight boxer in history had all of a sudden become very hittable. Lucky for him that Mother Nature had coincidentally blessed him with a granite jaw, because the 1970s version of Ali took some of the worst head-beatings in heavyweight history.

—October 2020

Idris Abdullah: In boxing, what are the techniques aimed at exhausting an opponent? And what methods are used against exhausted opponents?

J. A.: Remember the Rumble in the Jungle? It is probably the most iconic example of a boxing match in which the primary objective of the supposedly outmatched underdog was to cause his superior opponent to tire. As Ali himself famously commented on *Parkinson*, "George ran out of gas, and there was no filling station nearby!"

The technique that Ali used against Foreman later came to be known as the "rope a dope" tactic. The basic premise of this tactic was for Ali to lie on the ropes and absorb vicious punishment to the body but deny Foreman any kind of target to his head. Ali and his brilliant trainer Angelo Dundee had done their homework and knew from previous fights that Foreman was not the most accurate of body punchers. By nature, Foreman was a headhunter. So Ali maintained a high and tight defensive guard, ensuring his chin was totally covered up, and gave Foreman his body, so to speak. He leant way back on the ropes, further protecting his head. Every now and then he countered off the ropes with blinding hand speed, keeping Foreman on his toes, mostly from right crosses and one-twos. In the intense African heat, Foreman literally punched himself out and fell victim to pretty much the same one-two combination that Ali had been throwing all night long.

In all honesty, rope a dope is pretty crazy and suicidal. Ali was the only guy in the world who could have pulled it off. Ask any top boxing trainer and they will tell you that the last place you should be in a boxing ring, when you're up against a massive puncher, is on the ropes. But rope a dope worked a treat on the night. It was almost a classic case of drawing an apex predator into deeper waters and drowning him when he could no longer swim.

Any time you are outmatched in terms of punching power, I would say your main objective is to stay on your bike in the early rounds—what the old-timers used to call "milling on the retreat". Sugar Ray Leonard was great at this tactic and used it to good effect in the earlier rounds against stronger opponents such as Marvin Hagler. Boxing cautiously on the retreat, constantly switching your jab upstairs and downstairs is a good way of confusing your stronger opponent. In general body shots will tire out your opponent faster than headshots, so targeting your opponent's body is important. Repeated, accurately placed body shots will also restrict his mobility, as the cumulative effect of body punching eventually takes his legs away. If you want to see a masterclass in body punching and the devastating effect of repeated body shots on a fighter's mobility, then watch the clinic that Tyson gave against Tyrell Biggs in 1987. Biggs was noted for his movement and his silky boxing skills, but Tyson's precision body-punching literally took away his legs by round five.

Another method used by Ali and, in recent times, by Wladimir Klitschko is good old-fashioned wrestling—leaning on your opponent in the clinches and tying him up. If you are fitter than your opponent and have superior stamina, then you should in theory tire less than him at a given fight intensity. So plenty of road work never did a boxer any harm.

Once you have a tired opponent or one who is at least more tired than you, then I think your attacking options greatly increase. Whatever is your best and favourite power punch, use it as often as possible to finish him off. In this scenario you can afford to take a few risks, as his punches will lack any kind of sting—see Sugar Ray Leonard versus Thomas Hearns 1 for a great example of this tactic. Leonard was one of the best in the business at finishing off a hurt and tired opponent.

—January 2019

Joe Gleeson: Which heavyweight boxer had the highest ring IQ?

J. A.: There can be only one! The answer is simple: it's Muhammad Ali. When considering what constitutes an intelligent heavyweight boxer, the traits of Muhammad Ali come to mind. Why? Because he was the smartest heavyweight boxer of all time (with respect to Gene Tunney). And believe me, during the highly competitive 1970s, he needed every last IQ point he could muster, as he was often outmatched by physically superior opponents. In addition to facing much harder-hitting boxers, he was also well past his own physical prime. So on various occasions, he had to call on his ring smarts to bail him out of trouble.

Ali's now-legendary rope a dope tactic often inspires much retrospective banter and analysis. It's a crazy and bespoke fight tactic, almost suicidal in fact, and definitely not to be found in any coaching manual. But this was Ali; there surely had to be some method behind the madness.

Notice how high his gloves were against Foreman, almost mimicking the classic peekaboo guard, completely covering his head and chin. For Ali, this was a very unusual and uncharacteristic guard. He had spent the better part of his career to that point carrying his hands low. In this career-defining fight, he literally gave the headhunting Foreman no head target whatsoever but willingly allowed him to pound on his body with impunity.

In the intense African heat and humidity, the plan was obviously to wear out his stronger but dim-witted opponent by soaking up the body shots and literally going through the pain barrier. On the night, the rope a dope worked a treat, and Ali's all time legendary status was sealed, largely because of his high ring IQ. Years later, American rapper Ice-T commented, "You can be the hardest cat in the jungle, but when you get tired, a girl can knock you out."

The Foreman KO is probably the most famous exhaustion-facilitated knockout of all time. It had huge repercussions in boxing history. While he was lying on the canvas, Foreman's posture spoke a thousand words; he was down but he wasn't out. His version of events was that he was watching his chief second counting to ten, and that he had only reached the count of eight, whereas the referee had already completed the ten count. If you watch the fight footage closely, Foreman's version of events is accurate. That was indeed a notoriously fast ten count from a highly dubious referee.

Other than Ali, I think prime Tyson deserves to be mentioned, as he too had a surprisingly high fight IQ, especially given the fact he was a brawler. Larry Holmes was smart, as was the really old-school Gene Tunney. Lennox Lewis and Wladimir Klitschko also stand out in this department.

—August 2019

Samuele Bolotta: Was Muhammad Ali's IQ actually low?

J. A.: Apparently in the one documented IQ test that he sat, for the US Army, his score was below the "normal" score. In most commonly used standardised tests, this is a score of 100. Is it a big deal? So maybe he wasn't that good at IQ tests. This doesn't mean that he wasn't intelligent—by boxing standards, he was in fact very smart. IQ tests are credible tools, but the result has to be contextual and taken with a pinch of salt. After all, they only measure a specific form of intelligence, which is usually based on a set of multiple-choice questions. Maybe Ali didn't like multiple choice. Maybe he preferred a more creative type of test. Maybe he didn't give a shit and flunked on purpose.

Whatever the case, I think Ali was a very smart boxer and was probably of above-average intelligence compared to the population as a whole. By the same token, just because he could speak well and was funny doesn't mean he was the next Einstein. He was smart by boxer standards, and that's it.

Purely as an afterthought, do not read too much into IQ tests, because this is what the IQ test writers want you to believe—that they are the yardstick by which intelligence is measured. This is a fallacy.

—January 2019

Jacob Goldboe: What is the best way to win a fight when the odds are against you?

J. A.: According to Sun Tzu's *The Art of War*, "When your enemy is superior to you, then evade him." In general, I'd say this was pretty good advice and makes a lot of sense. But it is a general doctrine and cannot be applied universally across every fight in history.

Sticking to the boxing, then over the decades that I have followed the sport, many boxers have been outmatched by superior opponents but have prevailed by boxing smart and getting their tactics right on the night. In the modern era, a prime example of a boxer who won because of tactical supremacy was Sugar Ray Leonard against Marvin Hagler. The betting odds were stacked heavily against Sugar Ray Leonard, and on paper he was definitely outmatched. Hagler was the genuine middleweight, the harder puncher, the stronger, tougher, and more active fighter. Leonard's main advantages were speed, reflexes, and footwork, all of which were supposedly diminished due to inactivity.

Team Leonard pulled off two very significant tactical coups before a punch was ever thrown: they demanded a larger boxing ring and a twelve-round fight duration, as opposed to fifteen. Team Hagler were so confident that they incorrectly granted Leonard these "small" concessions. At the elite level of boxing, small details have big consequences. Both the larger ring and the shorter fight duration suited Leonard and proved decisive on the night. (So too did the judges' scoring, but that is another story altogether.) This was a prime example of an outmatched opponent manipulating environmental conditions to his advantage.

As a general rule of thumb, when the odds are against you, then tactics become very important. You have to fight smarter than the other guy. Evading your opponent early on in the fight is advisable, since his power advantage is greatest when he is fresh. Power advantages normally diminish with time. Ali, Leonard, and in recent times Floyd Mayweather have been masters at this evasion tactic. Movement and intelligent footwork are crucial components for success in a boxing match at any time, but doubly so when facing an opponent with superior firepower.

The timing of a fight is crucial. Sugar Ray Leonard has gone on record as saying that he only felt he could beat Hagler after the Mugabi fight— in other words, post-1986. There is no shame in delaying a fight and allowing other fighters to take some of the X factor out of your future adversary.

—January 2019

Sean Lim: Why couldn't anyone beat Floyd Mayweather?

J. A.: The main reason was that Floyd Mayweather was a defensive genius who was arguably the number-one defensive fighter all time. Not only did he consistently avoid clean punches throughout his career, but he was often able to neutralise dangerous opponents before they had a chance to throw heavy leather. Arguably the best exponent of defensive boxing when cornered on the ropes, he used the Philly shell shoulder roll to maximum benefit. He has also proven to be the number-one statistical boxer in history, according to CompuBox stats. Although statistical analysis in boxing has its limitations, in Mayweather's case, one is obliged to make an exception.

Secondly, Mayweather possessed possibly the highest ring IQ all time. He surely surpasses Ali and Sugar Ray Leonard in this facet of boxing. He was a very adaptable and versatile fighter who instinctively seemed to know how to fight against different and varied opposition. He could box to a given game plan or modify midstream—the true sign of a genius boxer.

Thirdly, his offense was very underrated— by no means the best ever, but world-class nonetheless. He had a good variety of punches, a great left jab to the body, and a great check hook. He was economical with his power punches, never wasteful, and he was one of the most accurate punchers ever.

—May 2018

Vincent Pisano: What are five things someone with a high fight IQ does differently than a fighter with low fight IQ?

J. A.:

- *Energy management or stamina*: In probably the most famous boxing match ever, Ali invented a new boxing tactic which was dubbed the rope a dope. The basic premise of this tactic was to allow his low-IQ opponent to pound on his body while Ali protected his head. The rationale was that the hardest puncher in the world would gas before he broke Ali's ribs! This crazy and suicidal tactic worked a treat on the night, as Foreman clearly couldn't see the trap and gassed by round eight.
- *Striking accuracy*: A high-IQ opponent values striking accuracy far more than power. If you attended your high school biology class (and listened to the teacher), you learned that the human liver is on the right side of the body; therefore practise the left hook.
- *Defence*: Legendary trainer Ray Arcel famously said that he would take brains over brawn any day. Though Arcel never trained Floyd Mayweather, Mayweather probably listened to those wise words. The main reason Floyd Mayweather remained unbeaten for his whole career was because of his flawless defence; the defensive aspects of boxing technique are clearly indicative of a high fight IQ.
- *Know-how*: The cross-arm defence is kind of catchy. Old Foreman realised that he was a sitting duck target in his "second coming" and could no longer rely on his vaunted punch to wipe out the opposition. He always had a granite chin, so he could take the headshots. But his old and flabby body had become vulnerable. So he adopted one of the best defensive guards in the business, and it worked a treat.
- *If it ain't broke, don't fix it*: When a young Tyson was under Cus D'Amato's watchful gaze, he was virtually unbeatable. In Tyson's own words, "The fighting is the easy part; the training is the hard part." He had the ultimate heavyweight plan A, so he didn't need plan B. When he deviated from the winning game plan, he rapidly declined.

—July 2019

Boyn Gwa: How did Mike Tyson defend against hooks?

J. A.: The key to prime Tyson's impregnable defence was precision head movement and rolling from the waist, which was described as a pendulum motion. On ESPN Classic, Teddy Atlas once described how it was one of Cus's main objectives to get this kid to "slip the jab" and "weave the round". As prime Tyson's style was so aggressive, it was absolutely imperative that he evaded the incoming counters while attempting to close the gap on a more rangy fighter.

In one instance—round four of the Tillis fight—Tyson gave a masterclass on how to avoid a left hook. Tillis lunged in with a sweeping left hook, which Tyson's eagle eye spotted a mile away. Tyson rapidly ducked to his right to avoid the punch, and in the process he got behind Tillis.

At this point, Tyson was in a perfect position to launch a blind-side attack, and he duly delivered his own counter-left hook, scoring a knockdown.

This sequence of Tyson moves was a perfect example of peekaboo defence transitioning into peekaboo offense. Tyson evaded a powerful left hook by ducking and weaving. In the process, he established an absolutely dominant blind-side position where only he could land.

At other times in the Tillis fight, Tyson employed an extreme crouch to get under the incoming punches. Such defensive manoeuvres were prime examples of stealth-based ninja tactics being brought into the heavyweight boxing arena. These defensive manoeuvres enabled Tyson to stay in the pocket, well within punching range, and throw his own counters from low down. By springing up from the crouch, Tyson was able to generate unprecedented amounts of power in short-range punches.

But what made Tyson appear invincible was his defence—specifically maintaining a high peekaboo guard, moving his head correctly, and rolling from the waist. His high guard enabled him to block many punches on his way inside, where Barry McGuigan once described him as the most ferocious in-fighter he had ever seen.

In addition to the above points, long-time Eurosport boxing commentator Steve Holdsworth once described Tyson as the best heavyweight gap closer he had ever seen. Tyson avoided hooks and punches in general through fleet-footedness, agility, head movement, and rolling from the waist.

—March 2019

John Palmer: What is the safest way to win a professional MMA fight with minimal damage?

J. A.: One word—Khabib. His tactics and fighting style appear to be optimally suited to ensuring a victory while sustaining little damage in return. He is similar to Floyd Mayweather in this respect, although he is far more aggressive.

In the dominant grappling positions Khabib often attains, he is almost invulnerable. Given the amount of pressure that he exerts on his opponents, any counter strikes coming his way have less sting because his opponents are almost always on the back foot.

He is also probably the most dominant grappler in UFC history. He is clearly a genetic freak at the weight. In many ways, his fighting style is a homage to the concept of mixed martial arts, in that he operates both as a human mauler and a human constrictor.

—January 2021

CHAPTER 9

BEWARE OF THE STEROID FREAK

MAX SHORTTE and JANGA ZILOTIN: Many people say Evander Holyfield used PEDs. That has never been proven to us. Where is the proof?

J. A.: If you are looking for a failed drugs test, then there isn't one. The closest thing to proof comes in the form of his alias name—Evan Fields. Numerous parcels and post from an illicit pharmacy were trackable to his home address, but mailed under the pseudonym of Evan Fields.

An undercover journalist called Holyfield's home phone number on a pretence, wishing to speak with the mysterious Evan Fields. Holyfield himself answered the phone and mistakenly told the journalist that he was indeed speaking to Evan Fields and confirmed that Fields had the same birth date as Evander Holyfield. The fact that a professional athlete confirmed an alias was big news. The fact that anyone reputable has an alias in the first place arouses suspicion, but a professional athlete—that's even worse.

Evan Fields's pharmacy has been linked to and implicated in the PEDs supply to other shady and suspicious athletes, who also coincidentally used pseudonyms which bore a resemblance to their real names.

Other "proof" comes in the form of Holyfield's abnormal ECG reading following his defeat by Michael Moorer in 1994. His abnormal heart reading was consistent with steroids and HGH users, but was covered up and conveniently repackaged as a misdiagnosis.

Further indirect proof comes in the form of his cranium size and shape, which has noticeably become larger and more irregular over the years. Steroids and HGH abuse cause well-known side effects of skull bossing, cranial enlargement, and drug-induced acromegaly—all of which can be seen in Holyfield. Further retrospective suspicion was aroused when his increased muscularity and masculinity appeared to coincide exactly with the time frame of his rapid and irregular hair loss.

Furthermore, his erratic and non-linear performances in the ring arouse even greater suspicion. Unusually and totally against the grain, his performances improved with the increasing quality of his opposition. This is the polar opposite of most elite boxers, who generally destroy lower-ranked opposition but struggle with equally ranked fighters.

The final anomaly of Holyfield's career path which raised the eyebrows of knowledgeable onlookers were the grossly skewed timelines of his physical and technical primes. From a physical standpoint, he clearly continued to improve and mature well into his late thirties, whereas his technical prime occurred much earlier.

—December 2020

Moh Ali: Was Evander Holyfield on steroids when he moved up to heavyweight?

J. A.: Does a bear take a shit in the woods? Does a horse piss where she pleases?

Anyone with approximately half a fully functioning brain, reasonable eyesight, and some common sense—and who has followed boxing for around thirty-five years—can easily tell there are certain modern boxers who look more muscular while being physically leaner at the weight, relative to their counterparts from yesteryear. Furthermore, if you have an eye for detail, you can easily notice that much of this steroid-acquired muscle is located in specific muscle groups, such as the traps. Believe me, a disproportionately enhanced trapezius muscle is a dead sure giveaway and is strongly indicative of steroid abuse.

Pay close attention to the Real Deal Holyfield's physique in the mid-1980s as a cruiserweight, and you can tell he was clean. To the seasoned observer, it is glaringly obvious that his 1980s physique pre-dated his steroid days.

In stark contrast to 1980s Holyfield, the late-1990s, unreal-deal Holyfield was way more muscular and ripped. What an amazing difference those twelve years and twenty thousand PEDs made. Can you see the difference?

There is widespread speculation, on social media and other internet sites, that Holyfield could never have boxed at heavyweight without usage of drugs. On one website page called "Top Ten Steroid Users in Boxing", Holyfield is named as the number-one steroid freak in boxing history. But don't take my word for it—google it.

—October 2020

Alexandre Puissant: What are the distinct features of a steroid skull?

J. A.: The skull morphology of late-1990s Holyfield is probably the quintessential example of a modern-day heavyweight steroid skull.

Strictly speaking, a "steroid skull" should be called a "steroid/HGH skull", as more often than not the PED abuser takes HGH in conjunction with steroids. Typically it is a skull which has deviated from the norm and has become asymmetric. The morphology of the skull often resembles that of an ancient and extinct human cousin known as a Neanderthal. In street slang, a PED abuser may be crudely labelled a "meathead". The simplest way to quantify a steroid skull is by using a measuring tape.

One side effect of PEDs is an increase in cranial size, and that increase is not one Mother Nature intended. PEDs cause an asymmetric increase in head size and width. To quantify this increase in size, we would simply measure head circumference at the brow line by wrapping the tape measure around the suspect's skull, and then compare the result to the measurement taken before the "medical therapy" was undertaken. Inevitably, you will find an increase in head circumference, with the magnitude depending upon the dose, duration, and type of PEDs consumed. As the increase in head size is gradual, it often goes unnoticed—at least in its fledgling stages. Other steroid skull features may include an increase in the protrusion of the chin, a widening of the jaw, scrunching up of the front teeth, and profound hair loss. To conceal the hair loss, the abuser typically shaves his whole head.

In summary, if you imagine taking a medication—any medication—the drug is eventually absorbed into the bloodstream. The blood supply to the head is simply downstream from the injection site. PEDs will eventually end up in your skull, causing hypertrophy of skull tissue and cranial bones. As with any other medication, there is a desired effect and a side effect.

—July 2019

Kinyanjui Kamau: Did Evander Holyfield's head and skull transformation from light-heavy to heavyweight help in his ability to take punches?

J. A.: One hundred per cent yes! If you analyse his late-1990s fights compared to his 1980s fights, then without doubt his punch resistance improved significantly with age. Analysing his trilogy with Riddick Bowe, you can see he's taking punches that he has no business taking. In the first Bowe fight, I believe he should have been KO'd. He always had a great chin, but it became superhuman after the juice.

In the late 1990s, he was often described as being "bombproof" by boxing journalists of the day. Now, anyone who knows anything about boxing surely realises that being bombproof is not possible in nature. But after chemical enhancement, literally anything is possible.

Looking at various before-and-after images of Holyfield, the "after" guy looks way tougher than the "before" guy. If you consider the increased width of his neck and the disproportionate development of his traps over the years, it is highly probable these anatomical features improved his ability to take a hit.

On top of these factors, Holyfield's skull morphology, by the mid 1990s, started to resemble that of Marvin Hagler. Hagler clearly had a naturally crash-helmet-shaped skull, which I believe Holyfield may have tried to imitate. It has been hypothesised that a Marvin Hagler type of skull is optimally suited to absorbing and perhaps deflecting the energy of an impact. So a savvy professional like Holyfield, fully realising he lacked the physical toolbox to mix it with the big boys, sought enhancement. He always had the boxing skills, but he lacked the physicality of a natural heavyweight.

—February 2020

Cameron Mccall: What is the worst example of cheating you have ever seen in boxing?

J. A.: How about a guy named Evan Fields? In the opinion of many neutral and knowledgeable fans, Fields, aka Evander Holyfield, is consistently the worst covert cheat in heavyweight history. He should rightfully be nicknamed the Unreal Deal. The funny thing is that people inside the boxing fraternity have known about Holyfield's exploits for decades. People on social media wonder why boxing's popularity is on the decline. His blatant PED usage has been facilitated and hushed up. Worst-case scenario, he has been part of an elaborate Frankenstein's monster experiment.

There is circumstantial evidence indicating that Holyfield started juicing in the early part of

1993, when he hooked up with a new training partner, an ex-Mr Olympia bodybuilder by the name of Lee Haney. This guy Haney clearly knew a thing or two about steroids. After Holyfield was outgunned by Riddick Bowe, in the fall of 1992, came the realisation that he lacked the intrinsic firepower, physicality, and strength to mix it with the big boys. The fight with Bowe was closer than most observers realised, but it was a classic case of a good big guy beating a good little guy. How could Holyfield circumvent Bowe's lean muscle weight advantage?

Holyfield weighed around 204 pounds for the first Riddick Bowe fight. Less than ten months later, he tipped the scales at a lean, mean 215 pounds for the second fight. Where did that 11 pounds of extra lean mass suddenly come from?

We have all seen *Rocky 4*, which dates back to the ancient days of Cold War politics. We can all recall Ivan Drago being injected with anabolic steroids. That was a movie, and in Drago's case the steroids enhanced his punching power to superhuman levels. Maybe PEDs do in reality improve punching power, but in my opinion, the main real-world benefit is that they enhance and maximise those physical and aerobic characteristics associated with being box-fit. In short, a steroid user won't get tired and will be physically stronger at a given weight. He will be bigger, stronger, and fitter. He will have better stamina and better recovery. This is precisely what we have witnessed with Holyfield since 1993. In addition to this, his misdiagnosed heart condition in early 1994 was some kind of a blip on the PEDs radar.

In retrospect, Holyfield was and still is the greatest cruiserweight ever. In those days, he was clean. But unfortunately, there is a huge, dark cloud looming over his excursions into the heavyweight division.

—January 2019

Daniel Prestwich: People are accusing Joshua of steroid abuse. What are your thoughts?

J. A.: A. J. has apparently gained approximately 2 stone of pure lean muscle mass in approximately four years. His weight gain equates to around 8 ounces (or half a pound) of muscle mass per calendar month. Anyone who has done natural weight training will probably be raising an eyebrow. It isn't impossible to gain two stone of lean muscle mass in four years, but it is *very* difficult. However, looking at A. J. over the years, he is—as yet—showing no signs of a steroid skull, which leads me to believe he is naturally trained.

A few years ago, his father came into the ring after one of his fights and addressed this very issue. "Natural and lots of hard work," he said, or words to that effect. The steroid alarm bells have been ringing for a while now—it is nothing new. Any pro boxer who gains significant muscle mass while staying totally ripped raises suspicion these days.

Looking at A. J.'s recent performances, which have been less than stellar, again leads me to conclude he is probably clean. He is a huge guy, a natural heavyweight with a big frame, so it is easier for him to gain muscle. In bodybuilding terminology, he may well be classified as an easy gainer.

In many ways, A. J. reminds me of another British boxer from yesteryear named Frank Bruno, who was also built like a Greek statue and similarly moved around the ring like one. Back in the day, Bruno had a real Mr Universe physique that was definitely natural. So it can be done naturally, particularly if you are on the right diet and lifting heavy.

—December 2019

Farooq E. Subhan: How much do steroids determine how good a boxer is?

J. A.: By now we've all probably seen *Rocky 4* many times. We can recall the steroid-charged lead antagonist Ivan Drago sending Apollo Creed to an early grave. Even casual fans will probably realise that Drago (fictitiously, of course) was a limited boxer—nothing more than a brute-force slugger. His chief asset was his freakish punching power, which in the film was measured at around 2,000 PSI. Simply put, he hit around three times as hard as a normal heavyweight boxer! His power was depicted as largely being the result of anabolic steroids. PEDs enhanced his punching power to superhuman, bone-crushing levels.

Obviously this was a Hollywood movie, and movies by their very nature tend to exaggerate the details. Broadly speaking, the effects of steroids on boxers can be better understood and visualised if you look at the sport of boxing as being represented by a double-edged sword. The first side of the sword is all about skill and technique, whereas the second is all about the physical aspects of boxing, e.g., strength, stamina, fitness, training intensity, recovery from training and injuries, punch resistance, punch power, and dynamics. Steroids act only to enhance edge two, the physical characteristics of a boxer.

What do we observe within the confines of a boxing ring in a boxer who has been doping? Typically, the seasoned observer notices a large and suspicious skew in his performances. The drugs produce a distortion in the abuser's performance which cannot be explained through boxing reasons alone. In *Rocky 4*, the skew in Drago's performance was his freakish punching power, which could not be explained and traced back to his mediocre punching technique alone. There had to be something else producing the enhancement.

In the real boxing world, we wouldn't see dopers hitting three times as hard as the average boxer. What we may observe in an abuser is perhaps a 25 to 50 per cent improvement in punching power. It will be a subtle change in power which may initially go unnoticed, but essentially it will give an otherwise outgunned fighter more equalising firepower. Other artefacts that we may observe is a fighter who doesn't seem to fatigue or who suddenly starts walking through punches that would previously have knocked him out.

Maybe the most easily observable artefact of steroids in a fighter is a distinct increase in lean muscle mass in a short space of time, such as that exhibited by Evander Holyfield. This gain in pure lean muscle will give him a big covert strength advantage in the clinches—invaluable to an in-fighter such as Holyfield. The illicit gain in muscle mass will not cause a corresponding loss in velocity, which is obviously highly suspicious.

Another performance alarm bell will be an anomalous fluctuation in his performance which once again cannot be explained through boxing technique alone. Typically the abuser will perform better against stronger opposition and relatively worse against inferior opposition—the exact opposite of what you would normally observe in an unenhanced world-class boxer. Essentially the steroids will act to dilute and spoil the skill factor of a superior, natural opponent.

Finally, the abuser will exhibit a big timeline differential between his technical peak and his physical peak; typically his physical prime will lag far behind his technical prime.

In summary, going back to the double-edged sword analogy, you will eventually end up with a lopsided, uneven sword because the drugs sharpen only *one* side of the sword.

—October 2019

Victoria Hartzema: Was Arnold Schwarzenegger only big because he was on steroids?

J. A.: Schwarzenegger was a big dude for various reasons, one of which was without doubt chronic, hardcore steroid abuse. According to legend and hearsay, in his heyday he was popping twenty-five Dianabol tablets a day with his one-time training partner, Sergio Oliva. I think most ethical medics and pharmacists would agree that this amount of Dianabol was slightly more than the recommended daily allowance.

Both guys were genetic freaks, at the very top of the bodybuilding food chain. Perhaps more sinisterly, both guys were also self-confessed steroid freaks. So I suppose you're wondering, what if a random couch-potato Joe Public took the same juice as Arnold? Would he not one day become just as well built as Arnold too? It's not quite so simple and straightforward—the steroids act as performance enhancers. The steroid doesn't create lean muscle all on its own but enhances what you have and your performance. So in theory, if the couch-potato guy trained as intensely as Arnold, consumed the same diet, took the same steroids, and had the same genetic profile, then I suppose he may one day be as big as Arnold.

But I can give you a prime example of what Arnold may have looked like minus the steroids. A legendary natural bodybuilder named Steve Reeves was virtually the same height and frame size as Arnold. He generally weighed around 15 1/2 stone in his heyday. Reeves was probably the last great natural bodybuilder before the dawn of the 'roid freaks forever changed the bodybuilding landscape. Steroids enabled Arnold to pack on about two stone of extra pure lean mass; otherwise Reeves was as good as Arnold.

—November 2019

George Wilkin: Did Mike Tyson ever take steroids? If so, at what point in his career did he start using them?

J. A.: Mike Tyson aged thirteen, weighed in at a whopping 190 pounds of lean mass! Teddy Atlas has explained it time and time again—he had to show people this kid's birth certificate to make them believe his age. Tyson was physically very mature at a young age. Some guys are just like this. It's called hormones—specifically testosterone. Tyson obviously had an unusually high testosterone level at a young age, which would also conveniently explain his unusual propensity to youth-based violence. If he doped as a youth, he would have had to start as a preteen, which is highly unlikely.

If you also look closely at images of Tyson age thirteen, you can clearly see that his muscles look natural, with no signs whatsoever of a steroid/HGH skull. He also has no signs whatsoever of hair loss or drug-induced acromegaly. This leads me to believe that he is indeed 100 per cent naturally trained and simply has exceptional genetics.

Moving along his timeline, at the age of eighteen, Tyson was preparing to make his pro debut in the spring of 1985. He had a well-muscled, natural look with no hair loss or facial asymmetry, such as a heavily pointed chin or a "pumpkin" face.

In early 1992, literally on his way to prison, Tyson again showed no hair loss, facial distortions, or signs of a Neanderthal-type skull. So I'm virtually 100 per cent sure that for the entire decade of the 1980s into the early 1990s, this guy was clean and boxed legit.

If he ever took steroids, which is a big if, it would have been after his defeat by Holyfield. Even then, I seriously doubt he took them. But if he did, in 1997 or later, he would have realised that he was up against a whole load of cheaters. It would be unsurprising if he adopted an attitude of "well, if I can't beat 'em, then I may as well join 'em". He did bulk up in the late 1990s, but that was due in large part to heavy weight training. Originally he only engaged in volume callisthenics, but he modified his routines under later trainers.

He was also involved with wrestling by the late 1990s and a more bulked-up look was preferred. Again, he showed no signs of hair loss, so I personally doubt he ever took steroids. Plenty of weed, yes, but no juice.

—November 2019

Younis Akram: Is Ronnie Coleman stronger than Arnold Schwarzenegger?

J. A.: Coleman is probably stronger overall than Schwarzenegger and is a prime candidate for the strongest bodybuilder ever. He has regularly been observed squatting six plates each side to failure, which equates to around 260 kilograms. Arnold has also squatted six plates each side, but only for one or two reps. So Coleman is definitely stronger in terms of lower body strength.

Arnold was also big on squats in the 1970s. But due to his longer legs, he couldn't consistently handle as much weight as Ronnie.

Judging by side-profile upper-body images of these two legends, again Coleman looks the stronger guy.

However on the bench press and inclined bench press, Schwarzenegger has racked up similar if not better numbers than Coleman. Both guys have benched in excess of 220 kilograms, which equates to five plates each side. So, given that Arnold has longer arms than Ronnie, it's likely that he had a stronger chest.

When it comes to dumbbell workouts, though, I think Coleman is probably in a league of his own. This guy could probably rival strongmen in terms of the weight of the dumbbells he has handled.

—November 2019

Farooq E. Subhan: How do Arnold Schwarzenegger's genes compare with Ronnie Coleman?

J. A.: One of the classic bodybuilding poses is the double biceps pose. Judging from this front-on pose, I think Schwarzenegger probably has the edge—that is, purely from a genetic standpoint. Additionally, from an aesthetic viewpoint, his midriff generally appears totally flat, whereas Coleman is showing clear signs of steroid or HGH gut. Coleman has a significantly larger lat spread, which was probably his biggest bodybuilding strength. But in general, his V-taper doesn't compare favourably with Schwarzenegger's, due to his larger waist measurement. As far as legs are concerned, there is no comparison—Coleman is way bigger.

At the end of the day, it all depends on what type of physique the judges of the day preferred. In Schwarzenegger's era, I think shape and symmetry superseded size. Since the early 1990s and the dawn of the mass monster, the intrinsic size of the muscle has become the major vote-winner.

In Schwarzenegger's era, the giant Lou Ferrigno was way bigger than the competition but never won a Mr Olympia contest. Apparently he lacked proportion, which supposedly was the result of slightly inferior genetics. To me, he looked equally as well built and symmetrical as Schwarzenegger, but obviously bodybuilding judges are ultra-critical and pick up on the smallest details.

In terms of pure bodybuilding genetics, Coleman is not the finest specimen of his generation.

A bodybuilder named Flex Wheeler supposedly had better genetics than Ronnie Coleman, but he couldn't compete with Coleman's sheer size. Staying with the Arnold versus Ronnie comparison, I would give Schwarzenegger the edge from a genetic standpoint. With his natural genetics combined with modern training methods (and advances in the juice), who knows how big he could have been today?

One thing is for sure: for his era, Arnold was a great blend of size, structure, and symmetry. But even he admits that he wasn't the number-one genetic freak of the 1970s. That accolade goes to a bodybuilder known as the Myth. His name was Sergio Oliva, and he had a physique that was superhero-grade material. Bodybuilding politics prevented this guy from being as famous as Schwarzenegger, but he was Arnold's one-time training partner. To this day, Sergio remains the only guy to defeat Arnold at a Mr Olympia contest.

—October 2019

Gregory Bolden: Who wins between a hardcore steroid user and a natural athlete?

J. A.: Take one look at almost any natural bodybuilder and compare him to maybe the number-one steroid freak in bodybuilding history, Ronnie Coleman, and you decide. As far as I can see, there is only one winner. While most natural bodybuilders still have fairly respectable physiques, without doubt they are all going to get kicked off the stage by Ronnie Coleman at a bodybuilding contest.

In almost any physical sport, the steroid freak wins easily, seven days a week, 365 days a year—as long as he or she is reasonably athletic in natural form. In other words, you can't just get an out-of-shape couch potato, feed him high-dose performance enhancers, and turn him into Superman in two weeks. It doesn't work like that. The steroid freak has to have decent genetics and some talent (and train hard) in the first place for the juice to be really beneficial.

Back in the day, I observed first-hand the benefits of juicing. This one steroid freak I weight-trained with, who was a good power lifter to begin with, turned into a gym monster over about a two-year period. His favourite exercise was the flat bench press. He started out at a very respectable standard, benching two plates each side, which equated to around 100 kilograms total. Shortly after he started sticking hypodermic needles into himself, you guessed it—his performance improved in a very short space of time. I can honestly say, as his spotter, that he went from benching 100 kilograms to 180 kilograms in about eighteen months! That is an improvement of 80 per cent on the same exercise in an eighteen-month period, which is physically impossible when training in the natural form.

For any young sports fans who have doubts about the true power of steroids, let's rewind the clock to the Seoul Olympics in 1988 and concentrate on the men's 100 metre sprint final. One of the favourites for the gold medal was a shady individual named Ben Johnson, who went on to become the most notorious 100 metre sprinter in history. At the time, this guy possessed a unique look: bulging red eyes and a well-muscled physique. Additionally he was destroying the opposition in the late 1980s.

His main competitor was a guy named Carl Lewis, who was without doubt, the best natural sprinter in the world. But Lewis simply could not match Johnson's absolutely explosive, flying starts out of the blocks. Hmm, I wonder why? Johnson tested positive for various banned substances and was immediately stripped of his gold medal. The drug-assisted world record he had set was wiped off the slate. In the short term, cheaters always win, but in the long term they generally lose (unless, of course, your name is Evan Fields).

—September 2019

FURQAN TARIQUE: What is the physique difference between Sylvester Stallone and Arnold Schwarzenegger?

J.A.: There is obviously a big difference in muscular size, bodyweight and intimidation potential, whereby Schwarzenegger has way more physical presence due to these aforementioned factors. For his era, Arnold was a symmetrical mass monster, whereas Stallone was a reasonably well muscled gym rat, who "punched" above his weight due to his filmography.

Hypothetically speaking, if Stallone was a pro bodybuilder in Arnold's era, he would probably have been in the same weight class as Arnold's one time training partner in Pumping Iron, Franco Columbo. Anyone who watched Pumping Iron back in the day would realise that Arnold was in the category known as "the tall man" class. Stallone who stands around 5ft9" would not have made that class.

In terms of specific muscle groups where there is literally no comparison is the chest and biceps— the showcase muscles of a bodybuilder. Even to this day, forty years later Arnold's chest and biceps are gold standard benchmarks for the industry... Make no mistake, Stallone at his peak, probably in Rocky 4 too had a very respectable physique and had notable definition but he never came close to attaining Arnold's muscular hypertrophy.

—May 2021

CHAPTER 10

LEGENDARY NIGHTS AT THE FIGHTS

LAURA HARMON: What are some of the best boxing fights of all time to watch (not including Muhammad Ali, George Foreman, or Mike Tyson)?

J. A.: In no particular order, the following are ten fights you need to see before you die:

Marvin Hagler versus Thomas Hearns (1985)

Just read the headlines with this one. It was the closest thing to all-out, full-intensity war in a boxing ring. There were no tactics, no strategy, and almost no defence; these two crazy guys simply stood toe to toe and traded bombs.

Alexis Arguello versus Aaron Pryor (1982)

This was another classic 1980s slugfest—q seriously bruising affair with almost as much action as a Rocky movie. The first time you see this fight, you'll be glued to your seat, as you simply don't know which guy is gonna come out on top.

Nigel Benn versus Gerald McClellan (1995)

Unfortunately this fight ended in tragedy, but it was an all-time classic—a real to-and-fro battle of wills and skills.

Arturo Gatti versus Micky Ward (2002)

No love was lost between these two career rivals. They had some of the most fierce exchanges I can remember in recent times. These two went to war in a classic machismo-filled, bruising trilogy which took its toll on both warriors.

Marco Antonio Barrera versus Erik Morales

These two legendary warriors went to war in a classic 2000s trilogy. My favourite was the first fight. It had plenty of machismo but also a lot of skill on show.

Vitali Klitschko versus Lennox Lewis (2003)

One of the great heavyweight showdowns of the twenty-first century occurred between these two huge and reasonably athletic guys. In the end, the fight was stopped because of cuts to Klitschko's face, which is always an unsatisfactory way to end a fight. Lewis was behind on the judges' scorecards at the time of the stoppage, and to this day boxing fans are still left wondering what might have happened.

Evander Holyfield versus Riddick Bowe (1992)

Hard to believe this fight happened almost thirty years ago, but it is one fight that is etched into my memory. It's perhaps the quintessential modern example of what happens when a good big guy takes on a good little guy. In the end, Bowe's heavier artillery proved decisive.

Thomas Hearns versus Roberto Duran (1984)

Because of the beatdown that Hearns inflicted on Duran, you'd be forgiven for thinking that Duran was a club fighter rather than a legend. The finishing punch from Hearns, for my money, was the most chilling unseen punch of the modern era.

Julio Caesar Chavez versus Edwin Rosario (1987)

This match showcases one of the best examples of pressure or in-fighting I can remember in recent times. Chavez was up against a very dangerous and world-class opponent, but on the night he put on a body-punching masterclass.

Jack Dempsey versus Jess Willard (1919)

This is my favourite fight from the really old-school days of boxing. Dempsey proved that a good little guy can, for a change, beat a good big guy.

—October 2020

Jeff Isozaki: What was the greatest rivalry (i.e., Ali–Frazier, Leonard–Hearns, Hagler–Hearns, etc.) in boxing?

J. A.: The following is a brief list of heated boxing rivalries of yesteryear:

Ali versus Frazier

This was probably the most heated, bitter, and well-publicised rivalry in boxing history. Frazier hated Ali and also the names that Ali had been calling him. He certainly used this hatred to fuel both his training workouts and real-time fighting intensity. On the other hand, Ali often clowned around and simply sold the fight to mass-market casual fans.

During their famous scuffle at ABC Studios in 1974, a distinctly agitated Frazier said to Ali's face, "You wanna do it right now?" Again, Ali was probably clowning around and goading Frazier, but Joe obviously had other ideas and an alternative sense of humour.

Benn versus Eubank

Make no mistake: there was a time when "the Dark Destroyer" Nigel Benn genuinely hated Chris "Simply the Best" Eubank. This wasn't a case of fake marketing hatred. No, this was genuine bad chemistry. In some respects, there were similarities in this all-British rivalry that mirrored that of Ali versus Frazier. Eubank thought of himself as an intellectual boxer who aspired to become a British aristocrat. He regarded Benn as a crazy animal who was merely another stepping stone on his road to riches.

Gatti versus Ward

Boxing fans do like their trilogies, and these two guys went to war in the early 2000s like a couple of old-school brawlers. Without doubt, some of the fierce exchanges between these two warriors were up there with the likes of the legendary Hagler versus Hearns war. See the 2010 Hollywood film *The Fighter* for a biographical account of Mickey Ward's boxing career.

Barrera versus Morales

If you like a bit of good old-fashioned Latin machismo, then look no further than this all-Mexican matchup. These two legends also went to war in a classic 2000s trilogy. As if there wasn't enough spice in the ring, there was also some genuine animosity on the outside. In one pre-fight interview, Barrera sucker-punched Morales in the face with a bare-knuckle fist.

Ali versus Norton

These two guys had probably the most intriguing stylistic matchup in heavyweight history. While Frazier may have been Ali's most stubborn adversary, Norton was Ali's stylistic bogeyman. In total, these two legends boxed for a total of thirty-nine rounds over the course of three "human chess matches" during boxing's golden era.

—December 2019

Matson Ruddell, Darren Blackburn, and one more: What is the best boxing match you have ever seen?

J. A.: In the good old days of boxing, the pre-fight stare-downs were genuine and intense encounters which often served as appetizers to the main course.

When Hagler and Hearns gave each other the evil eye, rest assured that you knew they meant business. Hagler looked tougher and more menacing, whereas Hearns looked more dangerous. During such stare-downs, it was interesting to note their vastly differing profiles, which were perhaps indicative of the vastly different punch resistance of these two warriors.

Theirs was the most action-packed and intense eight minutes of boxing in recent memory. US commentator Al Michaels summed the fight up perfectly: "It didn't last long, but it was a beauty." The manner in which these two legendary warriors laid into each other was the closest thing to a real-life version of Rocky Balboa versus Clubber Lang that I can recall. Tactics went out of the window, game plans were shredded, and the fight simply descended into an all-out backstreet war.

The build-up to this fight was electric and set the stage perfectly for the fight itself. Hagler referred to this fight simply as "the war" and frankly stated that there were only two things on his mind: "destruction and destroy." He was both angry and respectful of the Hitman. In one televised interview, Hagler praised Hearns for the two-round demolition job he had carried out on Roberto Duran. That same Duran had gone the distance with Hagler just six months earlier, and this fact was hard for Hagler to stomach. He threatened to "break every bone in Hearns's body". Hearns rebuffed Hagler and vowed to prove that his vaunted punch could also put the top middleweight to sleep.

The surprising thing at the time was that it was Hagler who initiated the all-out slugfest and from the outset went after Hearns with a vengeance. Hagler's highly aggressive approach was completely counter-intuitive. Most experts expected Hagler to be cautious in the early going, especially given the fact that Hearns was such a murderous early-rounds puncher. Hagler threw caution to the wind and simply went after Hearns to the body and head, going gung-ho for the knockout. He left himself wide open to counterpunches and almost paid the price. Hagler was surely the only middleweight on the planet who could have absorbed those right hands from Hearns. Ultimately it was Hagler's all-time great chin that proved to be the difference between the two fighters.

The punching exchanges were truly ferocious, with both fighters sustaining early damage. Hagler in particular prevailed against the odds, as he sustained a deep cut to his forehead which almost forced a referee's stoppage. Shortly after referee Richard Steele brought the cut to the doctor's attention, Hagler floored the gas pedal, went ballistic, and knocked out Thomas Hearns with his own peach of a right cross. It would have been interesting to see what may have transpired had Hearns not unfortunately fractured his own right hand in the first round.

—March 2019

ANONYMOUS: Do you think Lennox Lewis feared Vitali Klitschko to the point that he retired instead of having a rematch with him?

J. A.: One hundred per cent yes! Given his age at the time, do you really think Lewis wanted to taste Dr Iron Fist's right cross again? This power punch evaded Lewis's mediocre defence all too easily. Lewis made his bones during the late 1990s and early 2000s by being longer than the competition. In general, under Manny Steward, this formula worked a treat. Against Vitali, it clearly *didn't* work, as Lewis no longer had those physical advantages. On top of this, Vitali was a cerebral fighter, had decent athleticism for a giant, and had a well-known granite chin. With Father Time creeping up, if I were in Lewis's shoes, I would have done exactly the same thing—it was time for a sharp exit. It's always better to retire by choice than by force.

Having said the above, I don't think for a second that Lewis was afraid of Vitali. He was afraid of losing. There is a subtle difference. The rematch would have been a real fifty-fifty fight, and I suggest the timing of the fight favoured the Ukrainian. He was ahead on all the judges' scorecards when the fight was stopped. He generally had the upper hand in the early rounds, controlling the tempo of the fight and landing the harder shots.

Hypothetically speaking, if Lewis had, say, lost the rematch, this would have damaged his legacy. Any defeat is never good, but ending his career on a defeat to one of his heir apparents would have been much worse. In some respects it would have been the same as Carl Froch retiring on a losing note to George Groves. Froch was forced into a rematch with Groves due to public clamour, whereas the same couldn't be said about Lewis versus Vitali.

Lewis made a real mess of Vitali's face. This fact no doubt gave him satisfaction and consolatory peace of mind. That is to say, in general, the end of a boxing match is probably more important than the beginning. If Vitali had mashed up Lewis's face in the same way, there is no doubt there may have been more grounds for a rematch.

Ultimately by retiring, Lewis made a smart career decision and chose the lesser of two evils. He apparently claims that he took the fight with Vitali on very short notice, which is believable. No doubt the pay-off was worth the risk. In potentially taking a rematch with Klitschko, the risk would have far outweighed the reward, especially now that he also had hindsight as a decision maker. In the cold light of day, had he lost a potential rematch with Vitali, then his historical position as a top-ten heavyweight would have been in serious jeopardy. Even now, according to the majority of expert opinion, he only just about scrapes into the top ten.

—March 2019

ARROW JAYKRIS: In the first Clay–Liston fight, did Liston ever land a good shot on Clay?

J. A.: Judging from the cartoonish and nonchalant expression on Clay's face while he sat on his stool at the end of round one, I would say no. He was having fun in there against a harmless old bear.

Liston landed a few jabs and a few body shots but very few clean hooks or crosses to the head. In this fight, Clay's judgement of distance was near perfect, and he had surely practised his geometry.

The general game plan was for Clay to rotate in a clockwise direction around Liston, on a circle with a radius of approximately 42.5 inches. Literally every time he saw one of Liston's gloves move, he would either shuffle backwards or lean backwards.

Liston mostly punched thin air, as Clay's reflexes were too sharp for him. After two rounds of scouting, Clay realised there was no threat and so became more flat-footed. He started putting more sting into his combos.

In the later rounds, Liston had some fleeting success, particularly when Clay started complaining about the "mystery substance" that had gone into his eyes. But still nothing major landed and certainly not Liston's favourite left hook punch.

The main differences between the two boxers in that fight were hand and foot speed—Clay was way faster and made Liston look like an old man.

—December 2020

Jeffrey Dog: Did Sugar Ray Leonard really beat Marvin Hagler?

J. A.: Leonard got the decision, but he didn't beat Hagler. Almost thirty-five years later, this controversial split decision still inspires much banter and retrospective analysis, dividing boxing opinion right down the middle. One thing is for sure: the judge who scored that fight 118–110 in favour of Leonard was a disgrace. The other two scorecards of 115–113 apiece were fair and understandable.

The biggest in-fight mistake that Hagler made was starting the fight as a righty. That wasn't what he did best. While he was comfortable boxing from either stance, his best work was generally done as a southpaw. This tactical blunder cost him all the early rounds. It is entirely possible that Team Leonard had predicted the bluff and knew Hagler would start as a righty and switch stances later. But anyway Hagler was definitely behind going into the second half of the fight.

In the middle and later rounds, Hagler came on strong and generally bossed the action, but Leonard was always competitive in the exchanges. Leonard also made sure that he landed a few eye-catching flurries at the ends of rounds, which definitely influenced the judges. Throughout the fight a general pattern emerged, whereby Hagler's punches had more authority and Leonard's work was more eye-catching.

On my unofficial scorecard, I personally scored that legendary fight 114–114, an even draw, which would have been the fairest result. In the event of a draw, Hagler would have retained his belts, which surely would have led to an even more lucrative rematch.

In terms of the bigger picture, one area where Leonard did beat Hagler was in the tactical department. Team Leonard had insisted on a larger ring and a reduced twelve-round fight duration; Hagler nonchalantly conceded to both requests, which also backfired in the fight.

—January 2021

Monica R. Smith: In your opinion, what was Mike Tyson's greatest professional fight?

J. A.: There were many memorable Tyson fights, but the one against Trevor Berbick stands out the most. This was obviously the fight when Tyson became champion and truly announced his arrival on the global stage. For a change, all the pressure and expectation was on the challenger Tyson, and he more than lived up to his billing on judgement night.

Until this fight, critics had been saying that Tyson was beating nobodies. Berbick was definitely a big step up in class. His main claims to fame were finally retiring an ageing Muhammad Ali and giving a peak Larry Holmes a serious argument. So there were some experts who believed that Berbick would test Tyson.

They couldn't have been more wrong. A rampaging Tyson was equally rude to the WBC heavyweight champion of the world. Tyson settled the argument with a surreal and brutal second-round knockout, dropping Berbick three times with one punch! In many ways, this was an unprecedented knockout which served to highlight Mike Tyson's unique knockout power. In the process, Kid Dynamite made history, becoming the youngest-ever heavyweight champion of the world, aged just 20, and fulfilling the prophecy of his late, great trainer, Cus D'Amato. Cus had predicted that Tyson would one day become heavyweight champion of the world after first seeing him shadow-box at the age of 13!

—November 2019

Shaun Duggal: Did Foreman take a dive against Ali in 1974?

J. A.: If he did take a dive, it sure as hell was a thespian act worthy of an Academy Award. No, Foreman definitely did not take a dive against Ali; that was a 100 per cent legitimate knockout victory. However, it is a fairly well-established fact that it was largely an exhaustion-facilitated knockout, given the fact that Foreman had totally gassed. The final light one-two combo that Ali landed on Foreman's chin completely took the wind out of Foreman's sails and sent him over. On the canvas, it was clear from Foreman's posture that he was down but not out. He was literally 100 per cent fatigued and had completely run out of steam.

During the course of the fight, Ali landed many solid punches on Foreman, and there was nothing fake about any of them. In particular, he put a lot of sting into some of his right crosses and demonstrated that he could punch with bad intentions when the need arose. Ali was never renowned as being a hard puncher but still had good power when he was forced into a tight spot.

Just in case there is any confusion, the guy who more likely took a dive against Ali was Sonny Liston in their rematch in 1965. He went over in the first round from the so-called "phantom" punch, which was so fast that everybody missed it—including the intended target. The phantom punch did land, but it was a very soft punch. Ali himself didn't believe that it was hard enough to knock out a still-fresh Liston. After scoring this innocuous-looking knockdown, Ali screamed at Liston to get back up, as he thought Liston was play-acting.

Another reason that many people suspected this fight was fixed was because Liston was known to be a Mob-controlled fighter who owed debts. It has been speculated that he took a dive in a predetermined round at the behest of his Mafia bosses. This gambling spot-fix effectively wrote off Liston's debts.

Getting back to the Foreman fight, there is still some controversy and ambiguity, but that is more to do with external forces than Foreman himself. Both Ali's trainer Angelo Dundee and Foreman's trainer Dick Sadler were possibly involved in underhand practices before and during the fight. There is strong speculation that Dundee was allowed to loosen the ring ropes, which facilitated Ali's now legendary rope a dope tactic. Sadler had dual loyalties to both fighters, and it has been speculated that he gave Foreman the wrong advice during the fight. Fuel was added to the fire when, years later, Sadler became a member of Ali's entourage.

—October 2019

Otto Heinrich Heinz: What are the major mistakes Mike Tyson made against Lennox Lewis? How could he have beaten him?

J. A.: Smoking too much weed was definitely a big mistake!

The primary mistake Tyson made was to sign up for the fight in the first place. Had he not been in so much financial strife, that fight wouldn't have happened. It was a well-known inside-industry fact that in 2002, with his poor mental attitude and lack of training, Tyson had almost no chance of beating Lewis. By his own impeccable standards, he was a completely shot fighter.

But let's assume for a second that he took the fight with Lewis seriously. What could Tyson have done differently to improve his chances?

Mike Tyson was always a sixteen stone fighter. In the Lewis fight, he was carrying at least an extra stone of excess baggage. This is a lot of excess weight, particularly for a dynamic and explosive fighter like Tyson. So, bottom line, he came in too heavy.

He could have thrown way more punches and generally been busier all round. In his heyday, throwing "punches in bunches" was a hallmark of his famed peekaboo style. Against Lewis, his combinations were absent.

In the Lewis fight, Tyson seemingly couldn't avoid Lewis's jab. This punch was pivotal in determining the outcome of the fight. With Lewis, almost everything flows off his jab, and on the night, Tyson was a sitting-duck target. In the end, it was an easy night's work for Lewis because he couldn't miss Tyson with the jab.

—December 2020

Arne Van Lamoen: Why did Mike Tyson fail to knock out James Tillis in 1986?

J. A.: Having analysed this fight on various occasions, and also taking into consideration Tyson's post-fight interview, I believe James Tillis was used as something of a guinea pig.

"Going ten rounds in there for the first time, I was having some fun," said Tyson. This leads me to conclude that Team Tyson used Tillis to ensure that Tyson had sufficient stamina to go the distance, in readiness for world-class competition. There were several unknowns surrounding Tyson going into the Tillis fight. One of them was the question of whether he could take a solid power punch. Another was could he fight at a high tempo for the entire duration of a fight? The second question was conclusively answered by Tyson as he stormed over the finish line without gassing. Prior to the Tillis fight, he had mauled everybody into submission in double-quick time.

So his trainer, Kevin Rooney, needed to make sure Tyson's heart could cope with the intensity and pace of a long championship-grade bout.

It is interesting to note that Tyson didn't target Tillis's body with major intent. Tillis was a classic spoiler whose main tactic was "stick and move". If Tyson had wanted to restrict Tillis's movements, he would surely have punished him more to the body to take away his legs. Instead, Tyson operated almost exclusively as a headhunter. Again, this reinforces the theory that James Tillis was used as a guinea pig, the primary objective being to dispel any doubts surrounding Tyson's stamina.

British heavyweight Frank Bruno took on pretty much the same Tillis a year later, in 1987. The technically limited Bruno got Tillis out of there in five rounds—and yet Tillis had lasted the distance against Tyson. Of course fighting Bruno was a different matchup to Tyson, but something doesn't quite add up. Again, I suggest that if Tyson had really wanted to, he could easily have KO'd James Tillis. If Bruno could do it, then I see no reason why Tyson couldn't do the same—unless of course it was a pre-planned experiment.

—November 2019

Jovanne Rodriguez: Did Mike Tyson have a lot of trouble with Bonecrusher Smith? Watching the fight go the distance and seeing Bone Crusher land a significant hit seem to indicate that he had something Tyson's other opponents lacked.

J. A.: On the night, against prime Tyson, James Smith showed the world how technically proficient he was at the art of "hugging and mugging". The sight of him holding Tyson became an enduring image in a fight that the tabloid media labelled "the Bonecrusher Smith waltz". Smith hugged Tyson like a long-lost brother. When he wasn't hugging Tyson, he was running. It's a good job Tyson didn't have any money on him; otherwise Smith would definitely have robbed him!

So yes, on that night the Iron Man did have trouble dealing with Bonecrusher's grappling tactics. Smith had done his homework and refused point-blank to exchange any punches with Tyson in the kill zone. I can't really blame him. If I were in his shoes, I would have done the exact same thing: grab for dear life or run for your life! He made absolutely sure not to allow Tyson to unload with his patented combos in the kill-zone. Those were the days when Tyson was so fast and vicious, he could maul you into submission in a matter of seconds. So Smith employed a vaccine-type strategy, along the lines that prevention was better than cure.

Smith deserves some credit. He is an intelligent guy and a college graduate. His intelligence and his survival instincts were certainly two ingredients that many of Tyson's other opponents lacked. When you are totally outmatched in almost every boxing facet, then your best chance of survival is simply through spoiling. And Smith sure as hell proved to be a pretty good spoiler on the night! Additionally, he was a very strong man and needed every ounce of that strength to keep Pitbull Tyson muzzled on the inside.

Smith also had confidence in his ultra-negative game plan. He had a mindset that he was going to stick to this plan no matter what Tyson threw at him. His plan was simply not to engage with Tyson at all on the inside or in the mid range. Was Smith scared? Maybe he was, maybe he wasn't, but at least he didn't fall apart on the night like so many of prime Tyson's other opponents.

In interviews that he gave years and years later, he blamed media hype at the time for perpetuating the invincibility aura of heyday Tyson.

As for the big punch that he landed right at the end of the fight, let's just say he got lucky. Tyson was bored, frustrated, and tired. Smith did the same thing against Frank Bruno in 1983; he was well behind on the scorecards, but sucker-punched an unsuspecting Bruno in the last round. He cornered Bruno on the ropes shortly before scoring the against-the-tide knockout.

Make no mistake: Smith could bang and was what is known in the industry as a sneaky fighter who often liked playing possum. If he had tried to be aggressive against Tyson from the outset, he inevitably would have been mauled in the same way as most of Tyson's other opponents.

So Smith scores highly as far as ring IQ is concerned. He fulfilled one of Sun Tzu's ancient rules of combat: "When your enemy is superior to you, evade him at all costs."

—May 2019

Kinyanjui Kamau: What could Trevor Berbick have done differently in 1986 to prevent a young Mike Tyson from claiming his championship belt?

J. A.: The late Trevor Berbick was as brave and tough as they came—a true old-school warrior. He was the type of guy who, if you paid him the right amount of money, he'd have taken on a silverback. He had no fear whatsoever of any guy, not even prime Tyson. If I had been in his shoes, I would have relinquished the WBC belt and simply ducked Tyson. Berbick was always a proud champion, and in 1986 he bravely faced his mandatory challenger like a true warrior. I can think of many other guys in that era who would and indeed did duck Tyson like the plague.

Berbick's mentality on the night was to show everyone how brave and tough he was. To do so, he literally stood right in front of a rampaging Tyson, who himself had a lot to prove. At the time, standing in front of Tyson was a big mistake because Tyson was the hardest short-range puncher ever. But Berbick couldn't have cared less about Tyson's reputation and mistakenly decided to sample the eye of the storm.

Berbick generally stood way too close to Tyson. On various occasions in that short-lived fight, he almost invited Tyson to throw his right hook with full leverage. In slow motion, you can see Tyson targeting Berbick's left ear with a punishing right hook, trying to induce cauliflower ear. In one post-fight interview, Tyson admitted to going after Berbick's ears deliberately to upset his balance and equilibrium. There was literally no point in having a height and reach advantage if Berbick wasn't going to use it.

In the early going, Berbick had to box behind his jab and keep the fight going for as long as possible. Right from the get-go he was nowhere near busy enough with his jab. When Tyson got close, he needed to grab for dear life, but he failed to do this because of his own machismo. Other spoiling tactics he could have used were wrestling and roughhousing on the inside. To simplify, he really needed to tie his man up on the inside at all costs.

In summary, even if Berbick had adopted a less kamikaze approach, it would simply have delayed the inevitable. He may have lasted a few rounds longer had he used a more sensible approach, but he was still getting knocked out sooner or later. At that time, prime Tyson was the best gap closer in the business. He would inevitably have got to a game Berbick at some point in the fight.

—November 2019

Joshua Luttrell: What did Joe Frazier do wrong when fighting George Foreman, and what did he need to do?

J. A.: If you don't mind, let me turn the question on its head. What did he do right? Almost nothing, apart from throwing a lethal left hook which Foreman described as a "rifle shot" in the 1980s boxing documentary *Champions Forever.* It just grazed his whiskers. Other than this, Frazier did his usual "runaway freight train" thing. He didn't realise he was running into an immovable object. To cut a long story short, Foreman was a better and stronger grappler than Frazier. When they collided, Foreman simply pushed Frazier around like a grizzly bear, literally manhandling a one-dimensional pit bull terrier.

The 1973 "Sunshine Showdown" was a mismatch due to a clash of styles which heavily favoured the slugger (Foreman). In such matchups, the swarmer (Frazier) needs to avoid the slugger in the early rounds. Frazier clearly failed to do this. He literally walked head-first into huge punches, thereby doubling their impact. His famed bob-and-weave defence clearly failed against Foreman because he bobbed and weaved right in front of a massive puncher. Foreman was so powerful that he was able to punch right through Frazier's guard.

In stark contrast to Frazier, compare Ali's strategy when handling Foreman. Ali maintained an extremely high and tight head guard and denied Foreman any head target whatsoever, even when stood on the ropes. Against almost everyone else, Ali boxed with his hands low, but against Foreman, he knew he had to raise his guard. It is safe to say that Ali had a much higher ring IQ than Frazier and made the necessary adjustments to neutralise Foreman. It is also fairly apparent that Ali had superior glove control to Frazier.

In the rematch with Foreman in 1976, Frazier bulked up by a stone. This flawed tactic made little difference to the outcome. He lasted a few rounds longer but still walked head-first into huge, swinging punches. No one in boxing history can take several bombs in a row from a tremendous power man like prime Foreman; he was simply too powerful and strong early on. As Ali and Jimmy Young both demonstrated, a sensible and mobile counterpunching approach was required to beat Foreman.

—November 2019

Rodney Chin: Did George Foreman hurt Ali at all during their fight? It seems that he didn't connect any headshots.

J. A.: Having watched the fight a number of times, I think Foreman hurt Ali with body shots only (and the punches that landed on or were blocked by Ali's arms). Virtually none of his headshots landed cleanly, only as glancing blows. As Ali had a high pain tolerance, he simply sucked up the pain from the body pounding. As the fight progressed, he realised Foreman's power wasn't bothering him, as it wasn't precision power. Truth be told, Foreman was most effective from long range; his right cross was lethal at a certain distance. Ali's rope a dope tactic drew him in closer, thereby denying him his optimum leverage.

Foreman was never the best in-fighter, nor the most accurate of punchers. Ali made matters worse by upsetting his balance. Ali seemingly lay on the ropes for an eternity. Foreman had ample opportunity to execute the dreaded liver shot. Not once did he successfully land this punch. No matter who you are or how tough you are, it is a well-known fact that a really solid left hook to the liver causes temporary organ shutdown. Almost everyone goes down. So you would really have to question the effectivity of Foreman's body attacks. Nonetheless, with Foreman's heavy-handedness, body punches would still hurt, and the internal after-effects must have lasted for days or even weeks.

In my opinion, the rope a dope tactic remains a prime example of an appalling tactic which has become the stuff of legend because, on the night, it got the right result. If literally anybody else in the world had tried this stunt against Foreman, they would surely have been brutally knocked out. This legendary fight demonstrated why Ali was one of a kind.

—January 2019

Lee Leblanc: Did Mike Tyson train improperly for Lennox Lewis fight? Or was he just out of his prime and done?

J. A.: Both factors, really. By the time Mike faced off against Lewis in 2002, he was definitely washed up and all done. He spent half of that fight eating Lewis's signature right cross, so his once famed and impregnable defence was almost non-existent on the night. He was fourteen long years past his prime, which occurred in 1988 against Michael Spinks. After he split from his proper trainer, Kevin Rooney, shortly after the Spinks fight, he never again put in a full and proper training camp for any of his fights.

So when he fought Lewis, it was a money fight, pure and simple. He needed some big money fast because he was badly in debt. It is fair to say that had Mike not needed the money, he would never have contemplated facing a peak Lewis in the twilight of his own career.

In 2002, it was a stone-wall reality that Tyson had only a puncher's chance against Lewis. Even at his best, Lewis was always vulnerable to a big puncher, so Tyson tried his luck. But as we all saw during that dismal fight, Tyson barely threw a single hard punch with bad intentions. His box fitness, stamina, and cardio were literally a shell of his former self. On top of his physical decline, Tyson had some serious question marks over his mental health.

—June 2020

Brad Oxler: Which was a greater upset, Cassius Clay versus Sonny Liston or Muhammad Ali versus George Foreman?

J. A.: Leaving aside the bookies' odds for either fight (which can bias your opinion), I would say Ali upsetting Foreman was probably the bigger upset of the two. Liston 1 was still a big upset, but with the benefit of hindsight, we know that Liston's true biological age was greater than his documented age. This being the case, he was clearly well past his prime by the time a young braggart named Cassius Marcellus Clay got to him.

On the other hand, by 1974, Ali himself was slightly over the hill. He was still a great fighter but one in decline. This time round, the new ring monster on the scene was in his prime and at his fearsome best. In 1974, Foreman was a young, massive, and unstoppable juggernaut who was wiping away the opposition. He had significant momentum going into the Ali fight, and there were genuine fears for Ali's safety. In a great golden-era documentary called *Champions Forever*, Foreman remarked that he was being urged to use restraint and was being told, "Be careful, George—don't kill Muhammad." Against Liston, there were no such fears for Clay's safety.

—January 2020

Martin Asiner: How close did Henry Cooper come to beating Cassius Clay?

J. A.: Really close. Really, really close. So close, in fact, that Angelo Dundee, the brilliant trainer of Clay, had to tinker with his left glove in between rounds to buy some time. When Cooper threw his famous left hook, it landed clean and flush to Clay's jaw. It was a punch that Clay never saw coming—those are the ones that really get you. His legs totally buckled, and his body literally flopped into the ropes like the proverbial sack of spuds. He was virtually out and beat the count on instinct alone. Lucky for Clay—and indeed for the short-term financial future of heavyweight boxing—that punch landed right at the end of round four.

Cue lots of cold water, head massage, and the usual cornerman rantings. Dundee, ever the wily old fox, knew his fighter well and realised he needed more time to revive Clay. He spotted a small tear in Clay's glove and simply made it bigger. The tear was brought to the referee's attention, and the fight was temporarily halted while the torn glove was changed.

Needless to say, the few extra seconds ensured Clay was fully recuperated. He went back out to work on Cooper's cut, thereby fulfilling his fifth-round stoppage prediction: "If Cooper talks jive, he'll fall in five." According to Dundee's version of events, Clay could have stopped Cooper in round three, given the extent of the cut, but carried him to the fifth to make good his prediction. Alas, those were the days when he was selling fights based on his prophecies. He put tremendous pressure on himself making such round-specific predictions, but they sold tickets and the fight public of the day loved it. In the end, Clay survived a real scare and coincidentally showed the boxing world his first signs of vulnerability—good left hookers would haunt him for the rest of his career.

—December 2018

Michael Evans: Why was Buster Douglas so unmotivated when he became a champ?

J. A.: Buster Douglas was on an emotional high in the weeks before the Tyson fight due to the untimely passing of his mother. He used his family bereavement in a positive way and turned his sorrow into adrenaline and bravery. This highly charged emotional state only lasted for a short while—days or maybe a few weeks at the most.

After he pulled off the unthinkable, Douglas's hormones returned to normal, and he started enjoying his thirty-five minutes of fame and fortune. Approximately eight months and five hundred doughnuts later, he revealed his true colours and was exposed by Holyfield as nothing more than a one-hit heavyweight wonder. His weight for the Holyfield fight was 17 1/2 stone, and he looked sloppy to say the least. One tabloid headline of the day read, "Douglas floated like a buffalo and stung like a gnat". He collected his astronomical pay cheque and that was that.

—December 2020

LEVIATHAN CAMMOCK: I've been watching Muhammad Ali fights and noticed that he keeps his fists really low. How come?

J. A.: Guess what? Touché! I've also been watching Muhammad Ali fights and I too have noticed that he keeps his hands low.

Muhammad Ali had a lot of bad habits, and this was one of them. When you're a superior athlete with great reflexes, you can afford to have a few bad habits. To make a long story short, his defence was brilliant but flawed. He hardly ever blocked punches. Instead he chose to sway side to side or lean backwards. In his heyday, he was a dancing master and so could control the centre of the ring. Killers like Sonny Liston couldn't corner him. Ali could afford to drop his hands in Liston 1 because his fast feet kept him out of harm's way.

Fast-forward ten years. By the mid 1970s, Ali's reflexes had declined and he couldn't dance anymore—at least not for fifteen rounds. So against Foreman, his hands were up.

The other main reason Ali kept his hands low was for superior counterpunching opportunities. Quite often he baited opponents with verbal abuse and provocative physical gestures. The angry boxer lunged in, and Ali nailed him with a fast counter which he never saw. Ali's legendary "anchor" punch in the rematch with Sonny Liston was an example of such a counterpunch which came from low down. The punch that you don't see is the one that nails you. It's a classic sucker-punch tactic.

—December 2020

KINYANJUI KAMAU: Do you think that after the Thrilla in Manila, neither Frazier nor Ali were ever the same health-wise—that they both suffered permanent physical damage in some form?

J. A.: Yes, definitely. Neither guy was ever the same again, whether from a physical or mental standpoint. If ever there was a heavyweight fight that was almost too tough for words to describe, then the Thrilla in Manila was that fight. In fact, you will find that most boxing experts rate this fight as the toughest, most intense, and most bruising heavyweight title fight in history.

Ali's personal fight doctor was a guy named Ferdie Pacheco. In one post-fight interview, he said, "My guy was half dead and Frazier was more than half dead." I don't think for a second that Pacheco was joking.

As well as the scores of power punches that Ali and Frazier landed on each other, intensely hot and humid conditions defined that fight. Imagine fighting another Hall of Fame boxer for forty-two minutes in temperatures exceeding forty degrees Celsius. It can't possibly be good for your health. As a boxer, probably the last thing you want is to be hit when in a dehydrated state. So that fight was nuts for a variety of reasons.

In the years following that fight, Eddie Futch, Frazier's trainer, explained his decision to stop the fight at the end of the fourteenth round. In no uncertain terms, Futch explained that he felt that Frazier would have died in the ring had he not intervened.

In an ideal world, both legendary fighters should have promptly retired after this fight. But as always when boxing promoters dangle million-dollar carrots, it is hard to resist. Both guys campaigned for another six years after this most brutal of fights; Frazier had two more pro bouts, whereas Ali went to war ten more times.

—November 2020

Laura Harmon: How did Ali beat George Foreman when Foreman beat Frazier so easily and Frazier beat Ali once and gave him a good run twice?

J. A.: To cut a long story short, the Rumble in the Jungle was a prime example of a boxing match in which brains overcame brawn. On the night, Ali's brains—coupled with a well-executed game plan—were enough to confuse and tire an unsuspecting Foreman. From Foreman's perspective, he literally had no plan B and so when his basic bread-and-butter plan A failed, he was stuck.

The second main reason that Ali beat Foreman was that styles make fights. In pro boxing, at least in the gloved form of the sport as we know it, Ali's out-fighter style trumps Foreman's slugger style. This rule of thumb generally holds true—that is, as long as the out-fighter can take a punch. Foreman's slugger style was basic and very predictable, and his ring movements were telegraphed, so Ali knew exactly what to expect. The cannon balls that wiped out Frazier never landed on Ali's chin.

During much of that legendary fight, Ali controlled the range and the distance at which many of the exchanges occurred. At long range, he beat Foreman to the punch all night long.

Additionally, the location of the fight in Africa suited Ali down to the ground. Geography was big in this fight. Everyone in Zaire liked Ali and backed him as if he were a hometown fighter. On the other hand, Foreman hated it in Zaire, and Zaire hated him. Foreman's preparations for the fight were less than ideal. In a nutshell, fight psychology favoured Ali in a big way.

—October 2020

CHAPTER 11

THE MIGHTY BRUCE

Brent Deer: How well do you think Bruce Lee would have fared in MMA and UFC?

J. A.: As much as I would like to say Bruce Lee would have kicked ass, unfortunately, based on all the evidence, he would probably have fared quite poorly. If he fought in the way we all came to know and love in his movies, he would have got beaten up by the UFC's second-tier fighters. Grapplers rule the Octagon and always have from day one. Even the so-called world-class UFC strikers are really grapplers by nature who have simply learnt how to kick and dirty box.

A big indicator of how Bruce Lee would have done can be gauged from the recent showdown between McGregor and Khabib. McGregor is one of the best strikers in UFC and is also a very capable and versatile grappler. In fact, he is exactly the same as all the other top UFC fighters: he is first and foremost a grappler who has learned how to strike within the realms of UFC. Although the fight was competitive, in general Khabib had the upper hand from the outset. Why? Because he was by far the better grappler and is probably one of the most hyper-effective grapplers in the world. The term "mixed martial arts" has become something of a misnomer, as we are no longer watching old-school MMA but rather grapplers who have learnt how to kick and punch. Everyone is fighting in pretty much the same way.

This being the case, Bruce Lee would have to join the club and take some Brazilian ju-jitsu lessons before he set foot in the Octagon. To beat the grappler, you have to become the grappler, Grappling has shown itself to be by far and away the most dominant dilution technique in combat sports. The negative has become the positive. By grappling, you're exerting a big spoiling effect on the other technique. So Bruce Lee would have to learn Brazilian ju-jitsu as a contingency; it would be imperative for him to have any kind of success.

—January 2019

Michael Uzar: What was Bruce Lee's most impressive feat?

J. A.: As far as onscreen feats go, it has to be the nunchucks scene from *Enter the Dragon*. Still to this day for me, this remains a spine-tingling display of virtuoso skill, sublime technique, and overwhelming force. If ever a guy was sending a visual message to his adversaries, saying, "You guys don't stand a chance," then this was it. To pull off this feat would take a number of intertwined skill factors, which I doubt that too many (if any) other martial artists worldwide could pull off. Obviously it is a movie, so how much of it was real and how much was special effects (frame rate enhancement, modified nunchucks, etc.) is anybody's guess. Nonetheless, in my opinion it stands out as the most visually stunning display of onscreen weaponisation ever.

—January 2019

Thomas Gross: How do you think Bruce Lee would do against today's boxers if he could only punch?

J. A.: If it was an unregulated street fight, then I think Lee would stand a chance for a period of time, as long as he stayed at his mobile best. He had great footwork which could rival any boxer's, and this could potentially keep him out of harm's way. If he could distract the boxer and perhaps sucker-punch him with his infamous one-inch punch, then he may gain the upper hand. But remember one thing: pro boxers are usually a very tough breed when it comes to taking punches, so when and if the boxer gets close and gets off a bare-knuckle combo, you would expect that it's game over. At the end of the day, even the mighty Bruce Lee was only flesh and blood. As Mike Tyson once famously commented, "Everyone has a plan until they get punched in the face." Due consideration also has to be given to the environment of the street confrontation—an open space (parking lot) suited Lee, whereas a confined space (phone booth) probably suits the boxer.

If it was a proper, sanctioned boxing match—as in a ring with gloves on—Lee would stand almost no chance. Effectively this would now be an interdisciplinary fight, similar to Mayweather versus McGregor. This will suit the boxer down to the ground. In this instance, even the controlled environmental conditions of a boxing ring would be stacked against Lee. It is a classic case of a slow, stalking job for the boxer. With boxing gloves on, I seriously doubt if Lee would have the firepower to deter a pro boxer, even one who is in a similar weight class.

—August 2019

Andrew Tan and Julian Soto: In your opinion, if Bruce Lee and Mike Tyson were to fight, assuming each was at his peak physically, who would win?

J. A.: I can't see any other outcome than Tyson giving Bruce Lee a very bad, one-sided beating, and it wouldn't even be close. I asked a friend of mine who is a black-belt kickboxing instructor a similar question, but in my question, Bruce Lee's hypothetical opponent was the late Kimbo Slice. His instinctive reply was that Kimbo would beat Bruce Lee. I was slightly surprised but not shocked. Naturally I asked him the obvious: "Don't you think the greatest martial artist in history would be too fast and too skilful for Kimbo, have superior technique, and so on?"

He replied, "Yes, he would be too fast, too skilful, and technical for Kimbo. But when Kimbo lands one clean punch, it's over. There's no way that even Bruce Lee can overcome a seven stone lean muscle advantage."

This guy was talking about Kimbo, a heavyweight, backstreet, bare-knuckle brawler, who at the best of times was of average skill by professional boxing standards. What do you think Iron Mike would do? Tyson was probably at least 100 per cent more powerful than Kimbo, much faster, and much more skilful. He is a proper, professionally trained heavyweight boxer, and one of the best of all time at that. Bruce Lee was the best onscreen martial artist of all time, and we all love his films. But real-life fighting is an entirely different prospect to movie fighting. Pound for pound, Lee is probably the best fighter ever, but not even he can afford to give away a seven stone lean muscle advantage to a real-life ring monster like peak Tyson. It is a fight that an intelligent guy like Bruce Lee would never take because he would realise that he is completely outmatched and outgunned. If he weighed sixteen stone of solid lean muscle himself, with the exact same skill set, then it would be a different story. But Lee didn't weigh sixteen stone; he weighed no more than ten stone. This is why weight categories exist in the first place.

—April 2018

FURQAN TARIQUE: Who would win between Bruce Lee and Arnold Schwarzenegger if they had fought?

J.A.: Since you haven't specified any weapons or improvised weaponisation of the environment, then we have to assume this is a straight street fight. Essentially it is a matchup of a great martial artist vs a great bodybuilder with no formal fighting experience. This being the case, then one has to favour the more experienced Bruce Lee.

The only advantage that Schwarzenegger has is pure strength and in this matchup I don't think it will prove to be useful, unless of course he can grab a hold of the speedster. I don't see him getting close enough to execute a takedown and in doing so he will probably ship a lot of punishment.

As I see it, the most likely fight scenario is Lee circling around the bodybuilder and pot shotting him at his own leisure. After taking a few precision strikes from the master, Schwarzenegger will naturally get mad and over commit, similar to O'Hara in the movie, Enter the Dragon. As we saw Bruce Lee graphically demonstrate in that movie fight scene, he will feed off such mistakes and I can see this fight ending with a debilitating groin strike. Obviously Enter the Dragon was a movie, so the finisher against Schwarzenegger won't be as dramatic but you see the picture, right?

—March 2021

CHAPTER 12

WHO ATE ALL THE PIES?

Craig Knowles: Why are some heavyweight boxers fat?

J.A.: Ask yourself one question: between prime Tyson and Butterbean, who looks more powerful? It is debatable, but what Butterbean lacks in terms of definition, he surely makes up for in terms of sheer mass. What he lacks in terms of skill, he makes up for in terms of sheer brute force. As long as he can implement the fat weight through leverage, it will translate into tremendous punching power. Simply put, it is like bringing sumo tactics into heavyweight boxing.

The heavyweight division has no upper weight limit—it is limitless. As such, poorly conditioned athletes and pure in-fighters can gain an advantage by coming in fat. They can afford to be fat without facing any kind of penalty. Of course if their opponent is both a skilful boxer-mover and a good body puncher, it could turn out to be a long night. But the excess fat effectively translates into an advantage for a certain type of heavyweight, one who generally lacks skill and simply wants to wrestle and maul the other guy inside.

Another reason that heavyweights can be fat is simply appetite—some of them can eat like there is no tomorrow. Riddick Bowe was a world-class boxer who had well-documented appetite problems during the off season and was known to "battle with the refrigerator door". His optimum fight weight was around seventeen stone. Between fights, he could easily balloon to twenty stone-plus. As time goes by, it becomes harder and harder to shed this extra poundage come fight time.

Another guy with a massive appetite was a fringe contender from the 1980s named David Bey. He was nicknamed Bey of Pigs because of his uncontrollable appetite. Heavyweights don't have to make weight and so can afford to come in fat.

A prime example of this concept was seen in a 1986 heavyweight title fight between Frank Bruno and Tim Witherspoon. Bruno had a real Mr Universe physique, whereas Witherspoon was fat, flabby, and poorly conditioned. In Witherspoon's words, "From the start, I always had Frank Bruno's number." He knew he was technically superior to the limited Bruno, so his conditioning was largely irrelevant. If Witherspoon had been facing prime Tyson, you can bet your bottom dollar he would have come in lean and ripped.

In a small number of cases, a fat heavyweight boxer may have an underlying medical condition, such as a thyroid complication. This can contribute to weight gain which is difficult to lose later on. Muhammad Ali developed thyroid problems or something along those lines during his three-year enforced lay-off. In all of his 1970s fights, while not fat, he was no longer lean and ripped as he had been in his 1960s heyday. His optimum fight weight was around 210 pounds. He once commented that no matter how much road work he did, he simply couldn't shift his slight belly fat.

—February 2019

Leonnius Herbalies: How are some boxers fat and still have the stamina to fight twelve rounds?

J. A.: The boxer most well known for being fat was a guy named Eric Esch, better known as Butterbean. Do you think that Butterbean had the stamina to fight twelve rounds? The answer is debatable, because all of us will have a slightly different definition and viewpoint on what constitutes a fight. I am willing to say yes, he would be able to last twelve rounds against a certain type of opponent—namely an old and slow fighter. In 2002, Butterbean and a near-geriatric Larry Holmes plodded around the ring for ten of the most boring and uneventful rounds in recent heavyweight history, literally stinking up the joint. Anybody can go ten, twelve, or even fifteen rounds if you're moving at a snail's pace. It's as if I say that I can run a marathon—it just takes me two weeks to cover the twenty-six miles rather than three hours!

The intensity, pace, and volume of a fight are far more accurate indicators of a given fighter's stamina and fitness level than the number of rounds boxed. Butterbean was known as "the king of the four rounders", but against Larry Holmes he plodded through ten rounds, because he was largely inactive. In other words, his overall output and movement would have been virtually the same had it been a four-round fight. It is like spreading the same amount of margarine over a larger slice of toast.

Obviously Butterbean is an outlier. Not all fat heavyweights are this slow and sloppy.

The transformation of Tyson Fury from a fairly slim-looking heavyweight to a beer-bellied slob was interesting. In his first fight with Wilder, he was relatively fat but had undergone a decent training camp and had managed to shift a lot of the excess timber. He fought the full twelve rounds at a decent if not world-beating pace.

Just because a fighter may be slightly fat doesn't necessarily mean his stamina is poor. As a general rule of thumb, excess weight—be it fat or muscle—will cause a corresponding decrease in a fighter's stamina. But it doesn't necessarily prevent him from going the distance. The amount of time a given fighter's stamina will last is much more closely correlated with the pace and intensity of the fight. Truck versus car is a good analogy. The truck can comfortably cover the same distance as a car; it will simply take longer and use a lot more fuel.

—April 2019

Steve Pierce: Is Ruiz the most out-of-shape heavyweight champion ever?

J. A.: Between A. J. and Ruiz Junior, it is safe to assume that Ruiz is the more likely culprit for *eating all the pies*. If you believe in good old-fashioned BMI, then yes, Ruiz is the most out-of-shape heavyweight champion ever. He has an index value of 33, which makes him morbidly obese! Forget clinically obese, this guy is on death row according to BMI. And yet the fat guy, who looks like a Pizza Hut reject and boxes in his spare time, upset the world heavyweight champion—the same champion who not so long ago was supposedly up there with the likes of Muhammad Ali and Mike Tyson!

Ruiz is without doubt in appalling condition and must surely be the most obese heavyweight champion ever. I can't think of another guy who has been this fat, apart from Butterbean. There was one other guy from the 1980s called Tony "TNT" Tubbs whom Mike Tyson destroyed in two rounds. Tubbs was around 250 pounds of fat. Tyson mauled Tubbs on the inside and along the ropes. Judging by Tubbs's waistline, he was in very poor condition. But funnily enough Tubbs was still a fast puncher, and his fat weight didn't seem to adversely affect his hand speed. I would say Ruiz is in worse shape than Tubbs, although neither of their waistlines were characteristic of heavyweight champions.

Tim Witherspoon was another heavyweight champion who was renowned for his sloppy physique but who could definitely box. Witherspoon famously boxed another muscle-bound and statuesque British boxer, Frank Bruno, in 1986. In terms of muscle tone, there was no comparison between the two. Some would argue there was also no comparison when it came to boxing technique. Needless to say, technique once again conquered muscle.

—June 2019

Abhishek Modi: When punched hard in the stomach, who feels it most—the one with the six-pack abs or the one with a huge fat belly?

J. A.: Why don't we ask Andy Ruiz Junior? "Don't let Ruiz's rotund figure deceive you," said one of the commentators during Ruiz versus A. J. 1. Ruiz's midriff sure as hell carries plenty of mass but not a whole lot of definition. Maybe he is taking a page out of George Foreman's book. During his comeback, Foreman used to say that the fat was "protecting his cheeseburgers".

I know where you're coming from and what may be on your mind. Like many other fans around the world, you probably just watched the Ruiz Junior versus Joshua fight for perhaps the third time and are wondering how come the fat guy didn't get winded? How come the lean, ripped guy with a six-pack Mr Universe physique was the one who was breathing heavy? The answer is twofold. Firstly Joshua hardly went to Ruiz's body. You can't get winded if you aren't punched to the body. This situation simply highlighted Joshua's limitations as a boxer—he hardly ever goes to the body. Just because your opponent is shorter than you doesn't mean that you can't target his body.

Secondly Joshua's muscularity is one of the big contributory factors to him breathing heavily in this fight. Muscular guys are always at bigger risk of gassing, due to the increased oxygen demand of the muscle. It is kind of like a truck engine that is already redlining, even on a shallow incline. When the truck starts ascending a steeper incline, it slows down almost to a standstill. When Joshua got tagged to his vulnerable spot, he slowed down and fell apart because his cardiovascular system couldn't cope. In his post-fight analysis, Teddy Atlas remarked, "In this fight, Ruiz was breaking windows. He's got a tall building in front of him and there are plenty of windows that can be broken."

I think a guy with a six-pack will probably take the same body shot better than the fat guy—probably. But this assumes the body punch lands at exactly the same spot on both guys. For example, a six-pack isn't going to protect the liver or the small rib. A good body puncher will have studied anatomy and will readily target the muscular guy's weak spots.

In summary, a six-pack protects the lower abdomen more than the stomach, which is located above your belly button. The stomach is roughly at the level of the solar plexus, which is another weak spot that isn't protected by muscle. But to a fat and out-of-shape guy like Ruiz, who relies on the bulk to brawl, the fat itself will offer some protection. Clearly his core strength must be weak. So, in Ruiz's case, the fat at least provides cushioning to his lower torso. But there is also clearly the issue of pain tolerance. A great boxer is also normally a tough guy.

A. J.'s poor showing against Ruiz was hardly indicative of a tough guy, was it? The late great Marvin Hagler would have been watching this fight and shaking his head. When the going got tough, Joshua quit.

—August 2019

Matthew Culbertson: Why didn't Butterbean ever become a world champion? Would he have defeated Andy Ruiz or Anthony Joshua?

J. A.: Butterbean was known as "the king of the four rounders", as the vast majority of his professional fights were scheduled for just four rounds. It is unlikely that he would have had sufficient stamina to box in a twelve-round *championship* fight. He only ever fought once in a ten-round fight, and that was against a prehistoric Larry Holmes in 2002.

Given his immense weight and size, he had a surprisingly long boxing career and racked up an impressive number of wins. But he is a prime example of the concept of "it ain't the years, it's the mileage".

If he boxed either Ruiz Junior or Joshua in a four-round fight, then you have to give Butterbean a chance—being optimistic, say around a 33 per cent chance of success. If he can land a bomb on Joshua's suspect chin, then anything is possible. Given the fact that Ruiz tagged Joshua, then it isn't a stretch of the imagination that Butterbean could do the same—in a short fight.

If Butterbean fought either guy in a ten-rounder, then he would surely lose on points or by a technical knockout. Joshua would just stick and move and stay on his bike. Ruiz, being somewhat slimmer than Butterbean and the faster puncher, would probably TKO Butterbean as and when he started tiring—somewhere after round four.

—January 2021

CHAPTER 13

WHO'S THE GREATEST?

Fahad Nadeem and Praveen Yelleti: Can there be any doubt that Muhammad Ali is the greatest boxer of all time?

J. A.: Yes, substantial doubt, and in the wider boxing fraternity, unequivocal doubt. Once upon a time there was this dude named Walker Smith, more famously known as Sugar Ray Robinson. He is universally regarded as the greatest pound-for-pound pugilist all time by almost all impartial boxing experts. He was the closest thing to perfection as boxers go. He probably had no major weaknesses. He was a virtually flawless gem, whereas Mr. Ali was a flawed gem—there is a subtle difference.

In my humble opinion, it is almost a dead heat between these two legends. There is no doubt that Robinson was a better technical boxer than Ali—no doubt. Ali had several notable weaknesses. In no particular order, he hardly ever went to the body, he pulled his head back in straight lines from straight punches, and he held his hands habitually low throughout his career.

If you go by the coaching manual, then you will find that body punching is an extremely important and integral part of a fighter's offensive arsenal, even to an out-fighter like Ali. Ask any reputable boxing coach and you'll inevitably find that it isn't a good idea to pull your head back from punches. The correct defensive technique is either to block the punch or slip from side to side. With the exception of the Foreman fight, Ali almost always boxed with a low guard, and this habit cost him dearly against various opponents. He was dropped by left hooks from Henry Cooper, Sonny Banks, and, most notably, Smokin' Joe. He also had his jaw broken by Ken Norton in their first fight. All of these eventualities could have been avoided had he maintained a high defensive guard.

In stark contrast to Ali, you will find that it is extremely difficult to find a major weakness in Robinson's game. He was almost perfect. On top of this, he fought and won world titles in several weight categories. Indeed, this was the reason why pound-for-pound comparisons began.

However, there are some areas of boxing in which Ali was better than Robinson. Without doubt he was both faster and tougher than Robinson. In fact, it is a good job Ali was so tough; otherwise he would have been knocked out multiple times during the 1970s. However, Robinson was a significantly more destructive puncher than Ali, who was probably rated as a medium puncher by heavyweight standards. Ali even admitted, "I'm not known as a hard puncher. I'm a scientific boxer."

But one area where Ali closes the gap on Robinson is in terms of quality of opposition. I don't think any top boxer in history faced a tougher and more diverse selection of opponents than Ali. To be completely fair, the enforced three-year lay-off in Ali's prime also has to be factored into the equation. But these two guys are probably the top two boxers all time. It sometimes just boils down to personal preference and what sort of boxing style one prefers.

—January 2019

Steve Leyden: Can it still be argued that Muhammad Ali was the greatest heavyweight boxer of all time?

J. A.: Not at all—no need to argue, as there isn't really a serious argument. He is widely regarded as the GOAT heavyweight by most unbiased pundits and has been for the past thirty-eight years, since his retirement in 1981.

If you really want to be argumentative, then his chief competition comes from three Hall of Famers, in my humble opinion. They are Joe Louis, Rocky Marciano, and Mike Tyson.

If you polled, say, 100,000 boxing fans in America's Deep South, they would probably all vote for Joe Louis. But these would clearly be hometown votes, as Joe Louis is worshipped as a boxing god in states such as Alabama. Realistically speaking, though, Louis's run at the top was better than Ali's, and he still holds the record for the greatest number of successful heavyweight title defences. He is rated by *Ring* magazine as the greatest puncher in the division's history. He is also arguably one of the best combination-punching heavyweights all time, with probably the best and most effective footwork. It has to be said, though, Louis did fight his fair share of bums, infamously labelled as "the bum of the month club"; he also didn't face any seriously aggressive and well-muscled top-draw heavyweights such as Tyson or Liston.

Next there is the Brockton Blockbuster, Rocky Marciano, who was the only heavyweight champion to have ever creamed an entire division and retired undefeated. A legendary hard man, he had an all-action style that was extremely pleasing to the eye. He possessed a tremendous right-hand punch which he called his Susie Q. As with Louis, ask a certain demographic and they will tell you that the Rock was the greatest. He has certainly fared well against Ali in a number of computer-simulated fights over the years! His critics will no doubt cite the fact that he was really a modern-day cruiserweight—and a fairly crude one at that—who only had a miserly six world championship fights. Most of his notable victims were old and weak by the time he got to them. His most critically acclaimed victories were against fellow Hall of Famer Ezzard Charles.

And then there was Mike Tyson, who arguably had the most dominant reign ever as heavyweight champion and goes down as one of the most feared heavyweights of all time. At his best, his peak performances compare very favourably against any other top heavyweight in history. For a short period of time, he was touted by boxing critics the world over as the candidate GOAT and the heir apparent to Ali's throne—until, of course, a certain Buster Douglas upset the apple cart. However, nobody, not even Ali, rose to Tyson's level of prominence that quickly that early on in their career. Tyson's critics will no doubt question the quality of some of his opposition and his relatively short shelf life at the top.

Speaking of opposition, this is the one area in which Ali is surely unrivalled. This is the main reason why he generally gets the nod as the GOAT heavyweight. He emerged as the top dog from heavyweight boxing's golden era and arguably fought at the very highest level for the longest period of time. The toughness, quality, variety, and sheer depth of his opposition is undeniable and is probably the single best way to gauge and compare his form against the other contenders. Believe it or not, this is the main reason he is widely considered to be the GOAT heavyweight. To be the best, you have to beat the best, and Ali is the standout in this department. He literally fought everybody with no ducking, no jiving, and no delaying. He boxed sluggers, boxer-punchers, swarmers, crowders, out-fighters, in-fighters, brawlers, maulers, hard men, tall men, short men, fat men, thin men, wrestlers, and even the odd basketball player who wanted a piece of him!

—February 2019

Ed Smith: Would Mike Tyson have been the best heavyweight ever if he hadn't gone to prison?

J. A.: According to his one-time trainer Kevin Rooney, "He was on the road to going down as the best heavyweight ever, would have broken Rocky Marciano's record and probably gone undefeated his whole career." In your question, you are citing his prison sentence as perhaps being the cause of his decline, but I think prison finished him off. Many knowledgeable boxing pundits were describing Tyson as a shot fighter when he faced Razor Ruddock in 1991, and this was a year before he went to prison. Many technical errors had already crept into Tyson's game, and frankly he wasn't the same fighter without Rooney in his corner.

But sticking to the question, I think he still may have had a chance to recover lost ground had he not gone to prison. Those three years of heavy ring-rust were extremely difficult for Mike to shake off and were basically the beginning of the end. Legendary British heavyweight Henry Cooper stated that he felt Tyson was never the same physically or mentally after prison, and that he should never have mounted a comeback after being released. Had he not needed the money, maybe he would never have made a comeback, as virtually everything he did in the ring post-prison only served to damage his legacy.

But irrespective of how things turned out for Mike, I still think that at his best, he was an absolutely brilliant fighter and the second-best heavyweight of all time. He would arguably have been the most dangerous opponent for Ali to face.

—May 2018

JOE GLEESON: Who are the top ten greatest heavyweight boxers of all time, judged on who beats whom in their prime?

J. A.:

1. *Muhammad Ali*: A prime 1966 Ali landed a number of beautiful combos on Cleveland "Big Cat" Williams in what was probably the most prolific offensive showing of his career. In this fight, Ali is generally acknowledged to have given the number-one boxing performance in heavyweight history. It has also been speculated that in this form, he was

almost unbeatable. Williams was a heavy hitter but could only punch thin air. He was unfortunately left to chase Ali's shadow and took a bad beating in the process. Speed kills, and prime Ali had it in abundance.

2. *Mike Tyson*: How do you get 220 pounds of pure, ferocious muscle mass into a peach of a right hook-come-uppercut? Just ask the force of nature that was 1988 Tyson. "Speed, power, and timing—all your worst nightmares come true" was the comment of one ringside journalist. In the words of his former co-manager Bill Cayton, "Tyson was the second-best heavyweight ever in 1988." In ninety-one seconds of pure domination, Tyson landed all manner of precision power punches on a hapless and ridiculously overmatched Mike Spinks. In the process, he didn't take a single meaningful punch in return from a world-class and Olympic-standard boxer. Many people have long since forgotten that before this fight, Spinks was given a good chance of beating Tyson by such notable authorities as Sugar Ray Leonard.
3. *Sonny Liston*: Liston's legendary ramrod jab was a formidable weapon and was pivotal in many of his victories. His notorious failures against Ali are unfortunately what he is most remembered for, but during his boxing prime in the late 1950s, he was arguably the second most destructive heavyweight ever. He was also the first really well-muscled heavyweight who could box properly, with probably the number-one boxing genetics all time. With modern training methods and nutrition, Liston's frame could easily have accommodated 235 pounds of lean fighting mass, and he would have been a monster in any era.
4. *George Foreman*: If there was one heavyweight who was so strong and powerful that he could make other Hall of Fame fighters look bad, then Big George Foreman was your man. Foreman in 1973 was probably the most physically empowered specimen in heavyweight history. He was the second-hardest puncher ever and possessed one of the strongest chins in heavyweight history. Foreman once famously remarked, "When all else fails, I can always resort to brutality."
5. *Joe Louis*: Joe Louis's well-publicised fights against Max Schmeling were among some of the most significant and important fights in boxing history. Ask most experts who was the best boxer-puncher type of heavyweight ever, and Louis probably gets the nod. He is also generally regarded as having the most accurate and precise footwork of any heavyweight. Along with Liston and Tyson, he is probably one of the three best precision power punchers in the division's history: "A credit to his race—the human race."
6. *Jack Dempsey*: Dempsey is perhaps most fondly remembered for his legendary fists of steel. In terms of strength, size, and damage, his fists probably rank second all time—only just behind Sonny Liston's. Dempsey is generally regarded as the number-one mauler type of heavyweight all time and was renowned for punching well above his weight. He is generally regarded as the first Hall of Fame heavyweight who patented the use of leaping hooks to inflict massive damage on much larger and heavier opponents.
7. *Larry Holmes*: Holmes was the closest thing to an Ali clone that we have ever seen. He was also a masterful boxer. Nobody really likes copycats, but he was the one boxer who could do everything that Ali could. In fact, he was a slightly better technician than Ali

and ranks as having the second-best ramrod jab in heavyweight history. It's just a shame he came straight after Ali and was therefore always in his shadow.

8. *Joe Frazier*: Frazier was the best and most dangerous left hooker in the business, the quintessential heavyweight swarmer, one of the best body-punching heavyweights ever, and one of the best in-fighters ever. His boxing engine was none too shabby either. Imagine how good he could have been if he'd had a right-hand punch.
9. *Rocky Marciano*: Marciano was famous for his equalising punch, which he dubbed his Susie Q. His highly aggressive, all-action, and crowd-pleasing style was a joy to watch. This old-school brawler probably ranks as the number-one crowder type of heavyweight ever. Like Dempsey before him, Marciano punched well above his weight and had legendary toughness and stamina. He also knew a thing or two about covert dirty tactics.
10. *Lennox Lewis*: Lewis was the best of the super heavyweights, one of the best strategic out-fighters ever, and, in his prime, a real physical presence in the ring. Under Manny Steward's legendary tutelage, he became one of the most potent right-hand hitters in the division's history. He developed a prototype style that has been mimicked by one or two other well-known giants. Even at his best, though, always vulnerable, with both chin and defensive frailties.

—March 2019

Anonymous: Why is Muhammad Ali often underrated by modern fans despite the insurmountable evidence of his tremendous success?

J. A.: The main reason is probably to do with the old retro footage. When watching classic gladiators in action, one's viewpoint is limited by the quality of the film. If you watch Ali's early- to mid-1960s fights, they're largely in black-and-white. This has a big negative effect on a modern fan. Furthermore, if you watch his 1970s fights in glorious technicolour, then you will see that he took a lot of beatings. By 1975, Ali was a fighter in sharp decline.

On the other hand, people who watched his 1970s fights in real time still had clear memories of the 1960s speed-demon Ali. The 1970s beatings he sustained were taken with a pinch of salt by older fans. It is a generational bias: older fans are generally biased towards him and younger fans against him.

Now, Anthony Joshua has nothing directly to do with Ali or this question. But his physique is reportedly changing fast. The physical appearance of a boxer has a lot to do with how casual fans perceive his talent. You'd be surprised by how many young, casual boxing fans think that Joshua is better than Ali because he is the more well-built of the two!

Additionally, Ali's style may not be to the liking of everyone. Again, this is perhaps a generational thing, given the fact that Ali was a unique heavyweight in the 1960s. Most heavyweights of that era were bruisers who plied their trade via toughness and punching power. Ali was radically different in that he was probably the first slickster type heavyweight to have major success on the world stage. As time goes by, this novelty factor has simply worn off. Look at Larry Holmes: he was essentially an Ali clone but never came close to achieving even a smidgen of Ali's popularity.

—November 2019

Michael Harris: Who had faster hand and foot speed, a young Mike Tyson or a young Muhammad Ali?

J. A.: As far as hand speed is concerned, prime Ali had the fastest hands of any heavyweight ever. This is a scientific fact; his hand speed has been clocked and documented as the fastest. Probably the fastest heavyweight punch ever thrown was the phantom punch with which Ali dropped Liston in their rematch in 1965. Ali himself called this weak-looking punch his "anchor" punch. It was delivered like a bolt of lightning and was comfortably faster than the blink of an eye—hence the fact so many onlookers actually missed the punch.

In terms of hand speed, the Iron Man was also a speed demon, but he generally gets rated as the third-fastest heavyweight in history, Floyd Patterson being the second fastest. Ali has a slight edge in terms of hand speed.

In terms of foot speed, I think it is almost too close to call. Tyson generally gets rated as the number-one gap closer of the modern heavyweight era. In this respect, I think he is in a league of his own. Ali's best footwork was more often than not defensive. It was designed primarily to keep him out of harm's way. So it is a difficult and somewhat unfair comparison—Tyson's aggressive footwork versus Ali's defensive footwork.

Certainly the most spectacular display of footwork ever was the Ali shuffle, particularly in his finest hour versus Cleveland "Big Cat" Williams. In this fight, Ali was believed to be almost untouchable, and his footwork was dazzling to say the least.

Watching prime Tyson jump rope was also an awe-inspiring sight, especially given the fact that 220-pound guys don't usually defy the law of gravity so easily. A well-known American boxing writer once described prime Tyson as the boxing equivalent of Baryshnikov. In terms of pound-for-pound foot speed, it's dead even, given that Tyson was the more muscular and heavier guy.

—December 2019

Mohammed Saiful Alam Siddiqquee: Do you think George Foreman gets somewhat overrated just because he became the oldest heavyweight champion?

J. A.: By comparing the old, sloppy and overweight version of Foreman to the almost invincible, early 1970s ring monster, an interesting picture emerges.

You tell me which guy is better. To me, the answer is glaringly obvious. It really surprises me when people say that the old pot-bellied geezer who moved around the ring like a diplodocus was better than the all-time, fearsome, 1970s, T-Rex version of Foreman. All I can say is that if you rate Foreman highly because of his "second coming", then you don't really know boxing. But at the end of the day, it is all opinion.

The fact of the matter is that the old guy set a world record and the young guy didn't. Becoming a world champion at the age of 45 is very impressive, and no one is arguing with the merits of this achievement. It is a world record. But let's also not forget the fact that the guy whom he beat to set that world record was nothing more than a palooka, Michael Moorer. You can bet your bottom dollar that prime Foreman would probably have knocked out that same Moorer in under a round.

I think most knowledgeable boxing fans rate Foreman highly because of his 1970s exploits. The original Foreman was a truly massive puncher, stronger than an ox, with a granite chin. The old guy still had a great chin, was a good puncher, and was fairly strong. The only area where the old Foreman was better than the young Foreman was in terms of ring IQ. He grew wiser with age, like most humans do, and this wisdom translated into his 1990s fights. He paced himself much better.

In summary, I suggest Foreman's comeback has led to a certain amount of confusion among boxing fans. But from a purely boxing standpoint, he possessed the perfect style and genetics to campaign well into his forties and was amply assisted by some fairly mediocre opposition. In my book, I would never label Foreman as overrated. He was always a legitimate all-time great.

—July 2019

Anonymous: How did Mike Tyson get that much mass?

J. A.: It's largely down to genetics. At the age of thirteen, he weighed 190 pounds of virtually solid muscle, according to his one-time trainer Teddy Atlas. Tyson had also already beaten up a nineteen -year-old guy who killed one of his pigeons. Now, how many thirteen -year-olds can beat up a grown man? In school his nickname was Mighty Joe Young, so Tyson was clearly an early physical bloomer.

Desmond Lynam, a British TV broadcaster, interviewed Tyson in 1987, when he had just become champ. Lynam enquired about his impressive physique. Tyson confirmed that he did absolutely no weight training, only large amounts of callisthenic exercises, road work, skipping, and other boxing-specific exercises.

—March 2018

Anonymous: How was Mike Tyson's bulkiness not an issue for him in the ring?

J. A.: This was because much of Tyson's muscle was down to natural genetics and not artificially gained from weight training. His muscular development was the result of callisthenics or body-weight exercises and other boxing-specific exercises, which resulted in useful and proportionate muscle gain. At his peak, his cardiovascular fitness was outstanding, so his heart could comfortably support the muscle without any compromise to his ring movements or stamina. Furthermore, it was noticeable that much of Iron Mike's body weight was located in his legs, which positively assisted his mobility.

In reality, you will find that Tyson wasn't as bulky as he looked—appearances can be deceiving. He was ripped and had a six-pack, which made him appear bigger in the ring. In clothes, he looked big but not massive or bulky.

—April 2018

Ross Taylor: Is it true that Mike Tyson did very few weights, just practice boxing and callisthenics?

J. A.: During his peak years under Cus and Rooney, this is 100 per cent true—that is according to his own verbal testimony. He was interviewed by BBC Sports journalist Desmond Lynam in 1987, and Lynam naturally enquired about his impressive and natural-looking physique. On live British television, Tyson confirmed that he did no weight training, only callisthenics and boxing-specific exercises. Whether or not he lifted the odd dumbbell in the privacy of his own home is difficult to prove one way or the other. But the closest he came to gym weight training were added-weight dips and added-weight chin-ups, because his own body weight wasn't enough—he had become too strong. Dips and chins are still callisthenic exercises, but by strapping a metal weight to the body, the exercise becomes that much more difficult.

If you compare, say, a natural image of heyday Tyson doing one of his most impressive impact exercises (medicine ball abdominal strengthening) with his proper trainer, Kevin Rooney, to a product of twenty-first century biochemical engineering, such as Phil Heath, an interesting picture emerges.

There is clearly a big difference in the look and nature of these two guys' physiques. Tyson's physique clearly looks natural and proportional, without any significant bulges or muscular hypertrophy. Phil Heath clearly looks more synthetic, chemical, and hypertrophic—while being absolutely ripped to the bone. This extreme look is the result of very specific bodybuilding exercises, diet, and high-dose PEDs. Always pay close attention to the trapezius muscle and the gap on the pectoral muscle; these are classic signs of PED abuse. Also notice the bald head or premature receding hairline—no, this is not hereditary male pattern baldness!

Now what many casuals, haters, and mud-rakers simply don't understand is that Tyson was blessed with the genetics of the angels. He was a natural who weighed a whopping 190 pounds of lean muscle at the age of thirteen which his one-time trainer Teddy Atlas has confirmed many times over. Atlas's exact words on ESPN Classic were "physically he was a phenomenon before he ever set foot in the gym".

Looking at images of a teenage Tyson, it is fairly evident that his physical maturity belied his tender age. Some guys are simply like this naturally, largely due to hormones.

Furthermore, Tyson is what is known biologically as a *mesomorphic specimen*—or, in gym slang, an easy gainer. He was just big and muscular because of genetics, environment, and natural hormones.

Some people are also just fortunate that they were born with athletic genes. Lennox Lewis commented on this topic on the Joe Rogan podcast when he correctly described Tyson as an "early bloomer". It is fairly apparent that prime Tyson was both a genetic freak and possibly the top spartan-type trainer in heavyweight history. In a 1988 documentary called *Mike Tyson's Greatest Hits*, Tyson was almost in tears when describing the volume and intensity of his now-fabled callisthenic workouts.

—April 2019

Temi Ola: Given the importance of height and, as a consequence, boxing reach, why was a relatively short fighter like Joe Frazier successful as a heavyweight?

J. A.: It isn't the size of the dog in the fight but the size of the fight in the dog that really matters. Joe Frazier made up for his apparent lack of height and reach with excellence in many other boxing facets. Since Frazier was primarily an in-fighter, his average length was a moot point. He wanted to rumble with you inside a phone booth. Relatively shorter height and reach are suited to this type of confined environment.

Being shorter meant he was low to the ground like Tyson and Marciano, thereby making him more elusive. A shorter fighter is generally much more effective when boxing from a crouch. Frazier's punches mostly moved in an upward trajectory, which meant they had more leverage and disguise.

He also excelled in the delivery of the left hook to both head and body. He arguably possessed the best left hook in heavyweight history. When all or most of your opponents are taller than you, then you must go to the body. Frazier went to the body like a crazed SOB.

At the highest level of boxing, positional supremacy becomes very significant. Angles, distance, clockwise, anticlockwise, short range, long range, and so on—all these small details accumulate into the bigger picture. One thing that guys like Frazier and Tyson excelled at was closing the gap on the taller fighter. In general, this gap needs to be circumvented as quickly and efficiently as possible for the shorter fighter to be successful. Frazier used a legendary bob-and-weave motion, combined with fast footwork, to home in on his prey.

He also possessed terrific stamina, work rate, and fighting intensity. In the good old days of boxing, the athletes trained for fifteen rounds and fought hard for the entire duration of the fight. This is to say that Frazier and Marciano before him were probably the two most box-fit heavyweights in history. Frazier could throw scores and scores of punches in steady movements.

Finally, another big piece of the in-fighter's jigsaw puzzle is character. Frazier was as brave, tough, and stubborn as they came. When the going gets tough, the tough get going.

—January 2021

Piotr Gajda: Did Sonny Liston have any weaknesses as a fighter?

J. A.: All fighters have weaknesses, even the best of the best. Liston's weaknesses were mainly defensive in origin. His foot speed wasn't great for his body weight of approximately 217 pounds. It's not that he was sloppy, but his ring movements could have been sharper, particularly when he was on the back foot. He boxed a guy named Cleveland "Big Cat" Williams twice, and Williams had his fair share of success while the fights lasted, so Liston was always hittable. That same Williams boxed Ali and couldn't lay a glove on Ali.

Additionally, if you analyse Liston's defensive head movements closely, they are good but not great. Clay caught him with many straight punches which he could potentially have avoided had he possessed better side-to-side head movement.

Out of all the great historical heavyweights, Liston was the most famously heavy-handed. While his heavy-handedness was very useful to his offense, it detracted from his defence; carrying such heavy hands must have been tiring, and quite often his gloves are too low. To a speed demon like Clay, Liston proved to be a very easy target.

On the front foot, Liston was great. This no doubt contributed to his degree of complacency. When you are so physically strong and have so many attacking options, you can afford to have a few bad habits. But when you meet the Greatest, those same bad defensive habits are then more soundly punished.

—January 2021

Steve Moreby: They were both hard-hitting pugilists, but was Rocky Marciano also a better boxer than Mike Tyson?

J. A.: If they ever fought, it is difficult to imagine the outcome being anything other than a war.

"My defence is impregnable," ranted Tyson in 2000. Given that Tyson had a much better defence than Marciano, he surely would have had the edge in this matchup. Marciano was the type of slugger who took a punch to land a punch. To be successful with this old-school style required legendary toughness. By modern standards, his style was pretty crude and basic. Believe me, if he hadn't been as hard as nails, he would have been knocked out on several occasions in his career. He was very similar to George Foreman in this respect.

Prime Tyson, on the other hand, was as elusive as any brawler in heavyweight history. In fact, he was the best defensive heavyweight of the entire 1980s. Under Cus D'Amato and Kevin Rooney, his head movement was precise and well-drilled. For such a highly aggressive fighter, he took very few clean power shots during his heyday. Clearly the same cannot be said about Marciano, who absorbed significant punishment over the course of his career.

Marciano was slightly fitter and had greater stamina than Tyson. But after factoring in Tyson's two stone weight advantage, the box-fitness levels of these two warriors are not too dissimilar. Tyson's best fighting weight was 220 pounds, whereas Marciano generally tipped the scales at around 190 to 200 pounds. In Tyson's case, this extra weight was clearly pure lean muscle. At the end of the day, these two were tremendously conditioned and were probably the top two spartan trainers in heavyweight history.

In terms of pound-for-pound power, I think it is a dead heat, with Tyson hitting harder in absolute terms. Both guys garnered fearsome reputations for punching well above their body weight. Tyson had a big advantage in terms of hand-speed, but Marciano was no slouch either and could get the punch there pretty quickly.

Overall I would say Tyson was comfortably the more skilful, accomplished, and evolved boxer, although Marciano was tougher. They were both legendary warriors who deserve huge credit for encapsulating the ethos of putting bums on seats. When these two boxed, you can bet your bottom dollar there were no empty seats in the hall—true boxing fans would flock to see these guys brawl.

—August 2019

Stefan Rayka: Why do people rank Mike Tyson above Lennox Lewis, even though Lewis beat better opposition, including Tyson?

J. A.: In my humble opinion, the main reasons for rating Tyson above Lewis are natural boxing ability, dominance factor, peak performances, and historical impact. When you win the world heavyweight title at the age of twenty and in the process set a world record which has now lasted nearly thirty-five years, you are clearly going to raise a few eyebrows.

You don't destroy fully grown men at the age of nineteen or twenty by accident. The late British boxing commentator Reg Gutteridge joked about this very point: "Tyson isn't old enough to legally buy alcohol in New York State, and yet he's just knocked out the heavyweight champion of the world!" Tyson was a natural boxing prodigy, whereas Lewis wasn't.

Secondly, Tyson was absolutely dominant during his heyday. Even *Ring* magazine concedes the point that he was absolutely dominant during his prime. Most neutral and knowledgeable pundits opine that he was the most dominant heavyweight champion in history. In the mid to late eighties, he was in a league of his own, and the manner of his victories reinforced this fact. From a purely technical standpoint, he was almost perfect and way ahead of the competition. On top of this, he had a realistic shot at breaking the legendary Rocky Marciano's long-standing all-time record of 49–0. Had he remained with Kevin Rooney and his original management team, there was every chance Tyson would have gone on to break Marciano's record. He was 37–0 at the time of his first defeat.

In comparison to Tyson, Lewis had a relatively obscure and ignominious start to his pro career. Like Tyson, he had a very strong amateur pedigree but he didn't transition to the pro game anywhere near as efficiently as Tyson. He retained many amateurish traits, one of which cost him early in his career, against journeyman Oliver McCall. He always possessed a mediocre chin and defence, and McCall duly sparked him in September of 1994.

After this knockout defeat, Lewis was at a crossroads. Somewhat fortuitously, he used this setback to pave the way for a comeback. Lewis, always the smart cookie, hired Oliver McCall's coach, the legendary Emanuel Steward. Under Steward's tutelage, he slowly improved, both technically and physically.

Looking at Lewis's prime, circa 2000, and comparing it to Tyson's prime, circa 1988, there is clearly a big difference in the respective timelines. Even though the guys are roughly the same age, one peaked unusually early and the other peaked unusually late. To be perfectly fair, this makes a prime-versus-prime comparison all the more difficult, as boxing itself changes.

But consider the following upset: Lewis was once again sparked by a journeyman, but on this occasion the defeat came during his prime. In April 2001, he was knocked out cold by the unknown Hasim "the Rock" Rahman. This upset confirmed beyond any reasonable doubt that even at his best, Lewis was always a vulnerable fighter.

Compared to Tyson, Lewis clearly had greater longevity, and there are no grounds for argument on this point. Tyson had a supernova-type career; he shone extremely bright for a short period of time and then summarily crashed and burned. Lewis, on the other hand, was a late-blooming slow burner who had a much longer shelf life. It depends on personal preferences—do you prefer the shooting star or the red dwarf?

As for the quality of the opposition, do you really rate Lewis that highly for boxing a total of twenty-four rounds against a shopworn Holyfield? If he were that good, he should have put Holyfield to sleep. Instead he made hard work of both their fights. And as for beating Tyson—well, yes, we all know that he beat a name.

—October 2019

Joe Elliott: Why do people think Mike Tyson is better than Evander Holyfield, despite losing to him?

J. A.: It really depends on who you ask. The "people" in your question are probably knowledgeable and impartial neutrals, and I'm pretty sure that the vast majority of them will say prime Tyson was comfortably the better boxer. My own objective and subjective reasons for saying that prime Tyson was better than Holyfield are as follows:

- *Penitentiary time*: Tyson went to prison in 1992, at the age of twenty five, during his physical prime. Not only did he lose three years of his career, but he spent those three years behind bars. What do you think happened to his pristine boxing technique during that time? Anybody who knows anything about how human beings work surely realises that if you spend even three months, let alone three years, away from your specialism, your skills will rapidly erode. How would Holyfield have turned out if he spent three years in prison and then came out to fight 1988 Tyson? The point is, boxing is all about timing. When you fight a given opponent has a huge influence on the probable outcome of the fight. Tyson lost to Holyfield in the post-prison phase of his career, when he was merely a shell of his former self. Holyfield was on the up and up.
- *Punching power*: Even when Tyson was old and fooling around with wrestlers, he was way more powerful than Holyfield. At no point in Holyfield's career, even late on, did he possess a finishing punch. On the other hand, Tyson is consistently rated as one of the most devastating and destructive punchers in heavyweight history. So in terms of firepower, there really is no comparison.
- *Trainers and training regimens*: While Tyson was languishing in a prison cell, Holyfield was a very busy boy. He received a revolutionary, highly advanced, plyometrics-based training regimen.
- *Performance enhancements*: The 1990s version of Holyfield did not have a natural body. This was not the same guy that Tyson would have faced in 1991. What percentage enhancement did Holyfield receive from PEDs? From a scientific standpoint, it is a very difficult question to answer. In terms of body weight, he went from a 196-pound cruiserweight to a 220-pound heavyweight. This is roughly a gain of ten per cent of his body weight in pure lean muscle. A simple, linear analysis will reveal that he gained a minimum of ten per cent on the force and resistance components of boxing, with no corresponding loss of velocity or dynamics. In the real world, this is impossible

without chemical enhancement. I therefore estimate that by juicing, Holyfield gained an approximate twenty five per cent edge on Tyson overall.

- *Hand speed*: Anybody who hasn't seen a video of a fifteen-year-old Tyson shadow-boxing should watch it. The definition of blinding hand speed will become apparent. Holyfield was no slouch in the speed stakes, but he was never a speed demon.

—August 2019

Elisa Sirani: Is Mike Tyson a great boxer or just an aggressive person who was successful?

J. A.: Both!

If you saw a random, unknown Joe Public with a world-class, natural-looking physique, working the heavy bag with a legendary trainer like Cus D'Amato, would you say the guy looked like a great boxer? Would you say he had potential? The answer is debatable. Bear in mind that, in the early 1980s, Tyson was exactly that—just another random, unknown guy. In 1984 and 1985, aside from the immediate boxing fraternity, the outside world was pretty much oblivious to the existence of the young boxing prodigy that was Mike Tyson.

The point is that when the top boxing trainer in history invests a huge amount of time, expense, and effort into the development of a raw and uncut prospect, then surely he already knew that this kid smelt of opportunity. D'Amato was an old man who knew he didn't have much time and wanted to make the most of what he had left. He had literally waited a lifetime for his own Dempsey, his own Liston, his own avenging angel, so to speak.

So without elaborating too much on how good Tyson was in his prime, he was without doubt one of the best ever. I personally rate him as both the most dangerous and the most skilful heavyweight brawler in history. To knock out a bunch of professional boxers at the age of nineteen takes some doing. To continue that streak at the world level and become the youngest heavyweight champion ever is an all-time leading achievement. So Tyson was definitely a great boxer.

As for his aggression, he was also a natural in this respect. He had a genuinely aggressive fight face, and this was one of the reasons he became so successful and popular. In the 1980s, audiences worldwide had a big appetite for destruction, so he definitely benefited from audience demand. Good for him, because without boxing, he would surely have headed for a life of crime. At least boxing channelled his natural, primeval aggression in a positive way.

—July 2019

Jovanne Rodriguez: How could George Foreman compete at such a high level in his comeback career when he looked like he was so out of shape?

J. A.: That's because he was the same mean dude, but simply two to three stone fatter! Looks can also be deceiving. He was a lot wiser in his old age. He always possessed elite genetics, and this didn't change with age. Given that he boxed in the division of giants, being overweight wasn't really a big deal—especially if the other guy was fat too. See a guy named Andy Ruiz Junior or another one named Butterbean. There have been numerous heavyweights over the years who have boxed successfully with more than just a layer of fat. With age, the fat may well help a certain type of fighter—namely a slugger type, such as Foreman.

An ageing Foreman realised that his contemporaries in the late 1980s and early 1990s were, on average, more bulky than the heavyweights of his original era. Extra weight came in handy in the trenches.

Judging from his blubbery physique, it was obvious that old Foreman wasn't going to win a Mr. Universe contest, but the extra blubber served a protective function—especially given his reduced mobility. He was always a poor defensive boxer, and this wasn't going to improve in his forties. The extra fat ideally provided cushioning against any body shots coming his way.

His boxing toolbox, from a genetic standpoint, was always great, and again this wasn't going to change much with age. Whether he was old or young, Foreman was what he was, and that was a slugger. He could always take a hard punch and give a hard punch, and that was it, really. The clever part was realising that he would tire more quickly with age and extra weight, so in his second coming, he paced himself much better in his fights.

The final reason he became the oldest heavyweight champion ever was due to the level of competition he faced. The early 1990s heavyweight division was decent but not great. It lacked a great body puncher, so Foreman's vulnerability to the body wasn't really exploited. If Iron Mike Tyson hadn't been in prison during the early 1990s, then there would have been a distinct possibility that Foreman never regained the title.

—November 2019

Steve Moreby: They both were undisputed middleweight world champions, but was Marvin Hagler a better boxer than Bernard Hopkins?

J. A.: If these two legends of the sport ever fought, you could expect a classic—Hagler boxing from his favoured southpaw stance versus Hopkins from the classic orthodox stance. Hagler would need to be at his best to beat Hopkins. This would mean doing what he did best, and that was boxing southpaw. He made a big mistake in 1987 when he boxed Sugar Ray Leonard, beginning the fight from the orthodox stance. Anybody who really knew boxing realised right there and then that this was a tactical blunder. From the outset, he needed to be doing what he did best. Starting out as a righty was a bluff that Leonard predicted, and it inevitably led to Hagler ceding the early rounds.

Sticking with the question, deciding which boxer was better, Hopkins or Hagler, is kind of like deciding which car is better, a Lamborghini or a Ferrari. It really is a case of splitting hairs. It is such a close call that a given boxing pundit will likely have a different opinion on a different day. I also feel that pro boxers, past and present, would be split down the middle on this question. If you asked, say, Floyd Mayweather, I think he would say Hopkins is better. If you asked Sugar Ray Leonard, he is going to opt for Hagler. Comparing these two legends of the sport is going to expose a great deal of generational bias.

My own unbiased opinion (if there is such a thing as an unbiased opinion!) favours Hagler, due in large part to the intense competition in the middleweight division during the 1980s. He ruled at a time which was the golden era for the middleweight division, and undoubtedly faced some of the stiffest competition ever. Not that Hopkins didn't face his fair share of elite opposition too, but I think Hagler's opponents were on average tougher. Also the manner of Hagler's victories, on average, were slightly more dominant than Hopkins's best wins.

In a direct comparison between the two, I think Hopkins was marginally the better technician, particularly to the body. You don't earn the nickname the Executioner for nothing. There aren't too many historical boxers who could take out Oscar De La Hoya with the infamous liver shot, and Hopkins did it in fine style in 2004. So as far as precision power is concerned, I'm going with Hopkins.

On the outside, I favour Hagler with his legendary right jab. Both guys were as hard as nails, but Hagler was tougher. In fact he may have been the toughest boxer in history, alongside Jake LaMotta.

In terms of work-rate and volume of punches, both guys were great, and it is virtually a dead heat. As far as footwork is concerned, I think Hopkins was slightly more precise and cagier and could ghost into a dominant offensive position more easily than Hagler. In terms of guerrilla warfare (when the going gets really tough), Hagler had the edge—that guy would literally keep swinging until "all the heads were gone". In terms of ring IQ and defence, I think Hopkins was marginally the more intelligent boxer, although Hagler was more versatile. In terms of hand speed and power, it is too close to call.

In summary, if I were a middleweight boxer myself, I would fear Hagler more but perhaps respect Hopkins's toolbox more.

—September 2019

Jonathan Alexander: If you asked Sugar Ray Robinson who the greatest fighter of all time was, who would he say?

J. A.: Assuming he couldn't vote for himself, then I think he may say Homicide Hank, better known as Henry Armstrong. His is not exactly a household name, but he is extremely well known and respected within the boxing fraternity. Many boxing historians choose him as the number-two pound-for-pound boxer of all time. Like Sugar Ray Robinson, he campaigned in different weight divisions and held world titles in three separate weight classes. This achievement was much more significant in the old days, given that the adjacent weight classes were separated by at least seven pounds.

Armstrong is generally regarded as being the most prolific volume puncher in history. He could literally keep punching like a windmill, with textbook technique. He was also a great defensive fighter, as well as being a very skilful in-fighter. In short, he was a great all-rounder and not too dissimilar to Robinson.

Ask Joe Frazier who his favourite boxer was, and he would almost certainly reply that it was Henry Armstrong. In a 1980s documentary called *Champions Forever*, Frazier commented that his goal was to emulate Henry Armstrong and attempt to throw three hundred punches per round! This is probably a slight exaggeration on Joe's part, and arithmetic probably wasn't his strong point, but you can get the gist of what he's saying, right? The point of boxing is to box. That means throwing punches, and that is exactly what Armstrong did for three minutes of every round he boxed. *Ring* magazine rates Armstrong as the second-best boxer in history.

—January 2019

David Solomon: What is your review of Manny Pacquiao as a boxer?

J. A.: Manny Pacquiao was once described as the human equivalent of a Pacific typhoon. The quintessential modern-era volume puncher, who had a ubiquitous style that was incredibly difficult to read and deal with, he also just so happened to be a very awkward and cagey southpaw to boot. He surely had one of the best pound-for-pound boxing engines ever. He also had great footwork and could throw the dreaded southpaw left all night long.

It's hard to criticise a guy as great as Pac-Man (eight-weight world champion), but I think it would be an interesting experiment to see how good he would have been had he been an orthodox fighter. In other words, keep everything about him exactly the same except for switching him to a right-handed fighter. I personally think his southpaw left was even harder to read than normal. Without belittling his achievements, I think some of his victories were without doubt partly down to the "southpaw jinx". Certainly, the top Mexican fighters he beat seemed utterly bemused by his southpaw left down the middle.

This fairly simple-looking punch proved to be almost universally effective and covered a surprising amount of distance, given his diminutive size and reach. In some ways, he reminded me of a miniature Mike Tyson, in that he could cover a surprising amount of ground by punching while on the move. His fast footwork played a big part in his ability to close the gap. At his best, he really was a perpetual-motion punching windmill who had almost endless stamina. Certainly, this aspect of his game has been questioned. Fighters who don't fatigue do arouse suspicion.

Against the absolute best of the best, the southpaw jinx didn't work. Floyd Mayweather proved that what works against 99 per cent of the competition doesn't work against him. It would obviously have been interesting to see how the Mayweather fight would have gone had they fought when originally scheduled, in 2011–2012. The delay definitely suited Mayweather more.

In the end, I agree with Mayweather—Manny was a genuine pound-for-pound great, but he "didn't quite reach the pinnacle of the modern boxing pyramid". He will be remembered as a tremendous volume puncher and, along with Marvin Hagler, one of the two best lefties of the modern era.

—March 2019

Anonymous: Why is Rocky Marciano never considered a top heavyweight of all time?

J. A.: He is generally in the top ten, but almost no experts place him in the top five. Even though he is the only heavyweight champion to retire undefeated, his 0 has been criticised in the same way a certain Floyd Mayweather's 0 has also been. This is to say, even in Rocky's era, there was surely a little cherry picking of opponents that went on. It was, perhaps, more tolerated back in the day. Either way, the Rock's record does indeed flatter to deceive. Why? Only a miserly six of his forty-nine victories came in world championship bouts, which is pretty low.

Probably the main, universally acknowledged, objective criticism of Marciano is his lack of size and weight. He was a cruiserweight by modern standards. In those ancient days, there was no such thing as a cruiserweight division. He generally weighed less than 200 pounds. His reach was also among the lowest among Hall of Fame heavyweights, coming in at a paltry 68 inches. He wasn't the fastest nor all that subtle. Style-wise, he is generally regarded as the crudest of the great heavyweights.

He made up for some of his physical shortcomings with a legendary granite chin, great pound-for-pound power, and endless stamina. Would these three qualities be enough to translate into cross-era success? The general consensus among boxing experts is a resounding no. Indeed, Larry Holmes once infuriated many a Marciano fan by wrongly asserting, "Marciano couldn't carry my jockstrap!"

One of the oldest and most accurate adages in heavyweight boxing is "a good big guy almost always beats a good little guy". Marciano was a very good little guy who fought big, but his best probably wouldn't be enough to beat the top giants of the heavyweight division. At some point, when boxing ability and technique are fairly equal, an extra twenty pounds or so in weight generally proves decisive. See Holyfield versus Bowe 1 for a prime example of this phenomenon. Both guys were Olympic-standard boxers, but one outweighed the other by around twenty-five pounds of lean mass. Over the course of twelve rounds, Bowe's ten per cent of lean mass advantage translated into ten per cent more firepower, and that was that. In essence, this is the same problem that Marciano would face against many of the top modern heavyweight boxers, particularly from the 1960s onwards.

—January 2019

Chris Steele: Were George Foreman's skills as a boxer in his prime underrated?

J. A.: No, not at all. Big George was never all that skilful a boxer; he was the quintessential heavyweight slugger, pure and simple. Virtually all sluggers are fairly crude and basic technical boxers, and George was no different in this respect. His greatest skill was probably his ability to cut off the ring, along with his log-splitter jab.

So why is he an all-time great heavyweight then? This is because prime Foreman is ranked at or near the top in three categories: punching power, pure strength, and punch resistance. In terms of static punching power he is probably number one, at least on a target such as a heavy bag. He was an absolutely fearsome sight when he hit the heavy bag. His only historic rival on this apparatus was probably Sonny Liston. *Ring* magazine has consistently rated Foreman as the most fearsome puncher in recorded boxing history.

In terms of pure strength, Foreman was probably the most physically empowered specimen in boxing history. I don't think anybody was ever able to push him back in a real-time boxing match, although Smokin' Joe tried hard and failed miserably.

The final component of George's legendary triad was his granite chin, which is right up there with the very top chins in boxing history. This physical quality continued into the second phase of his career—well into his forties. With age, one normally sees a slight decline in punch resistance, but not with Foreman. He surely was a genetic freak.

Now let's talk about his cons. He had probably the lowest ring IQ of any hall of fame heavyweight, mediocre punch accuracy, and a so-so defence. In general, he threw punches one at a time and was therefore an average combination puncher. He was also often guilty of telegraphing his power punches. Intelligent slicksters like Muhammad Ali, Jimmy Young, and Gregorio Peralta were able to dodge, block, and neutralise many of his attacks.

In fact, his dismal display against Ali, according to Evander Holyfield, ranks as the single dumbest display of boxing ever in a heavyweight title fight. On that fateful night in Zaire in 1974, George basically had one tactic, and that was to keep marching forward in straight lines and letting those big guns fly until he literally ran out of steam. This tactic worked well against probably 98 per cent of the heavyweights he boxed because, most of the time, heavyweights don't actually box all that intelligently. When facing smart fighters who could really box on the fly, he came up short.

So I definitely don't think Foreman's skills were underrated. Big George was a tremendous power man, pure and simple.

—January 2019

Anonymous: Is Mike Tyson greater than Lennox Lewis in the all-time greatest heavyweight ranking? If so, give me reasons why Mike Tyson is greater than Lennox Lewis.

J. A.: Yes, I would say Tyson is definitely higher up in the all-time rankings than Lewis. I can honestly say, hand on heart, that if you asked one hundred knowledgeable ex-boxers and coaches to impartially assess this topic, then the majority would pick Tyson. But ask them specifically to compare *prime* for *prime*, and you'll find Tyson's peak is way higher than Lewis's. Don't get me wrong. I rate Lewis highly. He was without doubt a great long-range fighter and one of the best right-hand punchers in the division's history. But you'll find that he was, defensively, relatively weak and had a mediocre chin at the best of times.

I do have a number of other logical reasons underpinning why I rate Tyson higher. Prime Tyson was a more destructive two-handed puncher; indeed, ESPN rated Tyson as the most destructive force to ever enter the heavyweight arena. Lewis had a great right-hand punch but not a great left, and in my book, this ambidextrous advantage made Tyson twice as deadly.

As Rocky Balboa's trainer Mickey famously commented, "We need speed. Speed's what we need—greasy fast speed." Tyson is comfortably faster than Lewis and is generally rated as the third-fastest puncher in heavyweight history. Lewis was no slouch, but Tyson gets the punch there faster.

Other than prime Ali, no one had a better defence than prime Tyson—certainly not in terms of head movement, body shape, and waist movement. Within the boxing fraternity, Tyson is an accepted master of the peekaboo defence.

Prime Tyson had precision timing which was only really matched by Joe Louis. Tyson's ex-trainer Teddy Atlas commented on ESPN Classic, "Tyson was able to time punches perfectly in and around 1988."

Tyson is generally ranked as the second scariest boxer in history. He literally scared his opponents shitless, whereas Lewis didn't. In practical terms, this intimidation factor is priceless in a boxing match.

No heavyweight champion in history enjoyed a more dominant reign than peak Tyson. Even boxing experts who aren't that high on Tyson will concede this point. He was way better than his contemporaries. Like prime Sonny Liston twenty-five years before him, he was widely believed to be unbeatable.

According to my observations, Lewis is better than Tyson in terms of longevity at the top and versatility. In general, he could box in a more adaptable manner. It has to be said that Tyson boxed pretty much always in the same way.

Finally, in terms of natural boxing talent and instincts, I think Tyson is leagues ahead of Lewis. I know for a fact that two of the UK's most well-known and respected boxing pundits, Jim Watt and Barry McGuigan, would both pick Tyson over Lewis. (Both pundits were world champions in their respective weight classes.)

—January 2019

Alex Fricker: How much of Mike Tyson's fame is just down to his character, personality, and private life, as opposed to boxing skill?

J. A.: I'm guessing that you're a fairly young boxing fan, and so have only seen old and grainy YouTube footage of peak Tyson. Fortunately, I was privileged enough to see Kid Dynamite in his late 1980s heyday. Let me tell you something totally honest: I don't think any boxer in history came close to Tyson's instinctive boxing talent and ferocity. He was without doubt the most skilful brawler in heavyweight history and had the all-time greatest and most varied offensive arsenal. Tyson could knock you out with either hand from any angle. He was without question the most powerful short-range puncher in history. Let's now analyse one of his signature punches.

Mike Tyson's arching uppercut was arguably the most deadly punch in heavyweight history. He threw this nightmare of nature punch routinely, like most heavyweights throw jabs. He dropped a guy named Mike Jameson in 1986 with four consecutive uppercuts in a row! If this is not skill, I don't know what is. He was so talented that Nintendo released a video game named after him, specifically showcasing his signature punch.

No other fighter in history rose to Tyson's level of prominence so quickly. What does that tell you? In 1987, his private life was still private, and we didn't know that much about the man behind the myth. It was all about his perfect boxing skills, which the media of the day loved. Tyson produced the best knockout highlight reel in history. His fists quite literally put bums on seats. Boxing fans were addicted to his knockouts. In the 1980s, we knew the other guy didn't stand a chance. What was exciting was the expectation of the manner in which Tyson was gonna dish out the hurt. Was he gonna finish the argument with a cannon to the head? Would he punish the body? Or would he toy with his opponent and carry his sorry ass until the final bell?

But all of this is now ancient history. Many casual boxing fans have short memories, and many young fans have only seen rusty Mike. Trust me, Iron Mike is not one of those people who is famous for being famous. He isn't a Burt Reynolds; he is a Robert De Niro through and through.

—January 2019

John Dune: As Joe Louis was one of the best textbook boxers ever, why are there no contemporary boxers using his style?

J. A.: This may well be to do with the fact that he was just about as good as it gets. To use, borrow, or copy a classic fighter's textbook style is not always a good idea, particularly if you lack that guy's toolbox. It is kind of like saying, "Why hasn't there been another martial arts actor who can match the mighty Bruce Lee?" It has now been nearly fifty years since his untimely death, and there have been numerous martial artists over the years, but nobody has ever duplicated Lee's Jeet Kune Do style. In this same way, I don't think there is any contemporary heavyweight boxer who has the capability or boxing talent to copy the great Joe Louis.

So what exactly was his style? He has been described as a mechanical wonder, and back in the day, he was most notably described as "a machine of destruction". If you want to categorise his style, he was probably most accurately described as a boxer-puncher with a minimalistic approach. This is not to belittle his style, but it was fairly simple and was underpinned with textbook precision and very strong boxing fundamentals.

Hypothetically speaking, assuming a given boxer wanted to copy his style, then to land precision power punches like Joe Louis, using economic punching motions, would require his legendary shuffling footwork. According to the experts, he had the most precise footwork of any heavyweight in history. It enabled him to ghost into the perfect position to land a pinpoint bomb. How many contemporary guys are there who can match his footwork or even have the drive and determination to practise as hard as he did? Those were very hard times for boxers, and even the greats often struggled to make ends meet.

—January 2020

Mike Brown: Why do many hardcore fans say Tyson only beat bums? What makes Lewis's and Holyfield's résumés so much better than his, besides the fights that they had between each other?

J. A.: I think it all depends on which hardcore fans you ask. Tyson's career went from one extreme to the other, so it has led to much confusion, contradiction, and baseless speculation. During the 1980s, because he cleaned house from the basement to the attic, his critics now have a valid reason to rant that back in the day, he only "crushed tomato cans". In other words, his total dominance was short-lived and he dominated nobodies. Furthermore, during the second phase of his career, he was unable to get anywhere near those dizzying 1980s heights again. This further reinforces the theory of weak competition.

Now ask yourself an honest question. Would his critics and haters be accusing him of beating up on bums had he *never* mounted a comeback after prison? His comeback only served to damage his overall legacy. Hindsight is a fine thing. As far as I can recall, nobody was accusing him of beating up bums during the 1980s.

As for his career rivals having better résumés than Tyson, I argue that this is purely opinion rather than fact. Both Lewis and Holyfield (and Riddick Bowe for that matter) benefited hugely from the void left by prime Tyson. Those guys would have had vastly different careers had the Iron Man stayed on the straight and narrow. The way I see it is that the Buster Douglas defeat was a game changer and had far-reaching repercussions. It was like a *Back to the Future* moment in which the heavyweight timeline and landscape were horribly shifted to a new, alternate reality. Had Tyson stayed with his original trainer, Kevin Rooney, it is highly probable that prime Tyson would have retired Lewis and Holyfield in the same way that he retired Michael Spinks.

Boxing is all about timing. When a fight happens is perhaps the most important ingredient in determining the winner and the loser. Looking at old images taken in their respective youths, I don't think for a second that a juvenile Lewis could match a juvenile Tyson. When they finally met in 2002, Tyson was a mere shadow of his former self. Therefore the last impression of the two fighters has become more engraved in the memories of many fans.

—February 2020

Matt Arrington: How mean was George Foreman when he fought in the 1970s, and is he underrated?

J. A.: Quite simply put, he was very mean—one of the meanest and most brutal heavyweights ever. In his own words, "If all else fails, then I just resort to brutality." If you watch most of his 1970s fights, they were very reflective of this brutal and single-minded wrecking-ball attitude. It is safe to say that 1970s Foreman always went for the KO and never, ever looked to coast to a points victory.

His meanest and most brutal 1970s performances came against two Hall of Famers, namely Ken Norton and Joe Frazier. In 1973, he almost murdered Norton in one of the most brutal KOs in heavyweight history. This KO was all the more impressive and chilling given the fact that this same Norton had gone the distance twice with Muhammad Ali. But against Foreman, Norton did nothing other than get wiped out in two short rounds.

Foreman was equally rude to Smokin' Joe Frazier and just about bounced him up and down like a human yo-yo. Again, virtually this same version of Joe Frazier had gone the full distance with Ali.

As for whether Foreman was underrated, I would say probably not. He generally makes the cut in most all-time great, top ten heavyweight lists, and this is largely because of his 1970s exploits. But 1970s Foreman was a tremendous power man, pure and simple.

—October 2020

Gerardo Pleasant: Which pre-World War Two boxer on film looks most technically advanced?

J. A.: How about a guy named Joe Louis? He never ran and he certainly didn't hide. He was pure poetry in motion. If ever there was a 6-feet 2-inch, 200-pound ballet dancer who could punch like a mule kicks, then Joe Louis was that guy. Consistently rated by *Ring* magazine as the greatest puncher in heavyweight history, still to this day he is described by many old-school boxing anoraks as the GOAT heavyweight. He is the long-time record holder for the highest number of heavyweight title defences.

I personally rate Louis as the joint best combination puncher in heavyweight history, as having the most accurate and effective footwork in heavyweight history—yes, even better than Ali—and as having one of the highest ring IQs all time. Needless to say, he was a complete boxer in every sense, who had almost no weaknesses to his game. Louis was so precise with his power punches that he was once described by a journalist of the day as "a machine of destruction". I also loved his boxing quotes. He was a true credit to his race—the human race.

—December 2018

Sylvian Saurel: Where do you rank Lennox Lewis in the all-time heavyweight boxing rankings?

J. A.: In my list of top ten heavyweights, I have Lewis at number ten, just behind Rocky Marciano. Lewis was probably the best of the super heavyweights—a versatile, adaptable, and good all-round boxer who was essentially a thinking man's heavyweight. He was one of the best right-hand punchers in heavyweight history, and had great ring presence and athleticism for a guy of his size. Mediocre defence and chin let him down. I see him struggling in the 1970s golden era of heavyweights. I personally classify Lewis as a fringe great rather than a genuine great, as in my opinion true greats don't get knocked out by journeyman-grade opposition.

At times he performed like a world-beater, like when he destroyed Donovan "Razor" Ruddock in two short rounds and dismantled the overhyped Michael Grant. And then there were times when he looked pretty ordinary, as against the likes of Ray Mercer or the virtually unknown Zjelko Mavrovic. Over the course of most of his career, he blew hot and cold. It is this inconsistency that makes it all the more difficult to accurately assess his overall career standing.

With the benefit of hindsight, Lewis must be thanking his lucky stars that he ran into the late, great trainer of champions, Manny Steward. Steward was one of the best trainers ever and had a massive impact on Lewis's faltering career path. In the late 1990s, Steward remodelled Lewis's style into a more strategic, long-range-based game, which afforded better protection to his somewhat suspect chin. Steward also seemed to work wonders on Lewis's power and strength, as he was transformed into an intimidating physical presence. If you look at a pre-Manny Lennox Lewis, this physicality and power wasn't anywhere near so evident. But one thing Manny couldn't change was Lewis's chin strength, and against Rahman Lewis was crudely exposed.

Ultimately, I think Lewis looked fantastic against a certain type of opponent, when he could operate in a comfort zone. Whenever he was seriously pressured, there was a danger he could fall apart. Therefore I see him struggling against the top short-arm brawlers in heavyweight history. A guy like a prime Earnie Shavers would perhaps be Lewis's worst nightmare come true.

—December 2018

Bevan Narinesingh: Who was the better fighter, Jack Dempsey or George Foreman?

J. A.: You may as well toss a coin, because both fighters are all-time greats. It is almost too hard to call, but I think most fans will probably say Foreman, given his fights were captured in glorious technicolour. Believe me, this fact makes a big psychological difference when watching old footage. When you view Dempsey's old fights, they're literally from a bygone, prehistoric era. In addition to being in black-and-white, the footage is also very jerky due to the low frame rate of those ancient cameras. This doesn't really do Dempsey justice; he would look way better under modern cameras.

This comparison almost boils down to which type of style you prefer, whether it's the brute-force slugger approach of Foreman or the inside-mauling style of Dempsey. The guys do share major similarities in that they were both pressure fighters and massive punchers. They were also great at cutting the ring off on back-pedalling opponents. Dempsey was noticeably faster than Foreman and was also renowned for his use of leaping hooks. Foreman had a better jab and was physically stronger.

Each fighter carried out a legendary and timeless beatdown which has become part of boxing folklore. Dempsey destroyed the much larger Jess Willard, and Foreman destroyed fellow Hall of Famer Joe Frazier. On paper, both these fights were supposedly very close matchups but in reality they turned out to be huge mismatches. Such is the nature of top-level heavyweight boxing, in which fine margins have big consequences.

An easier question to answer would be who wins prime versus prime? If they ever shared a ring, I would go with Foreman based largely on his superior chin strength. The fight would no doubt be a war, with both guys landing home run shots but ultimately, I see Foreman absorbing Dempsey's power better than vice versa.

—January 2020

Rodney Chin: Excluding Holmes and Ruddock, who was the best boxer that Mike Tyson defeated?

J. A.: Most probably Michael Spinks, who received arguably the most dominant beating in the modern heavyweight era.

Poor old Michael Spinks was never to be heard from again. He was one of the best light heavyweights ever, a very slick and world-class boxer, and conqueror of the legendary Larry Holmes. Spinks didn't land a single telling blow on a rampaging Tyson, who was virtually unbeatable on this night. Sugar Ray Leonard's ringside comment was "Tyson is so destructive that he should be caged up." Another notable ringside pundit described Tyson as "speed, power and timing personified—your worst nightmare come true". Unfortunately for Michael Spinks, that nightmare became a cruel and brutal reality.

Like many of Tyson's victims, Spinks was clearly psyched out and fell victim to Tyson's aura of intimidation. It must have crossed his mind any number of times that "I beat Larry Holmes twice and this guy Tyson literally nailed that same Holmes to the canvas". With the benefit of hindsight, it was a fight that Spinks could not have won and should not have taken.

After Spinks, I think Tony Tucker was Tyson's next most impressive win. Tucker was a very tall, athletic guy who could box on the fly. In many ways, he perhaps gave the boxing world a glimpse of how a slick, mobile boxer could control Tyson, particularly in the very dangerous early rounds. Tucker was a very underrated boxer and far superior to the notorious Buster Douglas.

—January 2019

CHAPTER 14
MISCELLANEOUS

Maxine Short: Which was the bigger shock, Leon Spinks defeating Muhammad Ali or Buster Douglas defeating Mike Tyson?

J. A.: Douglas beating Tyson was a far bigger upset. He was a 42:1 betting underdog against the Iron Man in 1990. What these odds mean when they are converted into a probability is that Douglas had a two per cent chance of victory according to the bookies—in other words, he had almost no chance. Leon Spinks, on the other hand, was a 10:1 outsider against Ali in 1978, which means he had a ten per cent chance of victory. Simply put, according to the bookies, the Buster Douglas shock was approximately five times bigger than the Spinks shock.

The Buster Douglas upset occurred in Tokyo, Japan, which was a strong indication that literally no one was interested in the fight in the US, because there was no action. Prior to the Douglas fight, the last time that Tyson had fought abroad was coincidentally also in Tokyo—in fact at the same venue—two years earlier in 1988, Tyson had demolished Tony "TNT" Tubbs in another "foregone conclusion" type of defence.

Over the entire course of his career, Tyson only boxed overseas on five occasions. In chronological order, his opponents for these overseas fights were Tony Tubbs, Buster Douglas, Julius Francis, Lou Savarese, and Brian Nielsen. All of these fights on paper were either tune-up or keeping-busy fights.

—January 2021

Olorunfemi Bamiyo Ogundipe: In boxing, which is harder, moving up or coming down in weight class?

J. A.: When fighters change their weight class, they mostly move up. This evidence-based observation kind of answers the question. Based on the majority of the data, I think it is considerably harder to move down in weight class, given no one really does it.

Drawing a parallel to life in general, it is clearly easier to gain weight than to lose weight. To gain weight, one simply has to consume more calories than one burns, whereas to lose weight one has to diet and exercise. Clearly, eating like there is no tomorrow is much easier than dieting.

Real-world examples of high-profile boxers who famously moved up through the weights were Thomas Hearns, Sugar Ray Leonard, and Roberto Duran. Hearns and Leonard both started out as skinny welterweights but by the end of their careers had campaigned at light heavyweight. Duran, believe it or not, started out fighting in the super featherweight division and by the end of his career was campaigning in the super middleweight division.

At super middleweight, Duran famously defeated a much bigger man named Iran "the Blade" Barkley, in what was the fight of the year 1989. Although Duran was well past his best and boxing well out of his ideal weight class, he fully showed why he was nicknamed the Hands of Stone.

When fighters do on occasion move down in weight class, it is often a case of them moving back down to their original weight class, such as Roy Jones Junior. In this instance, the manipulation of his body weight had disastrous consequences for the latter part of his career. Jones was knocked out a total of five times in his career—and all those knockout defeats came after he moved back down in weight from heavyweight to light heavyweight.

—January 2021

Viv Pereira: Are left-handers at an advantage in boxing?

J. A.: As a general rule of thumb, yes, being left-handed does confer some natural advantages. The main reason is novelty, but there are also a number of secondary practical advantages. Being left-handed in boxing has been known for decades as giving rise to the southpaw jinx. There is an abundance of historical boxing data that can be called upon to explain how left-handedness was believed to be the decisive factor in major fights—hence the term *jinx*.

Along with the many unbelievable things that we see in the movies, once in a while we do also see common-sense things. The southpaw jinx was the basic common-sense premise behind the original *Rocky* movie. It gave the outmatched underdog some much-needed novelty value. Had Balboa been a righty with that exact same skill set, it is highly unlikely that he would have gone the distance with a superior athlete like Creed.

By boxing left-handed, Balboa did everything backwards. His trainer Mickey remarked upon this as being one of the root causes for his awkwardness and novelty. It is very similar to watching yourself shadow-box in front of a mirror, where everything is reversed.

But getting back to reality, being left-handed places you in a nine-to-one minority. The higher up the boxing food chain you go, the more significant this novelty value becomes. Prime examples of great fighters who became even better by virtue of being left-handed were the late Marvin Hagler and Manny Pacquiao. In Hagler's case, he was a brilliant switch-hitter and would change seamlessly between stances in the blink of an eye. In Pacquiao's case, his dreaded southpaw cross had greater disguise and novelty value than the conventional right cross. For many elite opponents, it proved to be a difficult punch to read.

Another major reason for having a good left-hand punch is because of the nightmare liver shot—you cannot deliver the same punch with the right hand. This is because Mother Nature placed the liver on the right-hand side of the body, in a relatively exposed position. To deliver the liver punch, the natural southpaw may well switch to orthodox on the inside, similar to Marvin Hagler. If this punch lands, it is usually a finisher. But the liver shot can only be executed by a left-hand punch.

Yet another advantage of being left-handed may well pertain to vision. This is more theory and intuition rather than an observation based on evidence. Normally, if you are right-handed, you are right eye dominant. If you are left-handed, you are left-eye dominant. As already stated, being left-handed puts you in the minority. So when an orthodox fighter faces a southpaw, from a visual standpoint it can throw him, particularly when trying to read the dreaded southpaw cross. The left cross follows a different visual trajectory to the conventional right cross, which makes it more difficult to see and therefore read. Simply put, the orthodox fighter faces far more unseen threats when facing the left-handed fighter.

Finally, we have the small matter of footwork. Any fan who has watched a number of boxing matches over the years will realise that the lead foot can become tangled. This generally happens when you have an orthodox versus southpaw clash. It is yet another complication that the orthodox fighter has to prepare for in sparring and in the real-time fight.

Speaking of sparring, it is not a foregone conclusion that an orthodox fighter will have access to sufficient high-quality left-handed sparring partners. This makes preparations for a southpaw opponent that much more difficult. On the other hand, for the southpaw boxer facing an orthodox boxer, it is simply business as usual.

—May 2019

Wyatt Thompson: Do boxing gloves protect the puncher's hand or the punch's recipient?

J. A.: Both! When a fist strikes an object, it exerts pressure on the object. How much pressure is exerted depends on the striking force and the contact area. The harder you punch the recipient, the greater the return force on your fist. The forces are exactly equal and opposite, according to Newton's third law.

The amount of pressure P can be calculated by the following equation:

P = F/A, where F = punching force and A = contact area

With the gloves on or off, clearly the main variable is contact area. Wearing a boxing glove obviously increases the surface area of a naked fist. So, for the same punching force, less pressure is applied. This means more headshots, longer fights, fewer cuts, fewer hand fractures, fewer facial bone fractures, and possibly more KOs. (This last point is debatable.) Ultimately, we as paying spectators get more bang for our buck and the fighters prolong their careers.

—May 2019

Anonymous: Has there ever been a Hispanic heavyweight boxing champion?

J. A.: The uncharismatic John Ruiz (no relation to Andy Ruiz Junior) had a brief stint as heavyweight champion in the early 2000s. He was known as the Quiet Man, and his most notable victory was over a shopworn Evander Holyfield. He did manage to drop Holyfield with a concussive right hand, which led many pundits to draw comparisons to Lennox Lewis. Ruiz managed to score a knock-down against Holyfield, which was something that a prime Lewis failed to achieve in twenty-four rounds of boxing Holyfield.

Ruiz suffered a notorious points defeat to a pumped-up Roy Jones Junior and was knocked out cold by a rampant David Tua. The knockout loss to Tua is often seen as one of the most brutal knockouts in heavyweight history.

—*June 2018*

Leonnius Herbalies: What are the natural advantages some boxers might have that can help them more easily become good boxers?

J. A.:

A boxer's physique

Ask yourself an honest question: If you saw a random guy with a Tysonesque or butcher-block body walking down the street with his top off, would you think he was a tough guy? Would you think he was naturally good at boxing? If this same random guy walked into your boxing gym, would you be willing to invest time and money into his training? The answer is debatable, but those in the know would instantly recognise an opportunity knocking. Prime Tyson's physique was largely a product of optimum genetics. He was muscular without being muscle-bound—there is a subtle difference.

Having a Tysonesque physique would no doubt help you with aggressive boxing, particularly at close range. As Tyson's physique was natural, it struck the perfect balance between the strength, power, speed, and dynamic aspects of boxing. Tyson's natural muscle tone was improved and refined through volume callisthenics, which are exercises that require flexibility in the first place and thereby facilitate explosive movements.

Boxing toolbox: hand size

Big hands means big fists. Sonny Liston had the biggest fists in boxing history. This resulted in more damage per punch due to his heavy-handedness. If you want to keep your money, then bet on Sonny!

Natural strength

Was Foreman the ultimate heavyweight strongman? George Foreman's feats of strength have become the stuff of legend. He also wasn't half bad wearing a pair of boxing gloves. Although strength can be significantly improved through environment and exercise, I don't think most mortals will be pulling jeeps uphill anytime soon!

Natural hand speed

Working the speed bag will no doubt improve your hand speed, but it will take you a lifetime to catch up to Ali!

Natural body coordination

Apparently Floyd Mayweather is the best ever at jumping rope. Mayweather's mastery of this classic boxing exercise maybe goes some way towards explaining his legendary body shape and fighting rhythm.

Natural toughness

Marvin Hagler and Roberto Duran were two of boxing's legendary hard men. Hagler possessed the strongest chin in boxing history, and Duran possessed possibly the most rock-solid fists ever. Surely these two boxing traits were largely genetic in origin.

Height, reach, and athleticism

Lennox Lewis was the best of the super heavyweights and a prime example of a big heavyweight who also learnt how to fight big. Heavyweight boxing has seen many giants over the years, but not many of them can boast Lewis's natural athleticism and ring savvy.

Cardiovascular fitness

Henry Armstrong isn't exactly a household name, but he possibly possessed the best ticker in boxing history. Joe Frazier idolised Armstrong and claims that he could throw three hundred punches in one round. Although we can all improve our cardio and become more box fit, Armstrong was a cardio freak!

Bodybuilder genetics

At heavyweight, Holyfield's upper body eventually began to resemble that of a real bodybuilder's. In a short space of time, he gained pure lean muscle mass while staying totally ripped and managed to maintain his original cruiserweight waist measurement. This classic bodybuilder V-taper enabled him to make maximal use of his frame size without sacrificing any of his dynamics and mobility.

A boxer's character

Ali and Frazier took bravery, grit, and determination to the next level. Frazier in particular would rather have died then quit in a fight. Some guys were maybe born to box?

—April 2019

Steve Pierce: How do you measure a boxer's reach and who had the longest?

J. A.: Reach pertains to a wingspan measurement: with your arms outstretched at your sides, the measurement is taken from the two extremities. In essence, when we talk about how long a boxer is, we're talking largely about reach and height. So why is reach important?

Sonny Liston was maybe the top genetic freak in heavyweight history, and he possessed a wingspan that many a jumbo jet would have been proud of. Relative to his height, this guy had by far the longest reach in history, coming in at a whopping 84 inches. In fact, Liston still has the highest reach-to-height ratio in boxing history at 1.15. In other words, his reach was 15 per cent longer than his height. You can just begin to imagine how dangerous and rangy his jab would have been. A long reach is particularly beneficial to punches that follow a straight-line trajectory—jabs and crosses.

It is interesting to observe a tale of the tape comparison between Liston and his bogeyman Mr. Clay. Even though Clay was two inches taller than Liston, his reach was five inches shorter than Liston's. Clay's reach-to-height ratio was still an impressive 1.05. Against everyone else, Liston's reach advantage was a decisive factor, but in the face of Ali's dazzling footwork, timing, and speed, it wasn't enough. To circumvent the other guy's reach advantage, you need fast feet!

Other heavyweight boxers with notable reach-to-height ratios are Lennox Lewis (1.09), Tyson Fury (1.05), and Wladimir Klitschko (1.04), all of whom are exceptionally tall. In the really modern era, Lewis is perhaps the standout boxer in terms of making his reach advantage count the most. Certainly Tyson Fury's reach advantage over Wladimir Klitschko was an important ingredient in his upset victory. At middleweight, Marvin Hagler (1.08) and Thomas Hearns (1.07) both had renowned reaches.

Ultimately, I suggest that having a reach advantage is all well and good, but knowing how to exploit it still relies on boxing ability. Sonny Liston was without doubt a genetic freak, but he still knew and learnt how to box.

—April 2019

Bill Dong: How important is strength versus speed in boxing?

J. A.: Speed kills! Strength wears the other guy out over a period of time. There is a delicate balance to be struck between the two. Unfortunately, gains in strength often come with corresponding sacrifices in speed and vice versa. If you asked me point-blank which boxing quality I value more if given a forced choice, then I would opt for speed. But in all honesty, a number of factors have to be taken into consideration when addressing this complex issue, such as your boxing style, body type, and skill set.

Observing the Foreman versus Frazier matchups, it is evident that Foreman's strength advantage was key to his manhandling of the smaller Frazier. Foreman's superior strength, coupled with his reach, proved to be consistently decisive against Frazier. If we asked Foreman which quality he valued more, he is obviously going to say strength, as much of his dominance flowed off his almost superhuman strength. If you asked most other heavyweight sluggers, I think they are generally going to opt for strength over speed.

Now if you asked an out-fighter like Ali, what do you think he's gonna say? To Ali, speed was absolutely crucial for him to be successful. His speed enabled him to beat the other guy to the punch—not to mention the fact that he had to land several hundred punches per fight to get the win. If you ask out-fighters like Ali, the two Sugars, Lennox Lewis, and Wladimir Klitschko, they would all probably say speed is more important to their style.

Next, let's consider the styles of the individuals in a classic matchup. Believe me, this complicates this equation even more. Remember the Rumble in the Jungle? At times in that fight, didn't Foreman look a tad frustrated? On the night, do you think it was Ali's speed or strength that proved to be the bigger thorn in Foreman's side? The answer is debatable. Ali showcased his all-round boxing ability, and on the inside, he was surprisingly strong and more than a match for Foreman in the grappling stakes. Under the very hot and humid conditions, Ali's rope a dope tactic relied on Ali being physically strong enough to tie his man up on the ropes The rope a dope has since been widely criticised, but on the night, due to a number of strange circumstances, it got the right result. Ali's physical strength was key to much of its success. Foreman could not manhandle Ali like he did Frazier.

In summary, I suggest that speed is more important to out-fighters, slicksters, and technicians. Strength is more important to sluggers, maulers, and in-fighters. Overall, I think speed is a more decisive ingredient to achieving success, because after all we are talking about boxing here and not wrestling. In a boxing match, the combatants are not in direct contact with each other the majority of the time

Finally, the duration of a fight also changes the balance of power between strength and speed.

Speed tends to be more significant in the early rounds, whereas strength comes to the fore in the later rounds, particularly if the fight turns into trench warfare.

—April 2019

Jack Mehoff: Why do boxers today look more rigid or stiff in competition than boxers of the past (1960s, 1970s, and 1980s)? Even the lumbering George Foreman moved more fluidly in his time.

J. A.: Too much weight! The scary super giant named Nikolai Valuev stood over seven feet tall and weighed well over twenty stone. There is a limit to which the human body can defy the laws of gravity, and the Beast from the East was surely well beyond that limit. This guy was so huge and cumbersome that he made a double-decker bus seem mobile. David Haye's words were "I thought I had seen some scary creatures in the *Lord of the Rings* until I saw this guy."

Obviously Valuev was an extreme outlier. Not every twenty-first-century heavyweight is as immobile as him. But heavyweights are seemingly getting bigger and heavier by the day. I personally believe that if a guy is too much over seventeen stone fight weight, his mobility, flexibility and suppleness will be adversely affected. The human heart and cardiopulmonary system struggles to cope with the stress caused by the excess weight. Hence the fact that a lot of these giants move around the ring like zombies. If you look at Lennox Lewis, Riddick Bowe, and Wladimir Klitschko, they were all approximately seventeen stone and were all reasonably mobile, but even they were pushing that physical boundary.

We all know that Big George Foreman was no Ali, but he moved much more fluidly than most of today's guys. He could just about bounce on his feet and was quite adept at cutting the ring off. But don't forget that he was a giant for his original era. In Foreman's case, as you correctly point out, he still had a lumbering and cumbersome look to his movements. Part of this would have been down to muscle weight, part to his training regimen, and part to his genetics. If there is too much muscle on a heavyweight, you get that stiff bodybuilder look—see Frank Bruno and Anthony Joshua.

Consider a physical comparison between prime Foreman, Frank Bruno, and Anthony Joshua. Bruno and A. J. appear more muscle-bound than Foreman, but at the same time, they don't necessarily look any tougher. Foreman looked more naturally trained, stronger, and more mobile than the two somewhat ponderous British fighters.

Some of this is no doubt the result of the different boxing cultures separating the two countries across the pond. But ultimately it boils down to the issue of weight—be it fat weight, water weight, or muscle weight, the extra weight is a burden on the most important muscle of all, the cardiac muscle. Unlike a car or a truck engine, which is mechanical and can therefore be modified, the cardiac engine is obviously biological and so cannot be modified to accommodate the extra body weight.

There is another, more subtle reason why boxers are more sloppy these days. It is simply a decline in skill and technique. As there is no weight limit in the heavyweight division, fighters are making up for their lack of skill with increased size and weight, without facing any kind of penalty. The added weight is obviously an advantage on the inside, particularly if the boxers start wrestling and the referees allow this kind of tactic to go unpunished. "Jab, jab and then grab."

—April 2019

Sean London: How did Mike Tyson have a 20-plus inch neck by the age of 18? Nature or training?

J. A.: One hundred per cent nature. Without doubt Tyson possessed some of the freakiest genetics in heavyweight history. His monster neck was perhaps his most talked-about freaky feature. In one of his very early fights, I remember the commentator drawing a comparison between Tyson's neck size and actress Shelley Duvall's waist! His neck was huge. Due to the squareishness of his build, it almost appeared to be an extension of his back, thereby giving him the classic pit-bull type of appearance. In other words, it almost appeared like he had no neck at all—quite similar to Tank Abbott in UFC, just more intimidating.

Watching prime Tyson doing full body weight neck rolls, the casual fan may be fooled into thinking they are watching an uncut scene from *The Exorcist*. To a hardcore boxing fan, this neck exercise is an impressive show from Tyson. In his prime, it sent a message to the competition: "Can any of you guys do this?"

No amount of neck rolls or neck exercises will get you to a Tysonesque neck. In Tyson's case, Mother Nature was at work in a big way, and it was the genetics that enabled him to perform such a difficult exercise so routinely.

One thing that did slightly surprise me was that, judging by his neck size, you would be forgiven for assuming that Tyson had the strongest chin in boxing history. There is a strong correlation between the size of one's neck and chin strength. However, Tyson had a very good chin but not quite granite. Obviously there are other anatomical characteristics which contribute to chin strength in addition to neck size.

—April 2019

Mario Thompson: Is natural talent the biggest foundation of becoming a pretty good boxer, or can anyone learn how to box on Mike Tyson's level?

J. A.: Tyson's physical appearance in his early teens created significant confusion and provoked many a raised eyebrow. Whether it was after seeing a photo of a 13-year-old Tyson or Tyson in person, many onlookers were left scratching their heads and thinking, "I wanna see the birth certificate." Believe it or not, at the age of 13, Tyson was already having to deny accusations of doping due to being blessed with the genetics of the angels.

The physical side of Tyson—the muscularity, the ambidextrous knockout punch, the aggression, the street-fighter mentality—all these traits were largely natural. The brilliant boxing technique that he subsequently acquired was all down to Cus. He effectively taught, trained, and bred Tyson into becoming a killer in the ring through tailored boxing technique. The system that D'Amato invented later came to be known as the peekaboo style, because of the hands held high and to the side of the head, similar to the game parents play with babies. The theory behind peekaboo was elusive aggression, and Tyson's natural physicality happened to be a perfect fit for the peekaboo template.

This is exactly the reason that Tyson created such a massive and unprecedented stir in the boxing industry: teenagers simply don't fight like Tyson. Someone was telling him what to do and how to do it.

Look for yourself through the annals of boxing history, and you will find that it is extremely rare for brawlers to be talked about in terms of their perfect boxing technique. Ultimately, to box like peak Tyson is a combination of nature and nurture. If I had to put a figure to it, I would say peak Tyson's brilliance was 40 per cent natural and 60 per cent taught.

—*August 2018*

PAUL BECHTOL: Did Mike Tyson plan on biting off Evander Holyfield's ear?

J. A.: It isn't all that difficult to imagine what happens after a 'roid- and HGH-hardened skull headbutts you. If you knew in advance that you might end up with a freaky, alien contusion on your head as Hasim Rahman did, would you prepare a contingency measure? I'm no mind reader, but I would say yes, the bite was indeed a pre-planned contingency. It was payback time. Team Tyson had insisted on a different referee to the first Holyfield fight, as they felt aggrieved that Holyfield's consistent use of his head had gone unpunished. A much more experienced referee in Mills Lane was brought in for the rematch.

In between rounds, the pain on the Iron Man's face after Headbutt Holyfield was having his wicked way spoke a thousand words. If you were in Tyson's shoes, how would you feel if you honestly believed that you were up against two fists *and* a 'roid skull instead of just two fists?

Because of the aftermath, casuals often forget the ferocity of some of the exchanges between these two career rivals. Holyfield had his own agenda; he wanted to *mentally torture* Tyson. Why? Holyfield had been part of the highly touted and close-knit US amateur team that struck gold at the LA Olympics in 1984. One of his teammates was heavyweight boxer Tyrell Biggs, whom Tyson dismantled in devastating fashion in the pros. Tyson played with Biggs in the same way that a domestic cat plays with a captured mouse. He visibly gloated in his victory and showcased Biggs as a trophy victim, which made Holyfield mad. Biggs was his amateur teammate and friend. In fact, Holyfield has stated that he dedicated his triumphs over Tyson to Tyrell Biggs, who was never again the same fighter post-Tyson.

The point is this: bad blood existed between Tyson and Holyfield dating back to their amateur days. They had sparred on various occasions as amateurs. On one occasion, what started out as a routine sparring session turned really nasty. They had to be broken up and physically restrained, as the exchanges had become way too physical and ferocious. Needless to say, that was the last time they ever sparred together.

Another simmering issue that many young fans won't be aware of is the fact that back in the day, Holyfield was privately jealous of Tyson's physique and the media attention it garnered. He was fully aware of the psychological benefits of having a macho-looking physique, particularly in a physical sport like boxing. So Holyfield was a very competitive guy and wanted to match Tyson in any and all possible ways. He would literally do and take anything to bridge the physical gap between himself and Tyson.

But getting back to the bite fight, we now know with hindsight that Tyson deliberately left out his mouthpiece in between rounds. This could not have been a random oversight. One of his entourage, who was conveniently nicknamed Crocodile, could be heard shouting at ringside, "It's time to bite, Mike!" This was verbal proof that Tyson had been planning his own dirty trick if Holyfield tried any rough stuff again. This is what happens when a boxing match turns into an alley war.

Holyfield got a taste of his own medicine. Judging by the look on his face after "the bite of the century", that medicine sure didn't taste too nice.

In the immediate post-fight aftermath, Tyson was absolutely defiant and remorseless. "I addressed it in the ring! I got one eye left, so he's got one ear left. I gotta go home and see my children with one eye closed!"

—April 2019

DANIEL PASSARELLI: Is it true that most of Tyson's opponents in the 1980s were mediocre fighters?

J. A.: The 1980s era that Tyson dominated has been described as relatively weak by some experts. While it wasn't the strongest decade, it certainly wasn't the weakest either. Considering that Tyson's era came shortly after the golden era, it was always going to receive some criticism for being relatively weak.

The majority of Tyson's early opponents were mediocre at best. Certainly the guys he destroyed in his first year of competition (1985) were hand-picked for harmlessness. So what's wrong with that? Isn't that exactly how you build up a young fighter's confidence? The great Joe Louis also fought his fair share of bums, which at the time was labelled "the bum of the month club".

In terms of name opponents, clearly the top scalp on Tyson's CV is that of Larry Holmes, whom he flattened in devastating fashion in 1988. After Holmes, Michael Spinks was the next most capable, and then Tony Tucker. If you call these three guys mediocre, then clearly you're a very harsh critic.

Who else could have taken care of Holmes like Tyson? No one, I'll tell you why: because no one else did. This was the only knockout defeat on Holmes's record. If Holmes was so mediocre, then why didn't Holyfield (+ PEDs) knock him out?

Larry Holmes was 42 years old when he gave Holyfield a good run for his money in 1992. So I guess, using the same deluded rationale, this means that 1992 Holyfield must be mediocre too, right?

Make no mistake, Tyson did not face the very stiff level of competition that Ali faced. Then again, no other historical world heavyweight champion did either.

—December 2020

SHAUN DUGGAL: Why did Tyson duck Foreman?

J. A.: The single main reason would've been the fact that Foreman was one of the toughest SOB's to ever lace up gloves.

At the grand old age of 41, Foreman took a serious beating from Holyfield, a guy who was thirteen years his junior at the time of the fight. This classic "battle of the ages" from yesteryear may well have been one of the material and factual reasons that dissuaded Tyson from sharing a ring with the Punching Preacher. Holyfield pounded on Foreman for twelve bruising rounds, and at no point did he stop him in his tracks. Without doubt, Foreman had a pure granite chin, arguably one of the strongest chins in the division's history. He could take a serious, serious beating and keep on fighting. In addition to this fact, I believe he had an unusually high tolerance for pain.

His persona, physical characteristics, and chin strength remind me of the scene from *Rocky 2* in which Apollo's trainer Tony tries in vain to convince Apollo to forget about the rematch with Balboa. "I saw you beat that man like you beat no other, and the man kept coming. We don't need that kind of man in our lives. Let's go after some easier meat." Creed should have listened to his trainer, as he gave Balboa an even worse beating in the rematch and still failed to score the knockout.

In real life, if you face a boxer who may well be as tough as a fictional boxer, this will inevitably play on your boxing psyche. There is also the realistic possibility that Tyson could have broken his own hands trying to pound on Foreman's rock-solid skull. Surely no boxer wants to be dealing with long-term debilitating hand injuries.

When analysing the Foreman matchup through the eyes of a knockout artist like Tyson, it is a very difficult pill to swallow. Probably the most dangerous heavyweight in history would possibly have insufficient firepower to take out an old, pot-bellied geezer who had been largely inactive for nearly a decade. To cut a long story short, fighting grandpa Foreman put Tyson in a no-win situation and in fact probably in a lose/lose scenario. Tyson's advisers probably suggested alternative and easier fights for roughly the same payday.

Something else that contributed to Tyson's reluctance was the advice and influence of his late, great trainer, Cus D'Amato. Tyson watched Foreman's 1970s fights extensively with Cus and apparently had been advised that the slugger (Foreman) versus the swarmer (Tyson) was a bad matchup. On an impressionable teenager, this advice would surely have had a long-lasting effect.

But in all honesty, irrespective of the issue of Tyson ducking old Foreman, Tyson wins the fight on points. It would probably have been very similar to the beatings that Holyfield and Morrison gave Foreman, but neither of those guys could stop this beast of a man from marching forward. So it may have been a known inside-industry fact that it was practically impossible to knock out Foreman, and this fact proved insurmountable—at least through Tyson's eyes.

—September 2019

Michael Uzar: Who was considered the "dirtiest" boxer?

J. A.: In the modern era of boxing, it is a close call between four shady pugilists. These are four professional foulers who have mastered the shady art of intermingling cheap shots with legal moves.

Evander "Headbutt" Holyfield

Taking a close look at this guy's fearsome cranium, it is easy to conclude that it was perhaps the largest, most dangerous, chemically enhanced, covert weapon to ever enter the modern heavyweight theatre. It surely must be way more than mere coincidence that over the course of his heavyweight career, Holyfield landed more "unintentional" headbutts than all the other modern heavyweight champions combined. Go figure.

George Foreman once described Holyfield, "He is the dirtiest motherfucker I have ever faced." Lennox Lewis on Holyfield: "Yeah, he definitely brings three weapons to the ring." Mike Tyson on Holyfield: "I got one eye left cause of the butts, so he's got one ear left." Holyfield's foul of choice was a one-two combo followed by a blind-side headbutt which most referees, onlookers, and intended targets would miss, as it was intermingled with the punches.

His headbutt on Hasim Rahman in 2002 has been described as the most damaging headbutt in boxing history.

Andrew Golota

If there was ever any doubt, then make no mistake: this guy knew exactly where a man's testicles are located. In two fights in 1996 against Riddick Bowe, Golota hit the target on several occasions with full-power low blows, right in front of the referee's face. Some observers would say that Golota gave a whole new meaning to the term *precision power*.

After Golota so blatantly and obviously brutalised Bowe's privates, the pained expression on Bowe's face spoke a thousand words. It is fair to say that Holyfield's head combined with Golota's low blows basically ended Bowe's short-lived heavyweight career—he was never the same fighter again.

Antonio Margarito

If he could have got away with it, then this guy would have hidden a horseshoe in his boxing gloves. Do you remember the now-debunked theory on how Jack Dempsey may have used plaster of Paris in his gloves when he fought the giant Jess Willard? Well, Margarito decided to take a leaf out of the old-school dirty fighter's manual and used the plaster of Paris trick against Miguel Cotto and Shane Mosley. Margarito is the only boxer in recent times to have been caught red-handed using tainted hand wraps.

Bernard "the Executioner" Hopkins

Hopkins knew a thing or two about holding and hitting. Some would even argue that he wrote the modern-day manual. Again, as with Holyfield, we see a fighter who would use any and all available covert means to gain an illicit advantage. Hopkins's specialty was holding his opponent on the referee's blind side and hitting him with his free and visible hand. Various opponents over the course of his career have cited Hopkins as being a consistent and crafty fouler. Without doubt he knew every trick in the book: low blows, elbows, thumbing in the eye, hitting on the break, rabbit punches, kidney punches, hitting after the bell sounds—you name it and at some point in his career, Hopkins has tried it.

—September 2019

Mark Adams: How skilful is an Olympic boxing gold medallist compared to an elite boxing world champion?

J. A.: It depends largely on which two fighters you compare. For example, if you compare Ali with Anthony Joshua, then both of them won gold medals at an Olympic Games: Ali at the Rome Olympics in 1960 and Joshua at London 2012. So as far as the amateur game is concerned, they are both equals, right? Just sticking to the facts and no opinions, they have roughly equal accomplishments as amateurs.

Comparing the same two guys in the professionals, there is clearly a big gulf in class that emerges. Had either Ali's or Joshua's skill set changed that much in the pros? I don't think their natural skill sets changed at all. What changed was the difficulty of the task at hand. The pro game is obviously way tougher than the amateur game, where you simply mucked about for three rounds with head-guards on. The pro game requires a much deeper and sharper toolbox.

So how do you acquire that deeper skill set? A large piece of the professional jigsaw puzzle is obviously your trainer. To make it big in the pros, you need a world-class trainer—Cus D'Amato for example—who can give you the know-how and expertise. You need a trainer who is right for you and one who improves your boxing technique, rather than preparing you for a Mr Universe contest. Does Joshua really need Mr Universe-sized biceps for boxing?

Another big piece of the professional jigsaw puzzle is genetics. You can't change your genes. To simplify the equation, you can't change your toughness all that much. You either are a tough guy or you're not. We know from the evidence to hand that Ali was as tough as they came, and clearly Joshua is not in the same class of tough guy. In the amateur game, your toughness and specifically your ability to take punishment is not really tested, whereas in the pros, your ability to take a hit is much more significant in dictating your chances of success or failure. Certainly Ali's longevity and long-term success was hugely dependent on his legendary chin strength.

Another big difference between the two forms of boxing is the concept of a learning curve. To make it to the elite class of pro boxer requires a long and steep learning curve. As far as I can see, Joshua has been exposed to roughly the same learning curve in both the amateur and professional games. Hence the fact he was so easily exposed by a half-decent but poorly conditioned counterpuncher in Andy Ruiz Junior. Can you honestly see that same Ruiz having any sort of success against a peak Ali? I certainly can't.

I think yet another differentiator between an Olympic medallist and an elite pro is character. This is again something that is largely natural and cannot be taught. Essentially, you either have it or you don't. As a professional, Ali was willing to go through the pain barrier to prevail. In several of his most famous fights, he took one helluva beating and crossed the finishing line largely on the basis of his character traits. Against Ruiz Junior, A. J. threw in the towel the moment the going got tough. What would he do if he were facing prime George Foreman? Chances are that he would avoid a guy like Foreman as if Foreman were carrying the plague. The character traits of a true legend like Ali come to the fore in the pro game.

—October 2019

Anthony Andranik Moumjian: What ruined boxing?

J. A.: How many belts does a real-world champion need?

If you ask a lot of knowledgeable boxing fans, I think the majority will say the primary reason for boxing's demise is the presence of too many alphabet group organisations. It was bad enough in the 1980s, when you had three governing bodies—the WBC, the WBA, and the IBF. If three sanctioning bodies weren't bad enough, then along came the fourth, the WBO.

Anybody with even a casual interest in boxing will realise that having up to four world champions per weight class at any given time leads to much confusion and a complete lack of transparency. Who is the real world champion? Who is the best fighter in the world? The fact there are potentially four different world champions per weight class clearly results in significant ambiguity in regards to who is the best fighter. Eventually this leads to a point where the value and prestige of a world championship belt is grossly diluted. In short, world titles no longer mean that much in boxing.

I grew up watching boxing at a time when the world heavyweight champion was perceived to be the main man. The heavyweight champ was believed to be the roughest, toughest guy in the world—at least in my mind. This is clearly no longer the case. The devaluation of the heavyweight crown has been a massive contributor to the overall demise of boxing. The heavyweight division had traditionally been the marquee and glamour division; it was regarded as the heart and soul of boxing. This hasn't been so for probably close to twenty years.

I personally think the slow death of the heavyweight division began in the mid 1990s, certainly in America. When you had guys like Ali or Tyson as the heavyweight champion, Joe Public related to them better and respected them way more than today's heavyweight champion.

Does Tyson Fury dressing up as Batman lend any credibility to the heavyweight division or boxing in general? After seeing Fury in such a ridiculous costume, the average person will think that he's more of a clown than a real champion.

Secondary factors contributing to ruining boxing are PPV, promotional disputes, and dodgy points decisions. The issue of PPV has been a long-running saga and has definitely been detrimental to the global audience. With regards to shady promoters in boxing, you could essentially write a book just on this topic. Finally, when you have big money involved, this inevitably leads to a degree of corruption and therefore dubious decisions. As we have seen time and again, when a big fight goes to the judges' scorecards, the best man on the night doesn't always win. You could write another book on incorrect and unfair points decisions. They contribute heavily to the theory of fight fixing.

—November 2019

David Mulata: What do they mean when they say two boxers were "fighting in a phone booth"?

J. A.: This is another boxing metaphor or a figure of speech. It pertains to a fight which takes place at very close quarters. Imagine two boxers who were so close that they were literally treading on one another's toes, so they may as well have fought in an old-fashioned phone booth.

A classic fight from 1987, between Julio Cesar Chavez and Edwin Rosario, may as well have been fought inside of a phone booth. Chavez was perhaps the best in-fighter of the late 1980s and early 1990s.

In their classic trilogy, Joe Frazier often tried to put Ali inside the phone booth so he could pound on Ali's body, thereby bringing his guard down, and then go upstairs with his trademark left hook. To put Ali inside the phone booth, he had to evade Ali's jab first and foremost. This was where Joe's legendary bob-and-weave style came to the fore. Frazier was perhaps the quintessential example of a heavyweight "phone booth" fighter.

When Frazier tried to put George Foreman inside the phone booth, he got smoked himself. Prime Foreman was way too strong and had superior glove control which Frazier couldn't deal with. Unfortunately, Frazier simply ran into a guy approximately the same size as Ali but way more powerful, and he couldn't avoid Foreman's big right hand. Some observers think it was Foreman's height and reach that defeated Frazier, and to an extent, this is true. But the primary reason for Foreman beating Frazier so easily was because styles make fights. Foreman's "stone" blunted Frazier's "scissors", and it didn't help one bit that Frazier was a slow starter.

—October 2019

Anonymous: In your opinion, which boxer has been robbed of victories by judges the most?

J. A.: A legendary hard man named Marvellous Marvin Hagler was robbed twice, both times in world middleweight title fights. Hagler suffered the most mental pain at the hands of his career nemesis, Sugar Ray Leonard, when they finally faced off in 1987.

It was a very, very close fight and way too close to call. It really should have been scored a draw. I personally scored the fight 114–114, and I can't even begin to imagine how one of the judges scored this fight 118–110 in favour of Leonard. Surely there can only be one feasible conclusion: this judge must have been bribed.

This wasn't the first time that Hagler was robbed by those judges. He had been robbed eight years earlier, also in Las Vegas. That time, his opponent was Italian hard man Vito Antuofermo. Hagler generally bossed the action and was expected to win a comfortable points decision—that is, according to unofficial ringside opinion. On this occasion in 1979, the judges scored the fight an even draw, and Vito Antuofermo held on to his middleweight title.

In terms of a major fight, Leonard versus Hearns 2 was probably the worst daylight robbery I can recall. Hearns generally bossed the action and had seemingly gotten his long-awaited revenge on Leonard, but once again the judges tore up the script. They decided to score the fight a draw. Again we saw a massive box-office draw in Leonard being the beneficiary of a highly dubious points decision. Incidentally, Hearns scored two big knockdowns in this fight, so those two rounds would automatically have been scored 10–8 in his favour.

If Holyfield hadn't got enough help from possessing the boxing world's largest and densest steroid skull, the judges also decided to give him a helping hand. Holyfield versus Lewis 1 was yet another disgraceful decision. The legendary Emanuel Steward, Lewis's trainer at the time, described it as "what's killing boxing".

—November 2019

Roger Cole: What's the hardest thing about boxing above your weight class?

J. A.: Thomas Hearns was a legendary fighter who was once known as the Hitman for a good reason. According to a lot of expert opinion, he was the most prolific and dangerous attacking boxer of the modern era. There was a time during the early 1980s when, if Hearns hit you cleanly with his "laser gun" right hand, it was pretty much a guarantee that you were going to sleep. He had an incredibly potent right hand which wreaked havoc in the middle divisions during the late 1970s and early 1980s.

In the fall of 1988, Hearns boxed a relatively unknown guy named James "the Heat" Kinchen, who was a natural super middleweight. Kinchen possessed a more robust and stocky physique compared to Hearns, had a good chin, and was taking Hearns's vaunted punching power surprisingly well. Hearns pounded on him with many clean right hands, but Kinchen stood tough throughout the entire twelve rounds. The main reason that Hearns didn't score a knockout was due to a decline in his relative punching power as he moved up through the weight classes. Boxing Kinchen at a heavier weight class, Hearns's punches had lost some of their sting and snap. In absolute terms, he hit harder at the higher weight class, but in relative terms, his power had declined.

At around the same time, Hearns boxed another genuinely tough middleweight boxer named Iran "the Blade" Barkley. Barkley again was the thicker and denser man, and he also took Hearns's power. Hearns gave this guy a tremendous body beating, with some of the hardest left hooks to the body I can recall. In the third round of their first meeting, after taking such a crippling body beating, Barkley sucker-punched Hearns and scored the against-the-tide knockout.

In this instance, Hearns was a much harder puncher than Barkley and landed way more clean leather. Yet he was the one who was knocked out. Clearly, boxing at a higher weight class had reduced Hearns's punch resistance. In other words, his pound-for-pound punch resistance was significantly lower at the higher weight class.

Other factors that also come into play when you box above your natural weight class are reduced hand speed, cardio, and stamina. For the same fight intensity, a boxer will tire more quickly at the higher weight class because his heart muscle is obviously more stressed at the higher weight. This is where those pesky little PEDs come in very handy.

In the case of Roy Jones Junior, moving up in weight class was perhaps the worst professional decision he ever made. Although he won a version of the world heavyweight title, I believe he was never again the same fighter once he moved back down in weight. In the mid 1990s, this guy was being touted as an heir apparent to Sugar Ray Robinson's pound-for-pound throne. He was almost unhittable, possessing some of the best feline reflexes to ever grace a boxing ring. When he moved up in weight, he lost the edge and was crudely exposed by Antonio Tarver in 2004. Subsequent to the Tarver loss, he suffered further knockout defeats which have irreparably tarnished his overall legacy.

—October 2019

Jovanne Rodriguez: How strong was George Foreman to be able to lift a cow? Could he have had a successful career as a professional strongman?

J. A.: George Foreman was famously photographed lifting a cow and carrying it on his back. If I had to guesstimate, the cow he lifted weighed somewhere in the region of 300 kilograms. The nearest powerlifting exercise that equates to this position is probably the squat, so I think we can assume that Foreman excelled at squatting. But I doubt very much that Foreman squatted the cow up from the ground. More likely the cow was loaded onto his back directly from a cattle truck.

Also you have to take into consideration the shape of the cow, which is more awkward than a conventional barbell in a gym. There is another variable to consider, and that is a live weight (a cow) versus a dead weight (a barbell.) Does the fact that the cow is alive assist George in this lift? I would suggest that it probably does, as its muscle weight supports some of its own body weight.

In the modern era of boxing, Foreman is generally regarded as the most physically empowered heavyweight specimen. His feats of pure strength are seriously freaky. He is also probably the only heavyweight boxer who has pulled a jeep uphill. Given that this vehicle weighed somewhere in the region of two tonnes, this was another jaw-dropping feet of strength—at least by boxing standards.

So Foreman was seriously strong, and he successfully incorporated this real-world strength into his boxing. When he manhandled Joe Frazier in 1973, that was as much to do with superior strength as it was with superior punching power. Several times he pushed Frazier away with comparative ease that was clearly the result of his superior strength.

Now, professional strong men pull aeroplanes. Although Foreman was tremendously strong, this strength has only been compared to other boxers. It is unlikely that he would have been strong enough to compete in professional strongman—not impossible, mind you, but he would probably finish last. Also remember that strongmen weigh well over 25 stone in the off season, whereas Foreman in his prime was around 20 stone in the off. In other words, it could be that Foreman's pound-for-pound strength was the equivalent of a pro strongman, but in order to successfully compete, he would surely have to bulk up.

—October 2019

Vincent Pisano: In boxing, what is a palooka?

J. A.: This is an American description for a fighter who creates smokescreens to deceive the mass-market casual fan. In reality, he is a limited fighter and is simply milking the system, until the public find out that he is really a "stumble bum". The first time I heard this word was when it was used to describe Michael Moorer after he was KO'd by George Foreman in 1994.

Many of the boxing fraternity's hard men raised a suspicious eyebrow when Moorer went down from the final knockout punch. The finishing punch was described as a "little tap" by ex-world champion and legendary British hard man Barry McGuigan. This fuelled speculation that Moorer was nothing more than a palooka, who went down and stayed down all too easily. Incidentally, this was the fight in which Foreman set his world record as the oldest boxer to ever become heavyweight champion of the world.

—January 2020

Jason Mitchell: What is the difference in Brock Lesnar from 2002 to 2019?

J. A.: In simple terms, Brock's transformation may be an extreme example of the middle-age spread. He also appears to be exhibiting well-known side effects of PEDs, such as steroid gut and steroid skull. Clearly he has lost much of his definition, and the muscle is inevitably turning into fat or being replaced by fat.

Everyone gains some weight in their late 30s and early 40s if their caloric intake remains the same, so Brock is no different. His weight gain due to fat and water retention will be more dramatic than the average Joe, as he is still consuming massive amounts of calories but not working out as hard. Additionally, his cardio intensity will also have reduced with age. Therefore he has incurred a daily net gain of calories, which inevitably turns into fat. He had better start detraining, as otherwise he may begin to resemble Butterbean.

In 2002 he was clearly ripped and dry, which had no doubt been facilitated by diuretics such as clenbuterol or an equivalent. When he stopped taking such supplements, he started retaining more water. Therefore his body metamorphosis mimicked that of a retired bodybuilder.

—February 2019

Benjamin Howard: What would happen if a boxer punched a spectator?

J. A.: In 1995, Eric Cantona executed his now-infamous kung fu kick on a football fan who was racially abusing him. Judging by the facial expressions of some of the onlookers, they were pretty shocked and confused. This was obviously a football match and not a boxing match, but what happened in the immediate aftermath? Not a lot. Cantona was quickly escorted off the pitch and down the tunnel by security. His actions could easily have triggered a riot. Luckily the kick was seen and heard as a response to extreme provocation, so effectively he was only targeting an individual and not a group of people.

Punching a boxing spectator could definitely be a flashpoint incident with wider-reaching consequences, particularly if it was a random spectator who perhaps only wanted an autograph. If the boxer was provoked as Cantona was, then I think his actions would be more justified and tolerated by onlookers. But a lot depends on the specific circumstances of the punch and who the spectator is. Worst-case scenario, if a disgruntled boxer simply went berserk and punched an elderly spectator, this would surely cause outrage, retaliation, and a potential riot.

In the long term, the boxer would face a lengthy ban, a big fine, and possibly criminal assault charges, depending on whether or not the spectator wanted to press charges. But off the top of my head, I can't recall a real-life boxer ever punching a spectator. Fictionally, Clubber Lang did in *Rocky 3* during his ring walk in the rematch with Balboa.

Riddick Bowe may also have had a go at punching the "fan man" who parachuted onto the ring apron during his 1993 rematch with Holyfield. That was again provocation by an idiot rather than a boxer kicking off the argument. Mike Tyson tried to punch a few police officers after biting Holyfield's ear in 1997. Shortly after the bite, Tyson could be seen loading up with a fierce-looking right-hand punch. Yet again, this isn't the same as punching a spectator. The police officers were simply doing their job and trying to defuse Tyson.

Ultimately any number of things could potentially happen if a boxer laid into a spectator, but the exact nature of the outcome would inevitably depend on the individual circumstances of the incident. Attacking a group of fans of the rival boxer could no doubt result in chaos, as Bernard Hopkins found out when he stamped on the Puerto Rican flag during a press conference in the build-up to his much-hyped clash with Felix Tito Trinidad.

—February 2019

Idris Abdullah: In boxing, how important is the advantage of a longer reach and a taller height? How can it be exploited, and how would a shorter boxer counter it?

J. A.: Lennox Lewis commented on this exact topic ages ago on Sky Sports. His words were "Height and reach do matter, but not as much as people think." Anybody who can remember back to 2011 in the run-up to David Haye's much-hyped clash with Wladimir Klitschko, one of Haye's favourite catchphrases was "It is not the size of the dog in the fight, but the size of the fight in the dog." Both these guys were world-class boxers and knew their stuff, and they both seemed to slightly play down the importance of size.

In my humble opinion, it depends on the individual style of the boxer and how they use their height and reach to maximise their boxing potential. Wladimir Klitschko was a great example of a tactical out-fighter who had almost perfected a style of long-range boxing that utilised his height and reach. But underpinning his style was world-class athleticism and top-notch footwork. His athleticism enabled him to fully exploit his height and reach.

For a shorter fighter to offset his length disadvantage, he must close the gap between himself and the taller fighter as quickly as possible. For the shorter guy to be successful, the fight must take place at mid range or close range. The shorter guy has to be fleet-footed and have efficient footwork. He has to be well versed in either Joe Frazier's classic bob and weave or Iron Mike's pendulum waist movement. It is imperative that he moves his head correctly to avoid eating the jab on his way inside.

Assuming the shorter guy gets inside often enough, then it is advantage to the small guy in a big way. On the inside, height and reach are irrelevant. The shorter guy can feast on the large target in front of him. At close range, the shorter guy can use the uppercut to devastating effect, and quite often the taller guy presents himself as a sitting duck to this punch.

On a final note, the smaller man should have superior timing, which is crucial. Mike Tyson once said, "Jabbing is all to do with timing. You can be 5 feet 10 inches tall and out-jab a guy who is 6 feet 4—if you have good timing." So it is entirely feasible for the shorter guy to use his jab as a weapon to get inside effectively, and it is not a foregone conclusion that he will automatically lose the battle of the jabs.

—January 2019

Robert Cicariello: An orthodox boxer decides to fight southpaw, out of the blue: What happens?

J. A.: Just ask Frank Bruno. In the third and decisive round of his second fight with Tyson in 1996, Bruno made a blunder which effectively sealed his fate. He was being soundly dominated by Tyson and was almost forced into a desperation tactic. On the spur of the moment, he switched stances from orthodox to southpaw. Tyson's eagle eye spotted the clumsy switch in slow motion. Almost the instant Bruno switched, Tyson jumped all over the mistake like a harbour shark, going to the body with the right, followed up immediately with a left hook upstairs. Perhaps three or four seconds after Bruno's ill-fated stance switch, Tyson finished him off in the ropes with his trademark uppercut.

Game over.

I doubt any knowledgeable boxing trainer would advise switch-hitting out of the blue. It obviously depends on who you're up against. In Tyson, Bruno was up against the wrong guy at the wrong time to try such a novelty trick. Switch-hitting clearly backfired on Bruno in a big way. I doubt if he had ever boxed southpaw in any of his previous professional fights, so this fact alone didn't really bode well.

But if you want to see a master class in stance switching and the right way to do it, then just watch any of Marvelous Marvin's 1980s fights.

—January 2020

Anonymous: Has Mike Tyson ever expressed any remorse for firing Kevin Rooney?

J. A.: I have never heard him talk about Rooney, let alone express remorse. In my humble opinion, the worst professional decision Tyson ever made was firing Rooney, if indeed he made it (see a guy named Don King). The last time Mike looked and fought like Iron Mike was the Spinks fight—more than thirty years ago! In his next fight against Frank Bruno, he looked frankly awful. What was the missing ingredient? No Kevin Rooney!

—February 2018

Timothy Soo: What caused Andrew Golota to throw a number of low blows during both his boxing matches against Riddick Bowe?

J. A.: Golota was a good old fashioned "nutter", and nothing he ever did inside the ring convinces me otherwise. He was one of those guys who had the capacity to do crazy things when under pressure and in the heat of the moment. He was more than holding his own against Riddick Bowe in the first fight, when he just appeared to lose the plot. I doubt whether the blatant low blows were premeditated in the first fight. Why throw so many, right in front of the referee? I think it probably stemmed from frustration that he couldn't finish Bowe off. Perhaps he felt he was gassing as the fight wore on. But he was just an unstable guy.

In the second fight, the low blows were probably premeditated and were intended to deliberately rattle Bowe and get some payback for Golota. He had been disqualified in the first fight, and in the immediate aftermath was attacked by one of Bowe's entourage. Some random guy entered the ring and hit Golota in the head with his mobile phone. So it could be that Golota deliberately turned the second fight into an alley war to get his revenge.

The low blows may also have been a follow-up to the war of words in the pre-fight build-up. Perhaps there was something personal there? It is entirely possible that Golota had a personal grudge to settle. But ultimately the main reason for the repeated low blows was that Golota was a genuinely unstable person, and an unstable person sometimes behaves randomly when subjected to a high-pressure situation. I don't think it was a case of him deliberatively fouling just to get himself disqualified, as has been suggested. He was just a crazy kind of guy.

—November 2018

Casey Hill: Is the per cent of knockouts for lighter-weight boxers (say a 135-pound fighter) much lower than for heavyweights (over 200 pounds)?

J. A.: Yes, this is true.

Deontay Wilder currently has a jaw-dropping 98 per cent knockout-to-wins ratio—one of the highest in history. However, he is a fundamentally flawed boxer who makes up for his many technical deficiencies with raw power and the choice to fight weak opponents.

Let's draw a comparison between Wilder and a certain legendary fighter named Roberto Duran. Duran is generally rated as the number-one pound-for-pound brawler in boxing history and probably the best lightweight ever. Yet his knockout-to-wins ratio is only 68 per cent. You see the problem with cold, hard stats, right?

In general, knockouts are more likely in the higher weight classes. If you prefer it the other way around, they are less likely in the lower weight classes. In simplest terms, a heavyweight boxer hits that much harder than a welterweight or a lightweight boxer and is therefore more likely to cause a concussion when he lands a clean punch. The reality of the situation is slightly more complex.

Broadly speaking, in pro boxing, punching power increases fairly linearly with increasing body weight. In other words, a pro boxer who weighs 10 per cent more than another pro boxer hits around 10 per cent harder, assuming that both guys have equal skill and technique.

The other big factor that affects the likelihood of a knockout is obviously the punch resistance of the recipient—his toughness, chin strength, and impact resistance. Unlike punching power, the matter of toughness is not linearly related to body weight. A lighter fighter can often be tougher than a heavier guy. Simply put, adding body weight, be it muscle, fat, or water weight, is not going to make you any tougher. Chin strength is mostly genetic.

If you want to be scientific, then the following simplified equation can be used to define the likelihood of a knockout:

Knockout potential = punch force ÷ chin strength

As stated, in general punching force increases linearly through the weight classes. However, punch resistance or chin strength does not follow a linear relationship through the weights. Hence the fact that we see many more boxing matches ending in a knockout in the higher weight divisions.

—November 2020

Emil Goubasarian: Has anyone ever kicked someone in a pro boxing fight?

J. A.: Yes. Quite a notable incident occurred in 1991. Riddick Bowe was involved in a boxing match with an unknown guy named Elijah Tillery. There was some bad blood between the two, and it spilled over into the boxing match. Bowe dominated the first round, scoring a knockdown. Tillery showed visible signs of anger. The bell sounded to end round one, at which point the two boxers exchanged harsh words. Bowe sucker-punched Tillery with a jab, and Tillery responded with several low kicks. Tillery ended up being pulled over the top rope by Bowe's manager, Rock Newman.

This strange incident occurred before Bowe became a household boxing name. Over the course of his career, he was surely involved in some crazy fights, and this was one of them. It became one of those infamous sporting incidents that appeared on a BBC Sports programme called *A Question of Sport* and came under the "what happened next" category.

—January 2019

Bonobox Redaniel: Who is the most strategic boxer of all time and why?

J. A.: It has to be "Dr Steel-Hammer" Wladimir Klitschko; he was always a cold, calculating, and robotic tactician in there.

Wladimir Klitschko was an intelligent boxer with very good long-range power who fully realised his own limitation in terms of punch resistance and therefore almost always boxed with a safety-first approach. You could almost argue that Klitschko thought of a boxing match as a real-life game of chess. He was arguably one of the most one-dimensional heavyweight champions ever, but he excelled in his boxing specialty, which was long-range out-fighting. His in-fighting skills were almost non-existent, and he could hardly brawl at all due to a notorious glass jaw.

The robotic style that he developed under the legendary Emanuel Steward's tutelage was very awkward and cagey to say the least. It basically revolved around the general premise of "jab, jab, and grab". He used his height, reach, footwork, and athleticism to great effect and proved to be the most difficult of all heavyweight champions to beat, due in large part to the complete lack of a world-class short-armed brawler during his long reign. When David Haye challenged Klitschko in 2011, he jokingly remarked that his main goal in the fight was to "make the robot malfunction".

Nonetheless, as a strategic boxer, Klitschko was second to none. His control of range was as good as any tall, rangy out-fighter in history. Unfortunately, his now-infamous loss to Tyson Fury in 2015 has had a damaging effect on his legacy, due in large part to the ignominious nature of the defeat. Many boxing experts have made the inevitable comparisons to the greats of yesteryear. There has been much speculation suggesting that those past greats would've easily dealt with Klitschko. As always, boxing is a game of levels, and Klitschko was undoubtedly dominant in a fairly weak era.

—February 2019

Mirco Giraudo: What are some strange curiosities about Mike Tyson?

J. A.: One such curiosity is the fact that his biological father's name was Kirkpatrick, which is clearly an Irish name. You can read into this fact any number of things.

In one Tyson documentary dating back to the early 1990s, the narrator was some guy named Montieth Illingworth. He recounted some disturbing childhood facts that may have made Tyson so violent and sociopathic. On a fairly regular basis, a juvenile Tyson witnessed bilateral domestic violence, in which his parents would pour boiling water on each other.

Tyson, believe it or not had a gentler side. He most often showed this through his affection for pigeons. One of his major early street fights was with a 19-year-old guy who had killed one of his pigeons. Tyson was only 13 at the time. You can just begin to imagine how tough Tyson was at such a tender age. Very few teenagers in history could have given up a six-year age gap and still expected to beat up a fully grown man.

In school, Tyson was so well built for his age that his classmates nicknamed him Mighty Joe Young. He regularly acted out, particularly at mealtimes, when he would throw cartons of milk against the wall if he wasn't fed on time.

A bizarre paradox in Tyson's character was the concept of fear. His one-time trainer, Teddy Atlas, recounts how a very young Tyson used to hide from bigger guys before he learned how to box. Tyson later became a seriously feared ring monster, but he was often equally scared of his opponents. In his own words, "I use fear as my friend, and I reflect it back on my opponents. If I don't have fear, then I don't fight." This statement gives us an insight into Tyson's boxing psyche and how the concept of fear was central to his psychological profile. In his amateur days, during the 1982 Junior Olympics, Teddy Atlas would regularly stop Tyson from crying before certain fights, as he was so fearful of failure.

—February 2019

Jan Patrick Pagtalunan: Which professional boxers do you think are freaks of nature?

J. A.: I would classify the following seven boxers as pure freaks of nature. In chronological order, they are Jack Dempsey, Henry Armstrong, Sonny Liston, Muhammad Ali, George Foreman, Marvin Hagler, and Mike Tyson. Five of these freaks coincidentally graced the heavyweight division.

Dempsey's finest hour came when he pounded on the giant Jess Willard, who was around six inches taller and seventy pounds heavier. In most experts' opinions, this was the most dominant weight-differential beatdown in boxing history. There was only ever one winner. In this instance, the tale of the tape was literally meaningless. The damage that Dempsey inflicted in a few minutes of boxing was at that time unprecedented and aroused all kinds of suspicion about dirty tricks, from horseshoes to plaster of Paris to even a railway spike embedded in Dempsey's glove! These conspiracy theories have since generally been debunked. It was just a case of Dempsey's genetic fists of steel doing the damage.

Henry Armstrong is not really a household name, but he's very well known in the boxing fraternity and is arguably the number-one volume puncher in boxing history. According to Joe Frazier, "Henry Armstrong could throw three hundred punches a round in steady movements." Henry's boxing engine may have been nuclear powered!

Sonny Liston came straight out of a comic book, with fists the size of Sandman and arms as long as Mr Stretch. Getting hit by Sonny was the closest thing to being hit by a hammer!

Muhammad Ali had the best set of legs ever seen on a heavyweight. In his prime, he could dance continuously for fifteen rounds—he was perpetual motion personified. His ring movements were incredible given the fact that he weighed around 210 pounds in his heyday.

George Foreman was the quintessential heavyweight beast who was also the epitome of a slugger. He is generally regarded as the most physically empowered specimen in heavyweight history and the most difficult boxer to push backwards—he was that strong. Interestingly, the only guy to make Foreman back off was Sonny Liston in sparring. Foreman also possessed a chin of pure granite.

If Foreman's chin was made of granite, then Hagler's was surely made of tungsten carbide. Hagler was so tough that British commentator Reg Gutteridge once jokingly remarked, "It appears Hagler has muscles even on his ears." If ever a boxer was bombproof, then Hagler was that man!

And finally we come to Kid Dynamite, who was 210 pounds of lean muscle mass at the age of 16. Surely no fighter in history was as naturally well-built and solid as Tyson at such a tender age, with a monster 20-inch neck to boot. When questioned about making a comeback, Sugar Ray Leonard once jokingly remarked, "Well, I can always fight Mike Tyson's neck—that must weigh around 160 pounds!"

—February 2019

Anonymous: How fair a trial do you think Mike Tyson received? Do you think Don King set him up? If no, do you think King exploited the circumstances to Tyson's ill benefit in any way?

J. A.: I think Mike Tyson received a fair trial, no question. The main reason, as I recall, for his conviction for rape being upheld was that his defence lawyer was largely believed to be incompetent. The stance that his lawyer took was that Desiree Washington should not have been alone after midnight in a hotel room with the womanising ex-heavyweight champion of the world, and as such was somehow asking for it. Apparently this was totally the wrong attitude to take when attempting to defend against a rape charge. Desiree Washington was represented by a very good & showy prosecutor by the name of Greg Garrison, who really knew what he was doing. He painted a very effective picture of her being a naive and vulnerable victim. The jury went with this.

In this instance, I doubt if Don King set Tyson up. Tyson was a cash register, so why would Don King want his prized possession to go to prison? He stood to gain nothing from Tyson's imprisonment; in fact he lost a ton of money. Of course he wanted to exploit Tyson—that's a different story altogether. The best way to rip Tyson off was by keeping him in the ring and fighting. So no, I seriously doubt King set him up. This was just a bad situation that Tyson got himself into because he became a sex addict.

—February 2019

Emmanuel Ibe: What really happens in a boxer's head at the moment of knockout?

J. A.: In terms of physiology and mechanics, the knockout punch creates a lateral and rotational force to the brain. This whiplash force is greatest when you hit the chin, which is the bullseye target. You can also regard the mechanical force from a punch as a leverage force, where the max force is achieved by a chin strike, which is the furthest point on the head away from the brain.

Medics generally call a knockout a concussion. There are many other ways to become concussed, such as falling off a horse and banging your head. You don't have to hit the chin, but the greatest whiplash effect for a given punching force is created by a chin strike. If you punch hard enough, you can knock someone out with a forehead punch, but that punch may need to be delivered with 100 per cent more power than the same punch to the chin.

So what exactly happens? Your brain is encased in your skull but is floating; it is not firmly attached to the skull. There is a slight gap between your outer brain and the inside of the skull, similar to an egg yolk inside an eggshell. When the knockout punch lands, your whole head is accelerated through the air due to the leverage force of the punch. Since your brain is not firmly attached to the inside of the skull, it is kind of left behind in space. When your skull stops accelerating or reaches the endpoint of the force, defined by the limits of your neck's extension, your brain catches up to the inside of your skull. At this point your brain literally collides with the inside of your skull. If the force of this collision is great enough, there is a bio-electrical short circuit; your brain temporarily stops sending signals to your body, and you are knocked out.

Punches that create the greatest knockout force are lateral hooks, followed by overhand hooks, crosses, and uppercuts. The weakest are jabs. Sonny Liston apparently was one of the few guys who could knock another pro boxer out with a jab. You will also find it is generally quite rare for professional boxers to be knocked out clean with an uppercut, even if it lands flush. Due to the anatomy of the skull, the leverage force from an uppercut is much less than the leverage force from a hook for the same given power.

Hence the fact Wladimir Klitschko absorbed a monster uppercut from Anthony Joshua in their 2017 meeting. This was a massive punch that spectacularly caused hyper-extension of Klitschko's neck. But because the force of an uppercut comes from below, it doesn't accelerate the skull to the same extent as a hook, which lands at right angles. If that same uppercut had been a hook, Klitschko would surely have been out for the count.

—February 2019

FURQAN TARIQUE: I believe that Mike Tyson and Anthony Joshua are real muscle-bound boxers. Is that a typical way of explaining it?

J. A.: Both guys have very well-muscled physiques. The tabloid media of their day often appear to be almost as interested in their muscles as their boxing. I personally would never describe prime Tyson as muscle-bound—muscular, yes, but not muscle-bound. In my book, a naturally muscular guy like prime Tyson was still supple and flexible. He retained much of his natural agility. On the other hand, a muscle-bound, statuesque guy like A. J. is not agile or rhythmic in his movements but often appears stiff and cumbersome. Hence the fact A. J. is such an easy target and prime Tyson was such a hard target.

Prime Tyson built his legendary physique doing volume callisthenics. During his heyday, he did no formal weight training. The real-world nature of callisthenics are far more beneficial to a boxer and no doubt facilitated Tyson's explosive movements. Boxing-specific exercises almost definitely enhanced prime Tyson's natural panther-like traits.

If one compares and contrasts A. J.'s strength training routines to prime Tyson's callisthenics workouts, then an interesting picture emerges. A. J. engaged in many powerlifting exercises which are not necessarily useful to a boxer. Do these exercises build muscle? Hell yeah, of course they do! But this weight-trained muscle also weighs you down and clearly reduces your aerodynamics, stamina, and mobility.

In summary, prime Tyson was a great boxer who also happened to possess a world-class natural physique. A. J. is a very muscle-bound guy who happens to be a decent boxer.

—January 2020

Dale Polekoff: Did professional MMA fighting begin because boxing just wasn't violent enough for the fans?

J. A.: No, I don't think so. That may have been a factor in some American states—Colorado, perhaps—but not right across the board. UFC began with the philosophy of attempting to discover which martial art was the most dominant within one universal arena, the Octagon. Using a regular eight-sided shape supposedly didn't favour any martial arts discipline. How the organisers chose an octagon shape as being neutral—well, your guess is as good as mine. Personally, I think it was pure bullshit and the reason they chose an octagon was because the organisers wanted a shape that was uniquely American. Since the stop sign in America is octagonal, they settled on this for marketing purposes.

The Gracie family was heavily involved in kick-starting the MMA movement. I remember a whole load of obscure street-fighting stats that were presented to us before a punch was ever thrown. "Did you know that most street fights end up on the ground?" Well, that thought never crossed my mind, but thanks for giving me a nice heads-up anyway. One of the commentators in the original UFC strongly predicted that Royce Gracie would win the tournament—almost like he knew something that the rest of us didn't. It certainly appeared that none of the other competitors knew anything about Brazilian ju-jitsu, other than perhaps Ken Shamrock. So there definitely appeared to be something going on in terms of UFC being used as a vehicle to launch a hitherto unknown martial art. But to be fair, BJJ has stood the test of time and is now a staple part of all MMA fighters' arsenals.

By the end of UFC 1, the violence factor that we all saw attracted a whole load of casual fans who basically wanted to see a guy on a stretcher. This casual violence factor was most evident when one of the original competitors had his teeth kicked out by a kickboxer. This was described by one commentator as "the kick that reverberated around the world", and it no doubt had a huge impact on the expectations of the casual fight fan.

I don't think the organisers of UFC calculatingly knew what was going to happen when the mixed martial arts concept was conceived. It was very much a hit-and-hope punt, as there were so many unknowns. Specifically, think of the situation of having no weight categories—that soon changed. This was clearly an amateurish oversight. In virtually all other combat sports, weight categories exist for a reason. Size and weight make a big difference—this isn't rocket science.

In more recent times, the violence factor in UFC has diminished slightly as MMA fighters have become more well-rounded due to cross training. There aren't quite so many ridiculous mismatches. It is kind of ironic that nowadays, everyone pretty much fights in a similar way: as an all-round fighter who uses a bit of every martial art.

—December 2018

STEVE PIERCE: Is there empirical proof that the golden-age fighters Ali, Frazier, and Foreman were better than the current crop of Wilder, Joshua, and Fury? Surely with better diets and training they are better now?

J. A.: I doubt if there is any experimental or absolute empirical proof that the golden-age guys were better than the current crop. The closest thing to scientific data corroborating any claims to supremacy is in the form of Ali's hand speed, which was clocked. Other than this, conclusions are mostly going to be opinion based on observations of fight footage. It is almost impossible to definitively prove that the classic 1970s fighters were better than the twenty-first century crop.

If you want to talk statistics, then there is a certain stat that indicates Deontay Wilder is a better puncher than the biggest guns of the golden era. Deontay fanboys will argue that Wilder is a bigger puncher than George Foreman based on his superior knockout-to-wins ratio. Of course this wouldn't be my own opinion, but based on cold, hard stats, then Wilder does in fact hit harder than either Shavers or Foreman. Wilder's knockout-to-wins ratio is an astonishing 98 per cent, whereas Shavers's and Foreman's knockout-to-wins ratios were around the 90 per cent mark.

With regards to improvements in training and diet, this school of thought does hold some water. Sports science has improved across virtually all sports and not just boxing. But you have to take into consideration the fact that the golden-era guys were much better natural athletes than modern-day lumbering giants. Certainly, Ali is universally recognised as an all-time great athlete. No amount of sport science or optimisation of diet is going to bridge the huge gulf in athletic class between Wilder and Ali.

In my humble opinion, one area which has seen a big drop in class over the years is boxing technique. It is difficult, if not impossible, to measure and quantify boxing technique. The golden era was the most competitive time in boxing history, particularly in the heavyweight division, so those guys had to be technical masters to survive. The strength in depth was also much greater in the 1970s. This is where statistics can give you a false viewpoint of the facts. What would Wilder's knockout-to-wins ratio be if he boxed in the 1970s against all-time great opposition?

—December 2019

Gray Summers: Can a 29-year-old heavyweight boxer who's been a pro for ten years and has a record of 29–0 be considered past his prime?

J.A.: Yes, absolutely.

Once upon a time there was this dude named Muhammad Ali, and he was already past his prime when he lost his 0. He was also approximately twenty nine years old at the time of his first defeat and had been a pro for around ten years. He was 31–0 when Joe Frazier decisioned him in 1971.

Many an unbeaten boxing record flatters to deceive—even Ali's. As the classic old saying goes, "You're only as good as your last fight." Ali's last unbeaten win came against the rugged Argentine slugger Oscar Bonavena in December of 1970. This was three very short months before the Fight of the Century with Frazier. A ring-rusty Ali struggled against the limited but tough Bonavena, eventually stopping him in the fifteenth round. I think a prime Ali would probably have taken care of Bonavena by the middle rounds.

If you want to go even further back in time, then you can focus on Rocky Marciano's legendary record of 49–0, probably the most famous unbeaten record of all. He is the only heavyweight in boxing history to retire unbeaten. He too was relatively young when he retired—in fact, only thirty two. But in Marciano's case, it was clearly a case of "it ain't the years, it's the mileage". The point is he must have been past his prime; otherwise he wouldn't have retired. His unbeaten record is almost a moot point, but clearly cynics will argue he retired in order to protect his 0.

—December 2020

Andrew Parker: What do Mike Tyson and George Foreman have in common with Muhammad Ali?

J. A.: This one's easy. All three legends are legitimate record breakers!

Mike Tyson was the youngest fighter to become heavyweight champion of the world, aged just twenty. This phenomenal record has now stood for thirty-four years and is testament to a child boxing prodigy. I don't see anyone breaking this record anytime soon—and if the heavyweight division stays in its current sorry state, maybe never.

George Foreman set the record for the oldest heavyweight champion of the world, aged forty five. His record has now stood for twenty-six long years, and again there appears to be little or no threat on the horizon.

Ali set the record for becoming the first heavyweight boxer to become world champion on three separate occasions. In 1964, he beat Sonny Liston to become champ for the first time. In 1974, he upset Foreman to become champion for the second time. Finally, he beat the relatively unknown Leon Spinks to reacquire the title for a third time in 1978.

—November 2020

Mark Adams: Why is it that a heavyweight boxer can easily knock out a featherweight boxer (and probably kill him) with one punch to the head, but is not likely to manage the same thing against another heavyweight? Human heads are basically identical.

J. A.: Human heads are similar in structure but not identical. You will find that a heavyweight boxer's head is a lot larger, wider, and heavier than a featherweight's head. Therefore the energy of a power punch will be better dissipated inside a heavyweight skull than a featherweight skull.

In his meeting with Marco Antonio Barrera, at one point Naseem Hamed was sent flying through the air. If that exact same punch had landed from a pro heavyweight, the force would obviously be much greater and the consequences more dire. The point is that there is more than just head shape and size involved when considering the physics of a knockout blow. A lighter boxer will suffer a much greater concussion than a heavier boxer, given the same punching force.

Let's turn our attention to prime Mike Tyson and specifically his monster 20-inch neck. A larger and thicker neck will clearly help to lessen the whiplash effect from a potential knockout punch. How many featherweight boxers have had a 20-inch neck?

Now let's concentrate on Evander Holyfield's head and compare it to a featherweight boxer's head e.g., Naseem Hamed. It is fairly obvious that Holyfield has a significantly larger skull than

Hamed. Therefore, based solely on the difference in skull size, we can conclude that Holyfield will withstand a much heavier punch.

Other important factors to consider are the width and area of the chin. Once again it is fairly obvious that a heavyweight boxer will have a larger and wider chin than a featherweight boxer.

Pressure = force/area

Assume that both the heavyweight and featherweight boxer take a punch to the chin with the same force. From the above equation, we can conclude that the featherweight boxer's chin will be exposed to a greater pressure than the heavyweight boxer's chin. This is because the featherweight boxer has a smaller chin with less surface area.

Finally, the hydration status of the brain and skull also needs to be considered. A large skull will inevitably contain more water and provide better cushioning to the brain. This obviously assumes that neither the heavyweight boxer nor the featherweight boxer are dehydrated.

—November 2020

Effayim Bulka: How old was Muhammad Ali when he lost to Larry Holmes?

J. A.: Ali was 38 years old. In 1980, in a fight dubbed the Last Hurrah, Larry Holmes gained a degree of unwanted notoriety for beating up on a boxing grandfather who may already have been suffering from undiagnosed Parkinson's.

What goes around comes around. Eight years later, in 1988, prime Tyson received much praise and adulation from Ali fans for giving Holmes a taste of his own medicine. Holmes too was coincidentally 38 years old when Tyson nailed him to the canvas.

—November 2020

Arrow Jaykris and Elliott Avant: Who have been some underrated professional heavyweight boxers?

J. A.: I can tell you one thing for sure: it would be much easier to answer, "Who was the most overrated heavyweight boxer?"

But staying with the question, the following is a list of heavyweight boxers who I believe to have been underrated for one reason or another.

Michael Spinks

The general public unfortunately often remembers a fighter by his last performance, and the sight of Spinks being flattened by a rampaging Tyson has become an enduring image down the years. The amount of unfair criticism that Michael Spinks has attracted because of his last professional outing has severely tarnished his overall career standing. Many, many casual fans forget that this guy was in fact a very slick boxer who is generally rated as the number-one light heavyweight of all time. In addition to this fact, casuals also forget that, on paper at least, he was a "live dog" in this hotly anticipated clash with Tyson. Obviously on the night, fear took hold of Spinks, and the rest is history

Tim Witherspoon

Tim Witherspoon was a very capable boxer and held his own against many of the best heavyweights of the 1980s. In the early 1980s, he gave Larry Holmes all the trouble he could handle and was most probably robbed of a points victory. On this night, both the judges and boxing politics went against Terrible Tim Witherspoon. Although he held a version of the heavyweight crown, he was never really regarded as a proper heavyweight champion and never became a household name.

Sonny Liston

While Liston is notorious for being the most feared boxer in history, his actual boxing abilities are overshadowed by his looming and fearsome persona. This guy could really box and had one of the best jabs in heavyweight history. His overall legacy has been tarnished by his two infamous failures against Ali. Many boxing historians have been particularly unkind to him because in the second Ali fight, it is widely believed he "took a dive" as part of a Mob-controlled betting fix.

Jimmy Young

You mention a golden-era slickster named Jimmy Young, and most casual fans will say, "Huh? What? Who you on about?" This guy not only had the guts to take on the beast that was 1970s George Foreman, but outboxed him and won a clear points decision. He also fought Ali and Ken Norton during that glorious era in heavyweight history. This guy was a strong candidate for the title of slipperiest heavyweight of the 1970s. Believe me, this guy was a genuinely talented boxer-mover, and yet he is now an almost forgotten name from a bygone era.

Ike Ibeabuchi

This guy was most renowned for his fearsome physique, but he could also box and had the potential to have gone on to great things. But for one reason or another, his boxing career stalled. It was all over before it ever began. He is most remembered for taming a seemingly mighty David Tua in 1997.

—November 2020

Jacob Holland: Did Mike Tyson duck any boxers in or out of his prime?

J. A.: During his prime years (1985 to 1988 inclusive) Mike ducked absolutely no one. Instead he took on all comers, leaving a trail of unprecedented concussions in his wake.

Prime Tyson spent many, many arduous hours fine-tuning his legendary side-to-side head movement, using the peekaboo slip bag. In his heyday, he was subjected to the most comprehensive defensive training regimen ever seen in the heavyweight division. For about a four-year period, he was almost unhittable by full power punches and therefore believed he couldn't lose. At the time, this fact alone gave him a valid reason to take on all comers.

Additionally, in the early years, Team Tyson were a close-knit bunch of individuals. Such harmony had a positive effect on an impressionable Tyson, in and out of the ring. He was once a happy boxer who loved fighting and training. He gained much confidence under his original team and was in a good place both mentally and physically, so there was no reason to duck any fighter during his heyday.

After the almost unthinkable defeat to Douglas happened, the Iron Man lost his mojo and never quite got it back

When he made his first comeback in 1990, Tyson was no longer Iron Mike. His original training and management team were long gone—they had left in 1988, and many technical errors had already crept into his game. Tyson was at least partially aware of the flaws in his game. As a result of this fact and the fact that old Foreman had a rock chin, he probably ducked Foreman in the early 1990s. Foreman was the only fighter that I can recall Tyson ducking, and there were many justifiable reasons for Tyson's reluctance to share a ring with him.

—*January 2020*

Den Jackson: Is it better not to have muscles in boxing so we don't gas out quickly?

J. A.: By comparing the physiques of Anthony Joshua and Deontay Wilder, one is able to better visualise the pros and cons of big muscles on a boxer. Joshua and Wilder are roughly the same height and have similar-sized natural frames, and yet Joshua outweighs Wilder by at least two stone. I can't see too much fat on either guy, so we can assume that Joshua's extra weight is down to lean muscle mass.

Now remember that lean muscle is very metabolically active. Also consider the fact that we are talking about boxing here and not bodybuilding Of the two, who do you think is gonna gas first? The answer is obviously Joshua, and the longer a fight goes on, the more fatigued he will become—even more so in relative terms. So as well as weighing Joshua down by an extra two stone of restricted mobility, the lean muscle tissue creates an increased oxygen demand on Joshua's cardiovascular system. This is not good in an intense action-packed fight, as he will inevitably tire faster than Wilder.

In boxing, muscle tissue is only really useful in terms of strength, which comes in handy when on the inside and in the clinches. If there is no actual physical contact between the fighters at close quarters, the strength doesn't make a difference. Remember, this is boxing and not wrestling. Furthermore, there is no real correlation between punching power and lean muscle tissue, which in this instance also doesn't look good for Joshua, as we know that Wilder has greater one-hit power. Punching power is generally derived from four main drivers, which are speed, timing, leverage, and torque. You could even argue that increased muscle mass has a negative effect on timing, mobility, and flexibility. So in general, I would say it is better to not have big muscles in boxing, especially when talking about the concept of stamina, which is often a decisive factor in world championship fights.

—*January 2019*

Joseph Ted: Why is boxing not as popular anymore as it was in the 1980s and 1990s?

J. A.: Multifactorial reasons are in play, really, but perhaps the main reason is a reduction in its entertainment value. Ask yourself, "What is boxing?" First and foremost, you should answer, "It is a spectator sport and has always been a spectator sport." When it ceases to be a spectator sport, then no one will watch. It really is that simple. Boxing fans want to see knockouts, exciting fights, to-and-fro momentum shifts, slugfests, and so on. How much of this kind of action have we seen over the last fifteen or so years? Other than the Klitschko versus Joshua fight, which was reasonably entertaining, when was the last great heavyweight slugfest? You will probably have to go back to 2003, when Lewis and Vitali Klitschko gave us some thrills and spills.

Another major factor is the lack of a genuinely great heavyweight fighter, which has a massive negative knock-on effect on all the divisions. The heavyweight division has traditionally been the marquee division since the year dot, and for the past twenty years it has been a division that is pretty much devoid of genuine boxing talent.

I have nothing against Wladimir Klitschko, great out-fighter and long-reigning champion that he was, but who did he actually beat? In all his years at the top, did he ever face a decent brawler, a decent swarmer, or even another decent boxer-puncher? He definitely didn't face a decent slugger. This isn't his fault—he can only fight who is in front of him—but I honestly can't ever remember the heavyweight division being in such a sorry state and so lacking in any kind of depth.

There are way too many alphabet group organisations, which have been killing boxing slowly for decades. In reality, you only want one world champion to be the real world champion. The best guy in the division is the world champion, and the second-best guy is the number-one ranked contender. That's how it used to be a long, long time ago, but that's certainly not how it is any more.

This lack of transparency creates confusion among the paying public. Who is the best guy? Is it Joshua, is it Fury, or is it Wilder? Who is the heavyweight champion of the world? The last time I checked, there is only one planet Earth. There is only one world that we all live in. So how can there be two world champions? Believe me, this is a big problem and will slowly kill off boxing as punters become more and more cynical and distrusting.

There is also a distinct lack of boxing rivalries, due in large part to the lack of great boxers. During the 1970s and 1980s, there were some tremendous rivalries between elite boxers, which kept boxing fans hungry for more. In particular, the US boxing audience has significantly reduced expectations and is simply pisspot bored.

—January 2019

M. Vincent Holguin: What is the first ability to go in an ageing boxer?

J. A.: Let's rewind the clock to 1971. In the Fight of the Century, Ali was still under 30 years old—hardly an old fighter. But the ageing process had been greatly accelerated in Ali due to his enforced three-year lay-off. None other than notable boxing scholar and great trainer Cus D'Amato predicted that Frazier would just about have enough in his locker to beat an ageing Ali. The primary reasons D'Amato cited were declines in Ali's reflexes and explosive movements. This is pretty much what we saw in that first meeting in 1971.

In his prime in 1966, Ali would surely have dodged many of Frazier's lethal left hooks. His legs would generally have kept him out of harm's way. For a number of reasons, he simply wasn't anywhere near as elusive in 1971 as before his three-year lay-off.

Ali always had a flawed defence—this was nothing new. Throughout the 1960s, he habitually carried his hands low and was always vulnerable to left hooks. Remember Henry's hammer? The left hook that floored Clay was one that he simply didn't see and therefore couldn't react to. I don't think it was down to a lack of reflexes. He was knocked down by Henry Cooper because of bad habits and perhaps a lapse in concentration.

The left hooks that Frazier repeatedly landed on him were different. Those were pre-planned punches, part of a strategy to exploit Ali's known weaknesses. It just so happened that there was also a significant decline in Ali's reflexes and movement due to premature ageing, caused primarily by inactivity and a thyroid condition.

After reflexes and movement, the next thing to go would be hand speed, which is linked to explosive movements. Again, looking at Ali in the 1970s. While he was hardly a slouch, it was noticeable that he didn't get the punch there quite as fast as in his 1960s heyday. A similar decline was observed in Tyson during his return to the ring after three years of incarceration. His legendary head movement was gone. So too was some of his hand speed, and his razor-sharp combinations had almost disappeared. Tyson's case was another example of the accelerated ageing process, due to inactivity and heavy ring rust.

Yet another example of a fight that I believe was lost partly because of the effects of Father Time was Hagler versus Leonard in 1987. In this fight, Hagler was caught by many punches that I believe he would have dodged or blocked in his prime. He also appeared slower than usual and more sluggish in his movements. His legs were going. Sugar Ray Leonard has gone on record as saying that he felt he couldn't have beaten a pre-1986 version of Hagler. In his 1986 war with John "the Beast" Mugabi, Hagler became significantly more shopworn, primarily due to a decline in his reflexes and explosive movements.

—February 2019

Anthony (A. J.) Valentino: Are modern boxers better than old boxers?

J. A.: No way! As a general rule, modern boxers are technically inferior to their older counterparts. Why do I say this? Check the cash register, and there is your proof-based answer. Madison Square Garden in America was once the Mecca of boxing, and this is no longer the case. A fringe pursuit such as UFC has become more popular in America than boxing. In 1993, when UFC was launched in a dingy location in Denver, Colorado, who would have predicted the revenue and momentum it would achieve a quarter of a century later? One of the reasons for this is that modern boxers are no longer capturing the public's imagination. They simply can't box. In particular, US fight fans are simply pisspot bored and are looking elsewhere for their combat fix. UFC is filling some of the void left by boxing—at least in America.

The single main reason for this is the sorry state of the heavyweight division. It is close to a shambling wreck of giants who are boxing simply because of gigantism. There is only one guy in the heavyweight division who can box in a reasonably fluid and unscripted manner, and that is Tyson Fury. Joshua is decent, with a great physique, but he is limited and is more suited to strongman. Wilder is a bum by world champion standards but can luckily punch hard.

In terms of sound technique, you have to look at the lower divisions, but even they are struggling. To thrill an audience, you need great fights. To have great fights, you need great fighters. As Apollo Creed clearly stated at the end of *Rocky 3*, "Rocky, you fight great but I'm a great fighter!" I see none of this kind of genuine charisma and bravado in boxing anymore.

If you want further ironclad proof of a lack of great boxers, just rewind the clock to 2017, when Mayweather had nothing more than a money fight against a huge box office name in Conor McGregor.

No disrespect intended—McGregor is a great UFC fighter—but as a boxer, he is nothing more than a name and would get beat by many an amateur. And yet this fight was huge in terms of PPV. Why? There weren't any other exciting fights out there, so the biggest name in boxing was left to fight the biggest name in MMA to keep the casual fanbase artificially entertained (and obviously generate a ton of money).

Many people on social media seem to cite the boxing doldrums as being a result of the huge influence of UFC. I am not one of those people. Boxing revenue is struggling because boxing itself is struggling. As a combat sports fan, I will happily watch two people fight in a cage as much as in a boxing ring. But I'm not gonna pay to watch bullshit. Who is the new Ali, the new Tyson, or the new Sugar Ray Leonard? Nobody. So, from a technical and charisma standpoint, modern boxers are definitely worse.

In summary, the main area in which modern boxers are better than the greats of yesteryear is in terms of commercial awareness and savvy. This is obviously an entirely different field to boxing technique. The issue of greed is also killing boxing. Titles these days are almost meaningless. Fighters simply want to be fast-tracked to the big paydays.

—April 2019

Den Jackson: Would Mike Tyson do well if he were a bodybuilder?

J. A.: If you saw a random guy walking down the street with his top off, and he possessed the same impressive and natural-looking physique as prime Tyson, and he told you, "I only do callisthenics and road work", would you believe him? These days, the majority of casual fans would blindly accuse him of PED abuse. And to be fair, this kind of sceptical viewpoint is entirely understandable, because more often than not the guys who are ripped and jacked at 220 pounds have probably experimented with performance-enhancing drugs.

But here's the news: most guys ain't Iron Mike Tyson and do not possess one-in-a-million genetics. To a casual fan, the concept of genetics is very much an alien one. It is much easier to point the finger of suspicion. But believe me, when Bobby Stewart brought Tyson to the attention of Cus D'Amato and Teddy Atlas, their eyes lit up like Christmas trees. They all knew that Tyson was a physical phenomenon before a jab, sit -up, or push-up was ever executed. Even as a child prodigy, Tyson truly was a natural genetic freak.

Regarding his bodybuilding potential, it is clear that his training regimen would have to be radically modified to incorporate heavy lifting. Intense free-weight training is clearly a staple part of every bodybuilder's training program. Weight training and PED abuse are two activities that prime Tyson never engaged in. Looking at Tyson's genetic potential, one would think he could have been a decent bodybuilder. However, it is an entirely different sport to boxing, and I don't think one can automatically assume that great boxing genetics = great bodybuilding genetics. Although they are both physical sports, not everyone responds to the drugs in exactly the same way.

Certainly if you look at the heavyweight story of Evander Holyfield, he has responded to the drugs miraculously. You could make a strong case that Holyfield would have made the best bodybuilder out of all major historical heavyweights. Certainly, Holyfield had one of the narrowest waist measurements of any heavyweight champion, which is a very desirable look for bodybuilding.

—July 2019

Zachary Barber: Are boxers scared of getting hit?

J. A.: Although I can't read the mind of every boxer—as a rule of thumb, I would say yes, they are afraid. They are only human, after all. Certainly, any fighter who has been knocked out early on in his career will be more scared than the average boxer. If you look at Lennox Lewis, for example, ever since he was knocked out by Oliver McCall in 1994, he has become somewhat gun-shy. Being gun-shy is basically being afraid of being hit. Lewis became a technical, long-range, and predominantly safety-first fighter. Even at his peak against David Tua in 2000, he didn't take any risks whatsoever. He knew Tua couldn't lay a glove on him, but the fear of being stretched out was still on his subconscious mind. If it weren't, a puncher of Lewis's calibre should be stepping up to the table and getting a crude slugger like David Tua out of there.

The same applies to Wladimir Klitschko, who had a notorious china chin. If it hadn't been for the legendary Emanuel Steward completely reinventing him, Klitschko would surely have faded into obscurity.

So on balance, it is likely that technical and strategic fighters tend to be more afraid of being hit. Conversely, brawlers such as Gatti, Chavez, and Duran—indeed, Latin fighters in general—tend to have a different mindset. They often have little or no fear and regard being hit as a sign of machismo. The legendary Jake LaMotta had absolutely no fear of being hit and regarded being punched as a form of masochism.

—April 2019

Anonymous: Mike Tyson was obese according to the BMI calculation. Is he a prime example of someone being big-boned, or was it all muscle?

J. A.: Prime Tyson was almost 100 per cent pure and solid lean muscle. At his peak he was 220 pounds, with around seven per cent body fat. He stood approximately 5 feet 11 inches tall and had a 34-inch waist and 26-inch thighs, which were bigger than many NFL players. Tyson was definitely a prime example of freak genetics.

But you are touching on a subtle point with regards to BMI, which is now well known to be a fundamentally flawed measurement. Almost every heavyweight boxer and bodybuilder in history is obese according to BMI. The calculation takes no account whatsoever of waist measurement or muscularity—in other words, it is pure bullshit. Believe it or not, when BMI was conceived, it was never intended to be used for analysis of an individual. Rather, it was meant for the analysis of obesity across a pool of un-athletic people. In knowledgeable circles, BMI has long been replaced by a measurement called *body volume index*.

—June 2018

Emile Collymore: Has anyone ever hit the referee in boxing, on purpose or on accident? What happened afterwards?

J. A.: Mike Tyson landed a powerful left hook on British referee John Coyle in 2000. It was entirely accidental; Tyson's intended target was his opponent, Lou Savarese. The referee was trying to stop the fight, but Tyson was so pumped up and hyper that he didn't realise. He continued to pound on Savarese—the referee simply got in the way. In this instance, Tyson wasn't punished for knocking the ref down, as it was an accident.

Tyson was summarily awarded the TKO victory. Straight after the fight, he went on to give his now-infamous rant: "I'm Sonny Liston, I'm Jack Dempsey, I'm from their cloth, my style is impetuous, my defence is impregnable!"

In terms of a deliberate attempt to KO the referee, Zab Judah went ballistic in 2001 after his stoppage loss to Kostya Tzyu. He cornered referee, Jay Nady, on the ropes and was observed loading up with a fierce right-hand punch. Thankfully, someone intervened, and the referee was spared from any unnecessary punishment.

—February 2021

Vincent Pisano: Why was UFC fighter Conor McGregor unbeatable, and then all of a sudden couldn't win a fight and had trouble with opponents?

J. A.: Styles make fights. To a lesser or greater extent, all combat sports share certain similarities, in that a given style can appear totally dominant against certain opponents and yet prove to be ineffective against others.

Although Royce Gracie and Dan Severn have nothing directly to do with McGregor, there was a time when Gracie was unbeatable and Brazilian ju-jitsu was considered the most dominant martial art. Gracie weighed around 180 pounds, and yet he defeated Severn, who weighed 260. If you transported that same 1995 Gracie to the modern era, can you for a second imagine him holding his own against Brock, Overeem, or Cain Velasquez? Of course he couldn't—he would get destroyed.

Gracie was dominated and manhandled by Matt Hughes at UFC 60, and at no point in that fight were any of his previously invincible techniques useful. What had changed? Matt Hughes was clearly a high-quality opponent who knew what he was doing, and he had made the necessary adjustments to neutralise Gracie's ju-jitsu.

In the same way, current UFC fighters will have observed footage of McGregor, spotted his strengths and weaknesses, and then made the appropriate adjustments. When McGregor fought Khabib, McGregor was dominated and fully realised what happens when you come up against a high-quality opponent.

In other words, the techniques that work against mid-range opposition don't necessarily work against the best. Additionally, in McGregor's specific case, the ageing process and motivational issues have contributed to his rapid decline.

—February 2021

Dimetries Smith: What kind of difficulties will a UFC fighter have in a boxing match?

J. A.: The more times I view the McGregor versus Mayweather "boxing match", the more I become convinced that Mayweather was carrying McGregor. When he did let his hands fly, it was surprising how easily Mayweather caught his freshman opponent. Power punches with either hand were landing flush, and McGregor was having difficulty reading his vastly superior opponent. To say there was a gulf in class is an astronomical understatement. Bear in mind the fact that Mayweather was also old and rusty. He only took the fight so that he could break Marciano's long-standing record and earn an easy payday. He does like his easy paydays.

The first and most obvious difficulty a UFC fighter will face is that he will likely be boxing a pro boxer in the boxing match. If the UFC fighter was involved in a boxing match against another UFC fighter, then his limitations in skill and technique would never be exposed. High-level boxing is a very skilful combat sport, and it is unfair to expect a bread-and-butter UFC striker to have any success.

In terms of specific examples of difficulties, then the footwork elements of pro boxing will be totally beyond a UFC fighter. A pro boxer will be floating in that boxing ring, whereas the UFC guy will appear to be stumbling as if on ice. The UFC fighter will have significant balance problems. Poor balance means poor leverage. The UFC guy will start swinging wildly, which will inevitably lead to fatigue, as we saw with McGregor.

On a fundamental level, hand striking in the Octagon is clearly different to punching with boxing gloves on. This basic but subtle difference will prove to be a big handicap to the UFC fighter. Those ten-ounce boxing gloves make a huge difference!

—January 2021

ANTON BRIGHAM: Why do professional boxers seem to go for runs very early in the morning rather than just have their run in the evening or night?

J.A.: "I run at 4am because I know the other guy is sleeping," said prime Tyson. This statement tells a deeper story about prime Tyson's competitive nature and that 4am run certainly never did him any harm...But Tyson wasn't the only one and other top pros have also utilized the dawn's early light for their roadwork.

From a logic perspective, running on an empty stomach will clearly tap into fat reserves better, so the fighter will get ripped faster. To a high octane fighter like Tyson, he clearly wants to be as streamlined as possible, so the early morning run increases his efficiency.

Other factors are the specific fighter's training regimen and schedule. Simply put, if one gets the tedious roadwork done early, then one can concentrate on the more interesting aspects of training in the afternoon e.g. sparring. Looking at it in reverse, it is highly unlikely that an elite pro will be sparring with another elite pro at 4am, because the sparring partner will obviously be asleep.

Also consider the famous scene from Rocky 2, where Balboa is running in the streets of Philadelphia hotly pursued by hundreds of latchkey kids. Clearly that was a movie and by their very nature, movies exaggerate the details; but in reality, a world famous fighter will attract a load of attention and distractions, if he too goes for a jog in broad daylight on a main road...And in reality, he doesn't want this kind of attention before fight night.

—March 2021

CHAPTER 15

HANGIN' TOUGH

David Mulata: What makes a boxer have a good chin?

J. A.: Pay close attention to a late, great hard man named Marvin Hagler and even closer attention to his skull shape and morphology—particularly the curvature just above his brow line. It has been speculated that Marvin Hagler's skull was the closest human equivalent to a motorcycle crash helmet ever seen. Much of his chin strength was the result of a tremendously strong and impact-resistant skull; it has been suggested that either his skull was double-coated or twice as thick and hard as a normal human skull. There was a very specific time when all this outlandish speculation began: April 15, 1985, to be exact.

On that April night in the Caesars Palace parking lot, Hagler's head was exposed to the most fearsome punishment ever seen in the modern era of boxing. During eight minutes of hell against the Hitman Thomas Hearns, he took all manner of clean headshots from probably the most murderous pound-for-pound puncher in boxing history. In the first round, Hagler was badly stunned and, I believe, was very, very close to being knocked out. By rights he should've been stretched out. But something strange happened. Something quirky and surreal kept him upright. You could visibly see his body and legs buckling beneath him, but his head somehow stood tough. It is believed that some of Hearns's hardest punches were being deflected off Hagler's head, similar to how a stealth bomber deflects radar. In other words, the impacts of those bombs were somehow being dissipated and channelled away from Hagler's brain by the unique crash-helmet curvature of his skull.

Chin strength is clearly mostly genetic but can be improved somewhat by neck exercises. A thick and strong neck is believed to lessen the whiplash effect to the brain. More often than not, you'll find that boxers with thick necks have good punch resistance. Oppositely, fighters with thin necks usually go over more easily. Another neck dimension which is critically related to chin strength is the vertical length of the neck and spine. A longer neck will inevitably contribute to a greater whiplash effect, and a shorter neck vice versa.

Finally, a more obscure factor which also contributes significantly to chin strength is the mechanical process during a chin strike. When a boxer or mixed martial artist receives a chin strike, their chin is depressed inwards and the upper skull is pulled forward and downwards, thereby creating a torsional force. The more the chin is depressed inwards, the greater the rotational force to the brain. I believe Hagler's freakishly unique jaw, neck, and skull structure was perfect for minimising this concussive force.

If one observes side profile head images of Hagler and Hearns, an interesting picture emerges. It is apparent that Hagler had a much longer horizontal jaw length than Hearns, but a shorter horizontal skull length at the top. These two dimensions contributed positively to Hagler's chin strength in terms of minimising the rotational force of a chin strike.

This is exactly what transpired during the fight. Hearns landed much the harder punches, and yet he was the one who was eventually knocked out. Yet again we find that at the highest level of boxing, punch power alone is not the decisive factor—it is relative punch power. Hagler and his team knew that he possessed greater relative punch power than Hearns, and this ingredient was most probably crucial in determining his crazy fight tactics. It was Hagler and not Hearns who initiated the war. Hagler shocked everyone by turning conventional boxing logic upside down. If anybody else in the world had tried this stunt against the Hitman, they would have risked serious injury, let alone the knockout. But when you're as tough as Hagler, you can afford to take those risks.

—May 2019

Gopal Rao: Who had the best chin in boxing history?

J. A.: Almost definitely, pound for pound, that accolade goes to Marvelous Marvin Hagler. Nobody ever legitimately knocked him down. Yet he faced some of the hardest punchers in middleweight history, including the Hitman Thomas Hearns, who had arguably the hardest right-hand punch in the history of middle division boxing. Well-known British boxer David Haye once described Thomas Hearns as having "freak show" power. In the now-legendary war at Caesars Palace in 1985, Hearns nailed Hagler with dozens of clean punches to the chin in the first round alone. He even stunned and hurt Hagler. But Marvin somehow stood tough.

Hagler fought fifteen intense and bruising rounds with the Hands of Stone Roberto Duran, and Duran couldn't hurt him, though he landed plenty of clean leather on Hagler. One of the best boxer-punchers in history, none other than Sugar Ray Leonard, couldn't stop Hagler in his tracks, let alone hurt him in twelve gruelling rounds. John "the Beast" Mugabi, another murderous puncher, fought a shopworn Hagler in a super-fight. Again, he landed plenty of clean power shots, but he couldn't deter Marvin. Hagler was a real throwback to some of the classic hard men of yesteryear and was probably the toughest guy to ever step into a boxing ring.

—April 2018

Anonymous: Who are the top five boxers with the toughest chins and/or biggest hearts?

J. A.:

1. *Marvelous Marvin Hagler*: According to the majority of expert opinion, Marvelous Marvin had the strongest pound-for-pound chin in boxing history. During his illustrious career Hagler faced off against some seriously tough fighters, including an Italian middleweight named Vito Antuofermo. In the early 1980s, Vito Antuofermo was probably the

pound-for-pound roughest, toughest guy in the whole of Italy. Vito Antuofermo was so tough-looking that film director Francis Ford Coppola gave him a cameo hoodlum role in *The Godfather 3*! In the face of Hagler's legendary toughness, a lot of other seriously tough guys were made to look fairly ordinary. In his whole pro career, Hagler wasn't once legitimately knocked down, and he faced some of the hardest hitters in middleweight history. Hagler was virtually bombproof. Notable boxing writer Michael Katz once speculated that Hagler's skull resembled a crash helmet in terms of its morphology. It seems there had to be something extra to account for his freakish punch resistance.

2. *The Raging Bull Jake LaMotta*: During the filming of *Raging Bull*, actor Robert De Niro got plenty of tough-guy advice from the real tough guy himself. According to boxing historian Bert Randolph Sugar, LaMotta was so tough that he would get annoyed if his opponents missed him with a punch! In six meetings with the pound-for-pound king, Sugar Ray Robinson, LaMotta was never floored once. In their sixth and final meeting, the fight was nicknamed the Saint Valentine's Day Massacre due to the monumental beating that LaMotta took off Sugar Ray. Still, he never went down. The head-banging scene from *Raging Bull* is surely evidence of both a damaged psyche and a man who had a head of rock.
3. *George Foreman*: George Foreman would have been knocked out multiple times during his career were it not for his legendary granite chin. The beating that he took off Holyfield in 1991 would have been impressive enough had it been in his prime but in fact he was seventeen years past his prime! How many forty-somethings could take this type of beating from a steroid freak, world heavyweight champion and still remain standing? He also absorbed many covert headbutts from Holyfield and never once complained to the referee. After the fight, he did say that Holyfield was the dirtiest fighter he had ever faced.
4. *Muhammad Ali*: Although Ali gave many brave performances during his stellar career, his toughest performance is hard to define. One thing is for sure: when he faced off against the puncher of the century, Earnie Shavers, he absorbed many lethal right crosses that were capable of felling a horse. This legendary fight with Shavers went the distance, with Ali taking way too many clean headshots from a murderous puncher. Ali was so tough and brave that he fought nearly twelve rounds with Ken Norton after sustaining a broken jaw in the second round of their first meeting. In terms of tolerance for pain, Ali may be number one all time—he was too tough for his own good.
5. *Smokin' Joe Frazier*: Anybody who gets in the ring with a prime George Foreman must be a serious tough guy. Anybody who gets knocked down by Foreman and gets back up as if nothing happened, then carries on fighting, must be a ludicrously tough guy. Anybody who gets knocked down six times by Foreman and keeps getting back up is simply crazy and possibly the most stubbornly resistant boxer ever. In terms of heart and fire, I would place Frazier at number one on this list.

Strong notable mention goes to Randall "Tex" Cobb. Against Larry Holmes, Cobb possibly gave the best impersonation ever of a human punching bag, which lasted the full course of fifteen painfully one-sided rounds. This was the type of beating that gave the anti-boxing lobby plenty of ammunition to call for a ban on this barbaric sport. This was one of several brutal, high-profile, early-1980s fights which ultimately led to the shortening of world championship fights from fifteen rounds to twelve.

Other notable mentions include Rocky Marciano, George Chuvalo, Arturo Gatti, Ray Mercer, Oliver McCall, Larry Holmes, Vitali Klitsckho, David Tua, and Jerry Quarry.

—April 2019

Timothy Soo: How did Tommy Morrison manage to survive twelve rounds and beat George Foreman in 1993?

J. A.: The tale of the tape can be very revealing in certain matchups. In this instance, two telling statistics jumped out at me and grabbed my attention. Essentially Morrison was fighting a guy who was old enough to be his father, both in terms of age and weight. This fight was a classic case of two big-punching sluggers facing off, but Morrison had the added advantages of youth and mobility.

During the fight, Foreman looked slow and sloppy and was taking way too long to cut the ring off. In the process, he was eating too many counters. In terms of punching power, I don't think there was much in it, so in the end, the busier and younger fighter justifiably got the decision. Obviously, if he'd faced prime George Foreman, it would have been a different story.

Going slightly off tangent, Foreman boxed a lesser-known fighter named Alex Stewart in 1992. The fight with Stewart followed a very similar pattern to the Morrison fight, and the younger and busier guy once again landed a ton of clean leather on old Foreman. But yet again we saw Foreman's chin hanging tough. In his second coming, Foreman was a sitting duck, but nobody seemed to have the KO punch to finish him off.

—December 2019

Shaun Duggal: Was Foreman's chin really made of granite?

J. A.: If you see the retired version of Foreman for the first time, it may be hard to believe that this old geezer was once one of the toughest guys ever to lace up gloves. Foreman had a tremendously strong and resilient chin, maybe the strongest ever. Who knows for sure? But referring to a boxer as having a "granite" chin is a metaphor rather than a literal description. It is simply a descriptive term which means that this guy can take a seriously heavy whack and still remain standing. "Granite" is an alternative word to "rock". It is like saying a boxer such as Marvin Hagler was as "hard as nails". We don't mean this literally; no one is literally as hard as nails. It is a metaphorical description of his unusual toughness and durability.

In case you harbour any doubts about Foreman's toughness, check out his classic slugfest with Ron Lyle from 1976. This fight had everything—toe-to-toe exchanges, machismo attitude, mean in-fight stare-downs, shifts in momentum, and so on. Ron Lyle possessed some seriously heavy firepower and had a pure no-fear mentality. He stood right in front of Foreman and happily traded bombs. The fight turned out to be one of the greatest slugger-versus-slugger matchups ever.

Lyle came really close to knocking Foreman out. Maybe one or two more clean headshots and he would have succeeded. But in the end, he came up just short, with Foreman winning by a stoppage. If you want iron-clad proof of Foreman's granite chin, then check out this fight. Ron Lyle probably gets rated in the top twelve hardest hitters in the heavyweight division's history.

—October 2019

Iqbal Hasan: Is there any fighter in the world, past or present, who could take a full power punch (with gloves on) from Deontay Wilder and not get knocked out?

J. A.: My money is on an old-school tough guy named George Chuvalo. Not only would he not get knocked out, he would remain standing. Chuvalo was a legendary hard man, as strong as an ox, and he had a no-fear mentality. He is also a very strong candidate for the toughest heavyweight ever. If there was an Oxford English Dictionary definition of a heavyweight bruiser, then this guy's picture would be next to the definition. This guy was tough, seriously tough, and then some.

In over ninety professional fights during the heavyweight division's golden era, this guy was never knocked down once. Big George Foreman pounded on Chuvalo and couldn't stop him. Chuvalo valiantly took the pain from Foreman and never went down. His corner pulled him out to save him from unnecessary punishment. Joe Frazier pounded on Chuvalo but couldn't discourage him. Eventually the referee stepped in due to a cut eye. Other golden-era sluggers such as Zora Foley, Buster Mathis, Cleveland Williams, and Oscar Bonavena all tried in vain to KO Chuvalo.

Even Ali got in on the act twice, but he couldn't dent this man's tough-guy ego. Both fights went the distance.

In real life, Chuvalo reminded me of Rocky Balboa's fictional toughness, particularly in *Rocky 4*, when Ivan Drago commented in disbelief, "He is like a piece of iron." So although Wilder is a huge one-hit puncher, I'd still back Chuvalo to take Wilder's best hit without going down.

—December 2019

Bevan Narinesingh: Has there ever been a heavyweight champion who could take a punch and recover better than a prime Muhammad Ali?

J. A.: Once upon a time there was a fighter who was nicknamed the Easton Assassin. His real name was Larry Holmes. One of his chief qualities was a granite chin that enabled him to absorb punishment like a dry sponge absorbs water. His chin was as good as any heavyweight in history, which he proved on multiple occasions. His standout tough-guy performances came against Earnie Shavers and Mike Tyson, two of the biggest hitters in the division's history. Both Shavers and Tyson knocked him down with huge right hands—but importantly, Holmes got back up, shook off the cobwebs, and soldiered on. Dare I say it, but could it be the case that his powers of recovery were even better than Ali's.

In his ill-advised meeting with prime Tyson, Holmes suffered several very heavy knockdowns, and the manner of the knockdowns suggested that he was badly concussed. He very bravely got up twice, temporarily shook off the cobwebs, and gamely carried on fighting against a rampaging Tyson, who would not be denied. And this was at the age of 38! If Anthony Joshua had taken those same punches from prime Tyson, he would probably have been comatose.

Holmes also absorbed numerous dangerous right crosses from big-punching Ken Norton in a legendary late 1970s slugfest. This same Norton was the guy who broke Ali's jaw in the early 1970s.

Holmes also came back from the brink of defeat against an obscure boxer named Renaldo Snipes. Holmes absorbed a huge right hand from Snipes in round seven of their 1981 meeting. He went down heavy, but once again got back up, stood tough—and went on to win.

In summary, I suggest that Holmes's chin was on a par with Foreman's and Ali's. Ali and Foreman perhaps had a higher tolerance for pain than Holmes, but Holmes certainly possessed faster powers of recuperation. Additionally, Holmes handled pressure extremely well. He was great under fire, and his survival instincts were the best in the business. At the highest level of boxing, taking the pain is as important as giving it, and Holmes was surely a master at dealing with a boxing crisis.

—July 2019

Annika Peacock: Was Mike Tyson's main weakness as a boxer his inability to take a punch?

J. A.: No, not at all! Mike had a very good chin. In the Buster Douglas fight, he took one of the worst and most sustained heavyweight beatings of the modern era. On that fateful night, he absorbed all manner of power punches from an adrenaline-charged Douglas, who gave his career-best performance. Douglas unloaded with many right crosses that landed flush on Mike's chin. Tyson was at his most hittable and, from a defensive standpoint, gave his career-worst performance. Only his legendary chin kept him in that fight until he finally succumbed in the tenth round, after absorbing an absolute ton of clean leather.

Another big puncher that Tyson faced was Donovan "Razor" Ruddock. At the time, in 1991, Ruddock's left hook, come uppercut was believed to be the hardest shot in boxing. This novelty punch was nicknamed the Ruddock Smash. Tyson has stated that he felt that Ruddock was the hardest puncher he had ever faced. In two legendary slugfests with Ruddock, Tyson never once tasted the canvas, even though he was hit cleanly on numerous occasions.

In my humble opinion, Tyson's main weakness as a fighter was mental rather than physical. In general, over the entire course of his career, he was always a big-time front-runner and exhibited a slight tendency to become disheartened when faced with adversity and stern resistance. In his early career, he had gotten very used to brushing aside the opposition, and in essence had become a boxing bully. Ultimately, his own inner demons were most likely his main weakness.

—February 2020

Tommy Hearns: Did Mike Tyson have a weak chin?

J. A.: No, not at all—the exact opposite, in fact!

I guess you must have missed his fight with Buster Douglas, which saw a jaded and unmotivated Tyson take a serious beating over ten very bruising rounds. Other than the proverbial kitchen sink, Buster Douglas basically landed every punch in the book, and still the Iron Man stood tough and soldiered on. It was one of the bravest and toughest displays in the modern boxing era. He couldn't even see out of one eye because his inept cornermen couldn't deal with a swollen eye!

What is the point of having a cut man in the corner if he can't deal with a swollen eye? As the old-timers would say, that cut man was "about as useful as a punctured spare tyre". The swelling to Tyson's left eye undoubtedly impaired his vision, leaving Tyson a sucker for Douglas's right cross, which he pretty much ate all night long.

Tyson also absorbed several very powerful left hooks from big punching Donovan "Razor" Ruddock in 1991. At the time, Ruddock was something of a Deontay Wilder figure, in that he could really bang but was technically flawed. In two meetings with Ruddock, by Tyson's own high standards, he was uncharacteristically caught with all manner of power punches that a Rooney-trained Tyson would easily have avoided. Thankfully, Tyson's chin hung tough, and his own punching power saw him over the finishing line.

James "Bonecrusher" Smith landed a sucker punch on Tyson in the last round of their 1987 meeting. Smith was a big hitter, and a big right-hand punch caught Tyson directly on the chin. It temporarily dazed Tyson, but once again the Iron Man stood tough.

Smith was yet another heavyweight whose boxing skills were limited, but he could put you to sleep in a split second. This huge right hand caught Tyson unawares in a fight that he otherwise totally dominated. As Tyson used to say himself, "The most dangerous punches are the ones that you don't see."

Big-punching British heavyweight Frank Bruno caught Tyson with some heavy shots in their first meeting in 1989. Lennox Lewis caught Tyson with some crunching right hands before Tyson finally succumbed in the eighth round of their 2002 meeting.

So Tyson was very tough. It would be unfair and somewhat unrealistic to say that Tyson was as tough as Ali or Foreman—those guys were legendary hard men. But make no mistake: the Iron Man was more than tough enough to get the job done in any era.

—October 2019

Mark Adams: Who had the weakest chins in heavyweight boxing history?

J. A.: Wladimir Klitschko has to be fairly high up on any list of china-chinned heavyweights. In fact, out of all the major heavyweight fighters over the years, W. Klitschko probably had the weakest chin. You didn't even need to hit him cleanly and he would go over. This was particularly evident in the early part of his career, before he hooked up with the late, great trainer of champions, Emanuel Steward. He was badly knocked out on three occasions by fairly modest opponents. In chronological order, they were Ross Purity, the late Corrie Sanders, and Lamon Brewster.

Against Corrie Sanders in 2003, he went over very easily. By heavyweight standards, the punches that Sanders landed were medium power at best, and yet they had a big concussive effect on a still-fresh Klitschko. On this occasion, he could not use the fatigue excuse. The only feasible explanation is that he was indeed china-chinned. Almost any type of reasonably clean headshot appeared to induce an almost punch-drunk state in Klitschko, with his body language becoming very negative and discombobulated. Throughout his career, Klitschko's chin proved to be his Achilles heel. Often he was up and down like a human yo-yo.

Another weak-chinned heavyweight who comes to mind is Michael Moorer, who was really a cruiserweight but nonetheless campaigned at heavyweight too. Moorer's chin was probably on a par with Wladimir Klitschko's, and he was also susceptible to soft punches.

An example of such a soft "tap" punch was delivered by old George Foreman in his 1994 meeting with Moorer. The finishing punch was maybe one of the weakest punches in heavyweight history, and by Foreman's own powerhouse standards, it really was a little tap. Yet Moorer went down and stayed down like the proverbial sack of spuds.

In more recent times, British heavyweight David Price has been notoriously chinny and has been badly knocked out by various opponents. He exhibits a weakness which appears to be synonymous with very tall boxers, in that when he gets nailed by a clean punch, he appears to lose all his body shape and coordination and simply stands there, wide open to follow-up punches.

When hit with power punches, Price consistently adopts extremely ungainly, stiff, and vulnerable looking positions. These postural issues were particularly evident when he was tagged cleanly by Tony Thompson and, more recently, by Alexander Povetkin. Price exhibits very poor survival instincts and often appears out on his feet. From his poor posture, it appears that his limbs are no longer obeying his brain's commands.

I think Joshua too falls into this undesirable category of weak-chinned heavyweights. Before the Ruiz fight, many knowledgeable fans already suspected that he was china-chinned, but this damaging defeat clearly confirmed their worst suspicions. In Joshua's case, though, I think his chin is made to appear worse than it actually is due to a very mediocre defence. For a world champion, he has very poor defensive movements and literally catches the full force of any punches coming his way.

Out of the classic heavyweight boxers of yesteryear, I would say Floyd Patterson probably had one of the weakest chins. Once again, he was really a cruiserweight campaigning at heavyweight, so he had a valid excuse. In his darkest hour, he was wiped out by the all-time fearsome Sonny Liston; there is no shame in being knocked out by Liston!

—June 2019

Leonnius Herbalies: Do boxers with wide or bigger heads naturally have better chins? I know your ability to take a punch is mostly with neck strength.

J. A.: If you pay close attention to the head structure and morphology of the brothers Klitschko, then an interesting picture emerges. From photographic analysis, it would appear that Vitali has the slightly wider head but also the shorter head. It also appears that he has a slightly thicker neck and a less protruding chin.

As anyone who has followed boxing even casually over the last twenty or so years knows, Vitali has a granite jaw, and yet his similar-sized sibling has a notorious glass jaw. Leaving aside genetics for the moment, I think we can conclude that facial geometry and morphology must play some part in overall chin strength. But I would certainly suggest that head width is a telling statistic and so too is neck thickness.

The most common way that knockouts are achieved in boxing is by a punch to the chin—it is the bullseye target, so to speak. A chin strike creates the greatest amount of torsional shock force to the brain. Therefore, for a given punching force, there will be a lesser rotational force to the brain with increased neck thickness or head width. To make a long story short, a thicker and shorter neck reduces the whiplash effect to the brain for a given punching force.

Another way to look at chin strength and how it relates to facial and neck structure is by looking at the other end of the spectrum. Boxers who have weak chins more often than not have a long and thin head with a similarly long and thin neck. Prime examples of well-known boxers who have known glass jaws are Wladimir Klitschko, Amir Khan, and David Price. All three guys have longish heads and relatively long and thin necks. This surely cannot be mere coincidence. Chin strength is largely genetic and is one boxing trait that is rarely improved to any significant degree.

—January 2019

CHAPTER 16
CURRENT AFFAIRS

Esther Bose Odejimi, Taurean Tyre and Five More: Who will win a fight between Tyson Fury and Deontay Wilder?

J. A.: My money is on Fury, largely because he is comfortably the better boxer. The fight is going to be close, but I think Fury will get the decision, as long as he can avoid Wilder's one-punch power. The main variables which may throw a spanner into the works are Fury's mental state and physical conditioning. As long as he is in shape and takes the fight seriously, like he did in the Klitschko fight, I think he gets the decision. But if he keeps abusing his body with large fluctuations in weight, there comes a point where the body can't deal with the associated strain. Simply put, he is clearly not a good off-season professional, and this may soon catch up with him. But I honestly don't think Fury is in the business for the long haul anyway.

—August 2018

Drew Hoover: How did Andy Ruiz Junior beat Anthony Joshua?

J. A.: To simplify matters, his noticeably poor conditioning wasn't really a factor in this fight. Despite carrying a lot of fat around his midsection, it didn't appear to detract from his hand speed. He had fast hands for a 260-pound man and was a decent counterpuncher. Also in his case, the fat weight contributed positively to his punching power, similar to using a Butterbean type of approach.

I do, however, think that fans are perhaps reading too much into this "upset". The fact that Joshua was exposed by a cheeseburger-guzzling slob shouldn't come as that much of a surprise, at least not to people in the know. While calling A. J. a paper champion is harsh and unfair, the reality of the situation is that he was a limited champion who has been grossly hyped.

To an extent, we judge a book by its cover—we are all guilty of this. Had Joshua been a well-rounded boxer with a deep skill set, he could have punished his overweight opponent with body shots. And yet he was the one who appeared to be breathing heavily. Ruiz went to Joshua's body rather than vice versa. In professional boxing, the value of body punching is huge. Joshua should use this loss as a lesson in self-improvement.

What is worrying is that he appears to have quit when the going got tough. I think this was largely because he didn't like the body shots, not one bit. His weakness to body shots was evident in previous fights and no doubt will still be a weakness in the rematch.

—June 2019

Bunyagun Naragsak Ak: Is Deontay Wilder gifted with freak genetics and the hardest hitter of all time?

J. A.: No and no! Deontay Wilder may be the most overrated heavyweight champion in history, at least by casual boxing fans. In a different era—say the 1970s—I very much doubt he would even have made contender grade. Journeyman grade is more likely. In terms of boxing technique, he is probably the poorest heavyweight champion in the modern era. His boxing technique is quite frankly mediocre at the best of times, especially given the fact he is a world champion. So why is he champion?

The current level of competition in the heavyweight division is anorexically thin; in terms of depth, it is probably the weakest the division has been in the post-World War Two era. People on Quora often ask why boxing's popularity is struggling, particularly in America. Well, the current state of the heavyweight division is one of the main reasons.

I don't think Wilder has freak boxing genetics at all. He has more of a basketball physique and is simply a reasonably athletic guy who has learned how to punch hard. And he can definitely punch, albeit in a telegraphed manner. Without doubt, he is the hardest puncher in the heavyweight division today. But the hardest hitter of all time? That is a long stretch of the imagination and a fairy-tale statement. He's a very hard puncher, but he is a *wild* hard puncher—wilder by name and even wilder by nature. For example, in his fight against King Kong Ortiz, it was surprising how often he missed with his power punches. His accuracy is pretty ordinary at the best of times, and a better counterpuncher than Ortiz would have made him pay a much heavier price.

So just how hard does Wilder hit? I estimate that his power punches carry roughly the same concussive force as Wladimir Klitschko's, although Wilder's shots do carry more shock power. His haymaker-type punches come from a long way out. No doubt some of his power comes from the physical length of his arms and body, creating a whip-like effect. But I can guarantee you, no way is he close to being the hardest hitter ever. He isn't even in the top ten all time. He isn't in the same league as the Foremans, the Shaverses, the Listons, and the Tysons of this world. I estimate that a fringe contender from the 1980s, named Gerry Cooney, probably hit harder than Wilder!

—March 2019

Robert Ciccariello: How is Anthony Joshua so good if he started boxing only at 18 years old?

J. A.: Who says that he is so good? Outside of his immediate fanbase, that is. He is a good world champion and a tremendous physical specimen, and he is as strong as an ox. Joshua is also a good boxer but not yet great, not at the moment. Right now, he has won most of his fights by steamrolling the opposition with an accumulation of strength, cumulative power, and volume of punches. He is also quite athletic for a guy of his size and can definitely box, albeit in a fairly limited and scripted manner. There's nothing wrong with this. His offense ain't the problem. It's his defence and his chin that are the main sources of concern.

On various occasions in key moments, his hands are too low. For a world champion, he still has some very amateurish habits and appears wide open to power punches, such as Klitschko's arrow right cross in round six of their 2017 meeting, which scored a heavy knockdown.

Going down from a right cross thrown by a boxer of Klitschko's calibre is no big deal. Many great fighters past and present have been caught with big punches and have gone down. Credit to Joshua, he got back up from that punch. What's concerning is how easily he was caught with power punches from a boxing grandfather. What's even more worrying is that the same Klitschko, in fact the younger and more active version, couldn't lay a meaningful glove on Tyson Fury. This is probably the single main reason the fight with Wilder is being delayed. If an ageing Klitschko can almost knock Joshua out, then Wilder can surely go one better.

To prove to his critics that he is so good—say in Lennox Lewis's class—then Joshua needs to beat both Wilder and Fury convincingly. Right now, there are no immediate signs that he is even willing to share a ring with his two foremost career rivals. Is he scared? Probably more wary than scared. As far as the Wilder fight is concerned, Team A. J. are using a good old-fashioned delaying tactic. That fight should happen somewhere down the line, but the longer it is put off, the more it suits Joshua, as he has four years of youth on Wilder.

The other main reason that I think Joshua isn't as good as the average casual fan perceives him to be is his chin. For a world-class boxer, he certainly doesn't have a world-class chin. On the several occasions where he has been caught cleanly with power punches, he has been badly shaken up and almost knocked out twice. In fact, he didn't look all that great against an old Povetkin either, and again looked wide open to right hands.

In summary, Joshua is good, and he's one of the best heavyweights in the world currently, but he is nowhere near being dominant or great. If I were his manager, I would be looking to hire a world-class defensive boxing coach sooner rather than later. Otherwise Joshua is going to remain a work in progress—a similar story to Frank Bruno.

—March 2019

Ashish Kumar: Was Andy Ruiz's win against Anthony Joshua a fluke?

J. A.: The initial big punch that concussed Joshua was a fast and well-timed counter left hook that appeared to have landed on or near Joshua's right ear. I don't think there was anything lucky or flukey about Ruiz's left hook. It was almost the same punch that Dillian Whyte landed on Joshua in 2015. Team Ruiz had clearly done their homework, and they fully realised that Joshua is wide open to counterpunches, even more so when he gets drawn into a brawl.

So I wouldn't say it was a fluke at all. It was an upset, and in fact a foreseeable upset. A fluke event is something that is solely luck-oriented, and in this fight, I can't say that I saw a great deal of luck influencing the eventual outcome. For a start, it wasn't a one-punch finish, so Joshua doesn't have the lucky punch excuse. In the end, he was worn down by a series of punches over a number of rounds. The body shots that Ruiz landed were perhaps even more significant than the headshots.

Having said the above, I do think there were a number of unusual circumstances that contributed to the upset. Firstly, Ruiz was not the original opponent. At world level, this was a complication that a script boxer like Joshua didn't really need. Joshua's preparations for a replacement opponent were clearly not as meticulous as if he had been facing his original opponent, Miller.

Secondly, I think the fight being in the US had a more negative psychological impact on A. J. than his team anticipated. It was another unknown which contributed to a degree of stage fright. Thirdly, A. J. apparently was carrying a mild concussion from his sparring preparations. But all of this boils down to one word, and that is *excuses*.

These excuses have only surfaced because the strong favourite lost. In reality, A. J. was a good but vulnerable champion and most definitely overrated. On the night, I think he was simply exposed by the better man, who, for a change, didn't look like the part. Ruiz was well out of shape but had nothing to lose and seized his opportunity convincingly. At the end of the day, this was a boxing match and not a bodybuilding contest. The rematch will give everyone a clearer picture of Ruiz's long-term abilities or lack thereof.

—July 2019

Anonymous: Did Tyson Fury really taste Deontay Wilder's blood?

J. A.: Knowing what Tyson Fury is like, it was probably play-acting! But the moment when his tongue got very close to Wilder's blood was unclear on the footage. One of the fight commentators definitely suggested that Fury was "drinking Wilder's blood". I personally doubt that his tongue actually made contact with the blood, but it came pretty damn close!

Since he's named after Mike Tyson, it may have been an improvised and provocative homage to the Iron Man?

—February 2020

Leroy Holiday: What was your reaction to the Wilder versus Fury 2 fight?

J. A.: I wasn't surprised that Fury won. I thought he would edge a close points decision. The exact manner of the victory was an eye opener. I definitely wouldn't have predicted an inside mauling job. And I would never have predicted a seventh-round stoppage victory. On the night, Wilder got brutalised up close and personal, in a similar manner to how Iron Mike Tyson would have hypothetically punished him. On this occasion, Wilder had no answer to Fury's strength and weight advantages.

Fury pounded on Wilder's beanpole body. It was the first heavyweight title fight in ages that I can remember a fighter being taken down by one clean body shot. Fury definitely took a page out of his namesake's book: "Pound the body and eventually the head will fall."

Wilder clearly can't box inside and had no answer to Fury's bulling/sumo tactics. He perhaps should have got on his bike and tried some "stick and move". But once again, this fight proved how unpredictable heavyweight boxing can be. Fury's mauling tactics were a real turn-up for the books. There was no luck involved. He had definitely pre-planned his inside fighting strategy, where his weight advantage proved decisive.

—February 2020

Kinyanjui Kamau: Should Wilder take a third fight with Fury? If so, would it not be a waste of time, as Wilder would have to rely on his only trick, a knockout right punch?

J. A.: From a financial perspective, yes, he should take the third fight with Fury. However, if he utilises a degree of common sense, I think he should try and avoid Fury for the foreseeable future. After the systematic mauling he sustained, his confidence must be at an all-time low. In a one-on-one combat sport like boxing, a badly beaten boxer should try to avoid an immediate rematch. Not only did Wilder lose, but he got manhandled by a giant human grizzly bear. I personally rate the beating that Wilder took as being in the same class as Foreman dominating Frazier, Tyson flattening Spinks, and Dempsey mauling Willard. It was absolutely dominant and a genuine mismatch.

As you assert in your question, outside of Wilder's haymaker right hand, what realistic chance does he have? He definitely cannot outbox Fury; we already knew this from the first fight. But in the rematch, he basically got owned by Fury in every single boxing department you can think of. So it definitely doesn't look good for Wilder against Tyson Fury. On top of this, Fury will be oozing confidence and will be looking to do an even worse demolition job on Wilder (if that is possible).

—March 2020

Timothy Soo: Is Deontay Wilder being disingenuous when making excuses for his defeat by Tyson Fury? Is he doing it with the sole intention of hyping the third fight?

J. A.: When you get your ass kicked on the world stage, then you need an excuse. He's definitely being disingenuous (for whatever reason). I personally don't think the third fight needs hyping—everybody's already watching. He's making excuses because on the night, he got owned by Tyson Fury both from a pugilistic standpoint and from a physical standpoint. The big boy's ego has taken a hammering!

Fury was the aggressor throughout this fight, systematically mauling Wilder on the inside. No one surely would have predicted this type of inside beatdown.

In the rematch, which on paper was supposed to be a fifty-fifty fight turned into a mismatch of epic proportions. Remember the bookies' odds? Wilder was a very slight betting favourite, so there are a lot of people out there who lost money on him. His lame-duck excuses are also probably directed towards disgruntled punters who backed him. But at the end of the day, he's not the first or last sore loser who will resort to making excuses as a cover-up.

—March 2020

The Michael H: Will the memory of Deontay Wilder's reign as champion get the Mike Tyson treatment, where fighting weaker opponents is overshadowed by the insane knockouts, or will he always be considered an overrated champion?

J. A.: At the best of times, Deontay Wilder couldn't even lace up Mike's gloves. So not at all—Wilder should never be compared to Tyson. I can't think of any knowledgeable pundits who would want to put Wilder into that kind of esteemed company. Other than the fact that Wilder boasts a very impressive knockout-to-wins ratio, there is almost no similarity between the two. Of course Wilder can really bang with his right hand, but his knockout highlight reel is nowhere near as impressive as Tyson's, and he is still a very limited boxer. Mike was a true great at the very top of the food chain, and in fact was the most technically skilled brawler in heavyweight history.

Wilder's record flatters to deceive because he has been fighting all-time weak opposition. This isn't entirely his fault. The current heavyweight division is basically like an episode out of the old TV show *Land of the Giants*. There are very few great boxers, if any, in the division, so Wilder has basically flattened a whole bunch of professionally trained giant tomato cans. Mike's era may not have been the golden era, but the competition he faced was way stiffer than this current crop.

As for labelling Tyson overrated, I personally think he's overrated in only one area, and that is in terms of absolute punching power. Although he hit like a mule, there were many other massive-punching historical heavyweights who do not receive anywhere near as much airtime as the Iron Man. What set Tyson apart from the heavyweight crowd was his punching effectivity; I believe he was the most dangerous puncher in heavyweight history. In terms of his overall boxing skill, you will find that Tyson was generally underrated, particularly at the time of his dominance.

Another factual area where there are no grounds for comparison is that Wilder is not undisputed champion and has never come anywhere near to exerting heyday Tyson's level of dominance. Tyson unified all the belts, effectively cleaned out the division, and was arguably the most dominant heavyweight champion in history. So Wilder is the unjustifiably overrated boxer and not Tyson. Anyone who calls prime Tyson overrated clearly knows little or nothing about pro boxing.

In the end, only time will tell how Wilder is remembered. This will inevitably depend on how he performs against his career rivals, namely A. J. and Tyson Fury.

—January 2020

Jovanne Rodriguez: How historically good is Tyson Fury? Is he benefiting from a weaker era, or can he hang with the greats?

J. A.: Fury is very good—good enough to win a version of a world title. As long as he is in shape—which by no means is a certainty—is properly motivated, and has put in a proper training camp, then I think he could hang in any era. At the end of the day, Fury is a giant with decent boxing skills who can also move fluidly, which is something of a rarity.

His signature win came against a slightly past-prime Wladimir Klitschko, and he matched Klitschko in virtually all boxing departments. Given that Klitschko is regarded as a generational great, this result speaks for itself. In other words, Fury has already hung with a fringe great.

To beat a guy as seasoned and as well schooled as Klitschko indicates that Fury can definitely box, has a high ring IQ, and can handle the pressure. Remember that the victory was away from home, in Klitschko's own backyard. This is a big positive for Fury. Boxing away from home indicates that he can do the business in unfamiliar territory, which is something that the true greats were renowned for.

Without doubt, the current era is relatively weak, particularly in terms of depth. The average heavyweight seems to be resorting to gigantism and strong-arm tactics of one form or another, rather than genuine boxing skills. So although Fury can box, his skills are slightly flattered due to the low level of the competition.

The biggest knock on Fury is that he generally lacks that equalising KO punch. When facing the true greats, this limitation in his offensive arsenal would be a big handicap. In the end, the combination of size and mobility he possesses would prove to be a handful in any era; therefore I see him being competitive against the greats but not a serious enough threat to actually beat them.

—December 2019

Mike Shaner: Could Andy Ruiz be a great fighter if he took it seriously and paid attention to strength and conditioning instead of eating doughnuts?

J. A.: I don't think Andy Ruiz Junior will ever be a great fighter or ever had such potential, irrespective of his new training regimen. Even if you asked a selection of impartial boxing experts this question immediately after he upset A. J. in June 2019, I think the majority would say that he is a limited boxer. To call Ruiz a one-trick pony may sound harsh, but it is probably a fairly accurate description. Unfortunately for A. J., he fell for that trick.

I think the boxing fraternity in general has found this last six months to have been quite amusing; to think that it took six months and a bad KO defeat for the heavyweight champion of the world to realise that you shouldn't stand and bang with a sumo wrestler-come-boxer is a pretty funny state of affairs.

However, if Ruiz totally changed his attitude to eating and training, it is highly probable that he would be an improved fighter. The weight loss would at least improve his foot speed and mobility, thereby making it much easier for him to cut off the ring on a back-pedalling boxer-mover. At a more sensible weight of, say, seventeen stone, he would also be a more elusive target and have vastly improved balance. This is where I think the strength training would also be beneficial. He wouldn't be so reliant on the fat weight to generate his power and momentum.

As for his doughnut-and-Snickers diet, it must surely be the worst diet of any heavyweight champion in history. Changing his diet would definitely make him look less like a cartoon. As Mike Tyson's former trainer Teddy Atlas jokingly commented in June 2019, "One hundred years' worth of sports science and nutrition just went out the window."

In summary, I think Ruiz is good at what he does, and that is reactive brawling. Improved diet and training will probably make him a better brawler but not a great boxer. If you stand in the pocket and have a pub brawl with him, he'll take you out. If you finesse him with angles and movement, he is reduced to a sitting duck because he is so heavy.

—December 2019

John K. Williamson: Did partying for three months instead of training contribute to Andy Ruiz Junior's defeat when he fought Anthony Joshua for the heavyweight world titles at Diriyah Stadium in Saudi Arabia?

J. A.: I doubt that Ruiz Junior can use the partying and distraction excuse. A more legitimate excuse is that for the last three months he's been guzzling Snickers bars like there was no tomorrow.

When you've got the body of a human hippo, it does beg the question: What kind of serious training is he capable of? Was the physical and cardio side of his training camp any better in June? He was badly out of shape in June, when he tipped the scales at the wrong end of nineteen stone. He was still badly out of shape in December, when he tipped the scales at the wrong end of twenty stone. Ask yourself an honest question: If you weren't told his body weights from the two weigh-ins, would you be able to tell that he was one stone fatter just by visual inspection alone?

In my humble opinion, the main reason that Ruiz lost was that A. J. made the correct adjustment. In the rematch, Joshua used a sensible stick-and-move style, which targeted Ruiz's deficiencies in conditioning and mobility. Ruiz was so heavy that he couldn't cut the ring off fast enough and was a sitting duck. He was also nowhere near aggressive enough in the early going and was literally incapable of punching while on the move, due to appalling balance. Also absent this time around were his body attacks, which did significant damage to A. J. in June.

In the end, I think Ruiz tried to use an even more extreme sumo/Butterbean tactic, which on the night backfired. He was banking on blitzing A. J. early on, and this time around A. J. simply wasn't there to be hit.

—December 2019

Bevan Narinesingh: Was Anthony Joshua's victory over Andy Ruiz a result of Ruiz being out of shape, as opposed to Joshua's boxing skills?

J. A.: Neither factor was decisive, really. The victory was more of a tactical coup. Joshua's safety-first points victory was more to do with sensible boxing, sensible weight loss, and adhering to a very strict game plan. Ruiz Junior was a nineteen stone hippo with boxing gloves on in June, and he was a twenty stone hippo with boxing gloves on in December. As far as Ruiz is concerned, all that has changed in six months is a stone of extra blubber.

As far as A. J. is concerned, he came in at his more natural fight weight of approximately seventeen stone, at which he had more mobility. On this occasion, when the hippo charged, Joshua could show some lateral movement to evade those crude attacks. In my humble opinion, an Olympic gold medallist (albeit a very vulnerable one) should have enough defensive skill to avoid a guy as sloppy as Ruiz Junior.

Hindsight is a fine thing, but it now appears A. J. was clearly underprepared in June, on top of which Ruiz was an unknown entity. In June, A. J. was also too muscular and heavy, and the law of diminishing returns worked against him. You will generally find that a heavyweight boxer should not weigh too much in excess of seventeen stone, unless of course they are exceptionally tall. Seventeen stone is a very good upper limit. Simply put, any weight above and beyond seventeen stone is a liability. If you check the history books, Lennox Lewis got himself knocked out by Hasim Rahman in April 2001, when he tipped the scales at a career-high eighteen stone. Big Daddy Bowe lost to Holyfield in their rematch, when he weighed close to eighteen stone. Similar to Ruiz, throughout his career Bowe had major appetite problems, which led to major fluctuations in body weight and therefore performance. The difference with Ruiz is that he is badly out of shape, full stop.

In summary, I think A. J.'s victory will not be remembered for too long. But he deserves some credit for handling the pressure, staying disciplined, and making the necessary and obvious adjustments. Primarily, I believe he lost in June because he committed a cardinal sin of boxing, and that is to "never brawl with a brawler".

—December 2019

Farooq E. Subhan: What were your thoughts on Anthony Joshua versus Andy Ruiz 2?

J.A.: The fight was an anticlimax. It reminded me of a dress rehearsal, but in this instance, it was a post-rehearsal of a play that went wrong the first time around. As Apollo Creed remarked in *Rocky 4*, "Some fellas have to learn the hard way." Perhaps A. J. needed to get KO'd to fully realise that he can't brawl? In essence, Ruiz was an unknown entity the first time around because he was a replacement opponent, albeit a very dangerous one. To a script fighter like A. J., an unknown entity is dangerous. On the other hand, Team Ruiz were perfectly prepared the first time out and had probably been stalking A. J.'s every move for years.

But credit to A. J., he was a guy under a lot of pressure and passed a tough test with flying colours. Ruiz on the night was a big let-down. He was an opportunistic, sloppy, fat guy who simply took advantage of an underprepared champion in June 2019. However, irrespective of the outcome of the rematch, Ruiz's brawler style still matches up very well against A. J.

The excess weight doesn't seem to affect Ruiz's hand speed, but it sure as hell slows down his foot speed. He took way too long to close the gap. If you break Ruiz's style down, he's clearly better at reactive brawling rather than proactive brawling and is definitely an opportunistic boxer. In the rematch, when he was forced to proactively apply pressure to a more defensive and negative A. J., he was too slow and sloppy with his footwork. On top of this, his balance was appalling—not surprising given his appalling conditioning.

To summarise, I think the rematch highlighted what a lot of people in the know already suspected. If they have a brawl, then Ruiz wins, but if they have a long-range boxing match, then A. J. wins. In the end, there is something called Newton's law of gravity, and it is equally applicable to muscle weight and fat weight.

—December 2019

Daniel Prestwich: Would Tyson Fury beat Anthony Joshua?

J. A.: If they fought tomorrow, I would go for Fury on points. All the evidence so far points towards a fairly cagey encounter which will not be too dissimilar to Fury versus Klitschko or even A. J. versus Parker. At this point in time, I rate a 38-year-old Klitschko as better than a 30-year-old A. J. If Fury out-spoiled Klitschko, he can do the same job on A. J. Klitschko was comfortably a better boxer than A. J. and a lot more dangerous. In hindsight, Fury made that fight look easy. The only quality that A. J. has above Klitschko is strength, and that's about it.

I think the fight should be close and will likely go the distance. If it goes to points, we are once again reliant on the judges' interpretation of the action. A. J. looked confused and somewhat ponderous against the fairly modest punching Joseph Parker, and Fury is a better boxer than Parker. On top of this, he will be physically stronger than Parker in the clinches and is an intimidating physical presence. As with Klitschko, A. J. is used to towering above his opponents, but against Fury he will be looking up at an even bigger man mountain.

All the above does assume that Fury doesn't gain around five stone in weight over the festive period, start experimenting with Class A drugs again, or suffer a mental breakdown.

—December 2018

Buck Leblanc: Was the Mike Tyson fight with Roy Jones Junior really a draw?

J. A.: I honestly wouldn't classify that "fight" as a fight. Even though it was nothing more than a sparring session minus head guards, I think Tyson won the fight on points. He clearly appeared to be taking it easy on Jones, particularly on the inside.

I think the judges' scorecards were really a moot point and may have been filled in prior to a punch being thrown. In other words, it was a pre-planned draw.

—December 2020

Nicollas Torres: How did Terence Crawford land a jab on Kell Brook with such power?

J. A.: It was an accurate and well-timed southpaw jab which had a double impact due to the fact that Brook walked onto the punch. It was another example of an "unseen" punch that causes a bigger concussion than you would otherwise expect. Every time Crawford switched to southpaw, he seemed to fare better, both offensively and defensively.

Right up until that point in round four, this fight looked fifty-fifty to me. That one big jab seemed to take an awful lot out of Brook. In years gone by, I think he would have taken those same punches much better—he is clearly looking a bit shopworn.

Crawford finished Brook off in somewhat underwhelming fashion in the ropes, just seconds after that big jab landed. I think the referee could have let this fight go on at least thirty seconds longer or until Brook went down properly—yet another premature referee stoppage in my book. Look at Brook's face and read his lips immediately after the stoppage. He's asking his cornermen what happened, because it was over so fast. Yes, he was concussed, but he was not badly hurt. After this defeat, it is hard to see where Brook goes other than a last big payday fight against Khan.

—November 2020

John Johansson: Now that Tyson Fury has said he will never fight again following defamation of character, will Wilder retire?

J. A.: Hard to say, really, because boxers say all sorts of things in the heat of the moment. If Tyson Fury is offered a substantially higher payday, who knows? He may well change his mind.

But if I were in Fury's shoes, I would most probably avoid a second rematch with Wilder. The reason is twofold. Firstly, Fury dominated Wilder in the rematch and stopped him in emphatic fashion. I think it is highly unlikely that he can repeat such a terrific, career-defining performance. Secondly, Wilder is still a very dangerous and massive one-hit puncher who can easily turn your lights out in the blink of an eye. Fury has it all to lose if they meet for a third time, so the fact that Wilder is goading him is really a moot point.

As for Wilder retiring? He can probably afford to retire! As the old saying goes, "It becomes much harder to train after waking up in silk pyjamas." But at the end of the day, if the money is right, we know from past history that fighters can be attracted back into the ring.

And before anyone retires, I think every genuine boxing fan wants to see A. J. and Wilder get it on.

—November 2020

Bevan Narinesingh: Will a fight between Deontay Wilder and Anthony Joshua (whoever wins) be more likely to end in a knockout, or will it go the distance?

J. A.: Based purely on hypothetical percentage probability, I would say there is a very high chance it will end in a KO or TKO. At the end of the day, this one's not rocket science. You've got two big punchers who both have average chins and suspect defensive technique, which is clearly a good recipe for a KO.

Apart from Tyson Fury, no one has lasted the distance against the massive-punching Wilder. A. J. like Wilder, has a great knockout-to-wins ratio, with only Parker and Ruiz Junior lasting the distance with him. So if you want to get statistical, then it looks like there is at least a 90 per cent chance of this fight ending in a stoppage.

Having said the above, both camps will also obviously know that their man is a bit on the chinny side. When you have a couple of china-chinned heavyweights who can both bang, it may be that both guys adopt an ultra-defensive strategy to offset the chance of the inevitable one-punch blowout. Certainly from A. J.'s perspective, he will want to avoid Wilder's windmill right hand like the plague, particularly in the early going. This being the case, he may avoid any and all scenarios where a big punch or combo can land.

But even if A. J. duplicates his safety-first approach from Ruiz Junior 2, I think Wilder is a much more dangerous banger than Ruiz. At some point during a twelve-rounder, Wilder should break through Joshua's suspect defence. He is also in way better shape than Ruiz, which is a big positive in Wilder's favour. Also consider the fact that the height and reach of Wilder and A. J. are very similar. This being the case, it will be much more difficult for A. J. to stick and move for thirty-six minutes against Wilder.

—January 2020

Yan Cao: Is there any heavyweight boxer in the world who can beat Deontay Wilder?

J. A.: Tyson Fury is clearly the most likely candidate. He has the physical tools (height and reach), boxing ability, and maybe most importantly the ring IQ to do a number on Wilder. Fury is comfortably a better boxer than Wilder. If they boxed again, say in the UK, he would easily decision him. Team Wilder knows this, which is why they want a piece of Joshua or Ruiz Junior instead. Wilder ideally wants to fight someone who will stand and trade bombs with him.

After Wilder knocked out Dominic Breazeale in devastating fashion, Fury commented, "If you stand in front of Wilder, he will take you out." While this is a fairly obvious statement (you shouldn't stand and bang with a massive puncher), then why doesn't everybody else simply box Wilder sensibly on the back foot? No doubt Wilder is the most dangerous heavyweight in the world and is a genuinely huge puncher, but he can be boxed, confused, and frustrated. Fury already did this in their original encounter last year, but at the same time was still floored twice over the course of twelve rounds. So if and when there is a rematch, you can be sure that Fury will try his best to avoid Wilder's windmill right hand.

On top of this, Team Wilder know that Fury is a smart, defensive boxer who prepares meticulously for his fights. They also know that Fury handled Wladimir Klitschko, which was a great achievement. In comparison to Klitschko, Wilder is in fact an easier boxing assignment.

Other than Fury, I think Wilder is currently number two in the world. I fancy he could probably knock out both Joshua and Ruiz.

—September 2019

G. Baines: What are the technical flaws in Anthony Joshua's boxing style?

J. A.:

- *Basic defensive frailties*: When under fire, Joshua's hands are too low, and his left hand in particular doesn't do all that much. Against Klitschko, his ability to block punches was poor. Without being ultra-critical, the defensive aspects of his game are still very amateurish, and to a seasoned observer this is glaringly obvious. He needs a much tighter head guard and way better head movement, which at the present time is almost non-existent. Simply put, at world level he is a sitting duck for a decent counterpuncher (Andy Ruiz Junior). He is wide open to body shots. In terms of body shape and rhythm, he has to do much more when he is not himself throwing punches.
- *Mediocre chin and weak survival instincts*: We all know that no fighter looks good after being knocked down, but after taking a big initial punch, Joshua kind of reminds me of Bambi stranded on ice. Alternatively, when he gets hurt or stunned, the red mist descends, and he mistakenly gets drawn into a brawl or does a silly, discombobulated dance. To me this indicates that he is simply an on-top fighter who is solely used to being a front runner, even in sparring sessions. He doesn't seem to have practised or rehearsed what to do in a boxing crisis. For a former world champion, this is worrying. When he's winning, he looks like a million dollars, but when the shoe is on the other foot and he has to take the pain, then he looks like an old and well-used ten-dollar bill. When hit cleanly, more often than not his posture and facial expression are indicative of a confused state. This disturbingly appears to be a reflex action—similar to opening your mouth automatically when looking up.
- *Over-reliance on the dominant hand*: It is pretty obvious that Joshua is right-handed. Most of us have a dominant hand, which is the power hand. I think he is right-hand trigger happy, and a crafty guy like Ruiz was reading his power punches all too easily. For that matter, so too were Wladimir Klitschko and Joseph Parker. Against all the other third- and fourth-tier opposition, this one-dimensional over-reliance on his right hand didn't

cost him. He also needs to work big time on his left jab and keep pumping it out with some authority and intent, rather than just pawing with it. A good stepping or stiff jab will keep a bulling fighter like Ruiz more honest and off balance.

- *Recovery of balance*: Every so often, even pro boxers miss the intended target by wide margins. Some miss more than others. No big deal, right? Joseph Parker made Joshua miss more than his previous opponents, but he didn't make him pay for his overcommitment on power punches. For a world champion, Joshua is too frequently off balance, particularly after missing with power punches. This is no surprise, given that he's lugging around 250 pounds of body weight. When off balance, everyone is vulnerable to a lesser or greater extent. However, the taller and heavier you are, the longer it takes to recover your balance, and this is when you are most vulnerable to fast counterpunchers like Ruiz Junior.
- *Joshua is a headhunter*: He has a great right cross, which has done its fair share of damage over the years. But he needs to work on his body punching. If the value of body punching hasn't yet sunk into his brain, then I guess it never will. The irony of his defeat to Ruiz was that the guy with the better body was the one who was breathing heavily. Ruiz went to Joshua's body like a seasoned pro and fulfilled yet another great old boxing adage: "Kill the body and eventually the head will fall." If you watch the fight closely, watch out for Ruiz's left body jab—it was a game changer and literally denied Joshua any breathing space. It isn't a finishing punch, but the body jab slowly pecks away at stamina, oxygen, and strength reserves.
- *Way too much emphasis on physicality instead of boxing technique*: Just in case Joshua hasn't realised, he is in the boxing business and not bodybuilding. He should save the V-shaped poses for when he's on the beach.

—August 2019

Steve Pierce: Should Ruiz Junior get in shape for the Anthony Joshua rematch, or should he stay as he is?

J. A.: Apparently Andy Ruiz Junior wants his body to look more beautiful for the rematch, so he may try and come in more lean and ripped. If he tries to take a leaf out of Joshua's book and look like Mr Universe, then it could be a big mistake. Looks can be very deceiving. As we all saw in June, the guy with the uglier body can be the better fighter on the night.

If I were his trainer, I would perhaps get him to trim up slightly, reducing his waistline by a couple of inches at the most. This would most probably equate to approximately one stone of pure fat loss, which would mean he tipped the scales at around 250 pounds fight weight. Given that he is around 6 feet 2 inches tall with a large frame, this is still more than enough weight to get the job done. In addition to sensible weight loss, I would also get him to work on his cardio, just in case the fight goes into the later rounds this time.

But other than conditioning, I would keep everything the same and just keep on brawling. I wouldn't change his fight tactics at all; they were nearly perfect the first time around. Other than getting knocked down, I can't see that he made any obvious mistakes. I think the trick to beating Joshua is aggressive and fast counterpunching, and then moving in on the inside and exploiting his weakness to body punching. From Joshua's perspective, I think he has to keep the fight much longer and box his man.

I think this intriguing matchup highlights the issue of what exactly is a good shape for a heavyweight boxer. Both guys are essentially extremophiles at the opposite ends of the spectrum. One guy is too muscular and the other guy too fat. At the end of the day, boxing technique is what matters the most. Personally, I've always felt that a heavyweight boxer should be around seventeen stone max. That is more than enough weight to get the job done, as long as you really know your way around a boxing ring.

—August 2019

Steve Pierce: Is there any way that Anthony Joshua can loosen up before the Ruiz fight? He reminds me a bit of Frank Bruno.

J. A.: That's funny, because from a defensive standpoint, he reminds me exactly of Frank Bruno—stiff, ponderous, muscle-bound, cumbersome, and unbalanced. He has bread-and-butter footwork and a weak chin, and he lacks any kind of head movement whatsoever. In general, after delivering his own punches, he hangs around like wet laundry, not doing much.

When comparing A. J. and Bruno under fire, there are a number of similarities that emerge. At close range in particular, both Brits are very poor under fire, catch the full force of counterpunches. They have weak survival instincts after being hit with the initial big punch. From the brawler's perspective, what I believe guys like Tyson and Ruiz Junior see when fighting upright, muscle-bound guys like Bruno and Joshua are sitting ducks. After getting tagged with the initial big shot, that sitting duck rapidly turns into a lame duck, and it's game over. Lennox Lewis commented on this issue after Bruno versus Tyson 2: "Tyson basically had a workout on a human heavy bag."

Can Joshua loosen up in readiness for the rematch? He has about four months to change the habits of a lifetime. I think he needs to trim down to seventeen stone tops, and that means losing at least a stone of excess muscle, which is simply weighing him down and causing him to gas more quickly. He urgently needs to get some defensive, proactive rhythm into his boxing. I would suggest jumping rope would help with this. So if he doesn't already know how to use a skipping rope, then now is a good time to start practising—that is. if his 250-pound strongman physique can overcome the well-known force of gravity.

In some respects, he finds himself in a situation similar to the fictional setting of *Rocky 3*, after Balboa was brutally knocked out by Clubber Lang. For the rematch, Apollo volunteered to train Rocky because Balboa's original trainer Mickey had died. But the point is that Apollo gave a limited and predictable slugger a fresh perspective on training. As Apollo explained to Rocky, "You need to stretch and use muscles that you never even thought you had." Rhythm and speed were two big features of the revamped Balboa in *Rocky 3*. Obviously that was a movie, but I think the message it conveyed was sound at world level. As the loser of the original fight, you have to do something quite different in order to reverse the result in the rematch.

In Joshua's case, I think this is more than just altering his poor tactics. He was simply too hittable to both body and head. On various occasions I've heard him say that he likes a tear-up:

"Mate, you ain't got the chin for brawling, not at world level anyways." I think he still has time to get himself a new trainer, one who concentrates on teaching boxing skills rather than lifting weights for a Mr Universe contest.

—*August 2019*

Jovanne Rodriguez: What does Andy Ruiz's future in boxing look like? Will he make a successful run as a champion or have a short career?

J. A.: Remember a certain guy by the name of Buster Douglas? I have a sneaky suspicion that Ruiz may be destined to follow in Buster Douglas's footsteps. While Joshua is certainly no Mike Tyson, I think Ruiz's performance on the night against Joshua was something of a déjà vu moment for boxing historians. There were a number of bizarre circumstances that all came together on the night to upset the applecart, as was the case with Douglas versus Tyson in 1990. Like Douglas before him, Ruiz suffered a fairly heavy knockdown, which provided him with the impetus to acquire a second wind. A wounded fighter turned brave is a very dangerous weapon. It is impossible to say for sure, but would Ruiz have come out swinging so intensely had he not been knocked down?

Most of Ruiz's short-term future obviously hinges on what happens in the rematch. It is obviously a massive fight. And make no mistake: in the rematch there will be a lot of pressure on both guys. Also Ruiz will no longer be an unknown entity, and I think this factor will be huge. If Ruiz modifies his game plan and becomes more passive, this will suit Joshua down to the ground. Ruiz needs to repeat exactly what he did in the first fight and be both aggressive and assertive from the outset. Also bear in mind that his flabby physique is clearly not suited to a protracted chess match—but then again, neither is Joshua's.

At the end of the day, the best way to predict the future is to look at the past. The majority of the time in the heavyweight division, a big underdog struggles against elite opposition and fades quite quickly. Prime examples of this phenomenon were observed when Leon Spinks, Michael Spinks, Buster Douglas, Oliver McCall, and Hasim Rahman *all* pulled off major boxing upsets. Coincidentally, all these guys generally went on to be nothings, and yet in their finest hours proved to be world-beaters.

The counter-argument is clearly that all these guys upset Hall of Fame-grade opposition, whereas Ruiz upset a very vulnerable and hyped champion in Anthony Joshua. I think Ruiz has a good chance to give Joshua a repeat dose of his original medicine, depending upon the location of the fight. Anthony Joshua is definitely a homeboy. If I were Ruiz, I would make Joshua fight him in the US again.

But even if Ruiz beats Joshua again, which is entirely feasible, how would he fare against the likes of Fury and Wilder? Only time will tell. I feel Wilder and Fury will be much tougher tests for Andy Ruiz. Certainly Tyson Fury will have many a trick up his sleeve and will be way more elusive than the statuesque Joshua.

—*June 2019*

CHAPTER 17

PUNCHES, COMBOS, AND SPECIAL MOVES

Jay Harewood: What is a check hook in boxing?

J. A.: The most notable example of a perfectly executed check hook was given by Floyd Mayweather in round ten of his 2007 clash with Ricky Hatton.

Throughout the fight, the highly aggressive Hatton consistently tried to bull his way into Mayweather's guard. As usual, Mayweather was happy to play the matador, drawing the bulling and unsuspecting Hatton deeper inside. At the last second, Mayweather spun out of the corner. Where Hatton thought Mayweather's ribcage was gonna be, now there was a perfectly timed check left hook waiting for him, which landed flush on his chin.

This was a great example of high-level counterpunching from Mayweather and a prime example of how to use the aggressor's momentum against him. But a check hook is usually a lead hook, whereby an elite boxer draws an aggressor onto a punch and simultaneously spins or swivels his own body out of harm's way at the last second. The body swivel and counterpunch happen together in one smooth motion, at least when Mayweather does it!

—October 2020

Chris Steele: If you have to have at least one foot on the canvas when throwing a punch in boxing, then how did Joe Frazier get away with his jumping hooks?

J. A.: Frazier was arguably the best left hooker in heavyweight history. Smokin' Joe's left hook was a great punch which he could throw at will all night long, with minimum backlift or wind up. But Joe wasn't the only one who mastered this punch. The leaping left hook was also a Jack Dempsey trademark. In more recent times, Floyd Patterson mastered this punch, along with middleweight great Marvin Hagler and, most notably, Iron Mike Tyson. Hagler landed a wicked leaping left hook on the unsuspecting British middleweight world champion Alan Minter in 1980.

By his own high standards, 1970s Muhammad Ali was something of a sitting duck for Frazier's lethal left hook. Frazier landed this punch with devastating effect in the fifteenth round of the Fight of the Century in 1971. The legendary trainer Cus D'Amato predicted that Frazier would beat Ali, citing Frazier's left hook as the main weapon in Ali's demise. D'Amato was a master coach and taught both Tyson and Patterson how to correctly throw the leaping left hook, with the proper disguise and technique.

The punch relies on a shifting of body weight from one foot to the other and is only really performed successfully by relatively short heavyweights. It requires powerful leg muscles, powerful glutes, and a very solid core. Tyson, like Frazier before him, had legendary lower body and core strength. The boxer propels his whole body forward and upward, so the punch often starts from a crouch. It can be viewed almost as a cobra strike, with the entire body unravelling. The fist is merely the end point of the strike. Jack Dempsey was probably the first heavyweight to utilise the leaping left hook to major effect, and he was a great proponent of using the whole body as a type of missile in boxing.

But ultimately, your feet are firmly planted on the canvas at the start of the punching motion. It is only at the end point of the strike that your feet are off the ground. It is kind of like a Bruce Lee flying kick but a flying punch instead. As both your feet are off the ground, then virtually the entire body weight of the boxer is incorporated into the punch.

—January 2019

Mobin Fathinajad: What are the most useful punches to learn and use for boxing and kickboxing?

J. A.: Believe it or not, there are only five different types of *fundamental* punches in boxing.

Firstly there are the straight-line punches, the jab and the cross. The jab is the most important punch to learn, as it traditionally travels the shortest straight-line distance. The jab is sometimes described as a lead punch or a "key to the lock" punch. To an out-fighter, it is an incredibly important punch; pretty much everything else flows off the jab. To an in-fighter, it is still important as it enables him to get inside more effectively.

After the jab comes the cross, which is so called because it is thrown with the rear hand. The punching hand has to cross a longer distance, typically the shoulder width of the boxer. It is also a straight-line punch, but more power can be generated in the cross due to greater leverage and body torque.

Next come the punches that follow a curved trajectory, starting with the hook. After this you have the uppercut, and finally the overhand hook. Since these punches travel along a curved path, they are easier to see and therefore easier to dodge. The advantage to the attacking fighter is that greater leverage can be implemented into these punches. Hooks are the most powerful punches.

So there you have it—only five punches to learn and practise, but an almost infinite number of combinations!

—January 2019

Ross Taylor: What is the standard boxing punch combo that you must know if you want to get to grips with the basics of the sport?

J. A.: The combo you must have is the one-two: the jab followed by the cross. The reason for this is fairly straightforward—the shortest distance between two points is a straight line. By keeping these basic punches as straight as possible, you cover the distance between yourself and your opponent as quickly as possible.

In recent times, Wladimir Klitschko mastered this bread-and-butter combo. By effectively utilising his long reach, he could land this standard combo from very long range. He threw this combo repeatedly (some would say robotically) against all his opponents. Over the years, it proved universally effective. Talk about a recent heavyweight boxer who had a high fight IQ and knew how to box to his strengths, then Klitschko comes to mind. It is a standard textbook combination, but in his case it was very dangerous, given his height and reach advantages.

Wladimir Klitsckho was one of those boxers whose looks were very deceiving. His opponents no doubt watched him on film and felt that what he did was fairly basic and one-dimensional, concluding that he therefore was easy to beat. But perhaps what his opponents didn't realise until they stepped into the ring with him was that he excelled in that one dimension. He was a great out-fighter with good footwork who executed the standard one-two combination with textbook precision.

Another of his basic combinations was the double jab followed by the right cross. When he threw the double jab, often the jabs were weakish, range-finding punches, with the follow-up right cross being the danger punch.

—July 2019

Stevie Van Zandt: Which heavyweight boxer had the most precise or dangerous jab of all time?

J. A.: Larry Holmes is a very strong candidate. Many of Holmes's opponents were undone by this simple but highly effective punch. He could stick and move virtually all night long, and his laser-guided jab would be in your face pretty much for the entire duration of the fight. It was simple but very effective. His fiercest critics would no doubt say, "Holmes simply jabbed his way to the world heavyweight title." This may be true, but if it was that simple and straightforward, then why didn't other heavyweights of his time follow suit?

In a number of his key title defences, Holmes's jab was almost definitely the decisive factor, particularly when he fought younger and physically stronger guys like Berbick, Cooney, and Witherspoon. His fight against Gerry Cooney was memorable for a variety of reasons, with many Cooney fans hoping for a quick knockout victory, similar to when Cooney blitzed Ken Norton early on. Norton had lasted the distance against Holmes in 1978, but against Cooney he was wiped out in the first round. Cooney could really bang but was a limited boxer, and many people felt that the Great White Hope stood a good chance of upsetting the apple cart. Against Holmes, Cooney couldn't land the big power punches. In fact he couldn't even solve the difficult and repetitive puzzle that was Holmes's legendary jab.

If you thought that Holmes looked old and rickety against prime Tyson, then you ain't seen nothing yet. He looked even older and ricketier against Holyfield in 1992. Yet at the grand old age of 42, that jab still gave Holyfield plenty of food for thought.

Another early 1980s opponent who couldn't solve Holmes's jab was the late Leon Spinks in 1981. The one-hit wonder that was Leon Spinks was badly exposed by a technically superior Holmes over the course of three very short rounds.

In closing, I suggest that Sonny Liston's jab was more powerful than Holmes's, but Holmes's was faster, more precise, and perhaps more influential in his victories. Everything else flowed off his jab. But it is generally a toss-up between Liston and Holmes as to whose jab was the best.

—July 2019

Logan Pettke: What is the most difficult punch to avoid or block?

J. A.: How about the uppercut? In my humble opinion, Mike Tyson's arching uppercut was consistently the most dangerous punch in heavyweight history. He landed this punch on almost all his opponents, so it was clearly a very difficult punch to block or avoid. When you nail so many professional boxers over a number of years with the same punch or combo, it has to be more than mere coincidence.

If you look at the uppercut from a technical standpoint, the punch comes from low down. Therefore, from the intended target's perspective, it is hard to see in its initial stages. The punch in its initial phase is not in your visual field; it starts off in your blind spot. This is kind of similar to a great white shark attack on an elephant seal. You can't avoid or block something that you can't see! Frank Bruno described Mike Tyson as a "harbour shark" when describing the manner of his stealth attacks. "He was on me before I could do anything."

The same punch landed on Bruno multiple times in his two meetings with Tyson. It is a great shot to throw at a taller and more upright opponent, which again was a consistent theme over the course of Tyson's career, as all his opponents were taller than him.

Tyson also landed his favourite punch on Buster Douglas in round eight of their 1990 fight. One such uppercut scored the knockdown that led to the famous long count which caused so much controversy. The referee didn't start his count until Douglas had already been down for three to four seconds, which is why there was a discrepancy between the referee's count and the timekeeper's count.

In their 1996 meeting, Tyson almost lifted Holyfield off his feet with a deadly looking uppercut. Tyson also nailed Jose Ribalta with this same punch in round two of their 1986 meeting. In this instance, he threw the uppercut off a right body shot, which was one of his patented combos. The body shot was more often than not a distraction tactic, with the immediately following uppercut being the danger shot.

The uppercut is the most difficult punch to defend against, both from a vision and a positional standpoint. To execute an uppercut correctly, you have to be close to the intended target and get your own body out of the way. Tyson was a master at ghosting into the correct position and set distance to throw this punch. The punch also relies on good timing, hand-eye coordination, and accuracy—you're obviously aiming for the natural gap between your opponent's gloves.

—July 2019

David Solomon: The flicker jab was utilised by some of the greatest boxers of all time, including the best ever—Muhammad Ali. Why isn't it used today?

J. A.: Is boxing in decline? You tell me. Judging by the number of great techniques that are no longer in use, then you would pessimistically say that boxing is indeed a sport on the slide. But this doesn't tell the full story. Ali was always unconventional and did many things in a boxing ring which were left of centre. He could afford to, as he was blessed with freak genetics and had tremendous hand speed. To use the flicker jab to good effect requires great hand speed, great reflexes, and low positioning of the hands. If you don't have the correct tools, then the punch can be too risky and becomes a liability.

What is the flicker jab? It is a quick jab that comes from a low-angle trajectory, intended to confuse, distract, and upset the balance of the intended target. Of course the punch, coming from low down, has the element of surprise also. Ali and other great fighters, such as Thomas Hearns, used this punch to great effect by flick-jabbing the body, thereby distracting their opponent's attention. In essence, the flicker jab is a high-level diversionary tactic, and the follow-up punches are the damaging shots.

The Hitman Thomas Hearns used the flicker jab to great effect against various opponents. Often his hands were held characteristically low. Was he gonna flick-jab or was he gonna throw that lethal right cross as a lead? Who knew? In 1984, the great Roberto Duran certainly didn't know. He was flattened by probably the most potent "unseen" right cross in modern boxing history, which was thrown immediately after a flicker jab to the body.

Lomanchenko is one guy who currently uses a type of flicker jab. His is called a circling jab, apparently.

The flicker jab is a high-level tactic which requires speed, timing, and hand-eye coordination. Having a reach advantage is also preferable, as ideally you want to keep your opponent at arm's length.

—April 2019

MOHAMMED: What is a Mike Tyson's gazelle punch? When, how, and why is it thrown?

The term *gazelle punch* referred to Tyson's leaping left hook, which was one of his most deadly punches. Many of Tyson's opponents were either finished off with this punch or were set up with it. More often than not, they didn't see it coming because it was so well disguised and fast. As Tyson literally threw the punch while on the move, it served a dual purpose in that it was both a strike and a gap closer. When Tyson threw the punch, it was like a cobra strike. His whole body came up from a crouch and unravelled, with his fist simply the end point of the strike. Normally both his feet were off the ground at impact. Tyson's stance was quite hard to define, as he was effectively airborne for a split second. But one thing was for sure: if you wanted a picture-perfect example of how to get near full body weight into a left hook, then look no further than Mike Tyson's gazelle punch. Notable examples of the Iron Man's gazelle punch were observed against Donnie Long in 1985 & Lou Savarese in 2000.

—August 2018

MASIMBA STIMBA AND MOHAMMED: What is the "D'Amato shift" move that Tyson used in his fights? When, why, and how is it used?

J. A.: The D'Amato shift referred to Tyson's most dangerous footwork manoeuvre, which resulted in a lightning-fast switching of stances and an accompanying shift in body weight from one foot to the other. As Tyson had natural knockout power in either hand, the D'Amato shift enabled him to fully exploit his ambidextrous nature. More often than not, Tyson punched while on the move. His punch served a dual purpose of closing the gap between himself and the taller opponent and, obviously, hitting the guy at the same time. So the D'Amato shift enabled him to throw power punches from either hand and either stance—and quite often from a neutral, squared stance also.

An important point is that prime Tyson's peekaboo style was all about movement. The D'Amato shift was all about foot movement, getting Tyson into the right position and distance to throw pinpoint bombs. Tyson fought a guy named Mark Young in December 1985, when he was a relative unknown. The fight, as usual, ended in a first-round knockout, but the Mark Young knockout created quite a stir in the boxing fraternity. Why? The D'Amato shift led to the knockout. Look for a lightning-fast stance switch from Tyson, orthodox to southpaw, followed immediately by a wicked right hook-come uppercut, which Young and most of the audience never saw. The knockout was a thing of beauty. Ex-world champion Ray "Boom " Mancini, who was a colour commentator on the fight, was utterly gobsmacked. Along with everyone else in real time, he missed the punch. Slow-motion replay was required. As a former pro boxer, he knew right there and then that there was no way a teenager could have acquired this kind of knockout punching technique on his own. Enter the boxing genius of Constantine D'Amato.

—August 2018

Muhd Danial: Why does Muhammad Ali shuffle his feet back and forth so fast? Is there a reason he does so?

J. A.: This was the most famous example of showboating in boxing history—the Ali shuffle! Watch his fight against Cleveland Williams to see the most dazzling display of footwork ever seen in a professional boxing ring. Ali destroyed Williams, but the amazing thing was that he found the time to do his patented Ali shuffle while pounding at the same time. First and foremost, by his very nature, Ali was a showman. If it put bums on seats, then Ali would do it. It was always his intention that the paying customer should be kept entertained, and the Ali shuffle was pure showmanship.

Indirectly, it could also be interpreted as Ali mind games. It sent a stark message to his rivals along the lines of "how many of you guys can do this?" Some would say that it was fight psychology, and it was Ali's intention to dominate his opponents psychologically as much as physically. In his own inimitable way, Ali too was a master of intimidation; he just did it in a different way to Mike Tyson and Sonny Liston.

—October 2020

BRAD OXLER: Why don't more boxers use the "smash punch" that Donovan "Razor" Ruddock was famous for?

J.A.: The Ruddock "Smash" was the most dangerous punch on the heavyweight scene during the early '90s. Mike Tyson fought Ruddock twice in 1991 and has confirmed that Razor Ruddock was the hardest puncher he faced and this is certainly high praise from Tyson. Whilst nobody in their right mind would want to taste Ruddock's hardest punch, it was a punch which was quite telegraphed and could therefore be avoided…This is to say that Tyson stood toe to toe with Ruddock in a show of machismo and therefore absorbed many left hooks from Ruddock, that heyday Tyson would have slipped or weaved.

The Smash itself can be described as something of a hybrid punch which started out as a low slung left hook that transitioned into an uppercut. What gave it more power and novelty was Ruddock's leg strength which he implemented into the punch through a "Jack in the box" effect. He literally sprang into the punch ensuring that nearly his full bodyweight was behind the punch.

The obvious answer why other heavyweights don't copy Ruddock is clearly that they lack his "toolbox" and specifically his leg strength. Also consider the fact that Ruddock was wide open to counters, given the fact he really loaded up with the shot and was often left off balance when he missed.

Lennox Lewis took full advantage of Ruddock's technical deficiencies way back in 1992 and at no point in this fight did Ruddock get close to landing his patented power punch.

—March 2021

The End